THE PRINCE
AND
THE DISCOURSES

MODERN LIBRARY
COLLEGE EDITIONS

THE PRINCE AND
THE DISCOURSES

By Niccolò Machiavelli

WITH AN INTRODUCTION
BY MAX LERNER
*Max Richter Professor of American Civilization,
Brandeis University*

The Modern Library • New York
Distributed by McGraw-Hill

ISBN: 0–07–553577–7

THE MODERN LIBRARY

is published by RANDOM HOUSE, INC.

29 30 BAH BAH 9 9 8

Manufactured in the United States of America

CONTENTS

v

THE DISCOURSES

First Book

SECOND BOOK

Third Book

INTRODUCTION

by MAX LERNER

WE LIVE today in the shadow of a Florentine, the man who above all others taught the world to think in terms of cold political power. His name was Niccolò Machiavelli, and he was one of those rare intellectuals who write about politics because they have had a hand in politics and learned what it is about. His portraits show a thin-faced, pale little man, with a sharp nose, sunken cheeks, subtle lips, a discreet and enigmatic smile, and piercing black eyes that look as if they knew much more than they were willing to tell.

There is little we can say for certain about his early years. He was born in 1469, of a family that was part of the small and impoverished gentry of Florence. His father, a lawyer, tried desperately to keep his family from slipping down into the ranks of the middle class. Niccolò must have had the sort of boyhood that most children had in the homes and on the streets of Florence in the *quattrocento*. He steps onto the threshold of history in 1498, already a young man of twenty-nine, only a month after the execution of the friar-politician Savonarola, who had dominated the last decades of the dying fifteenth century in Florence. At that time Machiavelli got a minor job as secretary to the Second Chancery—an office he was to hold for fourteen years.

He was what we should call today a Braintruster and bureaucrat. He loved his job as idea-man for some of the stuffed-shirt Florentine politicians. And because he was so

xxv

good at it, the stuffed shirts came to regard him as someone on whose shoulders they could place the burden of administrative work—the man who got papers drawn up and orders sent out and correspondence carried on and records kept. In due time—since Florence like the other Italian city-states in an age of intrigue depended on skilful diplomacy for its survival—they broadened the scope of his work and sent him on diplomatic missions. In the course of a decade he visited as an unofficial emissary every important city-state in Italy and several of the courts outside Italy. He sent back reports which may still be read for their tough understanding of diplomatic realities. Invariably he acquitted himself well; he met the movers and shakers of the world, and the narrow horizon of the Florentine expanded into the vistas of the European state-system.

It was thus that Machiavelli was in a position to become the first modern analyst of power. Where others looked at the figureheads, he kept his eyes glued behind the scenes. He sought the ultimate propulsion of events. He wanted to know what made things tick; he wanted to take the clock of the world to pieces to find out how it worked. He went on foreign missions, organized the armies of Florence, carried through successfully the long protracted siege of Pisa. Yet always he was concerned with what these experiences could teach him about the nature of power. In an age of portraiture it was natural that he too should be a painter, but his subjects never knew they were sitting for him. He studied Pope Julius II, the secular princes, the *condottieri;* above all he studied Caesar Borgia, the Duke Valentino, who came closer to embodying the naked ideal of power than any other person Machiavelli had met. There was in Machiavelli, as in Savonarola, an intense and searing flame, but it was a secular flame, and the things it fed on were not such things as religious dreams are made of.

A man like this might have lived out his days, tasted somewhat of power, known what it was to run a state from behind the scenes as an underling, and died leaving behind him some excellent diplomatic reports, a few plays, and some polished verses in the style of the time. But Machiavelli's destiny was different.

The petty dynasties and the bourgeois merchant princes who ruled the Italian city-states played their fateful game of chessboard diplomacy all through the fifteenth century until finally in the sixteenth it led to disaster for all of them. This is not the place to review the succession of maneuvers by which France, Spain, Germany and the Papacy vied for the supremacy over Italy. When, after the League of Cambrai, a split developed between France and the Papacy, Florence stuck to its basic alliance with France. When Julius II drove the French from Italy, Florence was lost; and not even the new citizen army that Machiavelli had trained could withstand the combined force of the Pope's prestige and his Swiss mercenaries. One of the conditions of the papal peace was the restoration of the Medici in Florence. And so Machiavelli, who had always been staunchly republican and anti-Medici, found himself in 1512 at the age of forty-three a dejected liberal without a job in a world that had come tumbling down about his ears.

He tried to make his peace with the Medici, but to no avail. There was a witch-hunting atmosphere in Florence, and everyone was suspect who had ever been identified with the liberal cause. Two ardent young republican conspirators had evidently made a list of those on whom they thought they might rely for aid, and Machiavelli's name was on the list. He was arrested, drawn by the rope, tortured. But he was plainly innocent, and finally was released. He slunk off to a small suburban farm near Florence, and for the next fourteen years until his death his letters are full of pleas to be reinstated in the favor of the Medici and the Pope, plans to recommend himself to them, strategies by which his abilities could be brought to their attention. It is, as so many commentators have pointed out, neither a pretty nor a graceful picture. Yet we must reflect that Machiavelli out of office felt himself a vessel without use. The letters he has left us during this period, for all their bitter pride and the unbreakable gaiety of their style, show that reinstatement in office spelled for him nothing less than a return to life.

Ironically, it was this period of his disgrace that represents the high-point of his creative power. The enforced leisure compelled him to fall back on himself. Finding himself after fourteen years deprived of his job, he felt shut in like a bird in an iron cage. The result was his books—his solitary song. More and more he retreated to his study and his mind. From them came *The Prince,* the *Art of War, The Discourses,* the *History of Florence;* various plays, among them a first-rate comedy, *Mandragola;* poetry, stories, biographical sketches. The civil servant, the politician, the diplomat, the military organizer had become a man of letters *malgré lui.*

There remains only the final ironic act. In 1527 the papal armies were defeated and Rome was sacked by the soldiers of Charles V. At this the popular party in Florence overthrew the Medici and for a short time restored democratic government. Machiavelli had hurried back to Florence, eager to regain his post as secretary. But he never stood a real chance. *The Prince,* circulated in manuscript, had made him enemies; the small dull men who had it in their power to dispense office feared his brilliance and his wit. Mercifully Machiavelli fell sick and never learned that the final vote of the Council was overwhelmingly against him. Before the news came he was dead. And so a man who had hoped for the ultimate glory of being restored to the Florentine civil service died, leaving behind him nothing but the memory of a few books he had written in his exile.

2

There is a famous letter from Machiavelli to his friend Vettori, the Florentine ambassador at the Papal Court in Rome, in which he describes the tenor of his life on the farm, and the relief that he finds among books in his study.

On the threshold I slip off my day's clothes with their mud and dirt, put on my royal and curial robes, and enter, decently accoutred, the ancient courts of men of old, where I am welcomed kindly and fed on that fare which is mine alone, and for which I was born: where I am not ashamed to address them and ask them the reasons for their action, and they reply considerately; and for two hours I forget all my cares, I know no more trouble, death loses its terrors: I am utterly translated in their company. And since Dante says that we can never attain knowledge unless we retain what we hear, I have noted down the capital I have accumulated from their conversation and composed a little book, *De Principatibus*, in which I probe as deeply as I can the consideration of this subject, discussing what a principality is, the variety of such states, how they are won, how they are held, how they are lost . . .[1]

It was the period of the great humanist revival of ancient learning. The books Machiavelli read were the traditional Latin authors and (since he probably did not know Greek) the Greek authors in Latin translation. And as he read there came crowding back into his mind the varied experiences

[1] I use here the translation made by Ralph Roeder in his *Man of the Renaissance* (1933).

of his life; and out of the fusion of reading and experience came new insights into politics, at first jotted down in the form of notes which eventually formed themselves into a vast book.

That book was not *The Prince*. There are clear indications that Machiavelli started to write what afterward became *The Discourses,* planned on a grand scale. But as he wrote in his study, things were happening in the world outside. There was a new Pope in Rome, a new regime in Italy; the Pope was carving out a new state in Italy and placing his nephew Giuliano at its head. What more natural than to wish to influence this new prince and recommend oneself to his favor? Perhaps one could once more thus have a hand in world affairs, and—who knows?—set in motion a train of forces that might arrest the decadence of the Italian communes and free Italy from the invaders. But *The Discourses* were too vast to finish quickly, and their form was far too sprawling for the purpose. And so, carving out of *The Discourses* certain sections and ideas, Machiavelli proceeded to recast them in the form of a short treatise, *De Principatibus.* Eventually he changed the title from the Latin abstract to the Italian personal, *Il Principe*. The book was written in 1513 at an almost white heat, in what was probably only a few months. Dedicated to Lorenzo de' Medici, it was presented to him and by him neglected and forgotten. It was, however, circulated in manuscript during Machiavelli's lifetime, surreptitiously copied and corrupted, and achieved an underground fame. Since his death it has been one of the half dozen books that have done most to shape Western thought.

What gives *The Prince* its greatness? It is not a great formal treatise on politics. It is bare of any genuine insights into social organization as the basis of politics. It has very little passion in it—so little that, because the final chapter crackles and glows with Machiavelli's fervor for the unification of Italy, some commentators have suggested that it is not an organic part of the book but was added as an afterthought. It has been pretty well proved, moreover, by recent scholarship that Machiavelli's little pamphlet on princes is not even original in form. It is part of a whole traditional literature on princes that stretches back to the Middle Ages. The structure of the book, its division into chapters and even some of the chapter headings follow the conventional form of what has been called the mirror-of-princes literature: the discussion of how to rule conquered territory, what advisers a prince should rely on, how he should conduct himself among the intrigues of diplomacy, whether he should depend mainly on fortified castles or entrenched camps in warfare.

But the intellectual spirit that pervades the book is quite another matter. Here we are in the presence of something little short of a revolution in political thinking. The humanists who had written books about princes had written in the idealistic and scholastic medieval tradition; they were ridden by theology and metaphysics. Machiavelli rejected metaphysics, theology, idealism. The whole drift of his work is toward a political realism, unknown to the formal writing of his time.

I say unknown to the *formal writing*. That does not mean it was unknown to his time. Machiavelli was expressing the realism that characterized the actual politics and the popular ethos of his time. Take, for example, some sentences from the famous eighteenth chapter, "In What Way Princes Must Keep Faith." The Achilles myth of the centaur, he writes, teaches us that we are "semi-animal, semi-human" and that "a prince must know how to use both natures." . . . "A prince being thus obliged to know well how to act as a beast must imitate the fox and the lion, for the lion cannot protect himself from traps, and the fox cannot defend himself from wolves." . . . "A prudent ruler ought not to keep faith when by so doing it would be against his interest, and when the reasons which made him bind himself no longer exist." "It is not, therefore, necessary for a prince to have all the above-named qualities, but it is very necessary to seem to have them." When Machiavelli wrote thus he was not creating a new ethos, whatever we may think of it; he was expressing the ethos of the late *quattrocento* and the early *cinquecento* not only in Florence but in the whole of Italy. Machiavelli was, in short, the child of his time—neither better nor worse than the other intellectuals, politicians, diplomats and civil servants of his time.

He was able, using the traditional humanist literary forms, to pour into them a realistic political spirit which his age was acting on but which had never before been so well expressed in political thought. He had the daring to turn against the whole idealistic preoccupation of the humanists. He had the clear-eyed capacity to distinguish between man as he ought to be and man as he actually is—between the ideal form of institutions and the pragmatic conditions under which they operate.

But if we have come close to his greatness here, we have not wholly succeeded in ensnaring it. There have been other men who have expressed the consciousness of their period. They have in very few instances achieved the highest rank in the history of ideas. And while those who content themselves with seeing Machiavelli thus in the context of his time may succeed thereby in countering the charges made against him of being a sort of anti-Christ who had created a new immorality, they do not thereby get at the roots of his greatness.

To take a further step in our analysis, we must see that Machiavelli, while he expressed the ethical consciousness of his time, was also a good deal ahead of his time in other respects. He lived in a period when economic growth had gone so far as to burst the bounds of existing political forms. What gave the city-states of Italy their Renaissance grandeur was not some mysterious flowering of the humanist spirit at the time. It was the fact that with the opening of the East by the crusades, the breakup of the manorial economy and the growth of trade and handicraft manufacture, the cities of Italy found themselves strategically placed with respect to the world trade routes. There followed what amounted to a communal revolution in Italy and a reorganization of the government of the Italian city-states under democratic and guild forms. The expansion of the economic power of these cities went on apace into the end of the fifteenth century. By the time Machiavelli came to the maturity of his powers, a sharp contraction had set in. The expansion had gone as far as the political limits of the communal organization allowed.

If the Italian city-states had been able to adjust themselves to the needs of an expanding economy by resolving their rivalries and joining in a united political structure, Italy might have been spared the two and a half centuries of humiliation and cultural aridness which followed the fall of the communes. Elsewhere, however, in France, in England, in Spain, the expansion of political forms kept pace with the economic expansion. Machiavelli lived in what, with our historical perspective, we now say to have been the beginnings of the Western nation-state system. As we know it, he was himself only dimly aware of it. He was in no sense an articulate nationalist, and the fervor of his national feeling has probably been overestimated by commentators. But two elements were historically to enter into the composition of the Western nation-state. One was national unity and the idea of a common tongue, common culture and common economic limits. The second was a realistic concentration of power at the center in order to break down divisive barriers. Machiavelli only dimly foresaw nationalism, but he very clearly expressed the second element—the realistic use of power from the center, the methods by which unity could be achieved.

Therein lies the importance of *The Prince* in the subsequent history of the Western world. Machiavelli wrote a grammar of power, not only for the sixteenth century, but for the ages that have followed. Read *The Prince* today and you will be struck by the detonations which its sentences set off in the corridors of our experiences with present-day rulers. Machiavelli seen only in his historical context does become intelligible; but his greatness does not emerge until we see that when he wrote his grammar of power he came close to setting down the imperatives by which men govern and are governed in political communities, whatever the epoch and whatever the governmental structure.

The Prince has become, for better or worse, a symbol of a whole body of literature and a whole approach to politics. Just as in literature and art we must always face, under whatever names, the polar conflict of classic and romantic, so in the history of political thinking we have always to face the polar conflict between the ethical and the ruthlessly realistic. *The Prince* is part of the world's polemical literature because it places itself squarely in the ranks of realism. It brushes aside, with an impatience in which Machiavelli scarcely cares to conceal his disdain, the tender-mindedness of reformers and idealists.

There is in all of us, along with the ethical and normative strain, a strain of hard-headedness and of the acceptance of the framework of human passions and social reality within which we have to work. One can trace it back to Aristophanes and the way in which he always deflated contemporary dreams and illusions by getting back to the essential limits of the human animal. In every generation since him the young men have been divided between the pursuit of some passionate ideal and the hard-bitten inquiry into how things actually get accomplished in a real political world. It is to that pole of our political thinking that *The Prince* gravitates. As long as this strain will remain in political thinking, so long will *The Prince* be found to have expressed in undying prose its intensity and its temper.

3

Very few who talk of *The Prince* have ever read more than a few sentences in it. But fewer still have read the work of Machiavelli which, without having the same *éclat* in history as *The Prince,* is nevertheless the saner, the more rounded, the more comprehensive work. I refer to *The Discourses.*

It was the longer work on which Machiavelli was engaged when, because of political opportunism, he made a sudden sortie to finish *The Prince.* He came back to it later. He seems to have worked on it intermittently for the better part of a decade. It bears to *The Prince* much the same relation that Marx's *Capital* bears to the *Communist Manifesto.* It is the considered, comprehensive treatise. Outwardly a commentary (unfinished) on the first ten books of Livy's *History of Rome,* it is actually a set of *pensées,* loosely gathered together into a book—reflections on politics which use Roman history as a point of departure. It is clearly not a book which ever had a chance for real fame. The very people who have written most about *The Prince* seem to have neglected *The Discourses,* and very few seem to have read it. When we talk of Machiavellianism, it is *The Prince* we have in mind. And that is perhaps as it should be. But when we talk of Machiavelli, we must have *The Discourses* in mind as well. For if we are to judge a man it is fairer to judge him by the book into which he sought to put his whole system of politics rather than by the pamphlet which he dashed off to win a friend and influence a personage.

Scholarship has not done well by *The Discourses.* The scholars pay lip service to it as the larger frame of reference within which *The Prince* can be understood. Yet having done so, they go on to talk of *The Prince.* Its structure is difficult and fragmentary. Precepts drawn from Livy form the chapter heads. There are whole sections that might easily be cut out to improve the book. A good editor today, receiving such a manuscript, would probably ask the author to cut it down to one-third and pull it together a bit. Yet once read, *The Discourses* stay in your mind as an impressive intellectual experience. And once read, whatever impression you have formed of Machiavelli through reading *The Prince* is rather drastically changed.

What was the intellectual tradition that lay back of *The Discourses?* In the case of *The Prince,* it was the mirror-of-princes medieval and humanist literature. Felix Gilbert has suggested in a recent article, and I think the suggestion is a sound one, that research into the literature of "the good state," both in Italian and in Greater European thought, might yield exciting results for an understanding of *The Discourses.*

However that may be, what are the basic ideas of *The Discourses?* I should say the following: first, the superiority of the democratic republic to every other political form;

second, the ultimate reliance even of despotic and authoritarian regimes on mass consent; third, the primary political imperative of cohesiveness, organic unity in a state, stability and survival; fourth, the great role of leadership (what Machiavelli calls the role of the law-giver, but what we should today call leadership) in achieving this cohesiveness and survival; fifth, the imperative of military power in insuring survival and the need for putting it on a mass base (he felt that war was the health of the state); sixth, the use of a national religion for state purposes, and the choice of one not for its supernatural validity, but for its power as a myth in unifying the masses and cementing their morale (Machiavelli's count against Christianity, like that of Nietzsche after him, was that by glorifying humility and pacifism and the weaker virtues, it dulled the fighting edge of a state); seventh, the need in the conduct even of a democratic state for the will to survive, and therefore for ruthless instead of half-hearted measures when ruthless measures were necessary; eighth, the idea—later to be found in Vico and in our day in Spengler—of the cyclical rise and fall of civilizations due to the decadence and corruption of the old and the reinvigoration of the new.

This is, of course, only a sampling of the vast riches to be found in *The Discourses*. It is not a single-themed, monolithic book, such as Marx or Mill wrote. It has a catholicity and vastness of resource which will make it yield different discoveries for every reader and on every reading.

This is not the place to discuss the themes I have mentioned. I want only to say that if *The Prince* is great because of its intensity, *The Discourses* are great because of their variety; if *The Prince* is great because it is polemical, *The Discourses* are great because they have balance; and if *The Prince* is great because it gives us the grammar of power for a government, *The Discourses* are great because they give us the philosophy of organic unity not in a government but in a state, and the conditions under which alone a culture can survive.

4

"The authentic interpreter of Machiavelli," Lord Acton has written in his erudite preface to Burd's great edition of *The Prince,* "is the whole of later history." In the same essay he strings out a remarkable series of quotations from the great writers and statesmen of the last three or four centuries which show the impact that Machiavelli had on the European mind. The history of that impact may be called the history of Machiavellianism.

It is clear that one element in the denunciation of Machiavellianism was the use of that symbol as a weapon of the Counter-Reformation. Machiavelli was utterly secular in his thinking. And when the Church, in assuming the aggressive against the religious reformers, sought something that could be set up as a secular devil-symbol in contrast to the ethical teachings of religion, it easily found what it sought in Machiavelli's writings. At the same time also the same symbol could serve to brand with infamy the methods that were being used to set up and consolidate the new nation-states of Europe, the power of whose sovereigns was one of the great threats to church power. And so the Church statesmen who had at first accepted *The Prince,* then ignored it, finally decided to attack it. Under Leo, Clement, Paul III, it was tolerated. But under Paul IV, in 1557, a generation after the Florentine's death, Machiavelli was put on the Index. What is somewhat ironic about this is that the Church princes, like the secular princes, were among the principal followers of Machiavelli's precepts. As Lord Acton (himself a Catholic) points out, the arguments used to excuse the massacres of the religious wars were drawn from Machiavelli.

There is another important element in the history of Machiavellianism—so far, at least, as the English-speaking secular world is concerned. Machiavelli entered our consciousness largely through the Elizabethan drama. Wyndham Lewis has written a provocative, although erratic, book with the title *The Lion and the Fox*. It takes its point of departure from a fact spelled out by scholars like Edward Meyer and more recently Mario Praz—that the figure of Machiavelli dominated the imagination of the Tudor dramatists. The meeting between Italian Renaissance culture and the Tudor mind contained an element of shock arising from novelty. The English were, as is true of all cultural borrowers, at once attracted and repelled by the Italians. Moreover, Tudor drama was enormously sensitive to world currents. The result was that not only were there, as Meyer has pointed out, some 400 direct references to Machiavelli in the Elizabethan literature; but the Machiavelli figure, whether directly or indirectly, dominates it as does no other. Iago was drawn from Machiavelli, as was Barabas. Webster, Massinger, Ford, Marston, Ben Jonson, Shakespeare—they were all fascinated by the image they constructed of subtle cunning, of treachery, of the gap between outward seeming and inward being, all of which they thought of as Machiavellianism. To the Tudor imagination, which has in turn so influenced our own, Machiavelli was the symbol that stood for the decadence, the corruption, the unfathomable depths of Renaissance Italy. It was probably due to the fusion of the influence of church and stage that Machiavelli became associated in the popular mind with the Devil himself. "Old Nick" became an epithet equally applicable to both.

It may therefore seem surprising that Tudor England had

scarcely read Machiavelli at all. *The Discourses* were not translated into English until 1636, *The Prince* until 1640. The Elizabethans got their knowledge of Machiavelli from a French book attacking him, Gentillet's *Anti-Machiavel*. And Gentillet gave just enough of Machiavelli to distort him, and not enough to make him either comprehensible or human. This should not surprise us. It is the essence of a symbol that its outlines should be shadowy. What has first been sifted through the intellect is unlikely to ensnare the imagination. Had the Elizabethans really read *The Discourses* and *The Prince,* they would no doubt have been more just to the author, but their drama would have suffered and one of its type figures would have had to be scrapped. By the time the translations were made, it was unfortunately—or shall we say fortunately?—too late to affect either their intelligence or their art. The symbol had become fixed.

I have spoken of various historical reasons why the Elizabethans should have responded to the Machiavelli symbol, and Wyndham Lewis adds the fascination which the diabolical holds for the Puritan genius in every age. Yet we come closer to the core of the truth when we remember that the Elizabethans had the same perverse and feverish preoccupation with the theme of death. And, I am inclined to guess, for much the same reason. It *unmasks* the human animal. But for this very reason Machiavelli became the subject of attack from still another source—the seventeenth- and eighteenth-century absolute monarchy. To be sure, we have a long roster of despots—benevolent and otherwise—who are reputed to have drunk in Machiavelli with their mothers' milk and were known as "Machiavellistae." But we must remember, so black had Machiavelli's reputation become that if you wanted to hit at a monarch, you had only to start a whispering campaign to the effect that he ruled according to Machiavelli's grammar. The supreme irony was that Frederick the Great of Prussia, while still a young man, wrote a refutation of Machiavelli. As Frederick's later career showed, Machiavelli had adumbrated the methods of the benevolent despots only too well. His offense had been only to unmask them, to lay bare to the world the mechanisms of power which were behind the authority of the ruler. Voltaire encouraged the young prince to write his treatise; but his comment on Frederick in his *Memoirs* is delicious:

> If Machiavelli had had a prince for disciple, the first thing he would have recommended him to do would have been to write a book against Machiavellism.

But if Machiavelli was a butt and a tool in the Age of Reason, he came into his own in the nineteenth century in the age of new nationalism. Men rediscovered Machiavelli the liberal, Machiavelli the democrat, Machiavelli the nationalist patriot. In Germany, during and after the Napoleonic wars, the intellectuals rediscovered Machiavelli, and turned their fine gifts of scholarship toward him, with the characteristic result of a spate of Machiavelli studies. The leader was Fichte, who made an analysis of Machiavelli part of his famous *Address to the German Nation;* and Hegel, who following Machiavelli made a cult of the state, taught that "the course of world history stands outside of virtue, blame and justice." And in Italy Cavour and the leaders of the Risorgimento found in Machiavelli their ideal symbol. What both the Italians and the Germans sought in him was what they needed for their movements of national liberation: the stress on cohesiveness, the pursuit of the main chance, the prime virtue of political survival. The Germans took from him the concept of *Staaträson*—opportunism justified by reasons of state policy; and in the field of foreign affairs, *Realpolitik*.

In country after country the rediscovery of Machiavelli seems to have had an almost magical efficacy in stirring latent national and even reformist energies. To complete the history of Machiavellianism, I need only point out that for the recent collectivist movements as well he became an evocative figure. H. G. Wells, in what is one of his really first-rate political novels, *The New Machiavelli,* dreamed of a "strengthened and perfected state" that blends Machiavelli with English Fabian humanitarianism. Both Lenin and Mussolini did their work in the shadow of the Florentine. The "old Bolshevik" Kamenev published a volume of Machiavelli selections with a sympathetic Introduction under the Soviet regime. Some years later, when he was tried and convicted in the purge trials, the Public Prosecutor used his Machiavelli editing job against him. Mussolini also wrote an introductory essay to an edition of *The Prince,* and it was included in Volume IV of his *Collected Works,* although for a time he banned his own works from the national library. Rauschning in his *Voice of Destruction,* which recounts his conversations with Hitler, asserts that Hitler ranked Machiavelli with Wagner as among the influences shaping his thought; and that he used to keep a copy of *The Prince* by his bedside.

5

It has become a truism to point out that Machiavelli is the father of power politics. Whether a truism or not, it is still true. Machiavelli, as ambassador and administrator, could not afford to do any wishful thinking. If he did, the penalty was swift and merciless—failure. Which may not be a bad idea as a school for political theorists. But to say that he was the father of power politics may have curiously erroneous implications—as if we were to say that Harvey was the father of the circulation of the blood. Power politics existed before Machiavelli was ever heard of; it will exist long after his name is only a faint memory. What he did, like Harvey, was to recognize its existence and subject it to scientific study. And so his name has come to be associated with it.

To be sure, Machiavelli's role is not wholly innocent. His grammar of power brought a whole new world to consciousness. With one of Moliere's characters, the princes of Europe became aware that all their lives they had been talking prose. And the awareness led them to perfect their prose. Frederick, Richelieu, Napoleon, Bismarck, Clemenceau, Lenin, Mussolini, Hitler, Stalin, have gone to school to Machiavelli. But by bringing the world to this awareness Machiavelli did what every creative figure does. We might as well blame Shakespeare because, by creating Hamlet, he has intensified the agony of the indecisive and divided liberal.

Machiavelli has also been accused, and it is true, of being the father of the martial spirit, of propaganda techniques and of the totalitarian spirit. But here again he anticipated things latent in the very texture of society and the state. A reading of *The Discourses* should show that his thinking fathered many movements, democratic as well as dictatorial. The common meaning he has for democrats and dictators alike is that, whatever your ends, you must be clear-eyed and unsentimental in pursuit of them and you must rest your power ultimately on a cohesive principle.

May I venture a guess as to the reason why we still shudder slightly at Machiavelli's name? It is not only the tradition I have described. It is our recognition that the realities he described *are* realities; that men, whether in politics, in business or in private life, do *not* act according to their professions of virtue; that leaders in every field seek power ruthlessly and hold on to it tenaciously; that the masses who are coerced in a dictatorship have to be wooed and duped in a democracy; that deceit and ruthlessness invariably crop up in every state; and that while the art of being ruled has always been a relatively easy one, the art of ruling ourselves is monstrously difficult. Machiavelli today confronts us with the major dilemma of how to adapt our democratic techniques and concepts to the demands of a world in which as never before naked power politics dominates the foreign field and determined oligarchies struggle for power internally. It is not an easy dilemma to resolve. And in a sense, just as the seventeenth- and eighteenth-century monarchs hated and feared Machiavelli because he had exposed their authority to the world, so today we hate and fear him because he has exposed our dilemma and made it visible to ourselves and the world.

Let us be clear about one thing: ideals and ethics are important in politics as norms, but they are scarcely effective as techniques. The successful statesman is an artist, concerned with nuances of public mood, approximations of operative motives, guesswork as to the tactics of his opponents, back-breaking work in unifying his own side by compromise and concession. Religious reformers have often succeeded in bringing public morale closer to some ethical norm; they have never succeeded as statesmen. Even in the theocracies of Savonarola in Florence, Cromwell and the Puritans in England, our own New England colonies, the men of God, when they came to power, learned to play the game of power. The only difference between them and others is that, since they had a certitude of having a pipeline to God, they did not have to reckon at all with the uneasy factor of their conscience. The most destructive imperialisms of the world have been those of men who have elevated their preferences to the pinnacle of moral imperatives and who have then confidently proceeded to impose those imperatives on others.

Today, as in Machiavelli's day, our world has become a collection of principalities struggling for survival, maneuvering for position, fighting over spoils. The scale is bigger but the proportions are the same. The strong men have come forward in every state, using the rhetoric of mass interest and national glory to extend their power and entrench their class. The first law of internal policy is to hold on to power, of external policy it is to extend your imperialism. Like Machiavelli, we live in a time of the breaking of nations.

Let it be said that Machiavelli in his day blundered as we are doing in ours. He could not make up his mind whether what he wanted was a democratic Florence or a unified Italy. I think he must have felt, when he wrote *The Prince,* that democracy would somehow follow if unity was achieved. There are some today who feel the same way about the attempts to achieve world integration through establishing a Russian Century or an American Century. There are others who feel that no integration is worth the candle if democratic rights and human decencies are scrapped in the process. In Machiavelli's writing you will find both attitudes, but more often the first.

This raises sharply, of course, the interminable question of ends and means. Machiavelli would, I think, shrug his shoulders at the whole problem. He himself, he would say, was an observer of politics. And as such he would find it irrelevant to impose his own ethical patterns on the torrential flow of world history. It is for that very reason that Machiavellianism, after everything has been said about it, fails to be an adequate philosophy for a way of life. Men are not only observers, not only participants; they are also valuing individuals. Without judgments life loses its hierarchial quality of being a choice between preferences. And losing that, it loses its savor.

Machiavelli sought to distinguish the realm of what ought to be and the realm of what is. He rejected the first for the second. But there is a third realm: the realm of what can be. It is in that realm that what one might call a humanist realism can lie. The measure of man is his ability to extend this sphere of the socially possible. We can start with our democratic values, and we can start also with Machiavelli's realism about tough-minded methods. To be realistic about methods in the politics of a democracy at home does not mean that you throw away all scruples, or accept the superior force of "reason of state," or embrace the police-state crushing of constitutional liberties. To be realistic about the massing of power abroad in the economic and ideological struggle for the support of men and women throughout the world does not mean that you abandon the struggle for peace and for a constitutional imperium that can grow into a world republic. We may yet find that an effective pursuit of democratic values is possible within the scope of a strong social-welfare state and an unsentimental realism about human motives.

March, 1940; May, 1950

BIBLIOGRAPHY

There is a new critical edition of Machiavelli's works in process, in the *Biblioteca di Classici Italiani* (Feltrinelli, Milano), of which volumes 1, 2, 6, and 7 have appeared; the two present works, *Il Principe e Discorsi*, comprise volume 1. The earlier standard edition was *Tutte le opere storiche e letterarie di Niccolò Machiavelli*, ed. Guido Mazzoni and Mario Casella (Firenze, 1929). The best biographies in English are Roberto Ridolfi, *The Life of Niccolò Machiavelli*, tr. by Cecil Grayson (New York, 1963); Pasquale Villari, *The Life and Times of Niccolò Machiavelli*, tr. by Linda Villari, 2 vols. (London, 1892). In Italian, in addition to Ridolfi and Villari, see Gennaro Sasso, *Niccolò Machiavelli, storia della suo pensiero politico* (Napoli, 1958). Sasso has also edited the standard edition of *The Prince*, in Italian, with an introduction, bibliography, and commentaries (Firenze, 1963). For the historical background of Machiavelli's work, see L. A. Burd, "Florence (II): Machiavelli," in *The Cambridge Modern History*, Vol. I (New York, 1934), 190–218: Jacob Burckhardt, *The Civilization of the Renaissance in Italy* (Oxford, 1945), pt. I, "The State as a Work of Art"; Ralph Roeder, *The Man of the Renaissance* (New York, 1933); and J. R. Hale, *Machiavelli and Renaissance Italy* (New York, 1960).

For the tradition of political thought into which Machiavelli's work was projected, see Allan H. Gilbert, *Machiavelli's "Prince" and Its Forerunners* (Durham, North Carolina, 1938), and the same author's "Introduction" to his edition of Machiavelli's *The Prince and Other Works* (Chicago, 1941), 1–76; also, Felix Gilbert, "The Humanist Concept of the Prince and *The*

Prince of Machiavelli," *The Journal of Modern History,* XI (1939), 449–483; and Frederico Chabod, *Machiavelli and the Renaissance* (London, 1958). (Readers of Italian may wish to study a larger collection of Chabod's writings on Machiavelli in his *Opere,* Vol. I, *Scritti su Machiavelli* (Torino, 1964). For a book of selected critical writings about the "Prince," see *Machiavelli's Prince: Cynic, Patriot or Political Scientist,* Problems in European Civilization series, D. C. Heath (Boston, 1960), and Garrett Mattingly, "Machiavelli's Prince: Political Science or Political Satire," *American Scholar,* August, 1958 (Washington, D.C.), 482. For *The Discourses,* see Felix Gilbert, "The Composition and Structure of Machiavelli's *Discorsi,*" *Journal of The History of Ideas,* XIV (1953), 136–156. See also Leslie J. Walker, S.J., *The Discourses of Niccolò Machiavelli,* 2 vols. (London, 1950), with a long critical introduction. On "reason of state" in Machiavelli, see the classic chapter in Friedrich Meinecke, "Die Idee der Staatsrason," in *Der Neueren Geschichte* (1925), translated as "Machiavellianism: The Doctrine of Raison d'Etat and its History" (1957); also, Carl J. Friedrich, *Constitutional Reason of State* (Providence, 1957). For the context of Renaissance political thought, see Felix Gilbert, *Machiavelli and Guicciardini: Politics and History in 16th Century Florence* (Princeton, 1965), which also contains a remarkably full bibliography. The best short introduction to Machiavelli is J. H. Whitfield, *Machiavelli* (Oxford, 1947), especially for his discussion of *virtù* and other terms. For other works on Machiavelli's concepts and vocabulary, see E. W. Mayer, *Machiavelli's Geschichtsauffassung und sein Begriff virtù* (München, 1921); Francesco Ercole, *La Politica di Machiavelli* (Roma, 1926). For his diplomacy and statecraft, see Herbert Butterfield, *The Statecraft of Machiavelli* (London, 1940), and G. P. Gooch, "Politics and Morals," in *Studies in Diplomacy and Statecraft* (London, 1942), 311–340.

For Machiavelli's place as a symbol in Elizabethan literature, see Mario Praz, *Machiavelli and the Elizabethans,* Annual

Italian Lecture, Proceedings of the British Academy (London, 1928), and Wyndham Lewis, *The Lion and The Fox: The Role of the Hero in the Plays of Shakespeare* (London, 1927; paperback, New York, 1966), 59–114. For his place in Italian literature, see Francesco de Sanctis, *History of Italian Literature,* tr. by Joan Redfern, Vol. II (New York, 1931), chap. 14, 535–597. For his quality as a writer, see T. S. Eliot, *For Lancelot Andrewes: Essays on Style and Order* (London, 1928), 49–66.

For varied approaches to his political thinking, see James Burnham, *The Machiavellians: Defenders of Freedom* (New York, 1943), pt. II; Jacques Maritain, "The End of Machiavellianism," *The Review of Politics,* IV (1942), 1–33; Leonardo Olschki, *Machiavelli the Scientist* (Berkeley, 1945); Ernst Cassirer, *The Myth of the State* (New Haven, 1946), 116–162; Harold J. Laski, "Machiavelli and the Present Time," in *Dangers of Obedience and Other Essays* (New York, 1930), 238–263; Leo Strauss, *Thoughts on Machiavelli* (Glencoe, Illinois, 1958); Sheldon S. Wolin, "Machiavelli and the Economy of Violence," in *Politics and Vision* (Boston, 1960), 195–238; and Alberto Moravia, "Machiavelli," in *Man as an End,* tr. by Bernard Wall (New York, 1966).

For the history of Machiavelli's reputation, the classic essay is Lord Acton's (John Emerich Edward Dalberg-Acton's) "Introduction" to L. Arthur Burd's Italian edition of *Il Principe di Niccolò Machiavelli* (Oxford, 1891), xix–xl, which has been reprinted under the title, "Introduction to L. A. Burd's Edition of *Il Principe* by Machiavelli" in Acton, *The History of Freedom and Other Essays,* ed. John N. Figgis and Reginald V. Laurence (London, 1907), 212–231; see also Grattan Freyer, "The Reputation of Machiavelli," *Hermathena,* LVI, Trinity College, Dublin (1940), 148–167; and Peter Gay, *The Enlightenment* (New York, 1966). Two recent novels that have been written around Machiavelli and his time are Maurice Samuel, *Web of Lucifer* (New York, 1947), and W. Somerset Maugham, *Then and Now* (New York, 1946).

THE PRINCE

Translated from the Italian by
Luigi Ricci

Revised by
E. R. P. Vincent

NICCOLO MACHIAVELLI

TO

LORENZO THE MAGNIFICENT

SON OF PIERO DI MEDICI

IT IS customary for those who wish to gain the favour of a prince to endeavour to do so by offering him gifts of those things which they hold most precious, or in which they know him to take especial delight. In this way princes are often presented with horses, arms, cloth of gold, gems, and such-like ornaments worthy of their grandeur. In my desire however, to offer to Your Highness some humble testimony of my devotion, I have been unable to find among my possessions anything which I hold so dear or esteem so highly as that knowledge of the deeds of great men which I have acquired through a long experience of modern events and a constant study of the past.

With the utmost diligence I have long pondered and scrutinised the actions of the great, and now I offer the results to Your Highness within the compass of a small volume: and although I deem this work unworthy of Your Highness's acceptance, yet my confidence in your humanity assures me that you will receive it with favour, knowing that it is not in my power to offer you a greater gift than that of enabling you to understand in a very short time all those things which I have learnt at the cost of privation and danger in the course of many years. I have not sought to adorn

3

my work with long phrases or high-sounding words or any of those superficial attractions and ornaments with which many writers seek to embellish their material, as I desire no honour for my work but such as the novelty and gravity of its subject may justly deserve. Nor will it, I trust, be deemed presumptuous on the part of a man of humble and obscure condition to attempt to discuss and direct the government of princes; for in the same way that landscape painters station themselves in the valleys in order to draw mountains or high ground, and ascend an eminence in order to get a good view of the plains, so it is necessary to be a prince to know thoroughly the nature of the people, and one of the populace to know the nature of princes.

May I trust, therefore, that Your Highness will accept this little gift in the spirit in which it is offered; and if Your Highness will deign to peruse it, you will recognise in it my ardent desire that you may attain to that grandeur which fortune and your own merits presage for you.

And should Your Highness gaze down from the summit of your lofty position towards this humble spot, you will recognise the great and unmerited sufferings inflicted on me by a cruel fate.

Chapter I

THE VARIOUS KINDS OF GOVERNMENT
AND THE WAYS BY WHICH THEY ARE ESTABLISHED

ALL states and dominions which hold or have held sway over mankind are either republics or monarchies. Monarchies are either hereditary in which the rulers have been for many years of the same family, or else they are of recent foundation. The newly founded ones are either entirely new, as was Milan to Francesco Sforza, or else they are, as it were, new members grafted on to the hereditary possessions of the prince that annexes them, as is the kingdom of Naples to the King of Spain. The dominions thus acquired have either been previously accustomed to the rule of another prince, or else have been free states, and they are annexed either by force of arms of the prince himself, or of others, or else fall to him by good fortune or special ability.

Chapter II

OF HEREDITARY MONARCHIES

I WILL not here speak of republics, having already treated of them fully in another place. I will deal only with monarchies, and will discuss how the various kinds described above can be governed and maintained. In the first place, the difficulty of maintaining hereditary states accustomed to a reigning family is far less than in new monarchies; for it is sufficient not to transgress ancestral usages, and to adapt one's self to unforeseen circumstances; in this way such a prince, if of ordinary assiduity, will always be able to maintain his position, unless some very exceptional and excessive force deprives him of it; and even if he be thus deprived, on the slightest mischance happening to the new occupier, he will be able to regain it.

We have in Italy the example of the Duke of Ferrara, who was able to withstand the assaults of the Venetians in 1484 and of Pope Julius in 1510, for no other reason than because of the antiquity of his family in that dominion. In as much as the legitimate prince has less cause and less necessity to give offence, it is only natural that he should be more loved; and, if no extraordinary vices make him hated, it is only reasonable for his subjects to be naturally attached to him, the memories and causes of innovations being forgotten in the long period over which his rule has extended; whereas one change always leaves the way prepared for the introduction of another.

Chapter III

OF MIXED MONARCHIES

BUT it is in the new monarchy that difficulties really exist. First, if it is not entirely new, but a member as it were of a mixed state, its disorders spring at first from a natural difficulty which exists in all new dominions, because men change masters willingly, hoping to better themselves; and this belief makes them take arms against their rulers, in which they are deceived, as experience later proves that they have gone from bad to worse. This is the result of another very natural cause, which is the inevitable harm inflicted on those over whom the prince obtains dominion, both by his soldiers and by an infinite number of other injuries caused by his occupation.

Thus you find enemies in all those whom you have injured by occupying that dominion, and you cannot maintain the friendship of those who have helped you to obtain this possession, as you will not be able to fulfil their expectations, nor can you use strong measures with them, being under an obligation to them; for which reason, however strong your armies may be, you will always need the favour of the inhabitants to take possession of a province. It was from these causes that Louis XII of France, though able to occupy Milan without trouble, immediately lost it, and the forces of Ludovico alone were sufficient to take it from him the first time, for the inhabitants who had willingly opened their gates to him, finding themselves deluded in the hopes they had cherished and not obtaining those benefits they had anticipated, could not bear the vexatious rule of their new prince.

How to conquer Italy

It is indeed true that, after reconquering rebel territories they are not so easily lost again, for the ruler is now, by the fact of the rebellion, less averse to secure his position by punishing offenders, unmasking suspects, and strengthening himself in weak places. So that although the mere appearance of such a person as Duke Ludovico on the frontier was sufficient to cause France to lose Milan the first time, to make her lose her grip of it the second time was only possible when all the world was against her, and after her armies had been defeated and driven out of Italy; which was the result of the causes above mentioned. Nevertheless it was taken from her both the first and the second time. The general causes of the first loss have been already discussed; it remains now to be seen what were the causes of the second loss and by what means France could have avoided it, or what measures might have been taken by another ruler in that position which were not taken by the King of France. Be it observed, therefore, that those states which on annexation are united to a previously existing state may or may not be of the same nationality and language. If they are, it is very easy to hold them, especially if they are not accustomed to freedom; and to possess them securely it suffices that the family of the princes which formerly governed them be extinct. For the rest, their old condition not being disturbed, and there being no dissimilarity of customs, the people settle down quietly under their new rulers, as is seen in the case of Burgundy, Brittany, Gascony, and Normandy, which have been so long united to France; and although there may be some slight differences of language, the customs of the people are nevertheless similar, and they can get along well together. Whoever obtains possession of such territories and wishes to retain them must bear in mind two things: the one, that the blood of their old rulers be extinct; the other, to make no alteration either in their laws or in their taxes; in this way they will in a very short space of time become united with their old possessions and form one state.

But when dominions are acquired in a province differing in language, laws, and customs, the difficulties to be overcome are great, and it requires good fortune as well as great industry to retain them; one of the best and most certain means of doing so would be for the new ruler to take up his residence there. This would render possession more secure and durable, and it is what the Turk has done in Greece. In spite of all the other measures taken by him to hold that state, it would not have been possible to retain it had he not gone to live there. Being on the spot, disorders can be seen as they arise and can quickly be remedied, but living at a distance, they are only heard of when they get beyond remedy. Besides which, the province is not despoiled by your officials, the subjects being able to obtain satisfaction by direct recourse to their prince; and wishing to be loyal they have more reason to love him, and should they be otherwise inclined they will have greater cause to fear him. Any external Power who wishes to assail that state will be less disposed to do so; so that as long as he resides there he will be very hard to dispossess.

The other and better remedy is to plant colonies in one or two of those places which form as it were the keys of the land, for it is necessary either to do this or to maintain a large force of armed men. The colonies will cost the prince little; with little or no expense on his part, he can send and maintain them; he only injures those whose lands and houses are taken to give to the new inhabitants, and these form but a small proportion of the state, and those who are injured, remaining poor and scattered, can never do any harm to him, and all the others are, on the one hand, not injured and therefore easily pacified; and, on the other, are fearful of offending lest they should be treated like those who have been dispossessed. To conclude, these colonies cost nothing, are more faithful, and give less offence; and the injured parties being poor and scattered are unable to do mischief, as I have shown. For it must be noted, that men must either be caressed or else annihilated; they will revenge themselves for small injuries, but cannot do so for great ones; the injury therefore that we do to a man must be such that we need not fear his vengeance. But by maintaining a garrison instead of colonists, one will spend much more, and consume all the revenues of that state in guarding it, so that the acquisition will result in a loss, besides giving much greater offence, since it injures every one in that state with the quartering of the army on it; which being an inconvenience felt by all, every one becomes an enemy, and these are enemies which can do mischief, as, though beaten, they remain in their own homes. In every way, therefore, a garrison is as useless as colonies are useful.

Further, the ruler of a foreign province as described, should make himself the leader and defender of his less powerful neighbours, and endeavour to weaken the stronger ones, and take care that they are not invaded by some foreigner not less powerful than himself. And it will be always the case that he will be invited to intervene at the request of

Take-no-prisoners; absolute all-or-nothing

those who are discontented either through ambition or fear,
as was seen when the Ætolians invited the Romans into
Greece; and in whatever province they entered, it was always at the request of the inhabitants. And the rule is that
when a powerful foreigner enters a province, all the less
powerful inhabitants become his adherents, moved by the
envy they bear to those ruling over them; so much so that
with regard to these minor potentates he has no trouble
whatever in winning them over, for they willingly join
forces with the state that he has acquired. He has merely to
be careful that they do not assume too much power and authority, and he can easily with his own forces and their
favour put down those that are powerful and remain in
everything arbiter of that province. And he who does not
govern well in this way will soon lose what he has acquired,
and while he holds it will meet with infinite difficulty and
trouble.

The Romans in the provinces they took, always followed
this policy; they established colonies, inveigled the less powerful without increasing their strength, put down the most
powerful and did not allow foreign rulers to obtain influence
in them. I will adduce the province of Greece as a sole example. They made friends with the Achæans and the Ætolians, the kingdom of Macedonia was cast down, and Antiochus driven out, nor did they allow the merits of the
Achæans or the Ætolians to gain them any increase of territory, nor did the persuasions of Philip induce them to be-
friend him without reducing his influence, nor could the
power of Antiochus make them consent to allow him to hold
any state in that province.

For the Romans did in these cases what all wise princes
should do, who consider not only present but also future
discords and diligently guard against them; for being fore-

seen they can easily be remedied, but if one waits till they are at hand, the medicine is no longer in time as the malady has become incurable; it happening with this as with those hectic fevers, as doctors say, which at their beginning are easy to cure but difficult to recognise, but in course of time when they have not at first been recognised and treated, become easy to recognise and difficult to cure. Thus it happens in matters of state; for knowing afar off (which it is only given to a prudent man to do) the evils that are brewing, they are easily cured. But when, for want of such knowledge, they are allowed to grow so that every one can recognise them, there is no longer any remedy to be found. Therefore, the Romans, observing disorders while yet remote, were always able to find a remedy, and never allowed them to increase in order to avoid a war; for they knew that war is not to be avoided, and can be deferred only to the advantage of the other side; they therefore declared war against Philip and Antiochus in Greece, so as not to have to fight them in Italy, though they might at the time have avoided either; this they did not choose to do, never caring to do that which is now every day to be heard in the mouths of our wise men, namely to enjoy the advantages of delay, but preferring to trust their own virtue and prudence; for time brings with it all things, and may produce indifferently either good or evil.

But let us return to France and examine whether she did any of these things; and I will speak not of Charles, but of Louis as the one whose proceedings can be better seen, as he held possession in Italy for a longer time; you will then see that he did the opposite of all those things which must be done to keep possession of a foreign state. King Louis was called into Italy by the ambition of the Venetians, who wished by his coming to gain half of Lombardy. I will not blame the king for coming nor for the part he took, because wishing to plant his foot in Italy, and not having friends in the country, on the contrary the conduct of King Charles having caused all doors to be closed to him, he was forced to accept what friendships he could find, and his schemes would have speedily been successful if he had made no mistakes in his other proceedings.

The king then, having acquired Lombardy, immediately won back the reputation lost by Charles. Genoa yielded, the Florentines became his friends, the Marquis of Mantua, the Dukes of Ferrara and Bentivogli, the Lady of Forlì, the Lords of Faenza, Pesaro, Rimini, Camerino, and Piombino, the inhabitants of Lucca, of Pisa, and of Siena, all approached him with offers of friendship. The Venetians might then have seen the effects of their temerity, how to gain a few cities in Lombardy they had made the king ruler over two-thirds of Italy.

Consider how little difficulty the king would have had in maintaining his reputation in Italy if he had observed the aforesaid rules, and kept a firm and sure hold over all those friends of his, who being many in number and weak, and fearful, one of the Church, another of the Venetians, were always obliged to hold fast to him, and by whose aid he could easily make sure of any who were still great. But he was hardly in Milan before he did exactly the opposite, by giving aid to Pope Alexander to occupy the Romagna. Nor did he perceive that, in taking this course, he weakened himself, by casting off his friends and those who had fled to his protection, and strengthened the Church by adding further temporal powers to the spiritual power, which gives it such authority. And having made the first mistake, he was obliged to follow it up, whilst, to put a stop to the ambition of Alexander and prevent him becoming ruler of Tuscany, he was forced to come to Italy. And not content with having increased the power of the Church and lost his friends, he now coveting the kingdom of Naples, divided it with the king of Spain; and where he alone was the arbiter of Italy, he now brought in a companion, so that the ambitious of that province who were dissatisfied with him might have some one else to appeal to; and where he might have left in that kingdom a king tributary to himself, he dispossessed him in order to bring in another who was capable of driving him out.

The desire to acquire possessions is a very natural and ordinary thing, and when those men do it who can do so successfully, they are always praised and not blamed, but when they cannot and yet want to do so at all costs, they make a mistake deserving of great blame. If France, therefore, with her own forces could have taken Naples, she ought to have done so; if she could not, she ought not to have shared it. And if the partition of Lombardy with the Venetians is to be excused, as having been the means of allowing the French king to set foot in Italy, this other partition deserves blame, not having the excuse of necessity.

Louis had thus made these five mistakes: he had crushed the smaller Powers, increased the power in Italy of one potentate, brought into the land a very powerful foreigner, he had not come to live there himself, nor had he established any colonies. Still these mistakes, if he had lived, might not have injured him, had he not made the sixth, that of taking the state from the Venetians; for, if he had not strengthened the Church and brought the Spaniards into Italy, it would have been right and necessary to humble them; having once taken those measures, he ought never to have consented to their ruin; because, had the Venetians been strong, it would have kept the others from making attempts on Lombardy

partly because the Venetians would not have consented to
any measures by which they did not get it for themselves,
and partly because the others would not have wanted to
take it from France to give it to Venice, and would not
have had the courage to attack both.

If any one urges that King Louis yielded Romagna to
Alexander and the Kingdom of Naples to Spain in order
to avoid war, I reply, with the reasons already given, that
one ought never to allow a disorder to take place in order to
avoid war, for war is not thereby avoided, but only deferred
to your disadvantage. And if others allege the promise
given by the king to the pope to undertake that enterprise
for him, in return for the dissolution of his marriage and for
the cardinalship of Rohan, I reply with what I shall say
later on about the faith of princes and how it is to be observed. Thus King Louis lost Lombardy through not observing any of those conditions which have been observed
by others who have taken provinces and wished to retain
them. Nor is this any miracle, but very reasonable and natural. I spoke of this matter with Cardinal Rohan at Nantes
when Valentine, as Cesare Borgia, son of Pope Alexander,
was commonly called, was occupying the Romagna, for on
Cardinal Rohan saying to me that the Italians did not understand war, I replied that the French did not understand politics, for if they did they would never allow
the Church to become so great. And experience shows us
that the greatness in Italy of the Church and also of Spain
have been caused by France, and her ruin has proceeded
from them. From which may be drawn a general rule,
which never or very rarely fails, that whoever is the cause
of another becoming powerful, is ruined himself; for that
power is produced by him either through craft or force; and
both of these are suspected by the one who has been raised
to power.

Chapter IV

WHY THE KINGDOM OF DARIUS, OCCUPIED BY ALEXANDER, DID NOT REBEL AGAINST THE SUCCESSORS OF THE LATTER AFTER HIS DEATH

CONSIDERING the difficulties there are in holding a newly acquired state, some may wonder how it came to pass that Alexander the Great became master of Asia in a few years, and had hardly occupied it when he died, from which it might be supposed that the whole state would have rebelled. However, his successors maintained themselves in possession, and had no further difficulties in doing so than those which arose among themselves from their own ambitions.

I reply that the kingdoms known to history have been governed in two ways: either by a prince and his servants, who, as ministers by his grace and permission, assist in governing the realm; or by a prince and by barons, who hold their positions not by favour of the ruler but by antiquity of blood. Such barons have states and subjects of their own, who recognise them as their lords, and are naturally attached to them. In those states which are governed by a prince and his servants, the prince possesses more authority, because there is no one in the state regarded as a superior other than himself, and if others are obeyed it is merely as ministers and officials of the prince, and no one regards them with any special affection.

Examples of these two kinds of government in our own time are those of the Turk and the King of France. All the Turkish monarchy is governed by one ruler, the others are his servants, and dividing his kingdom into "sangiacates,"

he sends to them various administrators, and changes or recalls them at his pleasure. But the King of France is surrounded by a large number of ancient nobles, recognised as
such by their subjects, and loved by them; they have their
prerogatives, of which the king cannot deprive them without danger to himself. Whoever now considers these two
states will see that it would be difficult to acquire the state
of the Turk; but having conquered it, it would be very easy
to hold it. In many respects, on the other hand, it would be
easier to conquer the kingdom of France, but there would
be great difficulty in holding it.

The causes of the difficulty of occupying the Turkish
kingdom are, that the invader could not be invited by
princes of that kingdom, nor hope to facilitate his enterprise
by the rebellion of those near the ruler's person, as will be
evident from reasons given above. Because, being all slaves,
and dependent, it will be more difficult to corrupt them, and
even if they were corrupted, little effect could be hoped for,
as they would not be able to carry the people with them for
the reasons mentioned. Therefore, whoever assaults the
Turk must be prepared to meet his united forces, and must
rely more on his own strength than on the disorders of
others; but having once conquered him, and beaten him in
battle so that he can no longer raise armies, nothing else is
to be feared except the family of the prince, and if this be
extinguished, there is no longer any one to be feared, others
having no credit with the people; and as the victor before
the victory could place no hope in them, so he need not fear
them afterwards.

The contrary is the case in kingdoms governed like that
of France, because it is easy to enter them by winning over
some baron of the kingdom, there being always malcontents,
and those desiring innovations. These can, for the reasons

stated, open the way to you and facilitate victory; but afterwards, if you wish to keep possession, infinite difficulties arise, both from those who have aided you and from those you have oppressed. Nor is it sufficient to suppress the family of the prince, for there remain those nobles who will take the lead in new revolutions, and being neither able to content them nor exterminate them, you will lose the state whenever an occasion arises.

Now if you will consider what was the nature of the government of Darius you will find it similar to the kingdom of the Turk, and therefore Alexander had first to overthrow it completely and invade the territory, after which victory, Darius being dead, the state remained secure to Alexander, for the reasons discussed above. And his successors, had they remained united, might have enjoyed it in peace, nor did any tumults arise in the kingdom except those fomented by themselves. But it is impossible to possess with such ease countries constituted like France. Hence arose the frequent rebellions of Spain, France, and Greece against the Romans, owing to the numerous principalities which existed in those states; for, as long as the memory of these lasted, the Romans were always uncertain of their conquest; but when the memory of these principalities had been extinguished and with the power and duration of the empire, they became unchallenged masters. When the Romans fell out amongst themselves, any one of them could count on the support of that part of the province where he had established authority. The Romans alone were recognised as rulers there after the extinction of the old line of princes. Considering these things, therefore, let no one be surprised at the facility with which Alexander was able to hold Asia, and at the difficulties that others have had in holding conquered territories, like Pyrrhus and many others; as this was not caused by the greater or lesser ability of the conqueror, but depended on the dissimilarity of the conditions.

Chapter V

THE WAY TO GOVERN CITIES OR DOMINIONS THAT, PREVIOUS TO BEING OCCUPIED, LIVED UNDER THEIR OWN LAWS

WHEN those states which have been acquired are accustomed to live at liberty under their own laws, there are three ways of holding them. The first is to despoil them; the second is to go and live there in person; the third is to allow them to live under their own laws, taking tribute of them, and creating within the country a government composed of a few who will keep it friendly to you. Because this government, being created by the prince, knows that it cannot exist without his friendship and protection, and will do all it can to keep them. What is more, a city used to liberty can be more easily held by means of its citizens than in any other way, if you wish to preserve it.

There is the example of the Spartans and the Romans. The Spartans held Athens and Thebes by creating within them a government of a few; nevertheless they lost them. The Romans, in order to hold Capua, Carthage, and Numantia, ravaged them, but did not lose them. They wanted to hold Greece in almost the same way as the Spartans held it, leaving it free and under its own laws, but they did not succeed; so that they were compelled to lay waste many cities in that province in order to keep it, because in truth there is no sure method of holding them except by despoiling them. And whoever becomes the ruler of a free city and does not destroy it, can expect to be destroyed by it, for it

can always find a motive for rebellion in the name of liberty
and of its ancient usages, which are forgotten neither by
lapse of time nor by benefits received; and whatever one
does or provides, so long as the inhabitants are not separated
or dispersed, they do not forget that name and those usages,
but appeal to them at once in every emergency, as did Pisa
after being so many years held in servitude by the Florentines. But when cities or provinces have been accustomed to
live under a prince, and the family of that prince is extinguished, being on the one hand used to obey, and on the
other not having their old prince, they cannot unite in
choosing one from among themselves, and they do not
know how to live in freedom, so that they are slower to
take arms, and a prince can win them over with greater
facility and establish himself securely. But in republics
there is greater life, greater hatred, and more desire for
vengeance; they do not and cannot cast aside the memory
of their ancient liberty, so that the surest way is either to
lay them waste or reside in them.

Emulate one another

Chapter VI

OF NEW DOMINIONS WHICH HAVE BEEN ACQUIRED BY ONE'S OWN ARMS AND ABILITY

LET no one marvel if in speaking of new dominions both
as to prince and state, I bring forward very exalted instances, for men walk almost always in the paths trodden
by others, proceeding in their actions by imitation. Not
being always able to follow others exactly, nor attain to
the excellence of those he imitates, a prudent man should
always follow in the path trodden by great men and

tate those who are most excellent, so that if he does not attain to their greatness, at any rate he will get some tinge of it. He will do as prudent archers, who when the place they wish to hit is too far off, knowing how far their bow will carry, aim at a spot much higher than the one they wish to hit, not in order to reach this height with their arrow, but by help of this high aim to hit the spot they wish to.

I say then that in new dominions, where there is a new prince, it is more or less easy to hold them according to the greater or lesser ability of him who acquires them. And as the fact of a private individual becoming a prince presupposes either great ability or good fortune, it would appear that either of these things would in part mitigate many difficulties. Nevertheless those who have been less beholden to good fortune have maintained themselves best. The matter is also facilitated by the prince being obliged to reside personally in his territory, having no others. But to come to those who have become princes through their own merits and not by fortune, I regard as the greatest, Moses, Cyrus, Romulus, Theseus, and their like. And although one should not speak of Moses, he having merely carried out what was ordered him by God, still he deserves admiration, if only for that grace which made him worthy to speak with God. But regarding Cyrus and others who have acquired or founded kingdoms, they will all be found worthy of admiration; and if their particular actions and methods are examined they will not appear very different from those of Moses, although he had so great a Master. And in examining their life and deeds it will be seen that they owed nothing to fortune but the opportunity which gave them matter to mould into what form they thought fit; and without that opportunity their powers would have been wasted,

and without their powers the opportunity would have come in vain.

It was thus necessary that Moses should find the people of Israel slaves in Egypt and oppressed by the Egyptians, so that they were disposed to follow him in order to escape from their servitude. It was necessary that Romulus should be unable to remain in Alba, and should have been exposed at his birth, in order that he might become King of Rome and founder of that nation. It was necessary that Cyrus should find the Persians discontented with the empire of the Medes, and the Medes weak and effeminate through long peace. Theseus could not have shown his abilities if he had not found the Athenians dispersed. These opportunities, therefore, gave these men their chance, and their own great qualities enabled them to profit by them, so as to ennoble their country and augment its fortunes.

Those who by the exercise of abilities such as these become princes, obtain their dominions with difficulty but retain them easily, and the difficulties which they have in acquiring their dominions arise in part from the new rules and regulations that they have to introduce in order to establish their position securely. It must be considered that there is nothing more difficult to carry out, nor more doubtful of success, nor more dangerous to handle, than to initiate a new order of things. For the reformer has enemies in all those who profit by the old order, and only lukewarm defenders in all those who would profit by the new order, this lukewarmness arising partly from fear of their adversaries, who have the laws in their favour; and partly from the incredulity of mankind, who do not truly believe in anything new until they have had actual experience of it. Thus it arises that on every opportunity for attacking the reformer, his opponents do so with the zeal of partisans, the others only defend him half-heartedly, so that between them he runs great danger. It is necessary, however, in order to investigate thoroughly this question, to examine whether these innovators are independent, or whether they depend upon others, that is to say, whether in order to carry out their designs they have to entreat or are able to compel. In the first case they invariably succeed ill, and accomplish nothing; but when they can depend on their own strength and are able to use force, they rarely fail. Thus it comes about that all armed prophets have conquered and unarmed ones failed; for besides what has been already said, the character of peoples varies, and it is easy to persuade them of a thing, but difficult to keep them in that persuasion. And so it is necessary to order things so that when they no longer believe, they can be made to believe by force. Moses, Cyrus, Theseus, and Romulus would not have been able to keep their constitutions observed for so long had they been disarmed, as happened in our own time with Fra Girolamo Savonarola, who failed entirely in his new rules when the multitude began to disbelieve in him, and he had no means of holding fast those who had believed nor of compelling the unbelievers to believe. Therefore such men as these have great difficulty in making their way, and all their dangers are met on the road and must be overcome by their own abilities; but when once they have overcome them and have begun to be held in veneration, and have suppressed those who envied them, they remain powerful and secure, honoured and happy.

To the high examples given I will add a lesser one, which, however, is in some measure comparable and will serve as an instance of all such cases, that of Hiero of Syracuse, who from a private individual became Prince of Syracuse, without other aid from fortune beyond the opportunity; for the

Syracusans being oppressed, elected him as their captain, from which post he rose by ability to be prince; while still in private life his virtues were such that it was written of him, that he lacked nothing to reign but the kingdom. He abolished the old militia, raised a new one, abandoned his old friendships and formed others; and as he had thus friends and soldiers of his own choosing, he was able on this foundation to build securely, so that while he had great trouble in acquiring his position he had little in maintaining it.

Chapter VII

OF NEW DOMINIONS ACQUIRED BY THE POWER OF OTHERS OR BY FORTUNE

THOSE who rise from private citizens to be princes merely by fortune have little trouble in rising but very much in maintaining their position. They meet with no difficulties on the way as they fly over them, but all their difficulties arise when they are established. Such are they who are granted a state either for money, or by favour of him who grants it, as happened to many in Greece, in the cities of Ionia and of the Hellespont, who were created princes by Darius in order to hold these places for his security and glory; such were also those emperors who from private citizens rose to power by bribing the army. Such as these depend absolutely on the good will and fortune of those who have raised them, both of which are extremely inconstant and unstable. They neither know how to, nor are in a position to maintain their rank, for unless he be a man of great genius it is not likely that one who has always lived in a private position should know how to command, and they are unable to maintain themselves because they possess no forces friendly and faithful to them. Moreover, states quickly founded, like all other things of rapid beginnings and growth, cannot have deep roots and wide ramifications, so that the first storm destroys them, unless, as already said, the man who thus becomes a prince is of such great genius as to be able to take immediate steps for maintaining what fortune has thrown into his lap, and lay afterwards those foundations which others make before becoming princes.

With regard to these two methods of becoming a prince, —by ability or by good fortune, I will here adduce two examples which have occurred within our memory, those of Francesco Sforza and Cesare Borgia. Francesco, by appropriate means and through great abilities, from citizen became Duke of Milan, and what he had attained after a thousand difficulties he maintained with little trouble. On the other hand, Cesare Borgia, commonly called Duke Valentine, acquired the state by the influence of his father and lost it when that influence failed, and that although every measure was adopted by him and everything done that a prudent and capable man could do to establish himself firmly in a state that the arms and the favours of others had given him. For, as we have said, he who does not lay his foundations beforehand may by great abilities do so afterwards, although with great trouble to the architect and danger to the building. If, then, one considers the procedure of the duke, it will be seen how firm were the foundations he had laid to his future power, which I do not think it superfluous to examine, as I know of no better precepts for a new prince to follow than may be found in his actions; and if his measures were not successful, it was through no fault of his own but only by the most extraordinary malignity of fortune.

In wishing to aggrandise the duke his son, Alexander VI had to meet very great difficulties both present and future. In the first place, he saw no way of making him ruler of any state that was not a possession of the Church. He knew that the Duke of Milan and the Venetians would not consent in his attempt to take papal cities, because Faenza and Rimini were already under the protection of the Venetians. He saw, moreover, that the military forces of Italy, especially those which might have served him, were in the hands of those who would fear the greatness of the pope, and therefore he could not depend upon them, being all under the command of the Orsini and Colonna and their adherents. It was, therefore, necessary to disturb the existing condition and bring about disorders in the states of Italy in order to obtain secure mastery over a part of them; this was easy, for he found the Venetians, who, actuated by other motives, had invited the French into Italy, which he not only did not oppose, but facilitated by dissolving the first marriage of King Louis. The king came thus into Italy with the aid of the Venetians and the consent of Alexander, and had hardly arrived at Milan before the pope obtained troops from him for his enterprise in the Romagna, which was made possible for him thanks to the reputation of the king. The duke having thus obtained the Romagna and defeated the Colonna, was hindered by two things in maintaining it and proceeding further: the one, his forces, of which he doubted the fidelity; the other the will of France; that is to say, he feared lest the arms of the Orsini of which he had availed himself should fail him, and not only hinder him in obtaining more but take from him what he had already conquered, and he also feared that the king might do the same. He had evidence of this as regards the Orsini when, after taking Faenza, he assaulted Bologna and observed their backwardness in the assault. And as regards the king, he perceived his designs when, after taking the dukedom of Urbino, he attacked Tuscany, and the king made him desist from that enterprise. Whereupon the duke decided to depend no longer on the fortunes and arms of others. The first thing he did was to weaken the parties of the Orsini and Colonna in Rome by gaining all their adherents who were gentlemen and making them his own followers, by granting them large remuneration, and appointing them to commands and offices according to their rank, so that their attachment to their parties was extinguished in a few months, and entirely concentrated on the duke. After this he awaited an opportunity for crushing the chiefs of the Orsini, having already suppressed those of the Colonna family, and when the opportunity arrived he made good use of it, for the Orsini seeing at length that the greatness of the duke and of the Church meant their own ruin, convoked a diet at Magione in the Perugino. Hence sprang the rebellion of Urbino and the tumults in Romagna and infinite dangers to the duke, who overcame them all with the help of the French; and having regained his reputation, neither trusting France nor other foreign forces, in order not to venture on their alliance, he had recourse to stratagem. He dissembled his aims so well that the Orsini made their peace with him, being represented by Signor Paulo whose suspicions the duke disarmed with every courtesy, presenting him with robes, money, and horses, so that in their simplicity they were induced to come to Sinigaglia and fell into his hands. Having thus suppressed these leaders and made their partisans his friends, the duke had laid a very good foundation to his power, having all the Romagna with the duchy of Urbino, and having gained the favour of the inhabitants, who began to feel the benefit of his rule.

And as this part is worthy of note and of imitation by others, I will not omit mention of it. When he took the Romagna, it had previously been governed by weak rulers, who had rather despoiled their subjects than governed them, and given them more cause for disunion than for union, so that the province was a prey to robbery, assaults, and every kind of disorder. He, therefore, judged it necessary to give them a good government in order to make them peaceful and obedient to his rule. For this purpose he appointed Messer Remirro de Orco, a cruel and able man, to whom he gave the fullest authority. This man, in a short time, was highly successful in rendering the country orderly and united, whereupon the duke, not deeming such excessive authority expedient, lest it should become hateful, appointed a civil court of justice in the centre of the province under an excellent president, to which each city appointed its own advocate. And as he knew that the harshness of the past had engendered some amount of hatred, in order to purge the minds of the people and to win them over completely, he resolved to show that if any cruelty had taken place it was not by his orders, but through the harsh disposition of his minister. And having found the opportunity he had him cut in half and placed one morning in the public square at Cesena with a piece of wood and blood-stained knife by his side. The ferocity of this spectacle caused the people both satisfaction and amazement. But to return to where we left off.

The duke being now powerful and partly secured against present perils, being armed himself, and having in a great measure put down those neighbouring forces which might injure him, had now to get the respect of France, if he wished to proceed with his acquisitions, for he knew that the king, who had lately discovered his error, would not give him any help. He began therefore to seek fresh alliances and to vacillate with France on the occasion of the expedition that the French were undertaking towards the kingdom of Naples against the Spaniards, who were besieging Gaeta. His intention was to assure himself of them, which he would soon have succeeded in doing if Alexander had lived.

These were the measures taken by him with regard to the present. As to the future, he feared that a new successor to the states of the Church might not be friendly to him and might seek to deprive him of what Alexander had given him, and he sought to provide against this in four ways. First, by destroying all who were of the blood of those ruling families which he had despoiled, in order to deprive the pope of any opportunity. Secondly, by gaining the friendship of the Roman nobles, so that he might through them hold as it were the pope in check. Thirdly, by obtaining as great a hold on the College as he could. Fourthly, by acquiring such power before the pope died as to be able to resist alone the first onslaught. Of these four things he had at the death of Alexander accomplished three, and the fourth he had almost accomplished. For of the dispossessed rulers he killed as many as he could lay hands on, and very few escaped; he had gained to his party the Roman nobles; and he had a great influence in the College. As to new possessions, he designed to become lord of Tuscany, and already possessed Perugia and Piombino, and had assumed the protectorate over Pisa; and as he had no longer to fear the French (for the French had been deprived of the kingdom of Naples by the Spaniards in such a way that both parties were obliged to buy his friendship) he seized Pisa. After this, Lucca and Siena at once yielded, partly through hate of the Florentines and partly through fear; the Florentines had no resources, so that, had he succeeded as he had done before, in the very year that Alexander died he would have gained such strength and renown as to be able to maintain himself without depending on the fortunes or strength of others, but solely by his own power and ability. But Alexander died five years after Cesare Borgia had first drawn his sword. He was left with only the state of Romagna firmly established, and all the other schemes in mid-air, between two very powerful and hostile armies, and suffering from a fatal illness. But the valour and ability of the duke were such, and he knew so well how to win over men or vanquish them, and so strong were the foundations that he had laid in this short time, that if he had not had those two armies upon him, or else had been in good health, he would have survived every difficulty. And that his foundations were good is seen from the fact that the Romagna waited for him more than a month; in Rome, although half dead, he remained secure, and although the Baglioni, Vitelli, and Orsini entered Rome they found no followers against him. He was able, if not to make pope whom he wished, at any rate to prevent a pope being created whom he did not wish. But if at the death of Alexander he had been well, everything would have been easy. And he told me on the day that Pope Julius II was elected, that he had thought of everything which might happen on the death of his father, and provided against everything, except that he had never thought that at his father's death he would be dying himself.

Reviewing thus all the actions of the duke, I find nothing to blame, on the contrary, I feel bound, as I have done, to hold him up as an example to be imitated by all who by fortune and with the arms of others have risen to power. For with his great courage and high ambition he could not have acted otherwise, and his designs were only frustrated by the short life of Alexander and his own illness. Whoever, therefore, deems it necessary in his new principality to secure himself against enemies, to gain friends, to conquer by force or fraud, to make himself beloved and feared by the people, followed and reverenced by the soldiers, to destroy those who can and may injure him, introduce innovations into old customs, to be severe and kind, magnanimous and liberal, suppress the old militia, create a new one, maintain the friendship of kings and princes in such a way that they are glad to benefit him and fear to injure him, such a one can find no better example than the actions of this man. The only thing he can be accused of is that in the creation of Julius II he made a bad choice; for, as has been said, not being able to choose his own pope, he could still prevent any one individual being made pope, and he ought never to have permitted any of those cardinals to be raised to the papacy whom he had injured, or who when pope would stand in fear of him. For men commit injuries either through fear or through hate. Those whom he had injured were, among others, San Pietro ad Vincula, Colonna, San Giorgio, and Ascanio. All the others, if elected to the pontificate, would have had to fear him except Rohan and the Spaniards; the latter through their relationship and obligations to him, the former from his great power, being related to the King of France. For these reasons the duke ought above all things to have created a Spaniard pope; and if unable, then he should have consented to Rohan being appointed and not San Pietro ad Vincula. And whoever thinks that in high personages new benefits cause old offences to be forgotten, makes a great mistake. The duke, therefore, erred in this choice, and it was the cause of his ultimate ruin.

Chapter VIII

OF THOSE WHO HAVE ATTAINED THE POSITION OF PRINCE BY VILLAINY

But as there are still two ways of becoming prince which cannot be attributed entirely either to fortune or to ability, they must not be passed over, although one of them could be more fully discussed if we were treating of republics. These are when one becomes prince by some nefarious or villainous means, or when a private citizen becomes the prince of his country through the favour of his fellow-citizens. And in speaking of the former means, I will give two examples, one ancient, the other modern, without entering further into the merits of this method, as I judge them to be sufficient for any one obliged to imitate them.

Agathocles the Sicilian rose not only from private life but from the lowest and most abject position to be King of Syracuse. The son of a potter, he led a life of the utmost wickedness through all the stages of his fortune. Nevertheless, his wickedness was accompanied by such vigour of mind and body that, having joined the militia, he rose through its ranks to be prætor of Syracuse. Having been appointed to this position, and having decided to become prince, and to hold with violence and without the support of others that which had been constitutionally granted him; and having imparted his design to Hamilcar the Carthaginian, who was fighting with his armies in Sicily, he called together one morning the people and senate of Syracuse, as if he had to deliberate on matters of importance to the republic, and at a given signal had all the senators and the

richest men of the people killed by his soldiers. After their
death he occupied and held rule over the city without any
civil strife. And although he was twice beaten by the Carthaginians and ultimately besieged, he was able not only to
defend the city, but leaving a portion of his forces for its
defence, with the remainder he invaded Africa, and in a
short time liberated Syracuse from the siege and brought
the Carthaginians to great extremities, so that they were
obliged to come to terms with him, and remain contented
with the possession of Africa, leaving Sicily to Agathocles.
Whoever considers, therefore, the actions and qualities of
this man, will see few if any things which can be attributed
to fortune; for, as above stated, it was not by the favour
of any person, but through the grades of the militia, in
which he had advanced with a thousand hardships and
perils, that he arrived at the position of prince, which he
afterwards maintained by so many courageous and perilous
expedients. It cannot be called virtue to kill one's fellow-
citizens, betray one's friends, be without faith, without pity,
and without religion; by these methods one may indeed gain
power, but not glory. For if the virtues of Agathocles in
braving and overcoming perils, and his greatness of soul in
supporting and surmounting obstacles be considered, one
sees no reason for holding him inferior to any of the most
renowned captains. Nevertheless his barbarous cruelty and
inhumanity, together with his countless atrocities, do not
permit of his being named among the most famous men.
We cannot attribute to fortune or virtue that which he
achieved without either.

In our own times, during the pontificate of Alexander
VI, Oliverotto da Fermo had been left as a young fatherless
boy under the care of his maternal uncle, Giovanni Fogliani, who brought him up, and sent him in early youth to

soldier under Paolo Vitelli, in order that he might, trained in that hard school, obtain a good military position. On the death of Paolo he fought under his brother Vitellozzo, and in a very short time, being of great intelligence, and active in mind and body, he became one of the leaders of his troops. But deeming it servile to be under others, he resolved, with the help of some citizens of Fermo, who preferred servitude to the liberty of their country, and with the favour of the Vitelli, to occupy Fermo; he therefore wrote to Giovanni Fogliani, how, having been for many years away from home, he wished to come to see him and his city, and as far as possible to inspect his estates. And as he had only laboured to gain honour, in order that his fellow-citizens might see that he had not spent his time in vain, he wished to come honourably accompanied by one hundred horsemen, his friends and followers, and prayed him that he would be pleased to order that he should be received with honour by the citizens of Fermo, by which he would honour not only him, Oliverotto, but also himself, as he had been his pupil. Giovanni did not fail in any due courtesy towards his nephew; he caused him to be honourably received by the people of Fermo, and lodged him in his own houses. After waiting some days to arrange all that was necessary to his villainous projects, Oliverotto invited Giovanni Fogliani and all the principal men of Fermo to a grand banquet. After the dinner and the entertainments usual at such feasts, Oliverotto artfully introduced certain important matters of discussion, speaking of the greatness of Pope Alexander, and of his son Cesare, and of their enterprises. To which discourses Giovanni and others having replied, he all at once rose, saying that these matters should be spoken of in a more private place, and withdrew into a room where Giovanni and the other citizens followed him. They were no

Violence worked to rid enemies

Take no prisoners

sooner seated than soldiers rushed out of hiding-places and killed Giovanni and all the others. After which massacre Oliverotto mounted his horse, rode through the town and besieged the chief magistrate in his palace, so that through fear they were obliged to obey him and form a government, of which he made himself prince. And all those being dead who, if discontented, could injure him, he fortified himself with new orders, civil and military, in such a way that within the year that he held the principality he was not only safe himself in the city of Fermo, but had become formidable to all his neighbours. And his overthrow would have been difficult, like that of Agathocles, if he had not allowed himself to be deceived by Cesare Borgia, when he captured the Orsini and Vitelli at Sinigaglia, as already related, where he also was taken, one year after the parricide he had committed, and strangled, together with Vitellozzo, who had been his teacher in ability and atrocity.

Some may wonder how it came about that Agathocles, and others like him, could, after infinite treachery and cruelty, live secure for many years in their country and defend themselves from external enemies without being conspired against by their subjects; although many others have, owing to their cruelty, been unable to maintain their position in times of peace, not to speak of the uncertain times of war. I believe this arises from the cruelties being exploited well or badly. Well committed may be called those (if it is permissible to use the word well of evil) which are perpetuated once for the need of securing one's self, and which afterwards are not persisted in, but are exchanged for measures as useful to the subjects as possible. Cruelties ill committed are those which, although at first few, increase rather than diminish with time. Those who follow the former method may remedy in some measure their condition, both with God

Machiavelli doesn't judge

and man; as did Agathocles. As to the others, it is impossible for them to maintain themselves.

Whence it is to be noted, that in taking a state the conqueror must arrange to commit all his cruelties at once, so as not to have to recur to them every day, and so as to be able, by not making fresh changes, to reassure people and win them over by benefiting them. Whoever acts otherwise, either through timidity or bad counsels, is always obliged to stand with knife in hand, and can never depend on his subjects, because they, owing to continually fresh injuries, are unable to depend upon him. For injuries should be done all together, so that being less tasted, they will give less offence. Benefits should be granted little by little, so that they may be better enjoyed. And above all, a prince must live with his subjects in such a way that no accident of good or evil fortune can deflect him from his course; for necessity arising in adverse times, you are not in time with severity, and the good that you do does not profit, as it is judged to be forced upon you, and you will derive no benefit whatever from it.

Chapter IX

OF THE CIVIC PRINCIPALITY

BUT we now come to the case where a citizen becomes prince not through crime or intolerable violence, but by the favour of his fellow-citizens, which may be called a civic principality. To attain this position depends not entirely on worth or entirely on fortune, but rather on cunning assisted by fortune. One attains it by help of popular favour or by the favour of the aristocracy. For in every city these two opposite parties are to be found, arising from the desire of the populace to avoid the oppression of the great, and the desire of the great to command and oppress the people. And from these two opposing interests arises in the city one of the three effects: either absolute government, liberty, or licence. The former is created either by the populace or the nobility, depending on the relative opportunities of the two parties; for when the nobility see that they are unable to resist the people they unite in exalting one of their number and creating him prince, so as to be able to carry out their own designs under the shadow of his authority. The populace, on the other hand, when unable to resist the nobility, endeavour to exalt and create a prince in order to be protected by his authority. He who becomes prince by help of the nobility has greater difficulty in maintaining his power than he who is raised by the populace, for he is surrounded by those who think themselves his equals, and is thus unable to direct or command as he pleases. But one who is raised to leadership by popular favour finds himself alone, and has no one, or very few, who are not ready to obey him. Besides which, it is impossible to satisfy the nobility by fair dealing and without inflicting injury on others, whereas it is very easy to satisfy the mass of the people in this way. For the aim of the people is more honest than that of the nobility, the latter desiring to oppress, and the former merely to avoid oppression. It must also be added that the prince can never insure himself against a hostile populace on account of their number, but he can against the hostility of the great, as they are but few. The worst that a prince has to expect from a hostile people is to be abandoned, but from hostile nobles he has to fear not only desertion but their active opposition, and as they are more far-seeing and more cunning, they are always in time to save themselves and take sides with the one who they expect will conquer. The prince is, moreover, obliged to live always with the same people, but he can easily do without the same nobility, being able to make and unmake them at any time, and improve their position or deprive them of it as he pleases.

And to throw further light on this part of my argument, I would say, that the nobles are to be considered in two different manners; that is, they are either to be ruled so as to make them entirely dependent on your fortunes, or else not. Those that are thus bound to you and are not rapacious, must be honoured and loved; those who stand aloof must be considered in two ways, they either do this through pusillanimity and natural want of courage, and in this case you ought to make use of them, and especially such as are of good counsel, so that they may honour you in prosperity and in adversity you have not to fear them. But when they are not bound to you of set purpose and for ambitious ends, it is a sign that they think more of themselves than of you; and from such men the prince must guard himself and look upon them as secret enemies, who will help to ruin him when in adversity.

One, however, who becomes prince by favour of the populace, must maintain its friendship, which he will find easy, the people asking nothing but not to be oppressed. But one who against the people's wishes becomes prince by favour of the nobles, should above all endeavour to gain the favour of the people; this will be easy to him if he protects them. And as men, who receive good from whom they expected evil, feel under a greater obligation to their benefactor, so the populace will soon become even better disposed towards him than if he had become prince through their favour. The prince can win their favour in many ways, which vary according to circumstances, for which no certain rule can be given, and will therefore be passed over. I will only say, in conclusion, that it is necessary for a prince to possess the friendship of the people; otherwise he has no resource in times of adversity.

Nabis, prince of the Spartans, sustained a siege by the whole of Greece and a victorious Roman army, and defended his country against them and maintained his own position. It sufficed when the danger arose for him to make sure of a few, which would not have sufficed if the populace had been hostile to him. And let no one oppose my opinion in this by quoting the trite proverb, "He who builds on the people, builds on mud"; because that is true when a private citizen relies upon the people and persuades himself that they will liberate him if he is oppressed by enemies or by the magistrates; in this case he might often find himself deceived, as were in Rome the Gracchi and in Florence Messer Georgio Scali. But when it is a prince who founds himself on this basis, one who can command and is a man of courage, and does not get frightened in adversity, and does not neglect other preparations, and one who by his own valour and measures animates the mass of the people, he will not find himself deceived by them, and he will find that he has laid his foundations well.

Usually these principalities are in danger when the prince from the position of a civil ruler changes to an absolute one, for these princes either command themselves or by means of magistrates. In the latter case their position is weaker and more dangerous, for they are at the mercy of those citizens who are appointed magistrates, who can, especially in times of adversity, with great facility deprive them of their position, either by acting against them or by not obeying them. The prince is not in time, in such dangers, to assume absolute authority, for the citizens and subjects who are accustomed to take their orders from the magistrates are not ready in these emergencies to obey his, and he will always in difficult times lack men whom he can rely on. Such a prince cannot base himself on what he sees in quiet times, when the citizens have need of the state; for then every one is full of promises and each one is ready to die for him when death is far off; but in adversity, when the state has need of citizens, then he will find but few. And this experience is the more dangerous, in that it can only be had once. Therefore a wise prince will seek means by which his subjects will always and in every possible condition of things have need of his government, and then they will always be faithful to him.

Chapter X

HOW THE STRENGTH OF ALL STATES SHOULD BE MEASURED

IN examining the character of these principalities it is necessary to consider another point, namely, whether the prince has such a position as to be able in case of need to maintain himself alone, or whether he has always need of the protection of others. The better to explain this I would say, that I consider those capable of maintaining themselves alone who can, through abundance of men or money, put together a sufficient army, and hold the field against any one who assails them; and I consider to have need of others, those who cannot take the field against their enemies, but are obliged to take refuge within their walls and stand on the defensive. We have already discussed the former case and will speak of it in future as occasion arises. In the second case there is nothing to be said except to encourage such a prince to provision and fortify his own town, and not to trouble about the surrounding country. And whoever has strongly fortified his town and, as regards the government of his subjects, has proceeded as we have already described and will further relate, will be attacked with great reluctance, for men are always averse to enterprises in which they foresee difficulties, and it can never appear easy to attack one who has his town stoutly defended and is not hated by the people.

The cities of Germany are absolutely free, have little surrounding country, and obey the emperor when they choose, and they do not fear him or any other potentate that they have about them. They are fortified in such a manner that every one thinks that to reduce them would be tedious and difficult, for they all have the necessary moats and bastions, sufficient artillery, and always keep food, drink, and fuel for one year in the public storehouses. Beyond which, to keep the lower classes satisfied, and without loss to the commonwealth, they have always enough means to give them work for one year in these employments which form the nerve and life of the town, and in the industries by which the lower classes live. Military exercises are still held in high reputation, and many regulations are in force for maintaining them.

A prince, therefore, who possesses a strong city and does not make himself hated, cannot be assaulted; and if he were to be so, the assailant would be obliged to retire shamefully; for so many things change, that it is almost impossible for any one to maintain a siege for a year with his armies idle. And to those who urge that the people, having their possessions outside and seeing them burnt, will not have patience, and the long siege and self-interest will make them forget their prince, I reply that a powerful and courageous prince will always overcome those difficulties by now raising the hopes of his subjects that the evils will not last long, now impressing them with fear of the enemy's cruelty, now by dextrously assuring himself of those who appear too bold. Besides which, the enemy would naturally burn and ravage the country on first arriving and at the time when men's minds are still hot and eager to defend themselves, and therefore the prince has still less to fear, for after some time, when people have cooled down, the damage is done, the evil has been suffered, and there is no remedy, so that they are the more ready to unite with their prince, as it appears that he is under an obligation to them, their houses having been burnt and their possessions ruined in his defence.

It is the nature of men to be as much bound by the benefits that they confer as by those they receive. From which it follows that, everything considered, a prudent prince will not find it difficult to uphold the courage of his subjects both at the commencement and during a state of siege, if he possesses provisions and means to defend himself.

Chapter XI

OF ECCLESIASTICAL PRINCIPALITIES

IT now only remains to us to speak of ecclesiastical principalities, with regard to which the difficulties lie wholly before they are possessed. They are acquired either by ability or by fortune; but are maintained without either, for they are sustained by ancient religious customs, which are so powerful and of such quality, that they keep their princes in power in whatever manner they proceed and live. These princes alone have states without defending them, have subjects without governing them, and their states, not being defended, are not taken from them; their subjects not being governed do not resent it, and neither think nor are capable of alienating themselves from them. Only these principalities, therefore, are secure and happy. But as they are upheld by higher causes, which the human mind cannot attain to, I will abstain from speaking of them; for being exalted and maintained by God, it would be the work of a presumptuous and foolish man to discuss them. However, I might be asked how it has come about that the Church has reached such great temporal power, when, previous to Alexander VI, the Italian potentates—and not merely the really powerful ones, but every lord or baron, however insignificant—held it in slight esteem as regards temporal power; whereas now it is dreaded by a king of France, whom it has been able to drive out of Italy, and has also been able to ruin the Venetians. Therefore, although this is well known, I do not think it superfluous to call it to mind.

Before Charles, King of France, came into Italy, this country was under the rule of the Pope, the Venetians, the King of Naples, the Duke of Milan, and the Florentines. These potentates had to have two chief cares: one, that no foreigner should enter Italy by force of arms, the other that none of the existing governments should extend its dominions. Those chiefly to be watched were the Pope and the Venetians. To keep back the Venetians required the alliance of all the others, as in the defence of Ferrara, and to keep down the Pope they made use of the Roman barons. These were divided into two factions, the Orsini and the Colonna, and as there was constant quarrelling between them, and they were constantly under arms, before the eyes of the Pope, they kept the papacy weak and infirm. And although there arose now and then a resolute Pope like Sextus, yet his fortune or ability was never able to liberate him from these evils. The shortness of their life was the reason of this, for in the course of ten years which, as a general rule, a Pope lived, he had great difficulty in suppressing even one of the factions, and if, for example, a Pope had almost put down the Colonna, a new Pope would succeed who was hostile to the Orsini, which caused the Colonna to spring up again, and he was not in time to suppress them.

This caused the temporal power of the Pope to be of little esteem in Italy. Then arose Alexander VI who, of all the pontiffs who have ever reigned, best showed how a Pope might prevail both by money and by force. With Duke Valentine as his instrument, and seizing the opportunity of the French invasion, he did all that I have previously described in speaking of the actions of the duke. And although his object was to aggrandise not the Church but the duke, what he did resulted in the aggrandisement of the Church, which after the death of the duke became the heir of his labours. Then came Pope Julius, who found the Church powerful, possessing all Romagna, all the Roman barons suppressed, and the factions destroyed by the severity of Alexander. He also found the way open for accumulating wealth in ways never used before the time of Alexander. These measures were not only followed by Julius, but increased; he resolved to gain Bologna, put down the Venetians and drive the French from Italy, in all which enterprises he was successful. He merits the greater praise, as he did everything to increase the power of the Church and not of any private person. He also kept the Orsini and Colonna parties in the condition in which he found them, and although there were some leaders among them who might have made changes, there were two things that kept them steady: one, the greatness of the Church, which they dreaded; the other, the fact that they had no cardinals, who are the origin of the tumults among them. For these parties are never at rest when they have cardinals, for these stir up the parties both within Rome and outside, and the barons are forced to defend them. Thus from the ambitions of prelates arise the discords and tumults among the barons. His holiness, Pope Leo X, therefore, has found the pontificate in a very powerful condition, from which it is hoped that as those Popes made it great by force of arms, so he through his goodness and infinite other virtues will make it both great and venerated.

Chapter XII

THE DIFFERENT KINDS OF MILITIA AND MERCENARY SOLDIERS

HAVING now discussed fully the qualities of these principalities of which I proposed to treat, and partially considered the causes of their prosperity or failure, and having also showed the methods by which many have sought to obtain such states, it now remains for me to treat generally of the methods, both offensive and defensive, that can be used in each of them. We have said already how necessary it is for a prince to have his foundations good, otherwise he is certain to be ruined. The chief foundations of all states, whether new, old, or mixed, are good laws and good arms. And as there cannot be good laws where there are not good arms, and where there are good arms there must be good laws, I will not now discuss the laws, but will speak of the arms.

I say, therefore, that the arms by which a prince defends his possessions are either his own, or else mercenaries, or auxiliaries, or mixed. The mercenaries and auxiliaries are useless and dangerous, and if any one supports his state by the arms of mercenaries, he will never stand firm or sure, as they are disunited, ambitious, without discipline, faithless, bold amongst friends, cowardly amongst enemies, they have no fear of God, and keep no faith with men. Ruin is only deferred as long as the assault is postponed; in peace you are despoiled by them, and in war by the enemy. The cause of this is that they have no love or other motive to keep them in the field beyond a trifling wage, which is not enough to make them ready to die for you. They are quite willing to be your soldiers so long as you do not make war, but when war comes, it is either fly or decamp altogether. I ought to have little trouble in proving this, since the ruin of Italy is now caused by nothing else but through her having relied for many years on mercenary arms. These did indeed help certain individuals to power, and appeared courageous when matched against each other, but when the foreigner came they showed their worthlessness. Thus it came about that King Charles of France was allowed to take Italy without the slightest trouble, and those who said that it was owing to our sins, spoke the truth, but it was not the sins they meant but those that I have related. And as it was the sins of princes, they too have suffered the punishment.

I will explain more fully the defects of these arms. Mercenary captains are either very capable men or not; if they are, you cannot rely upon them, for they will always aspire to their own greatness, either by oppressing you, their master, or by oppressing others against your intentions; but if the captain is not an able man, he will generally ruin you. And if it is replied to this, that whoever has armed forces will do the same, whether these are mercenary or not, I would reply that as armies are to be used either by a prince or by a republic, the prince must go in person to take the position of captain, and the republic must send its own citizens. If the man sent turns out incompetent, it must change him; and if capable, keep him by law from going beyond the proper limits. And it is seen by experience that only princes and armed republics make very great progress, whereas mercenary forces do nothing but harm, and also an armed republic submits less easily to the rule of one of its citizens than a republic armed by foreign forces.

Rome and Sparta were for many centuries well armed and free. The Swiss are well armed and enjoy great freedom. As an example of mercenary armies in antiquity there are the Carthaginians, who were oppressed by their mercenary soldiers, after the termination of the first war with the Romans, even while they still had their own citizens as captains. Philip of Macedon was made captain of their forces by the Thebans after the death of Epaminondas, and after gaining the victory he deprived them of liberty. The Milanese, on the death of Duke Philip, hired Francesco Sforza against the Venetians, who having overcome the enemy at Caravaggio, allied himself with them to oppress the Milanese his own employers. The father of this Sforza, being a soldier in the service of Queen Giovanna of Naples, left her suddenly unarmed, by which she was compelled, in order not to lose the kingdom, to throw herself into the arms of the King of Aragon. And if the Venetians and Florentines have in times past increased their dominions by means of such forces, and their captains have not made themselves princes but have defended them, I reply that the Florentines in this case have been favoured by chance, for of the capable leaders whom they might have feared, some did not conquer, some met with opposition, and others directed their ambition elsewhere. The one who did not conquer was Sir John Hawkwood, whose fidelity could not be known as he was not victorious, but every one will admit that, had he conquered, the Florentines would have been at his mercy. Sforza had always the Bracceschi against him which served as a mutual check. Francesco directed his ambition towards Lombardy; Braccio against the Church and the kingdom of Naples.

But let us look at what occurred a short time ago. The Florentines appointed Paolo Vitelli their captain, a man of great prudence, who had risen from a private station to the highest reputation. If he had taken Pisa no one can deny that it was highly important for the Florentines to retain his friendship, because had he become the soldier of their enemies they would have had no means of opposing him; and if they had retained him they would have been obliged to obey him. As to the Venetians, if one considers the progress they made, it will be seen that they acted surely and gloriously so long as they made war with their own forces; that it was before they commenced their enterprises on land that they fought courageously with their own gentlemen and armed populace, but when they began to fight on land they abandoned this virtue, and began to follow the Italian custom. And at the commencement of their land conquests they had not much to fear from their captains, their territories not being very large, and their reputation being great, but as their possessions increased, as they did under Carmagnola, they had an example of their mistake. For seeing that he was very powerful, after he had defeated the Duke of Milan, and knowing, on the other hand, that he was but lukewarm in this war, they considered that they would not make any more conquests with him, and they neither would nor could dismiss him, for fear of losing what they had already gained. In order to make sure of him they were there-fore obliged to execute him. They then had for captains Bartolommeo da Bergamo, Roberto da San Severino, Count di Pitigliano, and such like, from whom they had to fear loss instead of gain, as happened subsequently at Vailà, where in one day they lost what they had laboriously gained in eight hundred years; for with these forces, only slow and trifling acquisitions are made, but sudden and miraculous losses. And as I have cited these examples from Italy, which has now for many years been governed by mercenary forces, I will now deal more largely with them, so that having seen their origin and progress, they can be better remedied.

You must understand that in these latter times, as soon as the empire began to be repudiated in Italy and the Pope to gain greater reputation in temporal matters, Italy was di-vided into many states; many of the principal cities took up arms against their nobles, who, favoured by the emperor, had held them in subjection, and the Church encouraged this in order to increase its temporal power. In many other cities one of the inhabitants became prince. Thus Italy hav-ing fallen almost entirely into the hands of the Church and a few republics, and the priests and other citizens not being accustomed to bear arms, they began to hire foreigners as soldiers. The first to bring into reputation this kind of militia was Alberigo da Como, a native of Romagna. Braccio and Sforza, who were in their day the arbiters of Italy were, amongst others, trained by him. After these came all those others who up to the present day have commanded the armies of Italy, and the result of their prowess has been that Italy has been overrun by Charles, preyed on by Louis, tyrannised over by Ferrando, and insulted by the Swiss. The system adopted by them was, in the first place, to increase their own reputation by discrediting the infantry. They did this because, as they had no country and lived on their earnings, a few foot soldiers did not augment their reputation, and they could not maintain a large number and therefore they restricted themselves almost entirely to cavalry, by which with a smaller number they were well paid and honoured. They reduced things to such a state that in an army of 20,000 soldiers there were not 2,000 foot. They had also used every means to spare themselves and the soldiers any hardship or fear by not killing each other in their encounters, but taking prisoners without expectation of ransom. They made no attacks on fortifications by night; and those in the fortifications did not attack the tents at night, they made no stockades or ditches round their camps, and did not take the field in winter. All these things were permitted by their military code, and adopted, as we have said, to avoid trouble and danger, so that they have reduced Italy to slavery and degradation.

Chapter XIII

OF AUXILIARY, MIXED, AND NATIVE TROOPS

WHEN one asks a powerful neighbour to come to aid and defend one with his forces, they are termed auxiliaries and are as useless as mercenaries. This was done in recent times by Julius, who seeing the wretched failure of his mercenary forces, in his Ferrara enterprise, had recourse to auxiliaries, and arranged with Ferrando, King of Spain, that he should help him with his armies. These forces may be good in themselves, but they are always dangerous for those who borrow them, for if they lose you are defeated, and if they conquer you remain their prisoner. And although ancient

history is full of examples of this, I will not depart from
the example of Pope Julius II, which is still fresh. Nothing
could be less prudent than the course he adopted; for,
wishing to take Ferrara, he put himself entirely into the
power of a foreigner. But by good fortune there arose a third
cause which prevented him reaping the effects of his bad
policy; for when his auxiliaries were beaten at Ravenna,
the Swiss rose up and drove back the victors, against all
expectation of himself or others, so that he was not taken
prisoner by the enemy which had fled, nor by his own
auxiliaries, having conquered by other arms than theirs.
The Florentines, being totally disarmed, hired 10,000
Frenchmen to attack Pisa, by which measure they ran
greater risk than at any period of their struggles. The emperor of Constantinople, to oppose his neighbours, put 10,000
Turks into Greece, who after the war would not go away
again, which was the beginning of the servitude of Greece
to the infidels.

And one, therefore, who wishes not to conquer, would
do well to use these forces, which are much more dangerous than mercenaries, as with them ruin is complete, for
they are all united, and owe obedience to others, whereas
with mercenaries, when they have conquered, it requires
more time and a good opportunity for them to injure you,
as they do not form a single body and have been engaged
and paid by you, therefore a third party that you have made
leader cannot at once acquire enough authority to be able
to injure you. In a word, the greatest danger with mercenaries lies in their cowardice and reluctance to fight, but
with auxiliaries the danger lies in their courage.

A wise prince, therefore, always avoids these forces and
has recourse to his own, and would prefer rather to lose
with his own men than conquer with the forces of others,

not deeming it a true victory which is gained by foreign arms. I never hesitate to cite the example of Cesare Borgia and his actions. This duke entered Romagna with auxiliary troops, leading forces composed entirely of French soldiers, and with these he took Imola and Forlì; but as they seemed unsafe, he had recourse to mercenaries as a less risky policy, and hired the Orsini and Vitelli. Afterwards finding these uncertain to handle, unfaithful, and dangerous, he suppressed them, and relied upon his own men. And the difference between these forces can be easily seen if one considers the difference between the reputation of the duke when he had only the French, when he had the Orsini and Vitelli, and when he had to rely on himself and his own soldiers. His reputation will be found to have constantly increased, and he was never so highly esteemed as when every one saw that he was the sole master of his forces.

I do not wish to depart from recent Italian instances, but I cannot omit Hiero of Syracuse, whom I have already mentioned. This man being, as I said, made head of the army by the Syracusans, immediately recognised the uselessness of that militia which was organized like our Italian mercenary troops, and as he thought it unsafe either to retain them or dismiss them, he had them cut in pieces and thenceforward made war with his own arms and not those of others. I would also call to mind a symbolic tale from the Old Testament which well illustrates this point. When David offered to Saul to go and fight against the Philistine champion Goliath, Saul, to encourage him, armed him with his own arms, which when David had tried on, he refused saying, that with them he could not fight so well; he preferred, therefore, to face the enemy with his own sling and knife. In short, the arms of others either fail, overburden, or else impede you. Charles VII, father of King Louis XI, having through good fortune and bravery liberated France from the English, recognised this necessity of being armed with his own forces, and established in his kingdom a system of men-at-arms and infantry. Afterwards King Louis his son abolished the infantry and began to hire Swiss, which mistake being followed by others is, as may now be seen, a cause of danger to that kingdom. For by giving such reputation to the Swiss, France has disheartened all her own troops, the infantry having been abolished and the men-at-arms being obliged to foreigners for assistance; for being accustomed to fight with Swiss troops, they think they cannot conquer without them. Whence it comes that the French are insufficiently strong to oppose the Swiss, and without the aid of the Swiss they will not venture against others. The armies of the French are thus of a mixed kind, partly mercenary and partly her own; taken together they are much better than troops entirely composed of mercenaries or auxiliaries, but much inferior to national forces.

And let this example be sufficient, for the kingdom of France would be invincible if Charles's military organization had been developed or maintained. But men with their lack of prudence initiate novelties and, finding the first taste good, do not notice the poison within, as I pointed out previously in regard to wasting fevers.

The prince, therefore, who fails to recognise troubles in his state as they arise, is not truly wise, and it is given to few to be thus. If we consider the first cause of the collapse of the Roman Empire we shall find it merely due to the hiring of Goth mercenaries, for from that time we find the Roman strength begin to weaken. All the advantages derived from the Empire fell to the Goths.

I conclude then by saying that no prince is secure without his own troops, on the contrary he is entirely dependent on fortune, having no trustworthy means of defence in time of trouble. It has always been held and proclaimed by wise men 'quod nihil sit tam infirmum aut instabile quam fama potentiae non sua vi nixae.' One's own troops are those composed either of subjects or of citizens or of one's own dependants; all others are mercenaries or auxiliaries. The way to organise one's own troops is easily learnt if the methods of the four princes mentioned above be studied, and if one considers how Philip, father of Alexander the Great, and many republics and sovereigns have organised theirs. With such examples as these there is no need to labour the point.

Chapter XIV

THE DUTIES OF A PRINCE WITH REGARD TO THE MILITIA

A PRINCE should therefore have no other aim or thought, nor take up any other thing for his study, but war and its organisation and discipline, for that is the only art that is necessary to one who commands, and it is of such virtue that it not only maintains those who are born princes, but often enables men of private fortune to attain to that rank. And one sees, on the other hand, that when princes think more of luxury than of arms, they lose their state. The chief cause of the loss of states, is the contempt of this art, and the way to acquire them is to be well versed in the same.

Francesco Sforza, through being well armed, became, from private status, Duke of Milan; his sons, through wishing to avoid the fatigue and hardship of war, from dukes became private persons. For among other evils caused by being disarmed, it renders you contemptible; which is one of those disgraceful things which a prince must guard against, as will be explained later. Because there is no comparison whatever between an armed and a disarmed man; it is not reasonable to suppose that one who is armed will obey willingly one who is unarmed; or that any unarmed man will remain safe among armed servants. For one being disdainful and the other suspicious, it is not possible for them to act well together. And therefore a prince who is ignorant of military matters, besides the other misfortunes already mentioned, cannot be esteemed by his soldiers, nor have confidence in them.

He ought, therefore, never to let his thoughts stray from the exercise of war; and in peace he ought to practise it more than in war, which he can do in two ways: by action and by study. As to action, he must, besides keeping his men well disciplined and exercised, engage continually in hunting, and thus accustom his body to hardships; and meanwhile learn the nature of the land, how steep the mountains are, how the valleys debouch, where the plains lie, and understand the nature of rivers and swamps. To all this he should devote great attention. This knowledge is useful in two ways. In the first place, one learns to know one's country, and can the better see how to defend it. Then by means of the knowledge and experience gained in one locality, one can easily understand any other that it may be necessary to observe; for the hills and valleys, plains and rivers of Tuscany, for instance, have a certain resemblance to those of other provinces, so that from a knowledge of the country in one province one can easily arrive at a knowledge of others. And that prince who is lacking in this skill is wanting in the first essentials of a leader; for it is this which teaches how to find the enemy, take up quarters, lead armies, plan battles and lay siege to towns with advantage.

Philopœmen, prince of the Achaei, among other praises bestowed on him by writers, is lauded because in times of peace he thought of nothing but the methods of warfare, and when he was in the country with his friends, he often stopped and asked them: If the enemy were on that hill and we found ourselves here with our army, which of us would have the advantage? How could we safely approach him maintaining our order? If we wished to retire, what ought we to do? If they retired, how should we follow them? And he put before them as they went along all the contingencies that might happen to an army, heard their opinion, gave his own, fortifying it by argument; so that thanks to these constant reflections there could never happen any incident when actually leading his armies for which he was not prepared.

But as to exercise for the mind, the prince ought to read history and study the actions of eminent men, see how they acted in warfare, examine the causes of their victories and defeats in order to imitate the former and avoid the latter, and above all, do as some men have done in the past, who have imitated some one, who has been much praised and glorified, and have always kept his deeds and actions before them, as they say Alexander the Great imitated Achilles, Cæsar Alexander, and Scipio Cyrus. And whoever reads the life of Cyrus written by Xenophon, will perceive in the life of Scipio how gloriously he imitated the former, and how, in chastity, affability, humanity, and liberality Scipio conformed to those qualities of Cyrus as described by Xenophon.

A wise prince should follow similar methods and never remain idle in peaceful times, but industriously make good use of them, so that when fortune changes she may find him prepared to resist her blows, and to prevail in adversity.

Core of Machiavellian Philosophy

Chapter XV

OF THE THINGS FOR WHICH MEN, AND ESPECIALLY PRINCES, ARE PRAISED OR BLAMED

It now remains to be seen what are the methods and rules for a prince as regards his subjects and friends. And as I know that many have written of this, I fear that my writing about it may be deemed presumptuous, differing as I do, especially in this matter, from the opinions of others. But my intention being to write something of use to those who understand, it appears to me more proper to go to the real truth of the matter than to its imagination; and many have imagined republics and principalities which have never been seen or known to exist in reality; for how we live is so far removed from how we ought to live, that he who abandons what is done for what ought to be done, will rather learn to bring about his own ruin than his preservation. A man who wishes to make a profession of goodness in everything must necessarily come to grief among so many who are not good. Therefore it is necessary for a prince, who wishes to maintain himself, to learn how not to be good, and to use this knowledge and not use it, according to the necessity of the case.

Leaving on one side, then, those things which concern only an imaginary prince, and speaking of those that are real, I state that all men, and especially princes, who are placed at a greater height, are reputed for certain qualities which bring them either praise or blame. Thus one is considered liberal, another *misero* or miserly (using a Tuscan term, seeing that *avaro* with us still means one who is rapaciously acquisitive and *misero* one who makes grudging use of his own); one a free giver, another rapacious; one cruel, another merciful; one a breaker of his word, another trustworthy; one effeminate and pusillanimous, another fierce and high-spirited; one humane, another haughty; one lascivious, another chaste; one frank, another astute; one hard, another easy; one serious, another frivolous; one religious, another an unbeliever, and so on. I know that every one will admit that it would be highly praiseworthy in a prince to possess all the above-named qualities that are reputed good, but as they cannot all be possessed or observed, human conditions not permitting of it, it is necessary that he should be prudent enough to avoid the scandal of those vices which would lose him the state, and guard himself if possible against those which will not lose it him, but if not able to, he can indulge them with less scruple. And yet he must not mind incurring the scandal of those vices, without which it would be difficult to save the state, for if one considers well, it will be found that some things which seem virtues would, if followed, lead to one's ruin, and some others which appear vices result in one's greater security and wellbeing.

Chapter XVI

OF LIBERALITY AND NIGGARDLINESS

BEGINNING now with the first qualities above named, I say that it would be well to be considered liberal; nevertheless liberality such as the world understands it will injure you, because if used virtuously and in the proper way, it will not be known, and you will incur the disgrace of the contrary vice. But one who wishes to obtain the reputation of liberality among men, must not omit every kind of sumptuous display, and to such an extent that a prince of this character will consume by such means all his resources, and will be at last compelled, if he wishes to maintain his name for liberality, to impose heavy taxes on his people, become extortionate, and do everything possible to obtain money. This will make his subjects begin to hate him, and he will be little esteemed being poor, so that having by this liberality injured many and benefited but few, he will feel the first little disturbance and be endangered by every peril. If he recognises this and wishes to change his system, he incurs at once the charge of niggardliness.

A prince, therefore, not being able to exercise this virtue of liberality without risk if it be known, must not, if he be prudent, object to be called miserly. In course of time he will be thought more liberal, when it is seen that by his parsimony his revenue is sufficient, that he can defend himself against those who make war on him, and undertake enterprises without burdening his people, so that he is really liberal to all those from whom he does not take, who are infinite in number, and niggardly to all to whom he does not give, who are few. In our times we have seen nothing great done except by those who have been esteemed niggardly; the others have all been ruined. Pope Julius II, although he had made use of a reputation for liberality in order to attain the papacy, did not seek to retain it afterwards, so that he might be able to wage war. The present King of France has carried on so many wars without imposing an extraordinary tax, because his extra expenses were covered by the parsimony he had so long practised. The present King of Spain, if he had been thought liberal, would not have engaged in and been successful in so many enterprises.

For these reasons a prince must care little for the reputation of being a miser, if he wishes to avoid robbing his subjects, if he wishes to be able to defend himself, to avoid becoming poor and contemptible, and not to be forced to become rapacious; this niggardliness is one of those vices which enable him to reign. If it is said that Cæsar attained the empire through liberality, and that many others have reached the highest positions through being liberal or being thought so, I would reply that you are either a prince already or else on the way to become one. In the first case, this liberality is harmful; in the second, it is certainly necessary to be considered liberal. Cæsar was one of those who wished to attain the mastery over Rome, but if after attaining it he had lived and had not moderated his expenses, he would have destroyed that empire. And should any one reply that there have been many princes, who have done great things with their armies, who have been thought extremely liberal, I would answer by saying that the prince may either spend his own wealth and that of his subjects or the wealth of others. In the first case he must be sparing, but for the rest he must not neglect to be very liberal. The liberality is very necessary to a prince who marches with his armies, and lives by plunder, sack and ransom, and is dealing with the wealth of others, for without it he would not be followed by his soldiers. And you may be very generous indeed with what is not the property of yourself or your subjects, as were Cyrus, Cæsar, and Alexander; for spending the wealth of others will not diminish your reputation, but increase it, only spending your own resources will injure you. There is nothing which destroys itself so much as liberality, for by using it you lose the power of using it, and become either poor and despicable, or, to escape poverty, rapacious and hated. And of all things that a prince must guard against, the most important are being despicable or hated, and liberality will lead you to one or other of these conditions. It is, therefore, wiser to have the name of a miser, which produces disgrace without hatred, than to incur of necessity the name of being rapacious, which produces both disgrace and hatred.

Chapter XVII

OF CRUELTY AND CLEMENCY, AND WHETHER IT IS BETTER TO BE LOVED OR FEARED

PROCEEDING to the other qualities before named, I say that every prince must desire to be considered merciful and not cruel. He must, however, take care not to misuse this mercifulness. Cesare Borgia was considered cruel, but his cruelty had brought order to the Romagna, united it, and reduced it to peace and fealty. If this is considered well, it will be seen that he was really much more merciful than the Florentine people, who, to avoid the name of cruelty, allowed Pistoia to be destroyed. A prince, therefore, must not mind incurring the charge of cruelty for the purpose of keeping his subjects united and faithful; for, with a very few examples, he will be more merciful than those who, from excess of tenderness, allow disorders to arise, from whence spring bloodshed and rapine; for these as a rule injure the whole community, while the executions carried out by the prince injure only individuals. And of all princes, it is impossible for a new prince to escape the reputation of cruelty, new states being always full of dangers. Wherefore Virgil through the mouth of Dido says:

Res dura, et regni novitas me talia cogunt
Moliri, et late fines custode tueri.

Nevertheless, he must be cautious in believing and acting, and must not be afraid of his own shadow, and must proceed in a temperate manner with prudence and humanity, so that too much confidence does not render him incautious, and too much diffidence does not render him intolerant.

From this arises the question whether it is better to be loved more than feared, or feared more than loved. The reply is, that one ought to be both feared and loved, but as it is difficult for the two to go together, it is much safer to be feared than loved, if one of the two has to be wanting. For it may be said of men in general that they are ungrateful, voluble, dissemblers, anxious to avoid danger, and covetous of gain; as long as you benefit them, they are entirely yours; they offer you their blood, their goods, their life, and their children, as I have before said, when the necessity is remote; but when it approaches, they revolt. And the prince who has relied solely on their words, without making other preparations, is ruined; for the friendship which is gained by purchase and not through grandeur and nobility of spirit is bought but not secured, and at a pinch is not to be expended in your service. And men have less scruple in offending one who makes himself loved than one who makes himself feared; for love is held by a chain of obligation which, men being selfish, is broken whenever it serves their purpose; but fear is maintained by a dread of punishment which never fails.

Still, a prince should make himself feared in such a way that if he does not gain love, he at any rate avoids hatred;

for fear and the absence of hatred may well go together, and will be always attained by one who abstains from interfering with the property of his citizens and subjects or with their women. And when he is obliged to take the life of any one, let him do so when there is a proper justification and manifest reason for it; but above all he must abstain from taking the property of others, for men forget more easily the death of their father than the loss of their patrimony. Then also pretexts for seizing property are never wanting, and one who begins to live by rapine will always find some reason for taking the goods of others, whereas causes for taking life are rarer and more fleeting.

But when the prince is with his army and has a large number of soldiers under his control, then it is extremely necessary that he should not mind being thought cruel; for without this reputation he could not keep an army united or disposed to any duty. Among the noteworthy actions of Hannibal is numbered this, that although he had an enormous army, composed of men of all nations and fighting in foreign countries, there never arose any dissension either among them or against the prince, either in good fortune or in bad. This could not be due to anything but his inhuman cruelty, which together with his infinite other virtues, made him always venerated and terrible in the sight of his soldiers, and without it his other virtues would not have sufficed to produce that effect. Thoughtless writers admire on the one hand his actions, and on the other blame the principal cause of them.

And that it is true that his other virtues would not have sufficed may be seen from the case of Scipio (famous not only in regard to his own times, but all times of which memory remains), whose armies rebelled against him in Spain, which arose from nothing but his excessive kindness, which allowed more licence to the soldiers than was consonant with military discipline. He was reproached with this in the senate by Fabius Maximus, who called him a corrupter of the Roman militia. Locri having been destroyed by one of Scipio's officers was not revenged by him, nor was the insolence of that officer punished, simply by reason of his easy nature; so much so, that some one wishing to excuse him in the senate, said that there were many men who knew rather how not to err, than how to correct the errors of others. This disposition would in time have tarnished the fame and glory of Scipio had he persevered in it under the empire, but living under the rule of the senate this harmful quality was not only concealed but became a glory to him.

I conclude, therefore, with regard to being feared and loved, that men love at their own free will, but fear at the will of the prince, and that a wise prince must rely on what is in his power and not on what is in the power of others, and he must only contrive to avoid incurring hatred, as has been explained.

Chapter XVIII

IN WHAT WAY PRINCES MUST KEEP FAITH

How laudable it is for a prince to keep good faith and live with integrity, and not with astuteness, every one knows. Still the experience of our times shows those princes to have done great things who have had little regard for good faith, and have been able by astuteness to confuse men's brains, and who have ultimately overcome those who have made loyalty their foundation.

Keep "animal instinct"

You must know, then, that there are two methods of fighting, the one by law, the other by force: the first method is that of men, the second of beasts; but as the first method is often insufficient, one must have recourse to the second. It is therefore necessary for a prince to know well how to use both the beast and the man. This was covertly taught to rulers by ancient writers, who relate how Achilles and many others of those ancient princes were given to Chiron the centaur to be brought up and educated under his discipline. The parable of this semi-animal, semi-human teacher is meant to indicate that a prince must know how to use both natures, and that the one without the other is not durable.

A prince being thus obliged to know well how to act as a beast must imitate the fox and the lion, for the lion cannot protect himself from traps, and the fox cannot defend himself from wolves. One must therefore be a fox to recognise traps, and a lion to frighten wolves. Those that wish to be only lions do not understand this. Therefore, a prudent ruler ought not to keep faith when by so doing it would be against his interest, and when the reasons which made him bind himself no longer exist. If men were all good, this precept would not be a good one; but as they are bad, and would not observe their faith with you, so you are not bound to keep faith with them. Nor have legitimate grounds ever failed a prince who wished to show colourable excuse for the non-fulfilment of his promise. Of this one could furnish an infinite number of modern examples, and show how many times peace has been broken, and how many promises rendered worthless, by the faithlessness of princes, and those that have been best able to imitate the fox have succeeded best. But it is necessary to be able to disguise this character well, and to be a great feigner and dissembler; and men are

Since others are bad, good people must become bad to defend themselves

so simple and so ready to obey present necessities, that one who deceives will always find those who allow themselves to be deceived.

I will only mention one modern instance. Alexander VI did nothing else but deceive men, he thought of nothing else, and found the occasion for it; no man was ever more able to give assurances, or affirmed things with stronger oaths, and no man observed them less; however, he always succeeded in his deceptions, as he well knew this aspect of things.

It is not, therefore, necessary for a prince to have all the above-named qualities, but it is very necessary to seem to have them. I would even be bold to say that to possess them and always to observe them is dangerous, but to appear to possess them is useful. Thus it is well to seem merciful, faithful, humane, sincere, religious, and also to be so; but you must have the mind so disposed that when it is needful to be otherwise you may be able to change to the opposite qualities. And it must be understood that a prince, and especially a new prince, cannot observe all those things which are considered good in men, being often obliged, in order to maintain the state, to act against faith, against charity, against humanity, and against religion. And, therefore, he must have a mind disposed to adapt itself according to the wind, and as the variations of fortune dictate, and, as I said before, not deviate from what is good, if possible, but be able to do evil if constrained.

A prince must take great care that nothing goes out of his mouth which is not full of the above-named five qualities, and, to see and hear him, he should seem to be all mercy, faith, integrity, humanity, and religion. And nothing is more necessary than to seem to have this last quality, for men in general judge more by the eyes than by the hands,

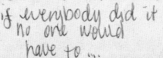
if everybody dyd it
no one would
have to ...

for every one can see, but very few have to feel. Everybody sees what you appear to be, few feel what you are, and those few will not dare to oppose themselves to the many, who have the majesty of the state to defend them; and in the actions of men, and especially of princes, from which there is no appeal, the end justifies the means. Let a prince therefore aim at conquering and maintaining the state, and the means will always be judged honourable and praised by every one, for the vulgar is always taken by appearances and the issue of the event; and the world consists only of the vulgar, and the few who are not vulgar are isolated when the many have a rallying point in the prince. A certain prince of the present time, whom it is well not to name, never does anything but preach peace and good faith, but he is really a great enemy to both, and either of them, had he observed them, would have lost him state or reputation on many occasions.

Chapter XIX

THAT WE MUST AVOID BEING DESPISED AND HATED

BUT as I have now spoken of the most important of the qualities in question, I will now deal briefly and generally with the rest. The prince must, as already stated, avoid those things which will make him hated or despised; and whenever he succeeds in this, he will have done his part, and will find no danger in other vices. He will chiefly become hated, as I said, by being rapacious, and usurping the property and women of his subjects, which he must abstain from doing, and whenever one does not attack the property or honour of the generality of men, they will live contented; and one will only have to combat the ambition of a few, who can be easily held in check in many ways. He is rendered despicable by being thought changeable, frivolous, effeminate, timid, and irresolute; which a prince must guard against as a rock of danger, and so contrive that his actions show grandeur, spirit, gravity, and fortitude; and as to the government of his subjects, let his sentence be irrevocable, and let him adhere to his decisions so that no one may think of deceiving or cozening him.

The prince who creates such an opinion of himself gets a great reputation, and it is very difficult to conspire against one who has a great reputation, and he will not easily be attacked, so long as it is known that he is capable and reverenced by his subjects. For a prince must have two kinds of fear: one internal as regards his subjects, one external as regards foreign powers. From the latter he can defend himself with good arms and good friends, and he will always have good friends if he has good arms; and internal matters will always remain quiet, if they are not perturbed by conspiracy and there is no disturbance from without; and even if external powers sought to attack him, if he has ruled and lived as I have described, he will always if he stands firm, be able to sustain every shock, as I have shown that Nabis the Spartan did. But with regard to the subjects, if not acted on from outside, it is still to be feared lest they conspire in secret, from which the prince may guard himself well by avoiding hatred and contempt, and keeping the people satisfied with him, which it is necessary to accomplish, as has been related at length. And one of the most potent remedies that a prince has against conspiracies, is that of not being hated by the mass of the people; for whoever conspires always believes that he will satisfy the people by the death of their prince; but if he thought to offend them by doing this, he would fear to engage in such an undertaking, for the difficulties that conspirators have to meet are infinite. Experience shows that there have been very many conspiracies, but few have turned out well, for whoever conspires cannot act alone, and cannot find companions except among those who are discontented; and as soon as you have disclosed your intention to a malcontent, you give him the means of satisfying himself, for by revealing it he can hope to secure everything he wants; to such an extent that seeing a certain gain by doing this, and seeing on the other hand only a doubtful one and full of danger, he must either be a rare friend to you or else a very bitter enemy to the prince if he keeps faith with you. And to express the matter in a few words, I say, that on the side of the conspirator there is nothing but fear, jealousy, suspicion, and dread of punishment which frightens him; and on the side of the prince there is the majesty of government, the laws, the protection of friends and of the state which guard him. When to these things is added the goodwill of the people, it is impossible that any one should have the temerity to conspire. For whereas generally a conspirator has to fear before the execution of his plot, in this case, having the people for an enemy, he must also fear after his crime is accomplished, and thus he is not able to hope for any refuge.

Numberless instances might be given of this, but I will content myself with one which took place within the memory of our fathers. Messer Annibale Bentivogli, Prince of Bologna, ancestor of the present Messer Annibale, was killed by the Canneschi, who conspired against him. He left no relations but Messer Giovanni, who was then an infant, but after the murder the people rose up and killed all the Canneschi. This arose from the popular goodwill that the house of Bentivogli enjoyed at that time, which was so great that, as there was nobody left after the death of Annibale who could govern the state, the Bolognese hearing that there was one of the Bentivogli family in Florence, who had till then been thought the son of a blacksmith, came to fetch him and gave him the government of the city, and it was governed by him until Messer Giovanni was old enough to assume the government.

I conclude, therefore, that a prince need trouble little about conspiracies when the people are well disposed, but when they are hostile and hold him in hatred, then he must fear everything and everybody. Well-ordered states and wise princes have studied diligently not to drive the nobles to desperation, and to satisfy the populace and keep it contented, for this is one of the most important matters that a prince has to deal with.

Among the kingdoms that are well ordered and governed in our time is France, and there we find numberless good institutions on which depend the liberty and security of the king; of these the chief is the parliament and its authority, because he who established that kingdom, knowing the ambition and insolence of the great nobles, deemed it necessary to have a bit in their mouths to check them. And knowing on the other hand the hatred of the mass of the people against the great, based on fear, and wishing to secure them, he did not wish to make this the special care of the king, to relieve him of the dissatisfaction that he might incur among the nobles by favouring the people, and among the people by favouring the nobles. He therefore established a third judge that, without direct charge of the king, kept in check the great and favoured the lesser people. Nor could any better or more prudent measure have been adopted, nor better precaution for the safety of the king and the kingdom. From which another notable rule can be drawn, that princes should let the carrying out of unpopular duties devolve on others, and bestow favours themselves. I conclude again by saying that a prince must esteem his nobles, but not make himself hated by the populace.

It may perhaps seem to some, that considering the life and death of many Roman emperors that they are instances contrary to my opinion, finding that some who always lived nobly and showed great strength of character, nevertheless lost the empire, or were killed by their subjects who conspired against them. Wishing to answer these objections, I will discuss the qualities of some emperors, showing the cause of their ruin not to be at variance with what I have stated, and I will also meanwhile consider the things to be noted by whoever reads the deeds of these times. I will content myself with taking all those emperors who succeeded to the empire from Marcus the philosopher to Maximinus; these were Marcus, Commodus his son, Pertinax, Julianus, Severus, Antoninus, Caracalla his son, Macrinus, Heliogabalus, Alexander, and Maximinus. And the first thing to note is, that whereas other princes have only to contend against the ambition of the great and the insolence of the people, the Roman emperors had a third difficulty, that of having to support the cruelty and avarice of the soldiers, which was such that it was the cause of the ruin of many, it being hardly possible to satisfy both the soldiers and the people. For the people love tranquillity, and therefore like pacific princes, but the soldiers prefer a prince of military spirit, who is insolent, cruel, and rapacious. They wish him to exercise these qualities on the people so that they may get double pay and give vent to their avarice and cruelty. Thus it came about that those emperors who, by nature or art, had not such a reputation as could keep both parties in check, were invariably ruined, and the greater number of them who were raised to the empire being new men, knowing the difficulties of these two opposite dispositions, confined themselves to satisfying the soldiers, and thought little of injuring the people. This choice was necessary, princes not being able to avoid being hated by some one. They must first try not to be hated by the mass of the people; if they cannot accomplish this they must use every means to escape the hatred of the most powerful parties. And therefore these emperors, who being new men had need of extraordinary favours, adhered to the soldiers rather than to the people; whether this, however, was of use to them or not, depended on whether the prince knew how to maintain his reputation with them. From these causes it resulted that Marcus, Pertinax, and Alexander, being all of modest life, lovers of justice, enemies of cruelty, humane and benign, all came to a sad end except Marcus. Marcus alone lived and died in honour, because he succeeded to the empire by hereditary right and did not owe it either to the soldiers or to the people; besides which, possessing many virtues which made him revered, he kept both parties in their place as long as he lived and was never either hated or despised. But Pertinax was created emperor against the will of the soldiers, who being accustomed to live licentiously under Commodus, could not put up with the honest life to which Pertinax wished to limit them, so that having made himself hated, and to this contempt being added because he was old, he was ruined at the very beginning of his administration.

Whence it may be seen that hatred is gained as much by good works as by evil, and therefore, as I said before, a prince who wishes to maintain the state is often forced to do evil, for when that party, whether populace, soldiery, or nobles, whichever it be that you consider necessary to you for keeping your position, is corrupt, you must follow its humour and satisfy it, and in that case good works will be inimical to you. But let us come to Alexander, who was of such goodness, that among other things for which he is praised, it is said that in the fourteen years that he reigned no one was put to death by him without a fair trial. Nevertheless, being considered effeminate, and a man who allowed himself to be ruled by his mother, and having thus fallen into contempt, the army conspired against him and killed him.

Considering, on the other hand, the qualities of Commodus, Severus, Antoninus, Caracalla, and Maximinus, you will find them extremely cruel and rapacious; to satisfy the soldiers there was no injury which they would not inflict on the people, and all except Severus ended badly. Severus, however, had such abilities that by maintaining the soldiers friendly to him, he was able to reign happily, although he oppressed the people, for his virtues made him so admirable in the sight both of the soldiers and the people that the latter were, in some degree, astonished and stupefied, while the former were respectful and contented.

As the deeds of this ruler were great and notable for a new prince, I will briefly show how well he could use the qualities of the fox and the lion, whose natures, as I said before, it is necessary for a prince to imitate. Knowing the sloth of the Emperor Julianus, Severus, who was leader of the army in Slavonia, persuaded the troops that it would be well to go to Rome to avenge the death of Pertinax, who had been slain by the Prætorian guard, and under this pretext, without revealing his aspirations to the throne, marched with his army to Rome and was in Italy before his departure was known. On his arrival in Rome the senate elected him emperor through fear, and killed Julianus. There remained after this beginning two difficulties to be faced by Severus before he could obtain the whole control of the empire: one in Asia, where Nigrinus, head of the Asiatic armies, had declared himself emperor; the other in the west from Albinus, who also aspired to the empire. And as he judged it dangerous to show himself hostile to both, he decided to attack Nigrinus and deceive Albinus, to whom he wrote that having been elected emperor by the senate he wished to share that dignity with him; he sent him the title of Cæsar and, by deliberation of the senate, he was declared his colleague; all of which was accepted as true by Albinus. But when Severus had defeated and killed Nigrinus, and pacified things in the East, he returned to Rome and charged Albinus in the senate with having, unmindful of the benefits received from him, traitorously sought to assassinate him, and stated that he was therefore obliged to go and punish his ingratitude. He then went to France to meet him, and there deprived him of both his position and his life.

Whoever examines in detail the actions of Severus, will find him to have been a very ferocious lion and an extremely astute fox, and will find him to have been feared and respected by all and not hated by the army; and will not be surprised that he, a new man, should have been able to hold so much power, since his great reputation defended him always from the hatred that his rapacity might have produced in the people. But Antoninus his son was also a man of great ability, and possessed qualities that rendered him admirable in the sight of the people and also made him popular with the soldiers, for he was a military man, capable of enduring the most extreme hardships, disdainful of delicate food, and every other luxury, which made him loved by all the armies. However, his ferocity and cruelty were so great and unheard of, through his having, after executing many private individuals, caused a large part of the population of Rome and all that of Alexandria to be killed, that he became hated by all the world and began to be feared by those about him to such an extent that he was finally killed by a centurion in the midst of his army. Whence it is to be noted that this kind of death, which proceeds from the deliberate action of a determined man, cannot be avoided by princes, since any one who does not fear death himself can inflict it, but a prince need not fear much on this account, as such men are extremely rare. He must only guard against committing any grave injury to any one he makes use of, or has about him for his service, like Antoninus had done, having caused the death with contumely of the brother of that centurion, and also threatened him every day, although he still retained him in his bodyguard, which was a foolish and dangerous thing to do, as the fact proved.

But let us come to Commodus, who might easily have kept the empire, having succeeded to it by heredity, being the son of Marcus, and it would have sufficed for him to follow in the steps of his father to have satisfied both the people and the soldiers. But being of a cruel and bestial disposition, in order to be able to exercise his rapacity on the people, he sought to favour the soldiers and render them licentious; on the other hand, by not maintaining his dignity, by often descending into the theatre to fight with gladiators and committing other contemptible actions, little worthy of the imperial dignity, he became despicable in the eyes of the soldiers, and being hated on the one hand and despised on the other, he was conspired against and killed.

There remains to be described the character of Maximinus. He was an extremely warlike man, and as the armies were annoyed with the effeminacy of Alexander, which we have already spoken of, he was elected emperor after the death of the latter. He did not enjoy it for long, as two things made him hated and despised: the one his base origin, as he had been a shepherd in Thrace, which was generally known and caused great disdain on all sides; the other, because he had at the commencement of his rule deferred going to Rome to take possession of the Imperial seat, and had obtained a reputation for great cruelty, having through his prefects in Rome and other parts of the empire committed many acts of cruelty. The whole world being thus moved by indignation for the baseness of his blood, and also by the hatred caused by fear of his ferocity, he was conspired against first by Africa and afterwards by the senate and all the people of Rome and Italy. His own army also joined them, for besieging Aquileia and finding it difficult to take, they became enraged at his cruelty, and seeing that he had so many enemies, they feared him less and put him to death.

I will not speak of Heliogabalus, of Macrinus, or Julianus, who being entirely contemptible were immediately suppressed, but I will come to the conclusion of this discourse by saying that the princes of our time have less difficulty than these in being obliged to satisfy in an extraordinary degree their soldiers in their states; for although they must have a certain consideration for them, yet any difficulty is soon settled, for none of these princes have armies that are inextricably bound up with the administration of the government and the rule of their provinces as were the armies of the Roman empire. If it was then necessary to satisfy the soldiers rather than the people, it was because the soldiers could do more than the people; now, it is more necessary for all princes, except the Turk and the Sultan, to satisfy the people than the soldiers, for the people can do more than the soldiers. I except the Turk, because he always keeps about him twelve thousand infantry and fifteen thousand cavalry, on which depend the security and strength of his kingdom; and it is necessary for him to postpone every other consideration to keep them friendly. It is the same with the kingdom of the Sultan, which being entirely in the hands of the soldiers, he is bound to keep their friendship regardless of the people. And it is to be noted that this state of the Sultan is different from that of all other princes, being similar to the Christian pontificate, which cannot be called either a hereditary kingdom or a new one, for the sons of the dead prince are not his heirs, but he who is elected to that position by those who have authority. And as this order is ancient it cannot be called a new kingdom, there being none of these difficulties which exist in new ones; as although the prince is new, the rules of that state are old and arranged to receive him as if he were their hereditary lord.

But returning to our matter, I say that whoever studies the preceding argument will see that either hatred or contempt were the causes of the ruin of the emperors named, and will also observe how it came about that, some of them acting in one way and some in another, in both ways there were some who had a fortunate and others an unfortunate ending. As Pertinax and Alexander were both new rulers, it was useless and injurious for them to try and imitate Marcus, who was a hereditary prince; and similarly with Caracalla, Commodus, and Maximinus it was pernicious for them to imitate Severus, as they had not sufficient ability to follow in his footsteps. Thus a new prince cannot imitate the actions of Marcus, in his dominions, nor is it necessary for him to imitate those of Severus; but he must take from Severus those things that are necessary to found his state, and from Marcus those that are useful and glorious for conserving a state that is already established and secure.

Chapter XX

WHETHER FORTRESSES AND OTHER THINGS WHICH PRINCES OFTEN CONTRIVE ARE USEFUL OR INJURIOUS

SOME princes, in order to hold their possessions securely, have disarmed their citizens, some others have kept their subject lands divided into parts, others have fomented enmities against themselves, others have endeavoured to win over those whom they suspected at the commencement of their rule: some have constructed fortresses, others have cast them down and destroyed them. And although one cannot pronounce a definite judgment as to these things without going into the particulars of the state to which such a deliberation is to be applied, still I will speak in such a general way as the matter will permit.

A new prince has never been known to disarm his subjects, on the contrary, when he has found them disarmed he has always armed them, for by arming them these arms become your own, those that you suspected become faithful and those that were faithful remain so, and from being merely subjects become your partisans. And since all the subjects cannot be armed, when you give the privilege of arms to some, you can deal more safely with the others; and this different treatment that they recognise renders your men more obliged to you. The others will excuse you, judging that those have necessarily greater merit who have greater danger and heavier duties. But when you disarm them, you commence to offend them and show that you distrust them either through cowardice or lack of confidence, and both of these opinions generate hatred against you. And as you cannot remain unarmed, you are obliged to resort to a mercenary militia, of which we have already stated the value; and even if it were good it cannot be sufficient in number to defend you against powerful enemies and suspected subjects. Therefore, as I have said, a new prince in a new dominion always has his subjects armed. History is full of such examples.

But when a prince acquires a new state as an addition to his old one, then it is necessary to disarm that state, except those who in acquiring it have sided with you; and even these one must, when time and opportunity serve, render weak and effeminate, and arrange things so that all the arms of the new state are in the hands of your soldiers who live near you in your old state.

Our forefathers and those who were esteemed wise used to say that it was necessary to hold Pistoia by means of factions and Pisa with fortresses, and for this purpose they fomented differences in some of their subject towns in order to possess them more easily. In those days when there was a balance of power in Italy, this was doubtless well done, but does not seem to me to be a good precept for the present time, for I do not believe that the divisions thus created ever do any good; on the contrary it is certain that when the enemy approaches, the cities thus divided will be at once lost, for the weaker faction will always side with the enemy and the other will not be able to stand.

The Venetians, actuated, I believe, by the aforesaid motives, fomented the Guelf and Ghibelline factions in the cities subject to them, and although they never allowed them to come to bloodshed, they yet encouraged these differences among them, so that the citizens, being occupied in their own quarrels, might not act against them. This, however, did not avail them anything, as was seen when, after the defeat of Vailà, a part of those subjects immediately took courage and seized the whole state. Such methods, besides, argue weakness in a prince, for in a strong government such dissensions will never be permitted. They are profitable only in time of peace, as by such means it is easy to manage one's subjects, but when it comes to war, the fallacy of such a policy is at once shown.

Without doubt princes become great when they overcome difficulties and opposition, and therefore fortune, especially when it wants to render a new prince great, who has greater need of gaining a great reputation than a hereditary prince, raises up enemies and compels him to undertake wars against them, so that he may have cause to overcome them, and thus climb up higher by means of that ladder which his enemies have brought him. There are many who think therefore that a wise prince ought, when he has the chance, to foment astutely some enmity, so that by suppressing it he will augment his greatness.

Princes, and especially new ones, have found more faith and more usefulness in those men, whom at the beginning of their power they regarded with suspicion, than in those they at first confided in. Pandolfo Petrucci, Prince of Siena, governed his state more by those whom he suspected than by others. But of this we cannot speak at large, as it strays from the subject; I will merely say that these men who at the beginning of a new government were enemies, if they are of a kind to need support to maintain their position, can be very easily gained by the prince, and they are the more compelled to serve him faithfully as they know they must by their deeds cancel the bad opinion previously held of them, and thus the prince will always derive greater help from them than from those who, serving him with greater security, neglect his interests.

And as the matter requires it, I will not omit to remind a prince who has newly taken a state with the secret help of its inhabitants, that he must consider well the motives that have induced those who have favoured him to do so, and if it is not natural affection for him, but only because they were not contented with the state as it was, he will have great trouble and difficulty in maintaining their friendship, because it will be impossible for him to content them. And on well examining the cause of this in the examples drawn from ancient and modern times it will be seen that it is much easier to gain the friendship of those men who were contented with the previous condition and were therefore at first enemies, than that those who not being contented, became his friends and helped him to occupy it.

It has been the custom of princes in order to be able to hold their state securely, to erect fortresses, as a bridle and bit to those who have designs against them, and in order to have a secure refuge against a sudden assault. I approve this method, because it was anciently used. Nevertheless, Messer Niccolò Vitelli has been seen in our own time to destroy two fortresses in Città di Castello in order to keep that state. Guid'Ubaldo, Duke of Urbino, on returning to his dominions from which he had been driven by Cesare Borgia, razed to their foundations all the fortresses of that province, and considered that without them it would be more difficult for him to lose the state again. The Bentivogli, in returning to Bologna, took similar measures. Therefore fortresses may or may not be useful according to the times; if they do good in one way, they do harm in another. The question may be discussed thus: a prince who fears his own people more than foreigners ought to build fortresses, but he who has greater fear of foreigners than of his own people ought to do without them. The castle of Milan built by Francesco Sforza has given and will give more trouble to the house of Sforza than any other disorder in that state. Therefore the best fortress is to be found in the love of the people, for although you may have fortresses they will not save you if you are hated by the people. When once the people have taken arms against you, there will never be lacking foreigners to assist them. In our times we do not see that they have profited any ruler, except the Countess of Forlì on the death of her consort Count Girolamo, for she was thus enabled to escape the popular rising and await help from Milan and recover the state; the circumstances being then such that no foreigner could assist the people. But afterwards they were of little use to her when Cesare Borgia attacked her and the people being hostile to her allied themselves with the foreigner. So that then and before it would have been safer for her not to have been hated by the people than to have had the fortresses. Having considered these things I would therefore praise the one who erects fortresses and the one who does not, and would blame any one who, trusting in them, recks little of being hated by his people.

Chapter XXI

HOW A PRINCE MUST ACT IN ORDER TO GAIN REPUTATION

NOTHING causes a prince to be so much esteemed as great enterprises and giving proof of prowess. We have in our own day Ferdinand, King of Aragon, the present King of Spain. He may almost be termed a new prince, because from a weak king he has become for fame and glory the first king in Christendom, and if you regard his actions you will find them all very great and some of them extraordinary. At the beginning of his reign he assailed Granada, and that enterprise was the foundation of his state. At first he did it at his leisure and without fear of being interfered with; he kept the minds of the barons of Castile occupied in this enterprise, so that thinking only of that war they did not think of making innovations, and he thus acquired reputation and power over them without their being aware of it. He was able with the money of the Church and the people to maintain his armies, and by that long war to lay the foundations of his military power, which afterwards has made him famous. Besides this, to be able to undertake greater enterprises, and always under the pretext of religion, he had recourse to a pious cruelty, driving out the Moors from his kingdom and despoiling them. No more miserable or unusual example can be found. He also attacked Africa under the same pretext, undertook his Italian enterprise, and has lately attacked France; so that he has continually contrived great things, which have kept his subjects' minds uncertain and astonished, and occupied in watching their result. And these actions have arisen one out of the other, so that they have left no time for men to settle down and act against him.

It is also very profitable for a prince to give some outstanding example of his greatness in the internal administration, like those related of Messer Bernabò of Milan. When it happens that some one does something extraordinary, either good or evil, in civil life, he must find such means of rewarding or punishing him which will be much talked about. And above all a prince must endeavour in every action to obtain fame for being great and excellent.

A prince is further esteemed when he is a true friend or a true enemy, when, that is, he declares himself without reserve in favour of some one or against another. This policy is always more useful than remaining neutral. For if two neighbouring powers come to blows, they are either such that if one wins, you will have to fear the victor, or else not. In either of these two cases it will be better for you to declare yourself openly and make war, because in the first case if you do not declare yourself, you will fall a prey to the victor, to the pleasure and satisfaction of the one who has been defeated, and you will have no reason nor anything to defend you and nobody to receive you. For, whoever wins will not desire friends whom he suspects and who do not help him when in trouble, and whoever loses will not receive you as you did not take up arms to venture yourself in his cause.

Antiochus went to Greece, being sent by the Ætolians to expel the Romans. He sent orators to the Achaeians who were friends of the Romans to encourage them to remain neutral; on the other hand the Romans persuaded them to take up arms on their side. The matter was brought before the council of the Achaeians for deliberation, where the ambassador of Antiochus sought to persuade them to remain neutral, to which the Roman ambassador replied: 'As to what is said that it is best and most useful for your state not to meddle in our war, nothing is further from the truth: for if you do not meddle in it you will become, without any favour or any reputation, the prize of the victor.'

And it will always happen that the one who is not your friend will want you to remain neutral, and the one who is your friend will require you to declare yourself by taking arms. Irresolute princes, to avoid present dangers, usually follow the way of neutrality and are mostly ruined by it.

But when the prince declares himself frankly in favour of one side, if the one to whom you adhere conquers, even if he is powerful and you remain at his discretion, he is under an obligation to you and friendship has been established, and men are never so dishonest as to oppress you with such a patent ingratitude. Moreover, victories are never so prosperous that the victor does not need to have some scruples, especially as to justice. But if your ally loses, you are sheltered by him, and so long as he can, he will assist you; you become the companion of a fortune which may rise again. In the second case, when those who fight are such that you have nothing to fear from the victor, it is still more prudent on your part to adhere to one; for you go to the ruin of one with the help of him who ought to save him if he were wise, and if he conquers he rests at your discretion, and it is impossible that he should not conquer with your help.

And here it should be noted that a prince ought never to make common cause with one more powerful than himself to injure another, unless necessity forces him to it, as before said; for if he wins you rest in his power, and princes must avoid as much as possible being under the will and pleasure of others. The Venetians united with France against the Duke of Milan, although they could have avoided that alliance, and from it resulted their own ruin. But when one cannot avoid it, as happened in the case of the Florentines when the Pope and Spain went with their armies to attack Lombardy, then the prince ought to join for the above reasons. Let no state believe that it can always follow a safe policy, rather let it think that all are doubtful. This is found in the nature of things, that one never tries to avoid one difficulty without running into another, but prudence consists in being able to know the nature of the difficulties, and taking the least harmful as good.

A prince must also show himself a lover of merit, give preferment to the able, and honour those who excel in every art. Moreover he must encourage his citizens to follow their callings quietly, whether in commerce, or agriculture, or any other trade that men follow, so that this one shall not refrain from improving his possessions through fear that they may be taken from him, and that one from starting a trade for fear of taxes; but he should offer rewards to whoever does these things, and to whoever seeks in any way to improve his city or state. Besides this, he ought, at convenient seasons of the year, to keep the people occupied with festivals and shows; and as every city is divided either into guilds or into classes, he ought to pay attention to all these groups, mingle with them from time to time. and give them an example of his humanity and munificence, always upholding, however, the majesty of his dignity, which must never be allowed to fail in anything whatever.

Chapter XXII

OF THE SECRETARIES OF PRINCES

THE choice of a prince's ministers is a matter of no little importance; they are either good or not according to the prudence of the prince. The first impression that one gets of a ruler and of his brains is from seeing the men that he has about him. When they are competent and faithful one can always consider him wise, as he has been able to recognise their ability and keep them faithful. But when they are the reverse, one can always form an unfavourable opinion of him, because the first mistake that he makes is in making this choice.

There was nobody who knew Messer Antonio da Venafro as the minister of Pandolfo Petrucci, Prince of Siena, who did not consider Pandolfo to be a very prudent man, having him for his minister. There are three different kinds of brains, the one understands things unassisted, the other understands things when shown by others, the third understands neither alone nor with the explanations of others. The first kind is most excellent, the second also excellent, but the third useless. It is therefore evident that if Pandolfo was not of the first kind, he was at any rate of the second. For every time the prince has the judgment to know the good and evil that any one does or says, even if he has no originality of intellect, yet he can recognise the bad and good works of his minister and correct the one and encourage the other; and the minister cannot hope to deceive him and therefore remains good.

For a prince to be able to know a minister there is this method which never fails. When you see the minister think more of himself than of you, and in all his actions seek his own profit, such a man will never be a good minister, and you can never rely on him; for whoever has in hand the state of another must never think of himself but of the prince, and not mind anything but what relates to him. And, on the other hand, the prince, in order to retain his fidelity ought to think of his minister, honouring and enriching him, doing him kindnesses, and conferring on him honours and giving him responsible tasks, so that the great honours and riches bestowed on him cause him not to desire other honours and riches, and the offices he holds make him fearful of changes. When princes and their ministers stand in this relation to each other, they can rely the one upon the other; when it is otherwise, the result is always injurious either for one or the other of them.

Chapter XXIII

HOW FLATTERERS MUST BE SHUNNED

I MUST not omit an important subject, and mention of a mistake which princes can with difficulty avoid, if they are not very prudent, or if they do not make a good choice. And this is with regard to flatterers, of which courts are full, because men take such pleasure in their own things and deceive themselves about them that they can with difficulty guard against this plague; and by wishing to guard against it they run the risk of becoming contemptible. Because there is no other way of guarding one's self against flattery than by letting men understand that they will not offend you by speaking the truth; but when every one can tell you the truth, you lose their respect. A prudent prince must therefore take a third course, by choosing for his council wise men, and giving these alone full liberty to speak the truth to him, but only of those things that he asks and of nothing else; but he must ask them about everything and hear their opinion, and afterwards deliberate by himself in his own way, and in these councils and with each of these men comport himself so that every one may see that the more freely he speaks, the more he will be acceptable. Beyond these he should listen to no one, go about the matter deliberately, and be determined in his decisions. Whoever acts otherwise either acts precipitately through flattery or else changes often through the variety of opinions, from which it follows that he will be little esteemed.

I will give a modern instance of this. Pre' Luca, a follower of Maximilian, the present emperor, speaking of his majesty said that he never took counsel with anybody, and yet that he never did anything as he wished; this arose from his following the contrary method to the aforesaid. As the emperor is a secret man he does not communicate his designs to any one or take any advice, but as on putting them into effect they begin to be known and discovered, they begin to be opposed by those he has about him, and he is easily diverted from his purpose. Hence it comes to pass that what he does one day he undoes the next, no one ever understands what he wishes or intends to do, and no reliance is to be placed on his deliberations.

A prince, therefore, ought always to take counsel, but only when he wishes, not when others wish; on the contrary he ought to discourage absolutely attempts to advise him unless he asks it, but he ought to be a great asker, and a patient hearer of the truth about those things of which he has inquired; indeed, if he finds that any one has scruples in telling him the truth he should be angry. And since some think that a prince who gains the reputation of being prudent is so considered, not by his nature but by the good counsellors he has about him, they are undoubtedly deceived. It is an infallible rule that a prince who is not wise himself cannot be well advised, unless by chance he leaves himself entirely in the hands of one man who rules him in everything, and happens to be a very prudent man. In this case he may doubtless be well governed, but it would not last long, for that governor would in a short time deprive him of the state; but by taking counsel with many, a prince who is not wise will never have united councils and will not be able to bring them to unanimity for himself. The counsellors will all think of their own interests, and he will be unable either to correct or to understand them. And it cannot be otherwise, for men will always be false to you unless they are compelled by necessity to be true. Therefore it must be concluded that wise counsels, from whoever they come, must necessarily be due to the prudence of the prince, and not the prudence of the prince to the good counsels received.

Chapter XXIV

WHY THE PRINCES OF ITALY HAVE LOST THEIR STATES

THE before-mentioned things, if prudently observed, make a new prince seem ancient, and render him at once more secure and firmer in the state than if he had been established there of old. For a new prince is much more observed in his actions than a hereditary one, and when these are recognised as virtuous, he wins over men more and they are more bound to him than if he were of the ancient blood. For men are much more taken by present than by past things, and when they find themselves well off in the present, they enjoy it and seek nothing more; on the contrary, they will do all they can to defend him, so long as the prince is not in other things deficient. And thus he will have the double glory of having founded a new realm and adorned it and fortified it with good laws, good arms, good friends and good examples; as he will have double shame who is born a prince and through want of prudence has lost his throne.

And if one considers those rulers who have lost their

position in Italy in our days, such as the King of Naples, the Duke of Milan and others, one will find in them first a common defect as to their arms, for the reasons discussed at length, then we observe that some of them either had the people hostile to them, or that if the people were friendly they were not able to make sure of the nobility, for without these defects, states are not lost that have enough strength to be able to keep an army in the field. Philip of Macedon, not the father of Alexander the Great, but the one who was conquered by Titus Quintius, did not possess a great state compared to the greatness of Rome and Greece which assailed him, but being a military man and one who knew how to ingratiate himself with the people and make sure of the great, he was able to sustain the war against them for many years; and if at length he lost his power over some cities, he was still able to keep his kingdom.

Therefore, those of our princes who had held their possessions for many years must not accuse fortune for having lost them, but rather their own remissness; for having never in quiet times considered that things might change (as it is a common fault of men not to reckon on storms in fair weather) when adverse times came, they only thought of fleeing, instead of defending themselves; and hoped that the people, enraged by the insolence of the conquerors, would recall them. This measure, when others are wanting, is good; but it is very bad to have neglected the other remedies for that one, for nobody would desire to fall because he believed that he would then find some one to pick him up. This may or may not take place, and if it does, it does not afford you security, as you have not helped yourself but been helped like a coward. Only those defences are good, certain and durable, which depend on yourself alone and your own ability.

Chapter XXV

HOW MUCH FORTUNE CAN DO IN HUMAN AFFAIRS AND HOW IT MAY BE OPPOSED

It is not unknown to me how many have been and are of opinion that worldly events are so governed by fortune and by God, that men cannot by their prudence change them, and that on the contrary there is no remedy whatever, and for this they may judge it to be useless to toil much about them, but let things be ruled by chance. This opinion has been more held in our day, from the great changes that have been seen, and are daily seen, beyond every human conjecture. When I think about them, at times I am partly inclined to share this opinion. Nevertheless, that our free-will may not be altogether extinguished, I think it may be true that fortune is the ruler of half our actions, but that she allows the other half or thereabouts to be governed by us. I would compare her to an impetuous river that, when turbulent, inundates the plains, casts down trees and buildings, removes earth from this side and places it on the other; every one flees before it, and everything yields to its fury without being able to oppose it; and yet though it is of such a kind, still when it is quiet, men can make provision against it by dykes and banks, so that when it rises it will either go into a canal or its rush will not be so wild and dangerous. So it is with fortune, which shows her power where no measures have been taken to resist her, and directs her fury where she knows that no dykes or barriers have been made to hold her. And if you regard Italy, which has been the seat of these changes, and who has given the impulse to them, you will see her to be a country without dykes or banks of any kind. If she had been protected by proper measures, like Germany, Spain, and France, this inundation would not have caused the great changes that it has, or would not have happened at all.

This must suffice as regards opposition to fortune in general. But limiting myself more to particular cases, I would point out how one sees a certain prince to-day fortunate and to-morrow ruined, without seeing that he has changed in character or otherwise. I believe this arises in the first place from the causes that we have already discussed at length; that is to say, because the prince who bases himself entirely on fortune is ruined when fortune changes. I also believe that he is happy whose mode of procedure accords with the needs of the times, and similarly he is unfortunate whose mode of procedure is opposed to the times. For one sees that men in those things which lead them to the aim that each one has in view, namely, glory and riches, proceed in various ways; one with circumspection, another with impetuosity, one by violence, another by cunning, one with patience, another with the reverse; and each by these diverse ways may arrive at his aim. One sees also two cautious men, one of whom succeeds in his designs, and the other not, and in the same way two men succeed equally by different methods, one being cautious, the other impetuous, which arises only from the nature of the times, which does or does not conform to their method of procedure. From this it results, as I have said, that two men, acting differently, attain the same effect, and of two others acting in the same way, one attains his goal and not the other. On this depend also the changes in prosperity, for if it happens that time and circumstances are favourable to one who acts with caution and prudence he will be successful, but if time and circumstances change he will be ruined, because he does not change his mode of procedure. No man is found so prudent as to be able to adapt himself to this, either because he cannot deviate from that to which his nature disposes him, or else because having always prospered by walking in one path, he cannot persuade himself that it is well to leave it; and therefore the cautious man, when it is time to act suddenly, does not know how to do so and is consequently ruined; for if one could change one's nature with time and circumstances, fortune would never change.

Pope Julius II acted impetuously in everything he did and found the times and conditions so in conformity with that mode of procedure, that he always obtained a good result. Consider the first war that he made against Bologna while Messer Giovanni Bentivogli was still living. The Venetians were not pleased with it, neither was the King of Spain, France was conferring with him over the enterprise, notwithstanding which, owing to his fierce and impetuous disposition, he engaged personally in the expedition. This move caused both Spain and the Venetians to halt and hesitate, the latter through fear, the former through the desire to recover the entire kingdom of Naples. On the other hand, he engaged with him the King of France, because seeing him make this move and desiring his friendship in order to put down the Venetians, that king judged that he could not refuse him his troops without manifest injury. Thus Julius by his impetuous move achieved what no other pontiff with the utmost human prudence would have succeeded in doing, because, if he had waited till all arrangements had been made and everything settled before leaving Rome, as any other pontiff would have done, it would never have succeeded. For the king of France would have found a thousand excuses, and the others would have inspired him with a thousand fears. I will omit his other actions, which were all of this kind and which all succeeded well, and the shortness of his life did not suffer him to experience the contrary, for had times followed in which it was necessary to act with caution, his ruin would have resulted, for he would never have deviated from these methods to which his nature disposed him.

I conclude then that fortune varying and men remaining fixed in their ways, they are successful so long as these ways conform to circumstances, but when they are opposed then they are unsuccessful. I certainly think that it is better to be impetuous than cautious, for fortune is a woman, and it is necessary, if you wish to master her, to conquer her by force; and it can be seen that she lets herself be overcome by the bold rather than by those who proceed coldly. And therefore, like a woman, she is always a friend to the young, because they are less cautious, fiercer, and master her with greater audacity.

Chapter XXVI

EXHORTATION TO LIBERATE ITALY FROM THE BARBARIANS

HAVING now considered all the things we have spoken of, and thought within myself whether at present the time was not propitious in Italy for a new prince, and if there was not a state of things which offered an opportunity to a prudent and capable man to introduce a new system that would do honour to himself and good to the mass of the people, it seems to me that so many things concur to favour a new ruler that I do not know of any time more fitting for such an enterprise. And if, as I said, it was necessary in order that the power of Moses should be displayed that the people of Israel should be slaves in Egypt, and to give scope for the greatness and courage of Cyrus that the Persians should be oppressed by the Medes, and to illustrate the pre-eminence of Theseus that the Athenians should be dispersed, so at the present time, in order that the might of an Italian genius might be recognised, it was necessary that Italy should be reduced to her present condition, and that she should be more enslaved than the Hebrews, more oppressed than the Persians, and more scattered than the Athenians; without a head, without order, beaten, despoiled, lacerated, and overrun, and that she should have suffered ruin of every kind.

And although before now a gleam of hope has appeared which gave hope that some individual might be appointed by God for her redemption, yet at the highest summit of his career he was thrown aside by fortune, so that now, almost lifeless, she awaits one who may heal her wounds and put a stop to the pillaging of Lombardy, to the rapacity and extortion in the Kingdom of Naples and in Tuscany, and cure her of those sores which have long been festering. Behold how she prays God to send some one to redeem her from this barbarous cruelty and insolence. Behold her ready and willing to follow any standard if only there be some one to raise it. There is nothing now she can hope for but that your illustrious house may place itself at the head of this redemption, being by its power and fortune so exalted, and being favoured by God and the Church, of which it is now the ruler. Nor will this be very difficult, if you call to mind the actions and lives of the men I have named. And although those men were rare and marvellous, they were none the less men, and each of them had less opportunity than the present, for their enterprise was not juster than this, nor easier, nor was God more their friend than He is yours. Here is a just cause; *'iustum enim est bellum quibus necessarium, et pia arma ubi nulla nisi in armis spes est.'* Here is the greatest willingness, nor can there be great difficulty where there is great willingness, provided that the measures are adopted of those whom I have set before you as examples. Besides this, unexampled wonders have been seen here performed by God, the sea has been opened, a cloud has shown you the road, the rock has given forth water, manna has rained, and everything has contributed to your greatness, the remainder must be done by you. God will not do everything, in order not to deprive us of freewill and the portion of the glory that falls to our lot.

It is no marvel that none of the before-mentioned Italians have done that which it is to be hoped your illustrious house may do; and if in so many revolutions in Italy and so many warlike operations, it always seems as if military capacity were extinct, this is because the ancient methods were not good, and no one has arisen who knew how to discover new ones. Nothing does so much honour to a newly-risen man than the new laws and measures which he introduces. These things, when they are well based and have greatness in them, render him revered and admired, and there is not lacking scope in Italy for the introduction of every kind of new organisation. Here there is great virtue in the members, if it were not wanting in the heads. Look how in duels and in contests of a few the Italians are superior in strength, dexterity, and intelligence. But when it comes to armies they make a poor show; which proceeds entirely from the weakness of the leaders, for those that know are not obeyed, and every one thinks that he knows, there being hitherto nobody who has raised himself so high both by valour and fortune as to make the others yield. Hence it comes about that for so long a time, in all the wars waged during the last twenty years, whenever there has been an entirely Italian army it has always been a failure, as witness first Taro, then Alexandria, Capua, Genoa, Vailà, Bologna, and Mestri.

If your illustrious house, therefore, wishes to follow those great men who redeemed their countries, it is before all things necessary, as the true foundation of every undertaking, to provide yourself with your own forces, for you cannot have more faithful, or truer and better soldiers. And although each one of them may be good, they will united become even better when they see themselves commanded by their prince, and honoured and favoured by him. It is therefore necessary to prepare such forces in order to be able with Italian prowess to defend the country from foreigners. And although both the Swiss and Spanish infantry are deemed terrible, none the less they each have their defects, so that a third method of array might not only oppose them, but be confident of overcoming them. For the Spaniards cannot sustain the attack of cavalry, and the Swiss have to fear infantry which meets them with resolution equal to their own. From which it has resulted, as will be seen by experience, that the Spaniards cannot sustain the attack of French cavalry, and the Swiss are overthrown by Spanish infantry. And although a complete example of the latter has not been seen, yet an instance was furnished in the battle of Ravenna, where the Spanish infantry attacked the German battalions, which are organised in the same way as the Swiss. The Spaniards, through their bodily agility and aided by their bucklers, had entered between and under their pikes and were in a position to attack them safely without the Germans being able to defend themselves; and if the cavalry had not charged them they would have utterly destroyed them. Knowing therefore the defects of both these kinds of infantry, a third kind can be created which can resist cavalry and need not fear infantry, and this will be done by the choice of arms and a new organisation. And these are the things which, when newly introduced, give reputation and grandeur to a new prince.

This opportunity must not, therefore, be allowed to pass, so that Italy may at length find her liberator. I cannot express the love with which he would be received in all those provinces which have suffered under these foreign invasions, with what thirst for vengeance, with what steadfast faith, with what love, with what grateful tears. What doors would be closed against him? What people would refuse him obedience? What envy could oppose him? What Italian would withhold allegiance? This barbarous domination stinks in the nostrils of every one. May your illustrious house therefore assume this task with that courage and those hopes which are inspired by a just cause, so that under its banner our fatherland may be raised up, and under its auspices be verified that saying of Petrarch:

> Valour against fell wrath
> Will take up arms; and be the combat quickly sped!
> For, sure, the ancient worth,
> That in Italians stirs the heart, is not yet dead.

DISCOURSES

ON THE

FIRST TEN BOOKS OF TITUS LIVIUS.

(Translated from the Italian by Christian E. Detmold)

NICCOLÒ MACHIAVELLI

TO

ZANOBI BUONDELMONTE AND COSIMO RUCELLAI,

GREETING

WITH this I send you a gift which, if it bears no proportion to the extent of the obligations which I owe you, is nevertheless the best that I am able to offer to you; for I have endeavored to embody in it all that long experience and assiduous research have taught me of the affairs of the world. And as neither yourselves nor any one else can ask more than that of me, you cannot complain that I have not given you more; though you may well complain of my lack of talent when my arguments are poor, and of the fallacies of my judgment on account of the errors into which I have doubtless fallen many times. This being so, however, I know not which of us has the greater right to complain,—I, that you should have forced me to write what I should never have attempted of my own accord, or you, that I should have written without giving you cause to be satisfied.

Accept it, then, as one accepts whatever comes from friends, looking rather to the intention of him who gives, than to the thing offered. And believe me, that I feel a satisfaction in this, that, even if I have often erred in the course of this work, I have assuredly made no mistake in having chosen you above all other friends to whom to dedicate these discourses. In doing this, I give some proof of gratitude, although I may seem to have departed from the ordinary usage of writers, who generally dedicate their works to some prince; and, blinded by ambition or avarice, praise him for all the virtuous qualities he has not, instead of censuring him for his real vices, whilst I, to avoid this fault, do not address myself to such as are princes, but to those who by their infinite good qualities are worthy to be such; not to those who could load me with honors, rank, and wealth, but rather to those who have the desire to do so, but have not the power. For to judge rightly, men should esteem rather those who are, and not those who can be generous; and those who would know how to govern states, rather than those who have the right to govern, but lack the knowledge.

For this reason have historians praised Hiero of Syracuse, a mere private citizen, more than Perseus of Macedon, monarch though he was; for Hiero only lacked a principality to be a prince, whilst the other had nothing of the king except the diadem. Be it good or bad, however, you wanted this work, and such as it is I send it to you; and should you continue in the belief that my opinions are acceptable to you, I shall not fail to continue to examine this history, as I promised you in the beginning of it. Farewell!

DISCOURSES

ON THE

FIRST TEN BOOKS OF TITUS LIVIUS.

FIRST BOOK *men jealous by nature*

INTRODUCTION

ALTHOUGH the envious nature of men, so prompt to blame and so slow to praise, makes the discovery and introduction of any new principles and systems as dangerous almost as the exploration of unknown seas and continents, yet, animated by that desire which impels me to do what may prove for the common benefit of all, I have resolved to open a new route, which has not yet been followed by any one, and may prove difficult and troublesome, but may also bring me some reward in the approbation of those who will kindly appreciate my efforts.

And if my poor talents, my little experience of the present and insufficient study of the past, should make the result of my labors defective and of little utility, I shall at least have shown the way to others, who will carry out my views with greater ability, eloquence, and judgment, so that if I do not merit praise, I ought at least not to incur censure.

When we consider the general respect for antiquity, and how often—to say nothing of other examples—a great price is paid for some fragments of an antique statue, which we are anxious to possess to ornament our houses with, or to give to artists who strive to imitate them in their own works; and when we see, on the other hand, the wonderful examples which the history of ancient kingdoms and republics presents to us, the prodigies of virtue and of wisdom displayed by the kings, captains, citizens, and legislators who have sacrificed themselves for their country,—when we see these, I say, more admired than imitated, or so much neglected that not the least trace of this ancient virtue remains, we cannot but be at the same time as much surprised as afflicted. The more so as in the differences which arise between citizens, or in the maladies to which they are subjected, we see these same people have recourse to the judgments and the remedies prescribed by the ancients. The civil laws are in fact nothing but decisions given by their jurisconsults, and which, reduced to a system, direct our modern jurists in their decisions. And what is the science of medicine, but the experience of ancient physicians, which their successors have taken for their guide? And yet to found a republic, maintain states, to govern a kingdom, organize an army, conduct a war, dispense justice, and extend empires, you will find neither prince, nor republic, nor captain, nor citizen, who has recourse to the examples of antiquity! This neglect, I am persuaded, is due less to the weakness to which the vices of our education have reduced the world, than to the evils caused by the proud indolence which prevails in most of the Christian states, and to the lack of real knowledge of history, the true sense of which is not known, or the spirit of which they do not comprehend. Thus the majority of those who read it take pleasure only in the variety of the events which history relates, without ever thinking of imitating the noble actions, deeming that not only difficult, but impossible; as though heaven, the sun, the elements, and men had changed the order of their motions and power, and were different from what they were in ancient times.

Wishing, therefore, so far as in me lies, to draw mankind from this error, I have thought it proper to write upon those books of Titus Livius that have come to us entire despite the malice of time; touching upon all those matters which, after a comparison between the ancient and modern events, may seem to me necessary to facilitate their proper understanding. In this way those who read my remarks may derive those advantages which should be the aim of all study of history; and although the undertaking is difficult, yet, aided by those who have encouraged me in this attempt, I hope to carry it sufficiently far, so that but little may remain for others to carry it to its destined end.

Chapter I

OF THE BEGINNING OF CITIES IN GENERAL, AND ESPECIALLY THAT OF THE CITY OF ROME

THOSE who read what the beginning of Rome was, and what her lawgivers and her organization, will not be astonished that so much virtue should have maintained itself during so many centuries; and that so great an empire should have sprung from it afterwards. To speak first of her origin, we will premise that all cities are founded either by natives of the country or by strangers. The little security which the natives found in living dispersed; the impossibility for each to resist isolated, either because of the situation or because of their small number, the attacks of any enemy that might present himself; the difficulty of uniting in time for defence at his approach, and the necessity of abandoning the greater number of their retreats, which quickly became a prize to the assailant,—such were the motives that caused the first inhabitants of a country to build cities for the purpose of escaping these dangers. They resolved, of their own accord, or by the advice of some one who had most authority amongst them, to live together in some place of their selection that might offer them greater conveniences and greater facility of defence. Thus, amongst many others were Athens and Venice; the first was built under the authority of Theseus, who had gathered the dispersed inhabitants; and the second owed its origin to the fact that several tribes had taken refuge on the little islands situated at the head of the Adriatic Sea, to escape from war, and from the Barbarians who after the fall of the Roman Empire had overrun Italy. These refugees of themselves, and without any prince to govern them, began to live under such laws as seemed to them best suited to maintain their new state. In this they succeeded, happily favored by the long peace, for which they were indebted to their situation upon a sea without issue, where the people that ravaged Italy could not harass them, being without any ships. Thus from that small beginning they attained that degree of power in which we see them now.

The second case is when a city is built by strangers; these may be either freemen, or subjects of a republic or of a prince, who, to relieve their states from an excessive population, or to defend a newly acquired territory which they wish to preserve without expense, send colonies there. The Romans founded many cities in this way within their empire. Sometimes cities are built by a prince, not for the purpose of living there, but merely as monuments to his glory; such was Alexandria, built by Alexander the Great. But as all these cities are at their very origin deprived of liberty, they rarely succeed in making great progress, or in being counted amongst the great powers. Such was the origin of Florence; for it was built either by the soldiers of Sylla, or perhaps by the inhabitants of Mount Fiesole, who, trusting to the long peace that prevailed in the reign of Octavian, were attracted to the plains along the Arno. Florence, thus built under the Roman Empire, could in the beginning have no growth except what depended on the will of its master.

The founders of cities are independent when they are people who, under the leadership of some prince, or by themselves, have been obliged to fly from pestilence, war, or famine, that was desolating their native country, and are seeking a new home. These either inhabit the cities of the country of which they take possession, as Moses did; or they build new ones, as was done by Æneas. In such case we are able to appreciate the talents of the founder and the success of his work, which is more or less remarkable according as he, in founding the city, displays more or less wisdom and skill. Both the one and the other are recognized by the selection of the place where he has located the city, and by the nature of the laws which he establishes in it. And as men work either from necessity or from choice, and as it has been observed that virtue has more sway where labor is the result of necessity rather than of choice, it is a matter of consideration whether it might not be better to select for the establishment of a city a sterile region, where the people, compelled by necessity to be industrious, and therefore less given to idleness, would be more united, and less exposed by the poverty of the country to occasions for discord; as was the case with Ragusa, and several other cities that were built upon an ungrateful soil. Such a selection of site would doubtless be more useful and wise if men were content with what they possess, and did not desire to exercise command over others.

Now, as people cannot make themselves secure except by being powerful, it is necessary in the founding of a city to avoid a sterile country. On the contrary, a city should be placed rather in a region where the fertility of the soil affords the means of becoming great, and of acquiring strength to repel all who might attempt to attack it, or oppose the development of its power. As to the idleness which the fertility of a country tends to encourage, the laws should compel men to labor where the sterility of the soil does not do it; as was done by those skilful and sagacious legislators who have inhabited very agreeable and fertile countries, such as are apt to make men idle and unfit for the exercise of valor. These by way of an offset to the pleasures and softness of the climate, imposed upon their soldiers the rigors of a strict discipline and severe exercises, so that they became better warriors than what nature produces in the harshest climates and most sterile countries. Amongst these legislators we may cite the founders of the kingdom of Egypt: despite the charms of the climate, the severity of the institutions there formed excellent men; and if great antiquity had not buried their names in oblivion, we should see that they deserved more praise than Alexander the Great and many others of more recent memory. And whoever has examined the government of the Pachas of Egypt and the discipline of their Mameluke militia before it was destroyed by the Sultan Selim of Turkey, will have seen how much they dreaded idleness, and by what variety of exercises and by what severe laws they prevented in their soldiers that effeminacy which is the natural fruit of the softness of their climate.

I say, then, that for the establishment of a city it is wisest to select the most fertile spot, especially as the laws can prevent the ill effects that would otherwise result from that very fertility.

When Alexander the Great wished to build a city that should serve as a monument to his glory, his architect, Dinocrates, pointed out to him how he could build a city on Mount Athos, which place he said, besides being very strong, could be so arranged as to give the city the appearance of the human form, which would make it a wonder worthy of the greatness of its founder. Alexander having asked him what the inhabitants were to live upon, he replied, "That I have not thought of"; at which Alexander smiled, and, leaving Mount Athos as it was, he built Alexandria, where the inhabitants would be glad to remain on account of the richness of the country and the advantages which the proximity of the Nile and the sea afforded them.

If we accept the opinion that Æneas was the founder of Rome, then we must count that city as one of those built by strangers; but if Romulus is taken as its founder, then must it be classed with those built by the natives of the country. Either way it will be seen that Rome was from the first free and independent; and we shall also see (as we shall show further on) to how many privations the laws of Romulus, of Numa, and of others subjected its inhabitants; so that neither the fertility of the soil, nor the proximity of the sea, nor their many victories, nor the greatness of the Empire, could corrupt them during several centuries, and they maintained there more virtues than have ever been seen in any other republic.

The great things which Rome achieved, and of which

Titus Livius has preserved the memory, have been the work either of the government or of private individuals; and as they relate either to the affairs of the interior or of the exterior, I shall begin to discourse of those internal operations of the government which I believe to be most noteworthy, and shall point out their results. This will be the subject of the discourses that will compose this First Book, or rather First Part.

Chapter II

OF THE DIFFERENT KINDS OF REPUBLICS, AND OF WHAT KIND THE ROMAN REPUBLIC WAS

I WILL leave aside what might be said of cities which from their very birth have been subject to a foreign power, and will speak only of those whose origin has been independent, and which from the first governed themselves by their own laws, whether as republics or as principalities, and whose constitution and laws have differed as their origin. Some have had at the very beginning, or soon after, a legislator, who, like Lycurgus with the Lacedæmonians, gave them by a single act all the laws they needed. Others have owed theirs to chance and to events, and have received their laws at different times, as Rome did. It is a great good fortune for a republic to have a legislator sufficiently wise to give her laws so regulated that, without the necessity of correcting them, they afford security to those who live under them. Sparta observed her laws for more than eight hundred years without altering them and without experiencing a single dangerous disturbance. Unhappy, on the contrary, is that republic which, not having at the beginning fallen into the hands of a sagacious and skilful legislator, is herself obliged to reform her laws. More unhappy still is that republic which from the first has diverged from a good constitution. And that republic is furthest from it whose vicious institutions impede her progress, and make her leave the right path that leads to a good end; for those who are in that condition can hardly ever be brought into the right road. Those republics, on the other hand, that started without having even a perfect constitution, but made a fair beginning, and are capable of improvement,—such republics, I say, may perfect themselves by the aid of events. It is very true, however, that such reforms are never effected without danger, for the majority of men never willingly adopt any new law tending to change the constitution of the state, unless the necessity of the change is clearly demonstrated; and as such a necessity cannot make itself felt without being accompanied with danger, the republic may easily be destroyed before having perfected its constitution. That of Florence is a complete proof of this: reorganized after the revolt of Arezzo, in 1502, it was overthrown after the taking of Prato, in 1512.

Having proposed to myself to treat of the kind of government established at Rome, and of the events that led to its perfection, I must at the beginning observe that some of the writers on politics distinguished three kinds of government, viz. the monarchical, the aristocratic, and the democratic; and maintain that the legislators of a people must choose from these three the one that seems to them most suitable. Other authors, wiser according to the opinion of many, count six kinds of governments, three of which are very bad, and three good in themselves, but so liable to be corrupted that they become absolutely bad. The three good ones are those which we have just named; the three bad

ones result from the degradation of the other three, and each
of them resembles its corresponding original, so that the
transition from the one to the other is very easy. Thus monarchy becomes tyranny; aristocracy degenerates into oligarchy; and the popular government lapses readily into licentiousness. So that a legislator who gives to a state which he
founds, either of these three forms of government, consti-
tutes it but for a brief time; for no precautions can prevent
either one of the three that are reputed good, from degen-
erating into its opposite kind; so great are in these the attractions and resemblances between the good and the evil.

Chance has given birth to these different kinds of governments amongst men; for at the beginning of the world the
inhabitants were few in number, and lived for a time dispersed, like beasts. As the human race increased, the necessity for uniting themselves for defence made itself felt; the
better to attain this object, they chose the strongest and
most courageous from amongst themselves and placed him
at their head, promising to obey him. Thence they began
to know the good and the honest, and to distinguish them
from the bad and vicious; for seeing a man injure his benefactor aroused at once two sentiments in every heart, hatred
against the ingrate and love for the benefactor. They blamed
the first, and on the contrary honored those the more who
showed themselves grateful, for each felt that he in turn
might be subject to a like wrong; and to prevent similar
evils, they set to work to make laws, and to institute punishments for those who contravened them. Such was the origin
of justice. This caused them, when they had afterwards to
choose a prince, neither to look to the strongest nor bravest,
but to the wisest and most just. But when they began to
make sovereignty hereditary and non-elective, the children
quickly degenerated from their fathers; and, so far from

trying to equal their virtues, they considered that a prince had nothing else to do than to excel all the rest in luxury, indulgence, and every other variety of pleasure. The prince consequently soon drew upon himself the general hatred. An object of hatred, he naturally felt fear; fear in turn dictated to him precautions and wrongs, and thus tyranny quickly developed itself. Such were the beginning and causes of disorders, conspiracies, and plots against the sovereigns, set on foot, not by the feeble and timid, but by those citizens who, surpassing the others in grandeur of soul, in wealth, and in courage, could not submit to the outrages and excesses of their princes.

Under such powerful leaders the masses armed themselves against the tyrant, and, after having rid themselves of him, submitted to these chiefs as their liberators. These, abhorring the very name of prince, constituted themselves a new government; and at first, bearing in mind the past tyranny, they governed in strict accordance with the laws which they had established themselves; preferring public interests to their own, and to administer and protect with greatest care both public and private affairs. The children succeeded their fathers, and ignorant of the changes of fortune, having never experienced its reverses, and indisposed to remain content with this civil equality, they in turn gave themselves up to cupidity, ambition, libertinage, and violence, and soon caused the aristocratic government to degenerate into an oligarchic tyranny, regardless of all civil rights. They soon, however, experienced the same fate as the first tyrant; the people, disgusted with their government, placed themselves at the command of whoever was willing to attack them, and this disposition soon produced an avenger, who was sufficiently well seconded to destroy them. The memory of the prince and the wrongs committed by him being still fresh in their minds, and having overthrown the oligarchy, the people were not willing to return to the government of a prince. A popular government was therefore resolved upon, and it was so organized that the authority should not again fall into the hands of a prince or a small number of nobles. And as all governments are at first looked up to with some degree of reverence, the popular state also maintained itself for a time, but which was never of long duration, and lasted generally only about as long as the generation that had established it; for it soon ran into that kind of license which inflicts injury upon public as well as private interests. Each individual only consulted his own passions, and a thousand acts of injustice were daily committed, so that, constrained by necessity, or directed by the counsels of some good man, or for the purpose of escaping from this anarchy, they returned anew to the government of a prince, and from this they generally lapsed again into anarchy, step by step, in the same manner and from the same causes as we have indicated.

Such is the circle which all republics are destined to run through. Seldom, however, do they come back to the original form of government, which results from the fact that their duration is not sufficiently long to be able to undergo these repeated changes and preserve their existence. But it may well happen that a republic lacking strength and good counsel in its difficulties becomes subject after a while to some neighboring state, that is better organized than itself; and if such is not the case, then they will be apt to revolve indefinitely in the circle of revolutions. I say, then, that all kinds of government are defective; those three which we have qualified as good because they are too short-lived, and the three bad ones because of their inherent viciousness. Thus sagacious legislators, knowing the vices of each of these systems of government by themselves, have chosen one that should partake of all of them, judging that to be the most stable and solid. In fact, when there is combined under the same constitution a prince, a nobility, and the power of the people, then these three powers will watch and keep each other reciprocally in check.

Amongst those justly celebrated for having established such a constitution, Lycurgus beyond doubt merits the highest praise. He organized the government of Sparta in such manner that, in giving to the king, the nobles, and the people each their portion of authority and duties, he created a government which maintained itself for over eight hundred years in the most perfect tranquillity, and reflected infinite glory upon this legislator. On the other hand, the constitution given by Solon to the Athenians, by which he established only a popular government, was of such short duration that before his death he saw the tyranny of Pisistratus arise. And although forty years afterwards the heirs of the tyrant were expelled, so that Athens recovered her liberties and restored the popular-government according to the laws of Solon, yet it did not last over a hundred years; although a number of laws that had been overlooked by Solon were adopted, to maintain the government against the insolence of the nobles and the license of the populace. The fault he had committed in not tempering the power of the people and that of the prince and his nobles, made the duration of the government of Athens very short, as compared with that of Sparta.

But let us come to Rome. Although she had no legislator like Lycurgus, who constituted her government, at her very origin, in a manner to secure her liberty for a length of time, yet the disunion which existed between the Senate and the people produced such extraordinary events, that

chance did for her what the laws had failed to do. Thus, if
Rome did not attain the first degree of happiness, she at
least had the second. Her first institutions were doubtless
defective, but they were not in conflict with the principles
that might bring her to perfection. For Romulus and all
the other kings gave her many and good laws, well suited
even to a free people; but as the object of these princes was
to found a monarchy, and not a republic, Rome, upon becoming free, found herself lacking all those institutions that
are most essential to liberty, and which her kings had not
established. And although these kings lost their empire, for
the reasons and in the manner which we have explained,
yet those who expelled them appointed immediately two
consuls in place of the king; and thus it was found that
they had banished the title of king from Rome, but not the
regal power. The government, composed of Consuls and a
Senate, had but two of the three elements of which we have
spoken, the monarchical and the aristocratic; the popular
power was wanting. In the course of time, however, the insolence of the nobles, produced by the causes which we shall
see further on, induced the people to rise against the others.
The nobility, to save a portion of their power, were forced
to yield a share of it to the people; but the Senate and the
Consuls retained sufficient to maintain their rank in the
state. It was then that the Tribunes of the people were
created, which strengthened and confirmed the republic,
being now composed of the three elements of which we have
spoken above. Fortune favored her, so that, although the
authority passed successively from the kings and nobles to
the people, by the same degrees and for the same reasons
that we have spoken of, yet the royal authority was never
entirely abolished to bestow it upon the nobles; and these
were never entirely deprived of their authority to give it to

the people; but a combination was formed of the three powers, which rendered the constitution perfect, and this perfection was attained by the disunion of the Senate and the people, as we shall more fully show in the following two chapters.

Chapter III

OF THE EVENTS THAT CAUSED THE CREATION OF TRIBUNES IN ROME; WHICH MADE THE REPUBLIC MORE PERFECT

ALL those who have written upon civil institutions demonstrate (and history is full of examples to support them) that whoever desires to found a state and give it laws, must start with assuming that all men are bad and ever ready to display their vicious nature, whenever they may find occasion for it. If their evil disposition remains concealed for a time, it must be attributed to some unknown reason; and we must assume that it lacked occasion to show itself; but time, which has been said to be the father of all truth, does not fail to bring it to light. After the expulsion of the Tarquins the greatest harmony seemed to prevail between the Senate and the people. The nobles seemed to have laid aside all their haughtiness and assumed popular manners, which made them supportable even to the lowest of the citizens. The nobility played this role so long as the Tarquins lived, without their motive being divined; for they feared the Tarquins, and also lest the ill-treated people might side with them. Their party therefore assumed all possible gentleness in their manners towards the people. But so soon as the death of the Tarquins had relieved them of their apprehensions, they began to vent upon the people all the venom they had so long retained within their breasts, and lost no opportunity to outrage them in every possible way; which is one of the proofs of the argument we have advanced, that men act right only upon compulsion; but from the moment that they have the option and liberty to commit wrong with impunity, then they never fail to carry confusion and disorder everywhere. It is this that has caused it to be said that poverty and hunger make men industrious, and that the law makes men good; and if fortunate circumstances cause good to be done without constraint, the law may be dispensed with. But when such happy influence is lacking, then the law immediately becomes necessary. Thus the nobles, after the death of the Tarquins, being no longer under the influence that had restrained them, determined to establish a new order of things, which had the same effect as the misrule of the Tarquins during their existence; and therefore, after many troubles, tumults, and dangers occasioned by the excesses which both the nobles and the people committed, they came, for the security of the people, to the creation of the Tribunes, who were endowed with so many prerogatives, and surrounded with so much respect, that they formed a powerful barrier between the Senate and the people, which curbed the insolence of the former.

Chapter IV

THE DISUNION OF THE SENATE AND THE PEOPLE RENDERS the REPUBLIC OF ROME POWERFUL AND FREE

I SHALL not pass over in silence the disturbances that occurred in Rome from the time of the death of the Tarquins to that of the creation of the Tribunes; and shall afterwards refute the opinion of those who claim that the Roman republic has always been a theatre of turbulence and disorder, and that if its extreme good fortune and the military discipline had not supplied the defects of her constitution, she would have deserved the lowest rank amongst the republics.

It cannot be denied that the Roman Empire was the result of good fortune and military discipline; but it seems to me that it ought to be perceived that where good discipline prevails there also will good order prevail, and good fortune rarely fails to follow in their train. Let us, however, go into details upon this point. I maintain that those who blame the quarrels of the Senate and the people of Rome condemn that which was the very origin of liberty, and that they were probably more impressed by the cries and noise which these disturbances occasioned in the public places, than by the good effect which they produced; and that they do not consider that in every republic there are two parties, that of the nobles and that of the people; and all the laws that are favorable to liberty result from the opposition of these parties to each other, as may easily be seen from the events that occurred in Rome. From the time of the Tarquins to that of the Gracchi, that is to say, within the space of over three hundred years, the differences between these parties caused but very few exiles, and cost still less blood; they cannot therefore be regarded as having been very injurious and fatal to a republic, which during the course of so many years saw on this account only eight or ten of its citizens sent into exile, and but a very small number put to death, and even but a few condemned to pecuniary fines. Nor can we regard a republic as disorderly where so many virtues were seen to shine. For good examples are the result of good education, and good education is due to good laws; and good laws in their turn spring from those very agitations which have been so inconsiderately condemned by many. For whoever will carefully examine the result of these agitations will find that they have neither caused exiles nor any violence prejudicial to the general good, and will be convinced even that they have given rise to laws that were to the advantage of public liberty. And if it be said that these are strange means,—to hear constantly the cries of the people furious against the Senate, and of a Senate declaiming against the people, to see the populace rush tumultuously through the streets. close their houses, and even leave the city of Rome,—I reply, that all these things can alarm only those who read of them, and that every free state ought to afford the people the opportunity of giving vent, so to say, to their ambition; and above all those republics which on important occasions have to avail themselves of this very people. Now such were the means employed at Rome; when the people wanted to obtain a law, they resorted to some of the extremes of which we have just spoken, or they refused to enroll themselves to serve in the wars, so that the Senate was obliged to satisfy them in some measure. The demands of a free people are rarely pernicious to their liberty; they are generally inspired by oppressions, experienced or apprehended; and if their fears are ill founded, resort is had to public assemblies where the mere eloquence of a single good and respectable man will make them sensible of their error. "The people," says Cicero, "although ignorant, yet are capable of appreciating the truth, and yield to it readily when it is presented to them by a man whom they esteem worthy of their confidence."

One should show then more reserve in blaming the Roman government, and consider that so many good effects, which originated in that republic, cannot but result from

very good causes. If the troubles of Rome occasioned the
creation of Tribunes, then they cannot be praised too highly;
for besides giving to the people a share in the public administration, these Tribunes were established as the most
assured guardians of Roman liberty, as we shall see in the
following chapter.

Chapter V

TO WHOM CAN THE GUARDIANSHIP OF LIBERTY MORE SAFELY BE
CONFIDED, TO THE NOBLES OR TO THE PEOPLE? AND WHICH OF
THE TWO HAVE MOST CAUSE FOR CREATING DISTURBANCES,
THOSE WHO WISH TO ACQUIRE, OR THOSE WHO DESIRE TO CON-
SERVE?

ALL the legislators that have given wise constitutions to republics have deemed it an essential precaution to establish a
guard and protection to liberty; and according as this was
more or less wisely placed, liberty endured a greater or less
length of time. As every republic was composed of nobles
and people, the question arose as to whose hands it was
best to confide the protection of liberty. The Lacedæmonians, and in our day the Venetians, gave it into the hands
of the nobility; but the Romans intrusted it to the people.
We must examine, therefore, which of these republics made
the best choice. There are strong reasons in favor of each,
but, to judge by the results, we must incline in favor of the
nobles, for the liberties of Sparta and Venice endured a
longer space of time than those of Rome. But to come to
the reasons, taking the part of Rome first, I will say, that
one should always confide any deposit to those who have
least desire of violating it; and doubtless, if we consider the

objects of the nobles and of the people, we must see that the first have a great desire to dominate, whilst the latter have only the wish not to be dominated, and consequently a greater desire to live in the enjoyment of liberty; so that when the people are intrusted with the care of any privilege or liberty, being less disposed to encroach upon it, they will of necessity take better care of it; and being unable to take it away themselves, will prevent others from doing so.

On the contrary, it is said, in favor of the course adopted by Sparta and Venice, that the preference given to the nobility, as guardians of public liberty, has two advantages: the first, to yield something to the ambition of those who, being more engaged in the management of public affairs, find, so to say, in the weapon which the office places in their hands, a means of power that satisfies them; the other, to deprive the restless spirit of the masses of an authority calculated from its very nature to produce trouble and dissensions, and apt to drive the nobles to some act of desperation, which in time may cause the greatest misfortunes. Rome is even adduced as an example of this; for having confided, it is said, this authority to the tribunes of the people, these were seen not to be content with having only one Consul taken from this class, but wanted both to be plebeians. They afterwards claimed the Censure, the Prætoriate, and all the other dignities of the republic. And not satisfied with these advantages, and urged on by the same violence, they came in the end to idolize all those whom they saw disposed to attack the nobles, which gave rise to the power of Marius and to the ruin of Rome.

And, truly, whoever weighs all these reasons accurately may well remain in doubt which of the two classes he would choose as the guardians of liberty, not knowing which would be least dangerous,—those who seek to acquire an authority which they have not, or those who desire to preserve that which they already possess. After the nicest examination, this is what I think may be concluded from it. The question refers either to a republic that desires to extend its empire, as Rome, or to a state that confines itself merely to its own preservation. In the first case Rome should be imitated, and in the second the example of Sparta and Venice should be followed; and in the next chapter we shall see the reasons why and the means by which this is to be done.

To come back now to the question as to which men are most dangerous in a republic, those who wish to acquire power or those who fear to lose that which they possess, I will remark that Menenius and M. Fulvius, both plebeians, were named, the one Dictator and the other Commander of the Cavalry, to make investigations on the occasion of a conspiracy formed at Capua against Rome. They were also commissioned to find out all those who from ambition and by extraordinary means sought to obtain the Consulate and the other important offices of the republic. The nobility, believing that such an authority given to the Dictator was aimed against them, spread the report throughout the city that it was not they who sought thus to arrive at these honors from ambition or by illicit proceedings, but rather the plebeians, who, trusting neither to their birth nor their personal merits, thus employed extraordinary means to obtain these honors, and they particularly charged it upon the Dictator himself. This accusation was so actively followed up that Menenius felt himself obliged to convoke an assembly of the people; where, after having complained of the calumnies spread against him by the nobles, he deposed the Dictatorship and submitted himself to the judgment of the people. The cause having been pleaded, Menenius was absolved. On that occasion there was much discussion as to which was the most ambitious, he who wished to preserve power or he who wished to acquire it; as both the one and the other of these motives may be the cause of great troubles. It seems, however, that they are most frequently occasioned by those who possess; for the fear to lose stirs the same passions in men as the desire to gain, as men do not believe themselves sure of what they already possess except by acquiring still more; and, moreover, these new acquisitions are so many means of strength and power for abuses; and what is still worse is that the haughty manners and insolence of the nobles and the rich excite in the breasts of those who have neither birth nor wealth, not only the desire to possess them, but also the wish to revenge themselves by depriving the former of those riches and honors which they see them employ so badly.

Chapter VI

WHETHER IT WAS POSSIBLE TO ESTABLISH IN ROME A GOVERN-
MENT CAPABLE OF PUTTING AN END TO THE ENMITIES EXISTING
BETWEEN THE NOBLES AND THE PEOPLE

WE have discussed above the effects of the quarrels between the people and the Senate. These same differences having continued to the time of the Gracchi, when they became the cause of the loss of liberty, one might wish that Rome had done the great things we have admired, without bearing within her bosom such cause of discords. It seems to me therefore important to examine whether it was possible to establish a government in Rome that could prevent all these misunderstandings; and to do this well, we must necessarily recur to those republics that have maintained their liberties without such enmities and disturbances; we must examine what the form of their government was, and whether that could have been introduced in Rome.

In Sparta we have an example amongst the ancients, and in Venice amongst the moderns; to both these states I have already referred above. Sparta had a king and a senate, few in number, to govern her; Venice did not admit these distinctions, and gave the name of gentlemen to all who were entitled to have a part in the administration of the government. It was chance rather than foresight which gave to the latter this form of government; for having taken refuge on those shallows where the city now is, for the reasons mentioned above, the inhabitants soon became sufficiently numerous to require a regular system of laws. They consequently established a government, and assembled frequently in council to discuss the interests of the city. When it seemed to them that they were sufficiently numerous to govern themselves, they barred the way to a share in the government to the newly arrived who came to live amongst them; and finding in the course of time that the number of the latter increased sufficiently to give reputation to those who held the government in their hands, they designated the latter by the title of "gentlemen," and the others were called the popular class. This form of government had no difficulty in establishing and maintaining itself without disturbances; for at the moment of its origin all those who inhabited Venice had the right to participate in the government, so that no one had cause to complain. Those who afterwards came to live there, finding the government firmly established, had neither a pretext for, nor the means of, creating disturbances. They had no cause, for the reason that they had not been deprived of anything; and they lacked the means, because they were kept in check by those who held the government, and who did not employ them in any affairs that might tempt them to seize authority. Besides, the new-comers in Venice were not sufficiently numerous to have produced a disproportion between the governing and the governed, for the number of nobles equalled or exceeded that of the others; and thus for these reasons Venice could establish and preserve that form of government.

Sparta, as I have said, being governed by a king and a limited senate, could maintain itself also for a long time, because there were but few inhabitants, and strangers were not permitted to come in; besides, the laws of Lycurgus had obtained such influence that their observance prevented even the slightest pretext for trouble. It was also the easier for the citizens to live in union, as Lycurgus had established equality in fortunes and inequality in conditions; for an equal poverty prevailed there, and the people were the less ambitious, as the offices of the government were given but to a few citizens, the people being excluded from them; and the nobles in the exercise of their functions did not treat the people sufficiently ill to excite in them the desire of exercising them themselves. This last advantage was due to the kings of Sparta; for being placed in this government, as it were, between the two orders, and living in the midst of the nobility, they had no better means of maintaining their authority than to protect the people against all injustice; whence these neither feared nor desired authority, and consequently there was no motive for any differences between them and the nobles, nor any cause for disturbances; and thus they could live for a long time united. Two principal causes, however, cemented this union: first, the inhabitants of Sparta were few in number, and therefore could be governed by a few; and the other was, that, by not permitting strangers to establish themselves in the re public, they had neither opportunity of becoming corrupt, nor of increasing their population to such a degree that the burden of government became difficult to the few who were charged with it.

In examining now all these circumstances, we see that the legislators of Rome had to do one of two things to assure to their republic the same quiet as that enjoyed by the two republics of which we have spoken; namely, either not to employ the people in the armies, like the Venetians, or not to open the doors to strangers, as had been the case in Sparta. But the Romans in both took just the opposite course, which gave to the people greater power and infinite occasion for disturbances. But if the republic had been more tranquil, it would necessarily have resulted that she would have been more feeble, and that she would have lost with her energy also the ability of achieving that high degree of greatness to which she attained; so that to have removed the cause of trouble from Rome would have been to deprive her of her power of expansion. And thus it is seen in all human affairs, upon careful examination, that you cannot avoid one inconvenience without incurring another. If therefore you wish to make a people numerous and warlike, so as to create a great empire, you will have to constitute it in such manner as will cause you more difficulty in managing it; and if you keep it either small or unarmed, and you acquire other dominions, you will not be able to hold them, or you will become so feeble that you will fall a prey to whoever attacks you. And therefore in all our decisions we must consider well what presents the least inconveniences, and then choose the best, for we shall never find any course entirely free from objections. Rome then might, like Sparta, have created a king for life, and established a limited senate; but with her desire to become a great empire, she could

not, like Sparta, limit the number of her citizens; and therefore a king for life and a limited senate would have been of
no benefit to her so far as union was concerned. If any one
therefore wishes to establish an entirely new republic, he
will have to consider whether he wishes to have her expand
in power and dominion like Rome, or whether he intends
to confine her within narrow limits. In the first case, it will
be necessary to organize her as Rome was, and submit to
dissensions and troubles as best he may; for without a great
number of men, and these well armed, no republic can ever
increase. In the second case, he may organize her like Sparta
and Venice; but as expansion is the poison of such republics, he must by every means in his power prevent her from
making conquests, for such acquisitions by a feeble republic always prove their ruin, as happened to both Sparta and
Venice; the first of which, having subjected to her rule
nearly all Greece, exposed its feeble foundations at the
slightest accident, for when the rebellion of Thebes occurred,
which was led by Pelopidas, the other cities of Greece also
rose up and almost ruined Sparta.

In like manner, Venice, having obtained possession of a
great part of Italy, and the most of it not by war, but by
means of money and fraud, when occasion came for her to
give proof of her strength, she lost everything in a single
battle. I think, then, that to found a republic which should
endure a long time it would be best to organize her internally like Sparta, or to locate her, like Venice, in some
strong place; and to make her sufficiently powerful, so that
no one could hope to overcome her readily, and yet on the
other hand not so powerful as to make her formidable to
her neighbors. In this wise she might long enjoy her independence. For there are but two motives for making war
against a republic: one, the desire to subjugate her; the

other, the apprehension of being subjugated by her. The two means which we have indicated remove, as it were, both these pretexts for war; for if the republic is difficult to be conquered, her defences being well organized, as I pre. suppose, then it will seldom or never happen that any one will venture upon the project of conquering her. If she remains quiet within her limits, and experience shows that she entertains no ambitious projects, the fear of her power will never prompt any one to attack her; and this would even be more certainly the case if her constitution and laws prohibited all aggrandizement. And I certainly think that if she could be kept in this equilibrium it would be the best political existence, and would insure to any state real tranquillity. But as all human things are kept in a perpetual movement, and can never remain stable, states naturally either rise or decline, and necessity compels them to many acts to which reason will not influence them; so that, having organized a republic competent to maintain herself without expanding, still, if forced by necessity to extend her territory, in such case we shall see her foundations give way and herself quickly brought to ruin. And thus, on the other hand, if Heaven favors her so as never to be involved in war, the continued tranquillity would enervate her, or provoke internal dissensions, which together, or either of them separately, will be apt to prove her ruin. Seeing then the impossibility of establishing in this respect a perfect equilibrium, and that a precise middle course cannot be maintained, it is proper in the organization of a republic to select the most honorable course, and to constitute her so that, even if necessity should oblige her to expand, she may yet be able to preserve her acquisitions. To return now to our first argument, I believe it therefore necessary rather to take the constitution of Rome as a model than that of any other

republic, (for I do not believe that a middle course between
the two can be found,) and to tolerate the differences that
will arise between the Senate and the people as an unavoid-
able inconvenience in achieving greatness like that of Rome.
Besides the other reasons alleged, which demonstrate the
creation and authority of the Tribunes to have been necessary for the protection of liberty, it is easy to see the advantage which a republic must derive from the faculty of
accusing, which amongst others was bestowed upon the
Tribunes, as will be seen in the following chapter.

Chapter VII

SHOWING HOW NECESSARY THE FACULTY OF ACCUSATION IS IN A REPUBLIC FOR THE MAINTENANCE OF LIBERTY

No more useful and necessary authority can be given to
those who are appointed as guardians of the liberty of a state,
than the faculty of accusing the citizens to the people, or to
any magistrate or council, for any attempt against public
liberty. Such a system has two very marked advantages for
a republic. The first is, that the apprehension of being
accused prevents the citizens from attempting anything
against the state, and should they nevertheless attempt it,
they are immediately punished, without regard to persons.
The other is, that it affords a way for those evil dispositions
that arise in one way or another against some one citizen to
vent themselves; and when these ferments cannot in some
way exhaust themselves, their promoters are apt to resort to
some extraordinary means, that may lead to the ruin of the
republic. Nothing, on the other hand, renders a republic

more firm and stable, than to organize it in such a way that the excitement of the ill-humors that agitate a state may have a way prescribed by law for venting itself. This can be demonstrated by many examples, and particularly by that of Coriolanus, which Titus Livius mentions, where he says that the Roman nobility was much irritated against the people, because they believed that the people had obtained too much authority by the creation of the Tribunes who defended them; and as Rome at the time was suffering greatly from want of provisions, and the Senate had sent to Sicily for supplies of grain, Coriolanus, who was a declared enemy of the popular faction, suggested to the Senate that it afforded a favorable opportunity for them to chastise the people, and to deprive them of the authority they had acquired and assumed to the prejudice of the nobility, by not distributing the grain, and thus keeping the people in a famished condition. When this proposition came to the ears of the people, it excited so great an indignation against Coriolanus, that, on coming out of the Senate, he would have been killed in a tumultuary manner, if the Tribunes had not summoned him to appear before them and defend his cause. This occurrence shows, as we have said above, how useful and necessary it is for a republic to have laws that afford to the masses the opportunity of giving vent to the hatred they may have conceived against any citizen; for if there exist no legal means for this, they will resort to illegal ones, which beyond doubt produce much worse effects. For ordinarily when a citizen is oppressed, and even if an injustice is committed against him, it rarely causes any disturbance in the republic; for this oppression has been effected by neither private nor foreign forces, which are most destructive to public liberty, but is effected solely by the public force of the state in accordance with the established laws, which have their prescribed limits that cannot be transcended to the injury of the republic.

And to corroborate this opinion by examples, let the case of Coriolanus suffice, and let any one reflect how much evil would have resulted to the Roman republic if he had been killed in that popular outbreak; for that would have been an offence of private individuals against a private individual, which kind of offences generate fear, and fear seeks for means of defence, and for that purpose seeks partisans, and from partisans arise factions in cities, and factions cause their ruin. But as the matter was disposed of by those who had the legal authority, it prevented all those evils that would have resulted from the exercise of private force. We have seen in our time what troubles occurred in Florence because the populace could not vent their anger against one of her citizens, in the case of Francesco Valori, who was almost like a prince in that city, and being looked upon by many as an ambitious man, who by haughtiness and audacity attempted to transcend the civil authority, and there being no way in Florence for resisting this except by a faction opposed to his, it resulted that Valori, having no fear of anything but some extraordinary proceeding, began to enlist partisans who might defend him. On the other hand, those who opposed him, being without legal means for repressing him, employed illegal ones, which naturally led to an armed conflict. But if he could have been reached by lawful means, the influence of Valori would have been crushed, and he would have been the only sufferer; but being obliged to resort to illegal measures, not only he, but many other noble citizens, suffered in consequence. We may also adduce in support of the above-expressed conclusion the incident which occurred in Florence in connection with Pietro Soderini, and which resulted wholly from the fact that there were no means in that republic for bringing charges against the ambition of powerful citizens. For to accuse a noble before only eight judges did not suffice; the number of the judges should be many, for the few are apt to favor the few in their decisions. Thus, if there had been in Florence a tribunal before which the citizens could have preferred charges against Soderini, their fury against him might have been assuaged without calling in the Spanish troops; or if he had not been liable to the charges, no one would have dared to bring them against him, for fear of being himself accused in turn; and thus on both sides the animosity would have ceased, which occasioned so much trouble.

Whence we may conclude that, whenever the aid of foreign powers is called in by any party in a state, it is to be ascribed to defects in its constitution, and more especially to the want of means for enabling the people to exhaust the malign humors that spring up among men, without having recourse to extraordinary measures; all of which can easily be provided against by instituting accusations before numerous judges, and giving these sufficient influence and importance. These things were so well organized in Rome that, with the many dissensions between the Senate and the people, neither the one nor the other, nor any private citizen, ever attempted to avail of foreign force; for having the remedy at home, there was no occasion to look for it elsewhere. And although the above examples are abundantly sufficient to prove this, yet I will adduce another, mentioned by Titus Livius in his history. At Chiusi (Clusium), in those days one of the most famous cities of Tuscany, a certain Lucumones had violated the sister of Arnutes, and, unable to revenge himself because of the power of the offender, Arnutes went to call in the aid of the Gauls, who at that time ruled over the country now called Lombardy, and

urged them to come with an armed force to Clusium, pointing out to them the advantage they would obtain for themselves by thus avenging him. Certainly, if Arnutes had been
able to secure redress by the laws of his city, he would never
have had recourse to the Barbarians.

But just as useful as accusations are in a republic, just so
useless and pernicious are calumnies, as we shall show in
the next chapter.

Chapter VIII

IN PROPORTION AS ACCUSATIONS ARE USEFUL IN A REPUBLIC, SO ARE CALUMNIES PERNICIOUS

DESPITE of the courage displayed by Furius Camillus in liberating Rome from the yoke of the Gauls, which caused all
the citizens of Rome to yield him the first place without
deeming themselves degraded thereby, Manlius Capitolinus
could not brook that so much honor and glory should be bestowed upon him; for, having himself saved the Capitol, he
considered that he had contributed as much to the salvation
of Rome as Furius Camillus, and that he was in no way inferior to him in military talents. So that, tormented by envy,
he could not rest on account of the glory of his rival; and,
finding that he could not sow discord amongst the Senators,
he turned to the people and spread various sinister reports
amongst them. Amongst other things, he circulated a state-
ment that the amount of money which had been collected
for payment to the Gauls had never been paid over to them,
but had been appropriated by some private citizens; and
that, if it were recovered from them, it might be most ad-
vantageously applied for the public good, by alleviating the

taxes of the people, or by the extinction of some other debt. These statements produced a great impression among the people; so that, many of them came together at the house of Manlius, and, at his instigation, commenced to create disturbances in the city. This greatly displeased the Senate, who, deeming the occasion momentous and perilous, created a Dictator, who should take cognizance of the facts and repress the audacity of Manlius; whereupon the Dictator had him promptly summoned. They met in the public place, the Dictator surrounded by the nobles, and Manlius in the midst of the people. Manlius was called upon to specify the persons who had appropriated the money in question, according to his reports, as the Senate was as anxious as the people to know them. To this Manlius made no particular reply, but in an evasive manner said that it was unnecessary to mention the names, as they knew them very well already; whereupon the Dictator had him incarcerated. This shows how much detested calumnies are in republics, as well as under any other government, and that no means should be left unemployed to repress them in time. Now, there is no more effectual way for putting an end to calumnies than to introduce the system of legal accusations, which will be as beneficial to republics as calumnies are injurious. On the other hand, there is this difference, namely, that calumnies require neither witnesses, nor confrontings, nor any particulars to prove them, so that every citizen may be calumniated by another, whilst accusations cannot be lodged against any one without being accompanied by positive proofs and circumstances that demonstrate the truth of the accusation. Accusations must be brought before the magistrates, or the people, or the councils, whilst calumnies are spread in public places as well as in private dwellings; and calumnies are more practised where the system of accusations does not

exist, and in cities the constitution of which does not admit
of them. The lawgiver of a republic, therefore, should give
every citizen the right to accuse another citizen without fear
or suspicion; and this being done, and properly carried out,
he should severely punish calumniators, who would have no
right to complain of such punishment, it being open to them
to bring charges against those whom they had in private
calumniated. And where this system is not well established
there will always be great disorders, for calumnies irritate,
but do not chastise men; and those who have been thus irritated will think of strengthening themselves, hating more
than fearing the slanders spread against them.

This matter, as has been said, was perfectly organized at
Rome, but has always been badly managed in our city of
Florence. And as in Rome this institution was productive
of much good, so at Florence the lack of it did much harm.
And whoever reads the history of that city will see to how
many calumnies those citizens were exposed who occupied
themselves with the most important public affairs. Of one
it was reported that he had robbed the public treasury; of
another, that he had failed in such or such an enterprise because he had been bribed; and of a third, that he had caused
this or that public inconvenience for the purpose of serving
his own ambition. This gave rise in every direction to
hatreds amongst the citizens, whence divisions arose, and
from these sprung factions that proved the ruin of the
state. If the system of accusations and the punishment of
calumniators had been established in Florence, those endless
scandals and disturbances that occurred would never have
taken place; for those citizens who had been either condemned or absolved could not have injured the city, and
there would have been a much less number accused than
there had been calumniated, as it would not have been as

easy to accuse as to calumniate any one. And amongst the other means which ambitious citizens frequently employed to achieve power was this practice of calumniating, which, when employed against one noble citizen who opposed the ambitious projects of another, did much for the latter; for by taking the part of the people and confirming them in the ill opinion which they had of the nobles, he made them his friends.

I might adduce many examples of this, but will content myself with only one. The Florentine army which besieged Lucca was under the command of Messer Giovanni Guicciardini, Florentine commissioner. Whether it was due to his bad management or to his ill fortune, the siege proved unsuccessful. Whatever the case may have been, Messer Giovanni was charged with having been bribed by the authorities of Lucca. This calumny, favored by his enemies, drove Messer Giovanni almost to desperation; and although he was anxious to place himself in the hands of the Captain to justify himself, yet he never was allowed the opportunity, there being no means in the republic that made such a course possible. This gave rise to the greatest indignation amongst the friends of Messer Giovanni, who constituted the majority of the nobles, and also amongst those who desired a change in the government of Florence. This difficulty, together with other similar causes, increased to that degree that it resulted in the ruin of the republic.

Thus Manlius Capitolinus was a calumniator, and not an accuser; and the Romans showed in his case how calumniators ought to be punished. For they ought to be made to be accusers; and, if the accusation proves true, they should be rewarded, or at least not punished; but if it proves not to be true, then they should be punished as Manlius was.

Murder of Brother

public

Politics is bloody

Chapter IX

TO FOUND A NEW REPUBLIC, OR TO REFORM ENTIRELY THE OLD INSTITUTIONS OF AN EXISTING ONE, MUST BE THE WORK OF ONE MAN ONLY

It may perhaps appear to some that I have gone too far into the details of Roman history before having made any mention of the founders of that republic, or of her institutions, her religion, and her military establishment. Not wishing, therefore, to keep any longer in suspense the desires of those who wish to understand these matters, I say that many will perhaps consider it an evil example that the founder of a civil society, as Romulus was, should first have killed his brother, and then have consented to the death of Titus Tatius, who had been elected to share the royal authority with him; from which it might be concluded that the citizens, according to the example of their prince, might, from ambition and the desire to rule, destroy those who attempt to oppose their authority. This opinion would be correct, if we do not take into consideration the object which Romulus had in view in committing that homicide. But we must assume, as a general rule, that it never or rarely happens that a republic or monarchy is well constituted, or its old institutions entirely reformed, unless it is done by only one individual; it is even necessary that he whose mind has conceived such a constitution should be alone in carrying it into effect. A sagacious legislator of a republic, therefore, whose object is to promote the public good, and not his private interests, and who prefers his country to his own successors, should concentrate all authority in himself; and a wise mind will never censure any one for having employed any extraordinary means for the purpose of establishing a kingdom or constituting a republic. It is well that, when the act accuses him, the result should excuse him; and when the result is good, as in the case of Romulus, it will always absolve him from blame. For he is to be reprehended who commits violence for the purpose of destroying, and not he who employs it for beneficent purposes. The lawgiver should, however, be sufficiently wise and virtuous not to leave this authority which he has assumed either to his heirs or to any one else; for mankind, being more prone to evil than to good, his successor might employ for evil purposes the power which he had used only for good ends. Besides, although one man alone should organize a government, yet it will not endure long if the administration of it remains on the shoulders of a single individual; it is well, then, to confide this to the charge of many, for thus it will be sustained by the many. Therefore, as the organization of anything cannot be made by many, because the divergence of their opinions hinders them from agreeing as to what is best, yet, when once they do understand it, they will not readily agree to abandon it. That Romulus deserves to be excused for the death of his brother and that of his associate, and that what he had done was for the general good, and not for the gratification of his own ambition, is proved by the fact that he immediately instituted a Senate with which to consult, and according to the opinions of which he might form his resolutions. And on carefully considering the authority which Romulus reserved for himself, we see that all he kept was the command of the army in case of war, and the power of convoking the Senate. This was seen when Rome became free, after the expulsion of the Tarquins, when there was no other innovation made upon the existing order of things

than the substitution of two Consuls, appointed annually,
in place of an hereditary king; which proves clearly that all
the original institutions of that city were more in conformity
with the requirements of a free and civil society than with
an absolute and tyrannical government.

The above views might be corroborated by any number
of examples, such as those of Moses, Lycurgus, Solon, and
other founders of monarchies and republics, who were enabled to establish laws suitable for the general good only by
keeping for themselves an exclusive authority; but all these
are so well known that I will not further refer to them. I
will adduce only one instance, not so celebrated, but which
merits the consideration of those who aim to become good
legislators: it is this. Agis, king of Sparta, desired to bring
back the Spartans to the strict observance of the laws of
Lycurgus, being convinced that, by deviating from them,
their city had lost much of her ancient virtue, and consequently her power and dominion; but the Spartan Ephores
had him promptly killed, as one who attempted to make
himself a tyrant. His successor, Cleomenes, had conceived
the same desire, from studying the records and writings of
Agis, which he had found, and which explained his aims
and intentions. Cleomenes was convinced that he would be
unable to render this service to his country unless he possessed sole authority; for he judged that, owing to the ambitious nature of men, he could not promote the interests of
the many against the will of the few; and therefore he
availed of a convenient opportunity to have all the Ephores
slain, as well as all such others as might oppose his project,
after which he restored the laws of Lycurgus entirely. This
course was calculated to resuscitate the greatness of Sparta,
and to give Cleomenes a reputation equal to that of Lycurgus, had it not been for the power of the Macedonians and

the weakness of the other Greek republics. For being soon after attacked by the Macedonians, and Sparta by herself being inferior in strength, and there being no one whom he could call to his aid, he was defeated; and thus his project, so just and laudable, was never put into execution. Considering, then, all these things, I conclude that, to found a republic, one must be alone; and that Romulus deserves to be absolved from, and not blamed for, the death of Remus and of Tatius.

Chapter X

IN PROPORTION AS THE FOUNDERS OF A REPUBLIC OR MONARCHY ARE ENTITLED TO PRAISE, SO DO THE FOUNDERS OF A TYRANNY DESERVE EXECRATION

OF all men who have been eulogized, those deserve it most who have been the authors and founders of religions; next come such as have established republics or kingdoms. After these the most celebrated are those who have commanded armies, and have extended the possessions of their kingdom or country. To these may be added literary men, but, as these are of different kinds, they are celebrated according to their respective degrees of excellence. All others—and their number is infinite—receive such share of praise as pertains to the exercise of their arts and professions. On the contrary, those are doomed to infamy and universal execration who have destroyed religions, who have overturned republics and kingdoms, who are enemies of virtue, of letters, and of every art that is useful and honorable to mankind. Such are the impious and violent, the ignorant, the idle, the vile and degraded. And there are none so foolish or so wise, so wicked or so good, that, in choosing between these two qualities, they do not praise what is praiseworthy and blame that which deserves blame. And yet nearly all men, deceived by a false good and a false glory, allow themselves voluntarily or ignorantly to be drawn towards those who deserve more blame than praise. Such as by the establishment of a republic or kingdom could earn eternal glory for themselves incline to tyranny, without perceiving how much glory, how much honor, security, satisfaction, and tranquillity of mind, they forfeit; and what infamy, disgrace, blame, danger, and disquietude they incur. And it is impossible that those who have lived as private citizens in a republic, or those who by fortune or courage have risen to be princes of the same, if they were to read history and take the records of antiquity for example, should not prefer Scipio to Cæsar; and that those who were (originally) princes should not rather choose to be like Agesilaus, Timoleon, and Dion, than Nabis, Phalaris, and Dionysius; for they would then see how thoroughly the latter were despised, and how highly the former were appreciated. They would furthermore see that Timoleon and the others had no less authority in their country than Dionysius and Phalaris, but that they enjoyed far more security, and for a much greater length of time. Nor let any one be deceived by the glory of that Cæsar who has been so much celebrated by writers; for those who praised him were corrupted by his fortune, and frightened by the long duration of the empire that was maintained under his name, and which did not permit writers to speak of him with freedom. And if any one wishes to know what would have been said of him if writers had been free to speak their minds, let them read what Catiline said of him. Cæsar is as much more to be condemned, as he who commits an evil deed is more guilty than he who merely has the evil intention. He will also see how highly Brutus was eulogized; for, not being allowed to blame Cæsar on account of his power, they extolled his enemy. Let him also note how much more praise those Emperors merited who, after Rome became an empire, conformed to the laws like good princes, than those who took the opposite course; and he will see that Titus, Nerva, Trajan, Hadrian, Antoninus, and Marcus Aurelius did not require the Prætorians nor the multitudinous legions to defend them, because they were protected by their own good conduct, the good will of the people, and by the love of the Senate. He will furthermore see that neither the Eastern nor the Western armies sufficed to save Caligula, Nero, Vitellius, and so many other wicked Emperors, from the enemies which their bad conduct and evil lives had raised up against them.

And if the history of these men were carefully studied, it would prove an ample guide to any prince, and serve to show him the way to glory or to infamy, to security or to perpetual apprehension. For of the twenty-six Emperors that reigned from the time of Cæsar to that of Maximinius, sixteen were assassinated, and ten only died a natural death; and if, amongst those who were killed, there were one or two good ones, like Galba and Pertinax, their death was the consequence of the corruption which their predecessors had engendered amongst the soldiers. And if amongst those who died a natural death there were some wicked ones, like Severus, it was due to their extraordinary good fortune and courage, which two qualities rarely fall to the lot of such men. He will furthermore learn from the lessons of that history how an empire should be organized properly; for all the Emperors that succeeded to the throne by inheritance, except Titus, were bad, and those who became Emperors by adoption were all good, such as the five from Nero to Mar' cus Aurelius; and when the Empire became hereditary, it came to ruin. Let any prince now place himself in the times from Nerva to Marcus Aurelius, and let him compare them with those that preceded and followed that period, and let him choose in which of the two he would like to have been born, and in which he would like to have reigned. In the period under the good Emperors he will see the prince secure amidst his people, who are also living in security; he will see peace and justice prevail in the world, the authority of the Senate respected, the magistrates honored, the wealthy citizens enjoying their riches, nobility and virtue exalted, and everywhere will he see tranquillity and well-being. And on the other hand he will behold all animosity, license, corruption, and all noble ambition extinct. During the period of the good Emperors he will see that golden age when every one could hold and defend whatever opinion he pleased; in fine, he will see the triumph of the world, the prince surrounded with reverence and glory, and beloved by his people, who are happy in their security. If now he will but glance at the times under the other Emperors, he will behold the atrocities of war, discords and sedition, cruelty in peace as in war, many princes massacred, many civil and foreign wars, Italy afflicted and overwhelmed by fresh misfortunes, and her cities ravaged and ruined; he will see Rome in ashes, the Capitol pulled down by her own citizens, the ancient temples desolate, all religious rites and ceremonies corrupted, and the city full of adultery; he will behold the sea covered with ships full of flying exiles, and the shores stained with blood. He will see innumerable cruelties in Rome, and nobility, riches, and honor, and above all virtue, accounted capital crimes. He will see informers rewarded, servants corrupted against their masters, the freedmen arrayed against their patrons, and those who were without enemies betrayed and oppressed by their friends. And then will he recognize what infinite obligations Rome, Italy, and the whole world owed to Cæsar. And surely, if he be a man, he will be shocked at the thought of re-enacting those evil times, and be fired with an intense desire to follow the example of the good. And truly, if a prince be anxious for glory and the good opinion of the world, he should rather wish to possess a corrupt city, not to ruin it wholly like Cæsar, but to reorganize it like Romulus. For certainly the heavens cannot afford a man a greater opportunity of glory, nor could men desire a better one. And if for the proper organization of a city it should be necessary to abolish the principality, he who had failed to give her good laws for the sake of preserving his rank may be entitled to some excuse; but there would be none for him who had been able to organize the city properly and yet preserve the sovereignty. And, in fine, let him to whom Heaven has vouchsafed such an opportunity reflect that there are two ways open to him; one that will enable him to live securely and insure him glory after death, and the other that will make his life one of constant anxiety, and after death consign him to eternal infamy.

Chapter XI

OF THE RELIGION OF THE ROMANS

ALTHOUGH the founder of Rome was Romulus, to whom like a daughter, she owed her birth and her education, yet the gods did not judge the laws of this prince sufficient for so great an empire, and therefore inspired the Roman Senate to elect Numa Pompilius as his successor, so that he might regulate all those things that had been omitted by Romulus. Numa, finding a very savage people, and wishing to reduce them to civil obedience by the arts of peace, had recourse to religion as the most necessary and assured support of any civil society; and he established it upon such foundations that for many centuries there was nowhere more fear of the gods than in that republic, which greatly facilitated all the enterprises which the Senate or its great men attempted. Whoever will examine the actions of the people of Rome as a body, or of many individual Romans, will see that these citizens feared much more to break an oath than the laws; like men who esteem the power of the gods more than that of men. This was particularly manifested in the conduct of Scipio and Manlius Torquatus; for after the defeat which Hannibal had inflicted upon the Romans at Cannæ many citizens had assembled together, and, frightened and trembling, agreed to leave Italy and fly to Sicily. When Scipio heard of this, he went to meet them, and with his drawn sword in hand he forced them to swear not to abandon their country. Lucius Manlius, father of Titus Manlius, who was afterwards called Torquatus, had been accused by Marcus Pomponius, one of the Tribunes of the people. Before the day of judgment Titus went to Marcus and threatened to kill him if he did not promise to withdraw the charges against his father; he compelled him to take an oath, and Marcus, although having sworn under the pressure of fear, withdrew the accusation against Lucius. And thus these citizens, whom neither the love of country nor the laws could have kept in Italy, were retained there by an oath that had been forced upon them by compulsion; and the Tribune Pomponius disregarded the hatred which he bore to the father, as well as the insult offered him by the son for the sake of complying with his oath and preserving his honor; which can be ascribed to nothing else than the religious principles which Numa had instilled into the Romans. And whoever reads Roman history attentively will see in how great a degree religion served in the command of the armies, in uniting the people and keeping them well conducted, and in covering the wicked with shame. So that if the question were discussed whether Rome was more indebted to Romulus or to Numa, I believe that the highest merit would be conceded to Numa; for where religion exists it is easy to introduce armies and discipline, but where there are armies and no religion it is difficult to introduce the latter. And although we have seen that Romulus could organize the Senate and establish other civil and military institutions without the aid of divine authority, yet it was very necessary for Numa, who feigned that he held converse with a nymph, who dictated to him all that he wished to persuade the people to; and the reason for all this was that Numa mistrusted his own authority, lest it should prove insufficient to enable him to introduce new and unaccustomed ordinances in Rome. In truth, there never was any remarkable lawgiver amongst any people who did not resort to divine authority, as otherwise his laws would not have been accepted by the people; for there are many good laws, the importance of which is known to the sagacious lawgiver, but the reasons for which are not sufficiently evident to enable him to persuade others to submit to them; and therefore do wise men, for the purpose of removing this difficulty, resort to divine authority. Thus did Lycurgus and Solon, and many others who aimed at the same thing.

The Roman people, then, admiring the wisdom and goodness of Numa, yielded in all things to his advice. It is true that those were very religious times, and the people with whom Numa had to deal were very untutored and superstitious, which made it easy for him to carry out his designs, being able to impress upon them any new form. And doubtless, if any one wanted to establish a republic at the present time, he would find it much easier with the simple mountaineers, who are almost without any civilization, than with such as are accustomed to live in cities, where civilization is already corrupt; as a sculptor finds it easier to make a fine statue out of a crude block of marble than out of a statue badly begun by another. Considering then, all these things, I conclude that the religion introduced by Numa into Rome was one of the chief causes of the prosperity of that city; for this religion gave rise to good laws, and good laws bring good fortune, and from good fortune results happy success in all enterprises. And as the observance of divine institutions is the cause of the greatness of republics, so the disregard of them produces their ruin; for where the fear of God is wanting, there the country will come to ruin, unless it be sustained by the fear of the prince, which may temporarily supply the want of religion. But as the lives of princes are short, the kingdom will of necessity perish as the prince fails in virtue. Whence it comes that kingdoms which depend entirely upon the virtue of one man endure but for a brief time, for his virtue passes away with his life, and it rarely happens that it is renewed in his successor, as Dante so wisely says:—

" 'T is seldom human wisdom descends from sire to son;
    Such is the will of Him who gave it,
    That at his hands alone we may implore the boon."

The welfare, then, of a republic or a kingdom does not consist in having a prince who governs it wisely during his lifetime, but in having one who will give it such laws that it will maintain itself even after his death. And although untutored and ignorant men are more easily persuaded to adopt new laws or new opinions, yet that does not make it impossible to persuade civilized men who claim to be enlightened. The people of Florence are far from considering themselves ignorant and benighted, and yet Brother Girolamo Savonarola succeeded in persuading them that he held converse with God. I will not pretend to judge whether it was true or not, for we must speak with all respect of so great a man; but I may well say that an immense number believed it, without having seen any extraordinary manifestations that should have made them believe it; but it was the purity of his life, the doctrines he preached, and the subjects he selected for his discourses, that sufficed to make the people have faith in him. Let no one, then, fear not to be able to accomplish what others have done, for all men (as we have said in our Preface) are born and live and die in the same way, and therefore resemble each other.

Chapter XII

THE IMPORTANCE OF GIVING RELIGION A PROMINENT INFLUENCE IN A STATE, AND HOW ITALY WAS RUINED BECAUSE SHE FAILED IN THIS RESPECT THROUGH THE CONDUCT OF THE CHURCH OF ROME

PRINCES and republics who wish to maintain themselves free from corruption must above all things preserve the purity of all religious observances, and treat them with proper reverence; for there is no greater indication of the ruin of a country than to see religion contemned. And this is easily understood, when we know upon what the religion of a country is founded; for the essence of every religion is based upon some one main principle. The religion of the Gentiles had for its foundation the responses of the oracles, and the tenets of the augurs and aruspices; upon these alone depended all their ceremonies, rites, and sacrifices. For they readily believed that the Deity which could predict their future good or ill was also able to bestow it upon them. Thence arose their temples, their sacrifices, their supplications, and all the other ceremonies; for the oracle of Delphos, the temple of Jupiter Ammon, and other celebrated oracles, kept the world in admiration and devoutness. But when these afterwards began to speak only in accordance with the wishes of the princes, and their falsity was discovered by the people, then men became incredulous, and disposed to disturb all good institutions. It is therefore the duty of princes and heads of republics to uphold the foundations of the religion of their countries, for then it is easy to keep their people religious, and consequently well conducted and united. And therefore everything that tends to favor religion (even though it were believed to be false) should be received and availed of to strengthen it; and this should be done the more, the wiser the rulers are, and the better they understand the natural course of things. Such was, in fact, the practice observed by sagacious men; which has given rise to the belief in the miracles that are celebrated in religions, however false they may be. For the sagacious rulers have given these miracles increased importance, no matter whence or how they originated; and their authority afterwards gave them credence with the people. Rome had many such miracles; and one of the most remarkable was that which occurred when the Roman soldiers sacked the city of Veii; some of them entered the temple of Juno, and, placing themselves in front of her statue, said to her, "Will you come to Rome?" Some imagined that they observed the statue make a sign of assent, and others pretended to have heard her reply, "Yes." Now these men, being very religious, as reported by Titus Livius, and having entered the temple quietly, they were filled with devotion and reverence, and might really have believed that they had heard a reply to their question, such as perhaps they could have presupposed. But this opinion and belief was favored and magnified by Camillus and the other Roman chiefs.

And certainly, if the Christian religion had from the beginning been maintained according to the principles of its founder, the Christian states and republics would have been much more united and happy than what they are. Nor can there be a greater proof of its decadence than to witness the fact that the nearer people are to the Church of Rome, which is the head of our religion, the less religious are they. And whoever examines the principles upon which that religion is founded, and sees how widely different from those principles its present practice and application are, will judge that her ruin or chastisement is near at hand. But as there are some of the opinion that the well-being of Italian affairs depends upon the Church of Rome, I will present such arguments against that opinion as occur to me; two of which are most important, and cannot according to my judgment be controverted. The first is, that the evil example of the court of Rome has destroyed all piety and religion in Italy, which brings in its train infinite improprieties and disorders; for as we may presuppose all good where religion prevails, so where it is wanting we have the right to suppose the very opposite. We Italians then owe to the Church of Rome and to her priests our having become irreligious and bad; but we owe her a still greater debt, and one that will be the cause of our ruin, namely, that the Church has kept and still keeps our country divided. And certainly a country can never be united and happy, except when it obeys wholly one government, whether a republic or a monarchy, as is the case in France and in Spain; and the sole cause why Italy is not in the same condition, and is not governed by either one republic or one sovereign, is the Church; for having acquired and holding a temporal dominion, yet she has never had sufficient power or courage to enable her to seize the rest of the country and make herself sole sovereign of all Italy. And on the other hand she has not been so feeble that the fear of losing her temporal power prevented her from calling in the aid of a foreign power to defend her against such others as had become too powerful in Italy; as was seen in former days by many sad experiences, when through the intervention of Charlemagne she drove out the Lombards, who were masters of nearly all Italy; and when in our times she crushed the power of the Venetians by the aid of France, and afterwards with the assistance of the Swiss drove out in turn the French. The Church, then, not having been powerful enough to be able to master all Italy, nor having permitted any other power to do so, has been the cause why Italy has never been able to unite under one head, but has always remained under a number of princes and lords, which occasioned her so many dissensions and so much weakness that she became a prey not only to the powerful barbarians, but of whoever chose to assail her. This we other Italians owe to the Church of Rome, and to none other. And any one, to be promptly convinced by experiment of the truth of all this, should have the power to transport the court of Rome to reside, with all the power it has in Italy, in the midst of the Swiss, who of all peoples nowadays live most according to their ancient customs so far as religion and their military system are concerned; and he would see in a very little while that the evil habits of that court would create more confusion in that country than anything else that could ever happen there.

Chapter XIII

HOW THE ROMANS AVAILED OF RELIGION TO PRESERVE ORDER IN THEIR CITY, AND TO CARRY OUT THEIR ENTERPRISES AND SUPPRESS DISTURBANCES

IT does not seem to me from my purpose to adduce here some examples to show how the Romans employed religion for the purpose of reorganizing their city, and to further their enterprises. And although there are many instances to be found in the writings of Titus Livius, yet I will content myself with the following. The Romans having created the Tribunes with consular powers, and selected all but one from the plebeian order, and a pestilence and famine having occurred in that year accompanied by some extraordinary phenomena, the nobles availed of this occasion of the new creation of the Tribunes, saying that the gods were angry because Rome had been wanting in respect to the majesty of her empire; and that there was no other way of placating the gods but by restoring the election of the Tribunes to its original plan. The result was, that the people, under the influence of religious fear, selected the Tribunes altogether from amongst the patricians.

It was also seen at the siege of the city of Veii, that the captains of the Roman army used religion to keep their soldiers disposed to any enterprise; for when the Lake Albano rose in that year in a very extraordinary manner, and the soldiers, tired of the long siege, wished to return to Rome, the leaders invented the story that Apollo and certain other oracles had predicted that the city of the Veienti would be taken in the year when Lake Albano should overflow its banks. The soldiers, having taken new hope from these predictions as to the capture of the city, bore the fatigues of the war and the siege cheerfully, and pushed the siege with so much energy that Camillus, who had been made Dictator, succeeded in taking that city after a siege of ten years' duration. And thus religion judiciously used promoted the capture of Veii, and the restitution of the tribunate to the patricians, either of which, without that means, would have been with difficulty accomplished.

I will not omit to cite another example much to the purpose. The Tribune Terentillus occasioned great disturbances by promulgating a certain law, for reasons which we shall explain further on; and one of the first means to which the patricians resorted for the suppression of these tumults was religion, which they employed in two different ways. The first was the exhibition of the Sibylline Books, which predicted that, in consequence of domestic dissensions, the liberties of Rome would be seriously imperilled in that year; the fraud, although discovered by the Tribunes, yet so filled the minds of the people with terror that they were no longer disposed to follow them. The second mode was when one Appius Erdonius, with a number of bandits and four thousand slaves, seized the Capitol at night, which caused general apprehension for the safety of the city itself, in case the Equeans and Volscians, eternal enemies of Rome, should attack her at that moment. The Tribunes nevertheless persisted with great obstinacy in the promulgation of the Terentillan law, saying that the capture of the Capitol was merely fictitious; whereupon Publius Rubetius, a grave citizen of great authority, left the Senate, and with alternate entreaties and menaces harangued the people, pointing out to them the unreasonableness of their demands, and constrained them to swear that they would not refuse obedience to the Consul. The people, thus forced to obedience, recovered the Capitol; but in the taking of it the Consul Publius Valerius lost his life, and in his stead Titus Quintius was immediately chosen Consul. He, not wishing to afford the people any repose or opportunity of thinking again of the Terentillan law, ordered them to leave Rome and to march against the Volscians; saying that they were bound to follow him, because of the oath they had taken to obey the Consul. To this the Tribunes objected, saying that the oath referred to the Consul that had been killed, and not to Titus Quintius. The people, however, according to Titus Livius, preferred to obey the Consul rather than believe the Tribunes, and he speaks as follows in favor of their ancient religion: "They had not yet come to that neglect of the reverence for the gods which prevails nowadays, nor to interpreting their oaths or the laws to suit themselves." And the Tribunes, fearing to lose all their authority, agreed with the Consul to submit to him, and that for one year nothing more should be said about the Terentillan law, and, on the other hand, that for one year the Consuls should not lead the people from Rome to war. And thus religion enabled the Senate to overcome that difficulty which without it they could never have done.

Chapter XIV

THE ROMANS INTERPRETED THE AUSPICES ACCORDING TO NECES-
SITY, AND VERY WISELY MADE SHOW OF OBSERVING RELIGION,
EVEN WHEN THEY WERE OBLIGED IN REALITY TO DISREGARD
IT; AND IF ANY ONE RECKLESSLY DISPARAGED IT, HE WAS
PUNISHED

THE system of auguries was not only, as we have said above,
the principal basis of the ancient religion of the Gentiles, but
was also the cause of the prosperity of the Roman republic.
Whence the Romans esteemed it more than any other institution, and resorted to it in their Consular Comitii, in com-
mencing any important enterprise, in sending armies into
the field, in ordering their battles, and in every other important civil or military action. Nor would they ever have ventured upon any expedition unless the augurs had first persuaded the soldiers that the gods promised them victory.
Amongst other aruspices the armies were always accompanied by a certain class of soothsayers, termed Pollari
(guardians of the sacred fowls), and every time before giving battle to the enemy, they required these Pollari to
ascertain the auspices; and if the fowls ate freely, then it was
deemed a favorable augury, and the soldiers fought confidently, but if the fowls refused to eat, then they abstained
from battle. Nevertheless, when they saw a good reason
why certain things should be done, they did them anyhow,
whether the auspices were favorable or not; but then they
turned and interpreted the auguries so artfully, and in such
manner, that seemingly no disrespect was shown to their
religious belief. This was done by the Consul Papirius on

the occasion of a most important battle with the Samnites, which forever enfeebled and broke the power of this warlike people. For Papirius in conducting the war against them found himself face to face with them; and as victory seemed to him certain, and wishing therefore to proceed to battle, he ordered the Pollari to ascertain the auspices. The fowls, however, did not eat; but the chief of the Pollari, seeing the great desire of the army to fight, and the confidence in victory which the general as well as the soldiers manifested, and being unwilling to deprive the army of this opportunity of achieving a success, reported to the Consul that the auspices were proceeding favorably; whereupon Papirius set his squadrons in order for battle. But one of the Pollari told certain soldiers that the fowls had not eaten, and they repeated it to Spurius Papirius, the nephew of the Consul; and when he reported this to his uncle, the latter promptly replied, that he expected him to do his duty well, and that, as regarded himself and the army, the auspices were favorable, and if the Pollarius had told a lie, it would come back upon him to his prejudice. And so that the result might correspond with the prognostication, he commanded his lieutenants to place the Pollari in the front ranks of the battle; and thus it happened that, in marching upon the enemy, the chief of the Pollari was accidentally killed by an arrow from the bow of a Roman soldier. When the Consul heard this, he said that all went well and with the favor of the gods, for by the death of this liar the army had been purged of all guilt, and that whatever anger the gods might have felt against him had been thereby appeased. And thus by apparently accommodating his designs to the auspices, Papirius resolved to give battle without letting his soldiers perceive that he had in any particular neglected his religious duties.

Appius Pulcher acted just the contrary way in Sicily during the first Punic war; for wishing to fight the Carthaginian army, he caused the Pollari to ascertain the auspices; and when they reported that the fowls did not eat, he said, "Then let us see whether they will drink," and had them thrown into the sea; he then went to battle, and was defeated. For which he was punished at Rome, whilst Papirius was rewarded; not so much because the one had been beaten and the other victorious, but because the one had contravened the auspices with prudence, and the other with temerity. Nor had this system of consulting the aruspices any other object than to inspire the soldiers on the eve of battle with that confidence which is the surest guaranty of victory. This system was practised not only by the Romans, but also by other peoples, of which it seems to me proper to adduce an example in the following chapter.

Chapter XV

HOW THE SAMNITES RESORTED TO RELIGION AS AN EXTREME REMEDY FOR THEIR DESPERATE CONDITION

The Samnites had been repeatedly defeated by the Romans, and had been completely routed in Tuscany, their armies destroyed, and their generals killed. Their allies, such as the Tuscans, Gauls, and Umbrians, had also been beaten, so that "they could not hold out any longer with their own forces, or with those of their allies; yet would they not desist from the war, and sooner than give up the unsuccessful defence of their liberty, they preferred risking defeat rather than not make one more attempt at victory"; and therefore resolved upon one last supreme effort. And knowing that to conquer they must inspire their soldiers with obstinate courage, for which there was no more efficient means than religion, they resolved, by the advice of Ovius Paccius, their high priest, to renew one of their ancient religious practices, which was arranged in the following manner. A solemn sacrifice was first made to their gods, and then, in the midst of the bleeding victims and smoking altars, they made all the chiefs of the army swear never to give up the fight. After this, they called in their soldiers one by one, and there, before these altars and surrounded by centurions with drawn swords in their hands, they made them swear, first, not to reveal anything they had seen or heard; and then, with horrid imprecations and incantations, they exacted an oath from them, and a pledge to the gods, promptly to go wherever commanded by their chiefs, and not to fly from the enemy, and to kill instantly whomever they saw flying; and if they failed in any particular in the compliance with this oath, it would be visited upon their families and descendants. Some of the men who were frightened and refused to swear were instantly put to death by the centurions; so that those who followed were terrified by the spectacle, and all took the oath. And by way of giving a more imposing effect to their assembled troops, they clothed one half of them in white, with crests and plumes on their casques; and thus they took position at Aquilonia. Papirius marched against them, and by way of encouraging his soldiers he said to them, "Those crests and plumes cannot inflict wounds, and neither will paint or gilding prevent Roman javelins from piercing their shields." And to diminish the impression which the oath of the enemy had produced upon his men, he said that such an oath was calculated to inspire fear, and not courage, in those who had taken it; for it caused them at the same time to fear their own citizens, their gods, and their enemies. So that, when they came to battle, the Samnites were defeated; for the Roman valor, and the fears of the Samnites, who remembered their former defeats, overcame all the obstinacy which their religion and their oath had infused into them. Nevertheless it showed that the Samnites knew of no more powerful means of reviving hope and reanimating their former courage; and proves in the most ample manner how much confidence religious faith, judiciously availed of, will inspire. And although this example might perhaps be deemed to belong elsewhere, as the event occurred amongst a foreign people, yet, as it refers to one of the most important institutions of the republic of Rome, I have thought it proper to mention it here in support of what I have said on that subject, and so as not to be obliged to recur to it hereafter.

Chapter XVI

A PEOPLE THAT HAS BEEN ACCUSTOMED TO LIVE UNDER A PRINCE PRESERVES ITS LIBERTIES WITH DIFFICULTY, IF BY ACCIDENT IT HAS BECOME FREE

MANY examples in ancient history prove how difficult it is for a people that has been accustomed to live under the government of a prince to preserve its liberty, if by some accident it has recovered it, as was the case with Rome after the expulsion of the Tarquins. And this difficulty is a reasonable one; for such a people may well be compared to some wild animal, which (although by nature ferocious and savage) has been as it were subdued by having been always kept imprisoned and in servitude, and being let out into the open fields, not knowing how to provide food and shelter for itself, becomes an easy prey to the first one who attempts to chain it up again. The same thing happens to a people that has not been accustomed to self-government; for, ignorant of all public affairs, of all means of defence or offence. neither knowing the princes nor being known by them, it soon relapses under a yoke, oftentimes much heavier than the one which it had but just shaken off. This difficulty occurs even when the body of the people is not wholly corrupt; but when corruption has taken possession of the whole people, then it cannot preserve its free condition even for the shortest possible time, as we shall see further on; and therefore our argument has reference to a people where corruption has not yet become general, and where the good still prevails over the bad. To the above comes another difficulty, which is, that the state that becomes free makes enemies for itself, and not friends. All those become its enemies who were benefited by the tyrannical abuses and fattened upon the treasures of the prince, and who, being now deprived of these advantages, cannot remain content, and are therefore driven to attempt to re-establish the tyranny, so as to recover their former authority and advantages. A state then, as I have said, that becomes free, makes no friends; for free governments bestow honors and rewards only according to certain honest and fixed rules, outside of which there are neither the one nor the other. And such as obtain these honors and rewards do not consider themselves under obligations to any one, because they believe that they were entitled to them by their merits. Besides the advantages that result to the mass of the people from a free government, such as to be able freely to enjoy one's own without apprehension, to have nothing to fear for the honor of his wife and daughters, or for himself,—all these, I say, are not appreciated by any one whilst he is in the enjoyment of them; for no one will confess himself under obligation to any one merely because he has not been injured by him.

Thus it is that a state that has freshly achieved liberty makes enemies, and no friends. And to prevent this inconvenience, and the disorders which are apt to come with it, there is no remedy more powerful, valid, healthful, and necessary than the killing of the sons of Brutus, who, as history shows, had conspired with other Roman youths for no other reason than because under the Consuls they could not have the same extraordinary advantages they had enjoyed under the kings; so that the liberty of the people seemed to have become their bondage. Whoever undertakes to govern a people under the form of either republic or monarchy, without making sure of those who are opposed to this new order of things, establishes a government of very brief duration. It is true that I regard as unfortunate those princes who, to assure their government to which the mass of the people is hostile, are obliged to resort to extraordinary measures; for he who has but a few enemies can easily make sure of them without great scandal, but he who has the masses hostile to him can never make sure of them, and the more cruelty he employs the feebler will his authority become; so that his best remedy is to try and secure the good will of the people. Although I have departed in this discourse from my subject, in speaking sometimes of a republic and sometimes of a prince, yet I will say a few words more, so as not to be obliged to come back to this matter.

A prince, then, who wishes the good will of a people that is hostile to him, (I speak of such princes as have been tyrants in their country,) should first of all ascertain what the people really desire, and he will always find that they want two things: one, to revenge themselves on those who have been the cause of their enslavement, and the other, to recover their liberty. The first of these desires the prince may satisfy entirely, and the second in part. As to the first, the following is an example in point. When Clearchus, tyrant of Heraclea, had been banished, a dissension arose between the people and the nobles of Heraclea. The latter, finding themselves the feebler of the two, resolved to recall Clearchus; and having conspired together, they placed him in opposition to the popular faction of the people of Heraclea, and thus deprived the people of their liberty. Clearchus, finding himself placed between the insolence of the nobles on the one hand, whom he could in no way content or control, and the rage of the popular faction on the other hand, who could not support the loss of their liberty, resolved suddenly to rid himself of the importunities of the nobles, and to secure to himself the good will and support of the people. Availing of a favorable opportunity, he had all the nobles massacred, to the extreme satisfaction of the people; and in this way he satisfied one of the wishes of the people, namely, the desire of revenge. But as to the other popular desire, that of recovering their liberty, the prince, not being able to satisfy that, should examine the causes that make them desire to be free; and he will find that a small part of them wish to be free for the purpose of commanding, whilst all the others, who constitute an immense majority, desire liberty so as to be able to live in greater security. For in all republics, however organized, there are never more than forty or fifty citizens who attain a position that entitles them to command. As this is a small number, it is easy to make sure of them, either by having them put out of the way, or by giving them such a share of the public honors and offices as, according to their condition, will in great measure content them. The others, who only care to live in security, are easily satisfied by institutions and laws that confirm at the same time the general security of the people and the power of the prince. When a prince does this, and the people see that by no chance he infringes the laws, they will in a very little while be content, and live in tranquillity. An example of this is the kingdom of France, where there would be no security but for the fact that the king there has bound himself by a number of laws that provide for the security of all his people. Those who organized that state wanted that the kings should dispose of the army and treasury at their own will, but that in all other matters they should conform to the laws. That sovereign, therefore, or that republic, which fails from the start to secure its authority, should do so on the first occasion, as the Romans did; and he who allows the opportunity to pass will repent too late not having done what he should have done in the beginning. The Romans, being not yet corrupted when they recovered their liberty, were able to maintain it after the death of the sons of Brutus and the expulsion of the Tarquins, by means of such laws and institutions as we have treated of above. But if the people had been corrupt, then there would have been no sufficient remedies found in Rome or elsewhere to maintain their liberty, as we shall show in the next chapter.

Chapter XVII

A CORRUPT PEOPLE THAT BECOMES FREE CAN WITH GREATEST DIFFICULTY MAINTAIN ITS LIBERTY

I THINK that it was necessary for royalty to be extinguished in Rome, else she would in a very short time have become feeble and devoid of energy. For the degree of corruption to which the kings had sunk was such that, if it had continued for two or three successive reigns, and had extended from the head to the members of the body so that these had become also corrupt, it would have been impossible ever to have reformed the state. But losing the head whilst the trunk was still sound, it was easy to restore Rome to liberty and proper institutions. And it must be assumed as a well-demonstrated truth, that a corrupt people that lives under the government of a prince can never become free, even though the prince and his whole line should be extinguished; and that it would be better that the one prince should be destroyed by another. For a people in such condition can never become settled unless a new prince be created, who by his good qualities and valor can maintain their liberty; but even then it will last only during the lifetime of the new prince. It was thus that the freedom of Syracuse was preserved at different times by the valor of Dion and Timoleon during their lives, but after their death the city relapsed under the former tyranny. But there is not a more striking example of this than Rome itself, which after the expulsion of the Tarquins was enabled quickly to resume and maintain her liberty; but after the death of Cæsar, Caligula, and Nero, and after the extinction of the entire Cæsarean line, she could not even begin to re-establish her liberty, and much less preserve it. And this great difference in the condition of things in one and the same city resulted entirely from this fact, that at the time of the Tarquins the Roman people was not yet corrupt, whilst under the Cæsars it became corrupt to the lowest degree. For to preserve her sound and ready to expel the kings in the time of the Tarquins, it sufficed merely that they should take an oath never to permit any of them ever to reign again in Rome; but in the time of the Cæsars the authority of Brutus with all the

Eastern legions was insufficient to keep her disposed to preserve that liberty which he, in imitation of the first Brutus,
had restored to her. This was the result of that corruption
which had been spread amongst the people by the faction
of Marius, at the head of which was Cæsar, who had so
blinded the people that they did not perceive the yoke they
were imposing upon themselves.

And although the example of Rome is preferable to all
others, yet will I cite on this subject some instances amongst
peoples known in our times. And therefore I say that no
change, however great or violent, could ever restore Milan
and Naples to liberty, because the whole people of those
states were thoroughly corrupt. This was seen after the death
of Philip Visconti, when Milan attempted to recover her
liberty, but knew not how, nor was she able to maintain it.
It was a great good fortune for Rome, therefore, that no
sooner did her kings become corrupt than they were expelled, before the corruption had time to extend to the heart
of the people. This corruption caused endless disturbances
in Rome; but as the intention of the people was good, these
troubles, instead of harming, rather benefited the republic.
And from this we may draw the conclusion that, where the
mass of the people is sound, disturbances and tumults do no
serious harm; but where corruption has penetrated the
people, the best laws are of no avail, unless they are administered by a man of such supreme power that he may cause
the laws to be observed until the mass has been restored to
a healthy condition. And I know not whether such a case
has ever occurred, or whether it possibly ever could occur
(as I have said above). For if a state or city in decadence,
in consequence of the corruption of the mass of its people,
is ever raised up again, it must be through the virtue of
some one man then living, and not by the people; and so

soon as such a man dies, the people will relapse into their corrupt habits; as was the case in Thebes, which by the virtue of Epaminondas could, during his lifetime, maintain the form of a republic and its dominion, but immediately upon his death relapsed into anarchy. And the reason of this is that one man cannot live long enough to have time to bring a people back to good habits which for any length of time has indulged in evil ones. Or if one of extreme long life, or two continuous virtuous successors, do not restore the state, it will quickly lapse into ruin, no matter how many dangers and how much bloodshed have been incurred in the effort to restore it. For such corruption and incapacity to maintain free institutions result from a great inequality that exists in such a state; and to reduce the inhabitants to equality requires the application of extraordinary measures, which few know how, or are willing, to employ; as will be shown more fully elsewhere.

Chapter XVIII

HOW IN A CORRUPT STATE A FREE GOVERNMENT MAY BE MAIN-
TAINED, ASSUMING THAT ONE EXISTS THERE ALREADY; AND
HOW IT COULD BE INTRODUCED, IF NONE HAD PREVIOUSLY
EXISTED

I BELIEVE it will not be amiss to consider whether in a state that has become corrupt a free government that has existed there can be maintained; or if there has been none before, whether one could be established there. Upon this subject I must say that either one of them would be exceedingly difficult. And although it is impossible to give any definite rules for such a case, (as it will be necessary to proceed according to the different degrees of corruption,) yet, as it is well to reason upon all subjects, I will not leave this problem without discussing it. I will suppose a state to be corrupt to the last degree, so as to present the subject in its most difficult aspect, there being no laws nor institutions that suffice to check a general corruption. For as good habits of the people require good laws to support them, so laws, to be observed, need good habits on the part of the people. Besides, the constitution and laws established in a republic at its very origin, when men were still pure, no longer suit when men have become corrupt and bad. And although the laws may be changed according to circumstances and events, yet it is seldom or never that the constitution itself is changed; and for this reason the new laws do not suffice, for they are not in harmony with the constitution, that has remained intact. To make this matter better understood, I will explain how the government of Rome was constituted and what the nature of the laws was, which together with the magistrates restrained the citizens. The constitution of the state reposed upon the authority of the people, the Senate, the Tribunes, and the Consuls, and· upon the manner of choosing and creating the magistrates, and of making the laws. These institutions were rarely or never varied by events; but the laws that restrained the citizens were often altered, such as the law relating to adultery, the sumptuary laws, that in relation to ambition, and many others, which were changed according as the citizens from one day to another became more and more corrupt. Now the constitution remaining unchanged, although no longer suitable to the corrupt people, the laws that had been changed became powerless for restraint; yet they would have answered very well if the constitution had also been modified at the same time with the laws.

And the truth that the original institutions were no longer suitable to a corrupt state is clearly seen in these two main points,—the creation of the magistrates, and the forms used in making the laws. As regards the first, the Roman people bestowed the consulate and the other principal offices only on such as asked for them. This system was very good in the beginning, because only such citizens asked for these places as deemed themselves worthy of them, and a refusal was regarded as ignominious; so that every one strove to make himself esteemed worthy of the honor. But when the city had become corrupt, this system became most pernicious; for it was no longer the most virtuous and deserving, but the most powerful, that asked for the magistratures; and the less powerful, often the most meritorious, abstained from being candidates from fear. This state of things did not come all at once, but by degrees, as is generally the case with other vices. For after the Romans had subjugated Africa and Asia, and had reduced nearly all Greece to their obedience, they felt assured of their liberty, and saw no enemies that could cause them any apprehension. This security and the weakness of the conquered nations caused the Roman people no longer to bestow the consulate according to the merits of the candidates, but according to favor; giving that dignity to those who best knew how to entertain the people, and not to those who best knew how to conquer their enemies. After that they descended from those who were most favored to such as had most wealth and power, so that the really meritorious became wholly excluded from that dignity. Now as to the mode of making the laws. At first a Tribune or any other citizen had the right to propose any law, and every citizen could speak in favor or against it before its final adoption. This system was very good so long as the citizens were uncorrupted, for it is always well in a state that every one may propose what he deems for the public good; and it was equally well that every one should be allowed to express his opinion in relation to it, so that the people, having heard both sides, may decide in favor of the best. But when the citizens had become corrupt, this system became the worst possible, for then only the powerful proposed laws, not for the common good and the liberty of all, but for the increase of their own power, and fear restrained all the others from speaking against such laws; and thus the people were by force and fraud made to resolve upon their own ruin.

It was necessary therefore, if Rome wished to preserve her liberty in the midst of this corruption, that she should have modified her constitution, in like manner as in the progress of her existence she had made new laws; for institutions and forms should be adapted to the subject, whether it be good or evil, inasmuch as the same form cannot suit two subjects that are essentially different. But as the constitution of a state, when once it has been discovered to be no longer suitable, should be amended, either all at once, or by degrees as each defect becomes known, I say that both of these courses are equally impossible. For a gradual modification requires to be the work of some wise man, who has seen the evil from afar in its very beginning; but it is very likely that such a man may never rise up in the state, and even if he did he will hardly be able to persuade the others to what he proposes; for men accustomed to live after one fashion do not like to change, and the less so as they do not see the evil staring them in the face, but presented to them as a mere conjecture.

As to reforming these institutions all at once, when their defects have become manifest to everybody, that also is most difficult; for to do this ordinary means will not suffice;

they may even be injurious under such circumstances, and therefore it becomes necessary to resort to extraordinary measures, such as violence and arms, and above all things to make one's self absolute master of the state, so as to be able to dispose of it at will. And as the reformation of the political condition of a state presupposes a good man, whilst the making of himself prince of a republic by violence naturally presupposes a bad one, it will consequently be exceedingly rare that a good man should be found willing to employ wicked means to become prince, even though his final object be good; or that a bad man, after having become prince, should be willing to labor for good ends, and that it should enter his mind to use for good purposes that authority which he has acquired by evil means. From these combined causes arises the difficulty or impossibility of maintaining liberty in a republic that has become corrupt, or to establish it there anew. And if it has to be introduced and maintained, then it will be necessary to reduce the state to a monarchical, rather than a republican form of government; for men whose turbulence could not be controlled by the simple force of law can be controlled in a measure only by an almost regal power. And to attempt to restore men to good conduct by any other means would be either a most cruel or an impossible undertaking. This, as I have related above, was done by Cleomenes, who for the sake of being alone in the government had all the Ephores massacred; and if Romulus for the same object killed his brother and the Sabine Titus Tatius, and if both he and Cleomenes afterwards employed their power well, we must nevertheless bear in mind that neither of them had to deal with a people so tainted with corruption as that we have considered in this chapter, and therefore they could desire the good and conform their measures accordingly to achieve it.

Chapter XIX

IF AN ABLE AND VIGOROUS PRINCE IS SUCCEEDED BY A FEEBLE
ONE, THE LATTER MAY FOR A TIME BE ABLE TO MAINTAIN
HIMSELF; BUT IF HIS SUCCESSOR BE ALSO WEAK, THEN THE
LATTER WILL NOT BE ABLE TO PRESERVE HIS STATE

IN carefully examining the characters and conduct of Romulus, Numa, and Tullus, the first three kings of Rome, we see that she was favored by the greatest good fortune in having her first king courageous and warlike, the second peace-loving and religious, and the third equally courageous with Romulus, and preferring war to peace. For it was important for Rome that in the beginning there should arise a legislator capable of endowing her with civil institutions; but then it was essential that the succeeding kings should equal Romulus in virtue and valor, otherwise the city would have become effeminate and a prey to her neighbors. Whence we may note that a successor of less vigor and ability than the first king may yet be able to maintain a state established by the genius and courage of his predecessor, and may enjoy the fruits of his labors. But if it should happen that his life be a long one, or that his successor should not have the same good qualities and courage as the first king, then the government will necessarily go to ruin. And so, on the contrary, if one king succeeds another of equally great abilities and courage, then it will often be seen that they achieve extraordinary greatness for their state, and that their fame will rise to the very heavens. David was beyond doubt a most extraordinary man in war, in learning, and in superior judgment; and such was his military ability that, having conquered and crushed his neighbors, he left a peaceful kingdom to his son Solomon, which he was able to maintain by the arts of peace and of war, and could thus happily enjoy the results of his father's virtue and valor. But he could not thus transmit it to his son, Rehoboam, who had neither the merits of his grandfather nor the good fortune of his father; and it was with difficulty, therefore, that he remained heir of the sixth part of the kingdom. The Sultan Bajazet of Turkey, although preferring peace to war yet could enjoy the labors of his father Mahomet, who, having, like David, crushed his neighbors, left him a firmly established kingdom, which he could easily preserve with the arts of peace. But the empire would have gone to ruin if his son Soliman, the present Sultan, had resembled the father, and not the grandfather; but it was seen that he even exceeded the glory of the grandfather.

I say then, that, according to these examples, the successor of a wise and vigorous prince, though himself feeble, may maintain a kingdom, even if it be not constituted like France, which is maintained by the force of its ancient institutions; and I call that prince feeble who is incapable of carrying on war. I conclude, then, that the genius and courage of Romulus were such that it left Numa competent to govern Rome for many years by the arts of peace. He was succeeded by Tullus, whose courage and warlike disposition exceeded even that of Romulus. After him came Ancus, who was gifted by nature to shine equally in peace and in war. At first he was disposed to follow the ways of peace, but he soon perceived that his neighbors regarded him as effeminate, and esteemed him but little; so that he concluded that, if he wished to maintain the Roman state, he must devote himself to war, and imitate Romulus, and not Numa Pompilius. Let all princes then who govern states take example from this, that he who follows the course of Numa may keep or lose his throne, according to chance and circumstances; but he who imitates the example of Romulus, and combines valor with prudence, will keep his throne anyhow, unless it be taken from him by some persistent and excessive force. And we may certainly assume that, if Rome had not chanced to have for her king a man who knew how by force of arms to restore her original reputation, she would not have been able, except with greatest difficulty, to gain a firm foothold and achieve the great things she did. And thus so long as she was governed by kings was she exposed to the danger of being ruined by a feeble or a wicked one.

Chapter XX

**TWO CONTINUOUS SUCCESSIONS OF ABLE AND VIRTUOUS PRINCES
WILL ACHIEVE GREAT RESULTS; AND AS WELL-CONSTITUTED
REPUBLICS HAVE, IN THE NATURE OF THINGS, A SUCCESSION OF
VIRTUOUS RULERS, THEIR ACQUISITIONS AND EXTENSION WILL
CONSEQUENTLY BE VERY GREAT**

AFTER Rome had expelled her kings she was no longer exposed to the dangers which we have spoken of above, as resulting from a succession of feeble or wicked kings; for the sovereign authority was vested in the Consuls, who obtained that authority not by inheritance, or fraud, or violent ambition, but by the free suffrages of the people, and were generally most excellent men. Rome, having the benefit of the virtue and good fortune of these men from time to time, was thus enabled to attain her utmost grandeur in no greater length of time than she had existed under the rule of kings. For if, as has been seen, two successive good and valorous princes are sufficient to conquer the world, as was the case with Philip of Macedon and Alexander the Great, a republic should be able to do still more, having the power to elect not only two successions, but an infinite number of most competent and virtuous rulers one after the other; and this system of electing a succession of virtuous men should ever be the established practice of every republic.

Chapter XXI

PRINCES AND REPUBLICS WHO FAIL TO HAVE NATIONAL ARMIES ARE MUCH TO BE BLAMED

Such princes and republics of modern times as have no national troops for defence or attack ought well to be ashamed of it; for they should bear in mind that, according to the example of Tullus, their not having armies of their own is not from the want of men fit for military service, but that the fault is wholly theirs, in not knowing how to make soldiers of their men. For when Tullus ascended the throne, after forty years of peace, he did not find a man that had ever borne arms in war; but as he contemplated making war, he neither attempted to avail himself of the Samnites, the Tuscans, nor of any other people accustomed to fight, but, like a most sagacious prince, he resolved to employ only his own subjects; and such was his skill and courage that he promptly created an excellent army within his own kingdom. And there is nothing more true than that, if there are no soldiers where there are men, it is not owing to any natural or local defect, but is solely the fault of the prince; in proof of which I cite the following most recent example. Everybody knows that quite lately the king of England attacked the kingdom of France, and employed for that purpose no other soldiers except his own subjects; and although his own kingdom had been for over thirty years in profound peace, so that he had at first neither soldiers nor captains who had seen any active military service, yet he did not hesitate with such troops to assail a kingdom that had many experienced commanders and good soldiers, who had been continually under arms in the Italian wars. He was enabled to do this because he was a sagacious prince, and his kingdom was well ordered, so that in time of peace the military art had not been neglected. Pelopidas and Epaminondas, both of Thebes, after having liberated that city and rescued her from the yoke of the Spartan rule, found themselves in a city accustomed to servitude, and in the midst of an effeminate people. Such, however, was their wisdom and valor that they did not hesitate to put the Thebans under arms, and to take the field with them against the Spartans, whom they defeated. The historian who tells this says, that these two great citizens proved in a short time that it was not Lacedæmon alone that gave birth to warriors, but that they were produced in all countries where men were found capable of instructing others in the art of war; as was seen in the case of Tullus, who trained the Romans to war. And Virgil could not state this fact and express his approbation of it better than in the following words: "And Tullus converted his indolent men into brave soldiers."

Chapter XXII

WHAT WE SHOULD NOTE IN THE CASE OF THE THREE ROMAN HORATII AND THE ALBAN CURATII

TULLUS, king of Rome, and Metius, king of Alba, agreed that that people should be master of the other whose three champions should overcome those of the other in an appointed combat. All three of the Curatii were killed, and only one of the Roman Horatii survived; and consequently Metius, king of the Albans, and his people, became subject to the Romans. When this surviving Horatius returned to Rome he met his sister, who was contracted in marriage to one of the slain Curatii; and when he heard her lamenting the death of her lover he killed her. He was judicially tried for this crime, and after a long discussion was acquitted, not so much on account of his own merit as on account of the prayers of his father. Now there are three things to be noted in these occurrences: the first, that one should never risk his whole fortune with only a portion of his forces; the second, that in a well-ordered state a man's merits should never extenuate his crimes; and the third, that it is never wise to enter into agreements the observance of which is doubtful. For the loss of independence is a matter of such supreme importance to a state that it is not to be supposed that any king or people will ever remain satisfied that the action of three of their citizens should subject them to servitude; as was seen in the case of Metius, who, although immediately upon the victory of the Horatii he confessed himself conquered and promised obedience to Tullus, yet on the very first expedition in which he had to take part against the Veienti he attempted by fraud to evade his obligations, like one who perceives too late the imprudence of the agreement he has made. Having said enough upon this third point, we will treat more fully of the others in the following chapters.

Chapter XXIII

ONE SHOULD NEVER RISK ONE'S WHOLE FORTUNE UNLESS SUP-
PORTED BY ONE'S ENTIRE FORCES, AND THEREFORE THE MERE
GUARDING OF PASSES IS OFTEN DANGEROUS

IT was never deemed wise to risk one's whole fortune without employing at the same time one's whole forces, and
which may be done in different ways. One is the acting
like Tullus and Metius, when they committed the entire
fortunes of their countries, and so many brave men as both
had in their armies, to the valor of only three of their citizens, who constituted but a minimum part of their respective forces. They did not perceive that by so doing all the
labors of their predecessors in organizing the republic so
as to insure it a long and free existence, and to make her
citizens defenders of their liberty, were as it were made
nugatory, by putting it in the power of so few to lose the
whole. On the part of the Romans, they could certainly not
have done a more ill considered thing. The same fault is
almost always committed by those who, upon the approach
of an enemy, attempt to hold the difficult approaches, and
to guard the passes; which course will almost always prove
dangerous, unless you can conveniently place all your
forces there, in which case that course may be adopted;
but if the locality be so rugged that you cannot keep and
deploy all your forces there, then it is dangerous. I am induced to think so by the example of those who, when assailed by a powerful enemy, their country being surrounded
by mountains and rugged places, never attempted to combat the enemy in the passes or mountains, but have always

gone either to meet him in advance of these, or, when they did not wish to do that, have awaited his coming in easy and open places; the reason of which is the one I have above alleged. For you cannot employ a large force in guarding rugged and mountainous places; be it that you cannot obtain provisions there for any length of time, or that the defiles are so narrow as to admit of only a small number of men, so that it becomes impossible to sustain the shock of an enemy who comes in large force. Now for the enemy it is easy to come in full force, for his intention is to pass, and not to stop there; whilst on the contrary he who has to await the approach of the enemy cannot possibly keep so large a force there, for the reason that he will have to establish himself for a longer time in those confined and sterile places, not knowing when the enemy may come to make the attempt to pass. And once having lost the pass which you had hoped to hold, and upon which your people and army had confidently relied, they are generally seized with such terror that they are lost, without your having even been able to test their courage; and thus you lose your whole fortune from having risked only a portion of your forces.

It is well known what difficulties Hannibal encountered in passing the Alps that separate Lombardy from France, as well as the mountains that divide Lombardy from Tuscany; nevertheless, the Romans awaited him first on the Ticino, and afterwards in the plains of Arezzo; for they preferred rather to expose their army to being defeated in a place where they themselves had a chance of being the victors, than to move it to the mountains, to be destroyed there by the difficulties of the locality. And whoever reads history attentively will find that very few of the best commanders have attempted to hold such passes, for the very reasons which I have given, and because they cannot close them all; the mountains being in that respect like the open country, in having not only well known roads that are generally used, but also many others, which, if unknown to strangers, are yet familiar to the people of the country, by whose aid any invader may always be guided to any desired point. Of this we have a most notable and recent example in 1515, when Francis I., king of France, wanted to enter Italy for the purpose of recovering the state of Lombardy. Those who opposed him in this attempt, relied mainly upon their confident expectations that the Swiss would arrest his march in the mountain passes. But the event proved that their confidence was vain, for the king of France, leaving aside the two or three passes that were guarded by the Swiss, came by another route hitherto quite unknown, and was in Italy and upon them before they knew anything of it; so that their terror-stricken troops retreated to Milan, and the entire Milanese population yielded themselves to the French, having been disappointed in their hopes that the French would be kept out by the difficulty of passing the Alps.

Chapter XXIV

WELL-ORDERED REPUBLICS ESTABLISH PUNISHMENTS AND REWARDS FOR THEIR CITIZENS, BUT NEVER SET OFF ONE AGAINST THE OTHER

THE services of Horatius had been of the highest importance to Rome, for by his bravery he had conquered the Curatii; but the crime of killing his sister was atrocious, and the Romans were so outraged by this murder that he was put upon trial for his life, notwithstanding his recent great services to the state. Now, in looking at this matter superficially, it may seem like an instance of popular ingratitude; but a more careful examination, and reflection as to what the laws of a republic ought to be, will show that the people were to blame rather for the acquittal of Horatius than for having him tried. And the reason for this is, that no well-ordered republic should ever cancel the crimes of its citizens by their merits; but having established rewards for good actions and penalties for evil ones, and having rewarded a citizen for good conduct who afterwards commits a wrong, he should be chastised for that without regard to his previous merits And a state that properly observes this principle will long enjoy its liberty; but if otherwise, it will speedily come to ruin. For if a citizen who has rendered some eminent service to the state should add to the reputation and influence which he has thereby acquired the confident audacity of being able to commit any wrong without fear of punishment, he will in a little while become so insolent and overbearing as to put an end to all power of the law. But to preserve a wholesome fear of punishment for evil deeds, it is necessary not to omit rewarding good ones; as has been seen was done by Rome. And although a republic may be poor and able to give but little, yet she should not abstain from giving that little; for even the smallest reward for a good action—no matter how important the service to the state—will always be esteemed by the recipient as most honorable. The story of Horatius Cocles and of Mutius Scævola is well known; how the one, single-handed, kept back the enemy to give time for the destruction of a bridge, and how the other burned his hand off for having erred in his attempt to take the life of Porsenna, king of the Tuscans. As a reward for their eminent services the city of Rome gave to each of them two acres of land. The story of Manlius Capitolinus is equally well known; having saved the Capitol from the Gauls who were besieging it, he received from each of those who had been shut up in it with him a small measure of flour, which (according to the current prices of things in those days in Rome) was a reward of considerable value and importance. But when Manlius afterwards, inspired by envy or his evil nature, attempted to stir up a rebellion, and sought to gain the people over to himself, he was, regardless of his former services, precipitated from that very Capitol which it had been his previous glory to have saved.

Chapter XXV

WHOEVER WISHES TO REFORM AN EXISTING GOVERNMENT IN A FREE STATE SHOULD AT LEAST PRESERVE THE SEMBLANCE OF THE OLD FORMS

HE who desires or attempts to reform the government of a state, and wishes to have it accepted and capable of maintaining itself to the satisfaction of everybody, must at least retain the semblance of the old forms; so that it may seem to the people that there has been no change in the institutions, even though in fact they are entirely different from the old ones. For the great majority of mankind are satisfied with appearances, as though they were realities, and are often even more influenced by the things that seem than by those that are. The Romans understood this well, and for that reason, when they first recovered their liberty, and had created two Consuls in place of a king, they would not allow these more than twelve lictors, so as not to exceed the number that had served the king. Besides this, the Romans were accustomed to an annual sacrifice that could only be performed by the king in person; and as they did not wish that the people, in consequence of the absence of the king, should have occasion to regret the loss of any of their old customs, they created a special chief for that ceremony, whom they called the king of the sacrifice, and placed him under their high priest; so that the people enjoyed these annual sacrificial ceremonies, and had no pretext, from the want of them, for desiring the restoration of the kings. And this rule should be observed by all who wish to abolish an existing system of government in any state, and introduce a new and more liberal one. For as all novelties excite the minds of men, it is important to retain in such innovations as much as possible the previously existing forms. And if the number, authority, and duration of the term of service of the magistrates be changed, the titles at least ought to be preserved. This, as I have said, should be observed by whoever desires to convert an absolute government either into a republic or a monarchy; but, on the contrary, he who wishes to establish an absolute power, such as ancient writers called a tyranny, must change everything, as we shall show in the following chapter.

Chapter XXVI

A NEW PRINCE IN A CITY OR PROVINCE CONQUERED BY HIM SHOULD ORGANIZE EVERYTHING ANEW

WHOEVER becomes prince of a city or state, especially if the foundation of his power is feeble, and does not wish to establish there either a monarchy or a republic, will find the best means for holding that principality to organize the government entirely anew (he being himself a new prince there); that is, he should appoint new governors with new titles, new powers, and new men, and he should make the poor rich, as David did when he became king, "who heaped riches upon the needy, and dismissed the wealthy empty-handed." Besides this, he should destroy the old cities and build new ones, and transfer the inhabitants from one place to another; in short, he should leave nothing unchanged in that province, so that there should be neither rank, nor grade, nor honor, nor wealth, that should not be recognized as coming from him. He should take Philip of Macedon, father of Alexander, for his model, who by proceeding in that manner became, from a petty king, master of all Greece. And his historian tells us that he transferred the inhabitants from one province to another, as shepherds move their flocks from place to place. Doubtless these means are cruel and destructive of all civilized life, and neither Christian nor even human, and should be avoided by every one. In fact, the life of a private citizen would be preferable to that of a king at the expense of the ruin of so many human beings. Nevertheless, whoever is unwilling to adopt the first and humane course must, if he wishes to maintain his power, follow the latter evil course. But men generally decide upon a middle course, which is most hazardous; for they know neither how to be entirely good or entirely bad, as we shall illustrate by examples in the next chapter.

Chapter XXVII

**SHOWING THAT MEN ARE VERY RARELY EITHER ENTIRELY GOOD
OR ENTIRELY BAD**

WHEN Pope Julius II. went, in the year 1505, to Bologna to
expel the Bentivogli from that state, the government of
which they had held for a hundred years, he wanted also
to remove Giovanpaolo Baglioni from Perugia, who had
made himself the absolute master of that city; for it was
the intention of Pope Julius to destroy all the petty tyrants
that occupied the possessions of the Church. Having arrived
at Perugia with that purpose, which was well known to
everybody, he did not wait to enter the city with his army
for his protection, but went in almost alone, although Giovanpaolo had collected a large force within the city for his
defence. And thus, with the customary impetuosity which
characterized all his acts, Julius placed himself with only
a small guard in the hands of his enemy Baglioni, whom
he nevertheless carried off with him, leaving a governor in
his stead to administer the state in the name of the Church.
Sagacious men who were with the Pope observed his temerity and the cowardice of Baglioni, and could not understand why the latter had not by a single blow rid himself
of his enemy, whereby he would have secured for himself
eternal fame and rich booty, for the Pope was accompanied
by all the cardinals with their valuables. Nor could they
believe that he had refrained from doing this either from
goodness or conscientious scruples; for no sentiment of
piety or respect could enter the heart of a man of such vile
character as Giovanpaolo, who had dishonored his sister

and murdered his nephews and cousins for the sake of obtaining possession of the state; but they concluded that mankind were neither utterly wicked nor perfectly good, and that when a crime has in itself some grandeur or magnanimity they will not know how to attempt it. Thus Giovanpaolo Baglioni, who did not mind open incest and parricide, knew not how, or, more correctly speaking, dared not, to attempt an act (although having a justifiable opportunity) for which every one would have admired his courage, and which would have secured him eternal fame, as being the first to show these prelates how little esteem those merit who live and govern as they do; and as having done an act the greatness of which would have overshadowed the infamy and all the danger that could possibly result from it.

Chapter XXVIII

WHY ROME WAS LESS UNGRATEFUL TO HER CITIZENS THAN ATHENS

In reading the history of republics we find in all of them a degree of ingratitude to their citizens; this, however, seems to have been the case to a less extent in Rome than in Athens, and perhaps less even than in any other republic. In seeking for the reason of this difference, so far as Rome and Athens are concerned, I believe it was because Rome had less cause for mistrusting her citizens than Athens. In fact, from the time of the expulsion of the kings until Sylla and Marius, no Roman citizen ever attempted to deprive his country of her liberty; so that, there being no occasion to suspect her citizens, there was consequently no cause for offending them inconsiderately. The very contrary happened in Athens, for Pisistratus had by fraud robbed her of her liberty at the very time of her highest prosperity; so soon as she afterwards recovered her freedom, remembering the injuries received and her past servitude, she resented with the utmost harshness, not only all faults, but the mere semblance of faults, on the part of her citizens. It was this that gave rise to the exile and death of so many of her illustrious men, and thence came the practice of ostracism and every other violence which that city exercised at various times against some of her noblest citizens. It is a very true saying of political writers, that those states which have recovered their liberty treat their citizens with greater severity than such as have never lost it. A careful consideration of what has been said on this subject will show that Athens is neither to be blamed, nor Rome to be praised, for their respective conduct, and that it necessarily resulted entirely from the difference of the events that occurred in those cities; for a penetrating observer will not fail to see that, if Rome had been deprived of her liberty in the manner Athens was, she would not have been more indulgent to her citizens than the latter. We may judge very correctly of this by her treatment of Collatinus and Publius Valerius after the expulsion of the kings; the first was exiled for no other reason than that he bore the name of the Tarquins, and the other was equally sent into exile because he had excited suspicion by building a house on Mount Cœlius. Seeing then how suspicious and severe Rome showed herself in these two cases, we may fairly judge that she would have been liable to the charge of ingratitude, the same as Athens, if she had been offended by her citizens in the beginning of her existence, before she had grown powerful. And so as not to be obliged to return to this subject of ingratitude, I shall continue what I have to say in relation to it in the next chapter.

Chapter XXIX

WHICH OF THE TWO IS MOST UNGRATEFUL, A PEOPLE OR A PRINCE

It seems to me proper here, in connection with the above subject, to examine whether the people or a prince is more liable to the charge of ingratitude; and by way of illustrating this question the better, I set out by saying that the vice of ingratitude springs either from avarice or fear. For when a people or a prince has sent a general on some important expedition where by his success he acquires great glory, the prince or people is in turn bound to reward him. But if instead of such reward they dishonor and wrong him, influenced thereto by avarice, then they are guilty of an inexcusable wrong, which will involve them in eternal infamy. And yet there are many princes who commit this wrong, for which fact Tacitus assigns the reason in the following sentence: "Men are more ready to repay an injury than a benefit, because gratitude is a burden and revenge a pleasure." But when they fail to reward, or rather when they offend, not from avarice, but from suspicion and fear, then the people or the prince have some excuse for their ingratitude. We read of many instances of this kind; for the general who by his valor has conquered a state for his master, and won great glory for himself by his victory over the enemy, and has loaded his soldiers with rich booty, acquires necessarily with his own soldiers, as well as with those of the enemy and with the subjects of the prince, so high a reputation, that his very victory may become distasteful, and a cause for apprehension to his prince. For as the nature of men is ambitious as well as suspicious, and puts no limits to one's good fortune, it is not impossible that the suspicion that may suddenly be aroused in the mind of the prince by the victory of the general may have been aggravated by some haughty expressions or insolent acts on his part; so that the prince will naturally be made to think of securing himself against the ambition of his general. And to do this, the means that suggest themselves to him are either to have the general killed, or to deprive him of that reputation which he has acquired with the prince's army and the people, by using every means to prove that the general's victory was not due to his skill and courage, but to chance and the cowardice of the enemy, or to the sagacity of the other captains who were with him in that action.

After Vespasian, whilst in Judæa, had been proclaimed Emperor by his army, Antonius Primus, who was at the head of an army in Illyria, took sides with him, and marched straight into Italy against Vitellius, then Emperor in Rome, and in the most gallant manner routed two Vitellian armies, and made himself master of Rome; so that Mutianus, who had been sent there by Vespasian, found everything achieved and all difficulties overcome. The reward which Antonius received for this service was that Mutianus deprived him of the command of the army, and gradually reduced his authority in Rome to nothing; so that Antonius, indignant, went to see Vespasian, who was still in Asia, who received him in such manner that, being soon after deprived of all rank, he died almost in despair. History is full of similar examples.

We have seen in our own day with how much courage and perseverance Gonsalvo de Cordova conducted the war in Naples for King Ferdinand of Aragon against the French; how he defeated them, and conquered the kingdom for Ferdinand; and how he was rewarded by his king, who left Spain and came to Naples, and first deprived Gonsalvo of his command of the army, and then took the control of the strong places from him, and finally carried him off with him to Spain, where Gonsalvo soon after died in obscurity.

Fear and suspicion are so natural to princes that they cannot defend themselves against them, and thus it is impossible for them to show gratitude to those who, by victories achieved under their banners, have made important conquests for them. If then a prince cannot prevent himself from committing such wrongs, it is surely no wonder, nor matter worthy of more consideration, if a people acts in a similar manner. For as a free city is generally influenced by two principal objects, the one to aggrandize herself, and the other to preserve her liberties, it is natural that she should occasionally be betrayed into faults by excessive eagerness in the pursuit of either of these objects. As to the faults that result from the desire for aggrandizement, we shall speak in another place; and those resulting from the desire to preserve her liberty are amongst others the following, namely, to injure those citizens whom she should reward, and to suspect those in whom she should place most confidence. And although the effects of such conduct occasion great evils in a republic that is already corrupt, and which often lead to despotism,—as was seen under Cæsar in Rome, who took for himself by force what ingratitude had refused him,—still, in a republic not yet entirely corrupt, they may be productive of great good in preserving her freedom for a greater length of time; as the dread of punishment will keep men better, and less ambitious.

It is true that, of all the people that ever possessed a great empire, the Romans were the least ungrateful; for it may be said that no other instance of their ingratitude can be cited than that of Scipio; for Coriolanus and Camillus were both exiled on account of the outrages which they had committed upon the people. The one was never pardoned, because he always preserved an implacable hatred against the people; but the other was not only recalled from exile, but was for the entire remainder of his life honored like a prince. The ingratitude to Scipio arose from jealousy such as never before had been felt towards any one else, and which resulted from the greatness of the enemy whom Scipio had conquered, from the great reputation which his victory after so long and perilous a war had given him, from the rapidity of his actions and the popular favor which his youth, his prudence, and other remarkable virtues had won for him. All of these were so great that everybody in Rome, even the magistrates, feared his influence and authority, which offended the intelligent men of Rome as an unheard of thing. And his manner of life was such that Cato the elder, who was reputed a man of the purest character, was the first to complain of him, saying that no city could call herself free where a citizen was feared by the magistrates. So that if in this case the people of Rome followed the opinion of Cato, they are entitled to that excuse which, as I have said above, those peoples and princes may claim who are ungrateful from suspicion and fear. In concluding, then, this discourse, I say that, as the vice of ingratitude is usually the consequence of either avarice or fear, it will be seen that the peoples never fall into this error from avarice, and that fear also makes them less liable to it than princes, inasmuch as they have less reason for fear, as we shall show further on.

Chapter XXX

HOW PRINCES AND REPUBLICS SHOULD ACT TO AVOID THE VICE OF
INGRATITUDE, AND HOW A COMMANDER OR A CITIZEN SHOULD
ACT SO AS NOT TO EXPOSE HIMSELF TO IT

A PRINCE, to avoid the necessity of living in constant mistrust or of being ungrateful, should command all his expeditions in person, as the Roman Emperors did in the beginning, and as the Sultan does at the present time, and as in fact all valiant princes ever have done and will do. For if victorious, all the glory and fruits of their conquests will be theirs; but if they are not present themselves at the action, and the glory of victory falls to the share of another, then it will seem to them that the conquest will not profit them unless they extinguish that glory of another which they have failed to achieve themselves. Thus they became ungrateful and unjust, and in that way their loss will be greater than their gain. But if from indolence or want of sagacity they remain idle at home, and confide the expedition to a commander, then I have no advice to give them but to follow their own inspirations. But I say to the commander, judging that he will not be able to escape the fangs of ingratitude, that he must do one of two things: either he must leave the army immediately after victory, and place himself at the disposal of his prince, carefully avoiding all show of insolence or ambition, so that the prince, deprived of all grounds of fear or suspicion, may reward him or at least not wrong him; or if this does not suit him, then he must boldly adopt the other course, and act in all respects as though he believed the conquest were for his own account, and not for his prince,—conciliating to himself the good will of his army and of the subjected people, forming friendships and alliances with the neighboring princes, occupying the strongholds with his own men, corrupting the chiefs of his army and making sure of such as he cannot corrupt,— and in this wise seek to punish his prince in advance for the ingratitude which he is likely to show him. And there is no other way for him to do. But, as I have already said, men neither know how to be entirely good nor wholly bad; and it so happens almost invariably that a general, after a great victory, is unwilling to leave his army, and to conduct himself with becoming modesty, and knows not how to take a decided course, which has in itself something honorable and grand; and thus he remains undecided, and whilst in this ambiguous state he is crushed.

A republic that wishes to avoid the vice of ingratitude cannot employ the same means as a prince; that is to say, she cannot go and command her own expeditions, and is obliged therefore to confide them to some one of her citizens. But it is proper that I should suggest as the best means to adopt the same course that Rome did, in being less ungrateful than others and which resulted from her institutions. For as the whole city, nobles and plebeians, devoted themselves to the business of war, there arose at all times in Rome so many brave and victorious generals, that the people had no cause for mistrusting any one of them, there being so many that they could watch each other. And thus they kept themselves so pure, and careful not to give the least umbrage, that they afforded the people not the least ground for suspecting them of ambition; and if any of them arrived at the dictatorship, their greatest glory consisted in promptly laying this dignity down again; and thus, having inspired no fear or mistrust, they gave no cause for ingratitude. A republic, then, that wishes not to have cause for ingratitude, should adopt the same system of government as Rome; and a citizen who desires to avoid the fangs of ingratitude should observe the same conduct as that of the Roman citizens.

Chapter XXXI

SHOWING THAT THE ROMAN GENERALS WERE NEVER SEVERELY PUNISHED FOR ANY FAULTS THEY COMMITTED, NOT EVEN WHEN BY THEIR IGNORANCE AND UNFORTUNATE OPERATIONS THEY OCCASIONED SERIOUS LOSSES TO THE REPUBLIC

THE Romans (as we have shown above) were not only less ungrateful than other republics, but were also more lenient and considerate in the punishment of the generals of their armies. For if their misconduct was intentional, they punished them humanely; and if it was caused by ignorance, they not only did not punish them, but rewarded and honored them nevertheless. This mode of proceeding had been well considered by them; for they judged that it was of the greatest importance for those who commanded their armies to have their minds entirely free and unembarrassed by any anxiety other than how best to perform their duty, and therefore they did not wish to add fresh difficulties and dangers to a task in itself so difficult and perilous, being convinced that, if this were done, it would prevent any general from operating vigorously. Suppose, for instance, that they had sent an army into Greece against Philip of Macedon, or into Italy against such tribes as had at first gained some victories over them. Now, the commander of such an expedition would naturally feel the weight of all the cares attendant on such enterprises, and which are very great. But if in addition to these anxieties the mind of the general had been disturbed by the examples of other generals who had been crucified, or otherwise put to death, for having lost battles, it would have been impossible for him, under the influence of such apprehensions, to have proceeded vigorously. Judging, therefore, that the ignominy of defeat would be sufficient punishment for such a commander, they did not wish to terrify him with other penalties.

The following is an instance of how they punished intentional faults. Sergius and Virginius were encamped before Veii, each commanding a separate division of the army; Sergius being placed on the side where the Tuscans could make an attack, and Virginius on the opposite side. It happened that, Sergius being attacked by the Faliscans and other tribes, he preferred being beaten by them and put to flight rather than apply to Virginius for assistance; and, on the other hand, Virginius, waiting for his colleague to humble himself, was willing rather to see his country dishonored, and the army of Sergius routed, than march unsolicited to his succor. Certainly a very bad case and worthy of note, and well calculated to cause unfavorable conjectures as to the Roman republic, if both these generals had not been punished. It is true that, whilst any other republic would have inflicted capital punishment upon them, they were subjected by Rome only to a pecuniary fine. Not but what their misconduct merited severer punishment, but because the Romans, for the reasons above explained, would not vary from their established custom.

As regards faults committed from ignorance, there is not a more striking example than that of Varro, whose temerity caused the defeat of the Romans by Hannibal at Cannæ, which exposed the republic to the loss of her liberty. Nevertheless, as it was from ignorance, and not from evil intention, they not only did not punish him, but actually rendered him honors; and on his return, the whole order of Senators went to meet him, and, unable to congratulate him on the result of the battle, they thanked him for having returned to Rome, and for not having despaired of the cause of the republic.

When Papirius Cursor wanted to have Fabius put to death for having, contrary to his orders, given battle to the Samnites, amongst the other reasons which the father of Fabius opposed to the obstinacy of the Dictator was this,—that after the most bloody defeats the Roman people had never treated their generals as Papirius Cursor wanted to treat his victorious son.

Chapter XXXII

REPUBLIC OR A PRINCE SHOULD NOT DEFER SECURING THE GOOD WILL OF THE PEOPLE UNTIL THEY ARE THEMSELVES IN DIFFICULTIES

ALTHOUGH the Romans happily always treated the people with liberality, yet when danger came upon them, and Porsenna attacked Rome for the purpose of restoring the Tarquins, the Senate was doubtful whether the people might not rather accept the restoration of the kings than undergo a war; and to assure themselves of the people, they relieved them of the impost on salt and of all other taxes, saying that the poor did enough for the public benefit in rearing their children; and although in consequence of this liberality the people submitted to the hardships and privations of siege, famine, and war, yet let no one, trusting to this example, defer securing the good will of the people until the moment of danger; for they will never succeed in it as the Romans did. For the masses will think that they do not owe the benefits you have bestowed upon them to you, but to your adversaries; and fearing that, when the danger is past, you will again take from them what under the pressure of danger you conceded to them, they will feel under no obligations to you. The reason why this proceeding turned out well for the Romans was that the government was still new and not yet firmly established, and the people had seen that other laws had been enacted for their benefit, such, for instance, as that of the appeal to the people; and thus they were easily persuaded that the relief from taxation which had been granted to them was not caused so much by the approach of the enemy as by the disposition of the Senate to favor them. Besides this, the memory of the kings, by whom they had been wronged and maltreated in various ways, was still fresh in their minds. And as it is rare that similar circumstances concur, so it is equally rare that similar remedies avail; and therefore republics as well as princes should think in advance what adversities may befall them, and of whom they may have need in time of trouble, and then they should comport themselves towards these in the manner they might deem necessary in case danger should come upon them. And whoever acts differently, whether prince or republic, and more especially a prince, and supposes from the above-related fact that it is time enough by benefits to secure the good will of the people when danger has come upon him, deceives himself greatly; for not only will he fail to obtain the good will of the people, but he will accelerate his own destruction.

Chapter XXXIII

WHEN AN EVIL HAS SPRUNG UP WITHIN A STATE, OR COME UPON
IT FROM WITHOUT, IT IS SAFER TO TEMPORIZE WITH IT RATHER
THAN TO ATTACK IT VIOLENTLY

As the Roman republic grew in reputation, power, and dominion, the neighboring tribes, who at first had not thought
of how great a danger this new republic might prove to
them, began (too late, however) to see their error; and wishing to remedy their first neglect, they united full forty tribes
in a league against Rome. Hereupon the Romans resorted,
amongst other measures which they were accustomed to
employ in urgent dangers, to the creation of a dictator; that
is to say, they gave the power to one man, who, without
consulting any one else, could determine upon any course,
and could have it carried into effect without any appeal.
This measure, which on former occasions had proved most
useful in overcoming imminent perils, was equally service-
able to them in all the critical events that occurred during
the growth and development of the power of the republic.
Upon this subject we must remark, first, that when any
evil arises within a republic or threatens it from without,
that is to say, from an intrinsic or extrinsic cause, and has
become so great as to fill every one with apprehension, the
more certain remedy by far is to temporize with it, rather
than to attempt to extirpate it; for almost invariably he who
attempts to crush it will rather increase its force, and will
accelerate the harm apprehended from it. And such evils
arise more frequently in a republic from intrinsic than extrinsic causes, as it often occurs that a citizen is allowed to

acquire more authority than is proper; or that changes are permitted in a law which is the very nerve and life of liberty; and then they let this evil go so far that it becomes more hazardous to correct it than to allow it to run on. And it is the more difficult to recognize these evils at their origin, as it seems natural to men always to favor the beginning of things; and these favors are more readily accorded to such acts as seem to have some merit in them, and are done by young men. For if in a republic a noble youth is seen to rise, who is possessed of some extraordinary merits, the eyes of all citizens quickly turn to him, and all hasten to show him honor, regardless of consequences; so that, if he is in any way ambitious, the gifts of nature and the favor of his fellow-citizens will soon raise him to such a height that, when the citizens become sensible of the error they have committed, they have no longer the requisite means for checking him, and their efforts to employ such as they have will only accelerate his advance to power.

Many instances of this might be cited, but I will confine myself to one which occurred in our own city of Florence. Cosimo de' Medici, to whom the house of Medici owes the beginning of its greatness, obtained such reputation and authority through his own sagacity and the ignorance of his fellow-citizens, that he became a cause of apprehension to the government, and that the other citizens judged it hazardous to offend him, but more dangerous still to allow him to go on. At that time there lived in Florence Niccolo Uzzano, reputed a man of consummate ability in matters of state, who, having committed the first error of not foreseeing the danger that might result from the great influence of Cosimo, would never permit the Florentines, so long as he lived, to commit the second error of trying to destroy Cosimo, judging that any such attempt would lead to the ruin of the state, as in fact proved to be the case after his death. For the citizens, regardless of the counsels of Uzzano, combined against Cosimo and drove him from Florence. The consequence was that the partisans of Cosimo, to resent this insult, shortly afterwards recalled him and made him prince of the republic, which position he never would have attained but for the previous hostility manifested towards him. The same thing happened in Rome with regard to Cæsar, who by his courage and merits at first won the favor of Pompey and of other prominent citizens, but which favor was shortly after converted into fear; to which Cicero testifies, saying "that Pompey had begun too late to fear Cæsar." This fear caused them to think of measures of safety, which however only accelerated the ruin of the republic.

I say, then, that inasmuch as it is difficult to know these evils at their first origin, owing to an illusion which all new things are apt to produce, the wiser course is to temporize with such evils when they are recognized, instead of violently attacking them; for by temporizing with them they will either die out of themselves, or at least their worst results will be long deferred. And princes or magistrates who wish to destroy such evils must watch all points, and must be careful in attacking them not to increase instead of diminishing them, for they must not believe that a fire can be extinguished by blowing upon it. They should carefully examine the extent and force of the evil, and if they think themselves sufficiently strong to combat it, then they should attack it regardless of consequences; otherwise they should let it be, and in no wise attempt it. For it will always happen as I have said above, and as it did happen to the neighboring tribes of Rome; who found that it would have been more advantageous, after Rome had grown so much in power, to placate and keep her within her limits by peaceful means, than by warlike measures to make her think of new institutions and new defences. For their league had no other effect than to unite the people of Rome more closely, and to make them more ready for war, and to cause them to adopt new institutions that enabled them in a brief time to increase their power. One of these was the creation of a Dictator, by which new institution they not only overcame the most imminent dangers, but obviated also an infinity of troubles in which they would otherwise have been involved.

Chapter XXXIV

THE AUTHORITY OF THE DICTATORSHIP HAS ALWAYS PROVED BENEFICIAL TO ROME, AND NEVER INJURIOUS; IT IS THE AUTHORITY WHICH MEN USURP, AND NOT THAT WHICH IS GIVEN THEM BY THE FREE SUFFRAGES OF THEIR FELLOW-CITIZENS, THAT IS DANGEROUS TO CIVIL LIBERTY

SOME writers have blamed those Romans who first introduced the practice of creating Dictators, as being calculated in time to lead to despotism in Rome; alleging that the first tyrant of that city governed her under the title of Dictator, and saying that, if it had not been for this office, Cæsar never could under any other public title have imposed his despotism upon the Romans. Evidently the subject could not have been thoroughly considered by those who advance this opinion, so generally adopted without good reasons; for it was neither the name nor the rank of the Dictator that subjected Rome to servitude, but it was the authority which citizens usurped to perpetuate themselves in the government. And if the title of Dictator had not existed in Rome, some other would have been taken; for power can easily take a name, but a name cannot give power. And it is seen that the dictatorship, whenever created according to public law and not usurped by individual authority, always proved beneficial to Rome; it is the magistracies and powers that are created by illegitimate means which harm a republic, and not those that are appointed in the regular way, as was the case in Rome, where in the long course of time no Dictator ever failed to prove beneficial to the republic. The reason of this is perfectly evident: first, before a citizen can be in a position to usurp extraordinary powers, many things must concur, which in a republic as yet uncorrupted never can happen; for he must be exceedingly rich, and must have many adherents and partisans, which cannot be where the laws are observed; and even if he had them, he would never be supported by the free suffrages of the people, for such men are generally looked upon as dangerous. Besides this, Dictators were appointed only for a limited term, and not in perpetuity, and their power to act was confined to the particular occasion for which they were created. This power consisted in being able to decide alone upon the measures to be adopted for averting the pressing danger, to do whatever he deemed proper without consultation, and to inflict punishment upon any one without appeal. But the Dictator could do nothing to alter the form of the government, such as to diminish the powers of the Senate or the people, or to abrogate existing institutions and create new ones. So that, taking together the short period for which he held the office, and the limited powers which he possessed, and the fact that the Roman people were as yet uncorrupted, it is evident that it was impossible for him to exceed his powers and to harm the republic; which on the contrary, as all experience shows, was always benefited by him.

And truly, of all the institutions of Rome, this one deserves to be counted amongst those to which she was most indebted for her greatness and dominion. For without some such an institution Rome would with difficulty have escaped the many extraordinary dangers that befell her; for the customary proceedings of republics are slow, no magistrate or council being permitted to act independently, but being in almost all instances obliged to act in concert one with the other, so that often much time is required to harmonize their several opinions; and tardy measures are most dangerous when the occasion requires prompt action. And therefore all republics should have some institution similar to the dictatorship. The republic of Venice, which is pre-eminent amongst modern ones, had reserved to a small number of citizens the power of deciding all urgent matters without referring their decisions to a larger council. And when a republic lacks some such system, a strict observance of the established laws will expose her to ruin; or, to save her from such danger, the laws will have to be disregarded. Now in a well-ordered republic it should never be necessary to resort to extra-constitutional measures; for although they may for the time be beneficial, yet the precedent is pernicious, for if the practice is once established of disregarding the laws for good objects, they will in a little while be disregarded under that pretext for evil purposes. Thus no republic will ever be perfect if she has not by law provided for everything, having a remedy for every emergency, and fixed rules for applying it. And therefore I will say, in conclusion, that those republics which in time of danger cannot resort to a dictatorship, or some similar authority, will generally be ruined when grave occasions occur. It is well to note with reference to this institution how wisely the Romans had provided the mode of electing the Dictator. For as his creation reflected in some measure discredit upon the Consuls, who as chiefs of the republic had to submit to his authority the same as the other citizens, and apprehending that this might possibly excite indignation amongst the citizens, it was decided that the nomination of the Dictator should be made by the Consuls themselves; so that when an emergency occurred in which Rome needed this quasi regal power, the Consuls, having the right of creating it themselves, might thus be less sensitive than if it were imposed upon them by others. For the wounds and every other evil that men inflict upon themselves spontaneously, and of their own choice, are in the long run less painful than those inflicted by others. In later times, however, the Romans, instead of appointing a Dictator, used to confer that extraordinary power upon the Consuls in these words: "Let the Consuls see that the republic suffers no detriment." But to return now to our subject, I conclude that the neighboring tribes of Rome, in attempting to oppress her, caused her not only to adopt new means for defending herself, but also to prepare with greater force, abler counsels, and greater authority to attack them.

Chapter XXXV

THE REASON WHY THE CREATION OF DECEMVIRS IN ROME WAS INJURIOUS TO LIBERTY, NOTWITHSTANDING THAT THEY WERE CREATED BY THE FREE SUFFRAGES OF THE PEOPLE

THE election of ten citizens by the Roman people to make the laws in Rome, who in course of time became tyrants, and regardlessly destroyed her liberty, seems to be in contradiction with what I have said in the preceding chapter;

namely, that the authority which is violently usurped, and not that which is conferred by the free suffrages of the people, is hurtful to republics. In this, however, there are two things to be considered; namely, the manner in which the authority is bestowed, and the length of time for which it is given. For when full power is conferred for any length of time (and I call a year or more a long time) it is always dangerous, and will be productive of good or ill effects, according as those upon whom it is conferred are themselves good or bad. And if we examine the power given to the Decemvirs and that of the Dictators, we shall find that of the former beyond comparison the greater. For at the creation of a Dictator, the Tribunes, the Consuls, and the Senate all remained with their respective powers, of which they could not be deprived by the Dictator. And even if he could have removed any one from the consulate or from the Senate, yet he could not abrogate the senatorial order and make new laws himself. So that the Senate, the Consuls, and the Tribunes, remaining in full authority, served as it were as a guard to watch that the Dictator did not transcend his powers. But in the creation of the Decemvirs just the opposite was the case; for their appointment cancelled that of the Consuls and Tribunes, and to the Decemvirs the power was given to make new laws, and in fact to do everything that the Roman people were competent to do. So that, finding themselves alone, without Tribunes or Consuls, and without the necessity of appealing to the Roman people, and having therefore no one to watch them, they were enabled in the second year, instigated by the ambition of Appius, to become overbearing, and to abuse their power. And therefore, when we said that an authority conferred by the free suffrages of the people never harmed a republic, we presupposed that the people, in giving that power, would limit it, as well as the time during which it was to be exercised. But if from having been deceived, or from any other reason, they are induced to give this power imprudently, and in the way in which the Roman people gave it to the Decemvirs, then the same thing will happen to them as happened to the Romans. This is easily proved by examining the causes that kept the Dictators within the limits of their duties, and those which made the Decemvirs transcend theirs; and by examining, further, the conduct of those republics that were well constituted, in giving power for any length of time, as the Spartans did to their kings, and as the Venetians gave to their Doges. In both these cases we see that guardians were appointed to watch that neither the king nor the Doge could abuse the power intrusted to him. Nor is it of any advantage in such a case that the mass of the people is not corrupt, for absolute authority will very quickly corrupt the people, and will create friends and partisans for itself. Nor is it any disadvantage to be poor and without family influence, for riches and every other favor will quickly run after power, as we shall show in the case of the creation of the Decemvirs.

Chapter XXXVI

CITIZENS WHO HAVE BEEN HONORED WITH THE HIGHER OFFICES SHOULD NOT DISDAIN LESS IMPORTANT ONES

THE Romans had made Marcus Fabius and C. Manilius Consuls, and had gained a most glorious victory over the Veienti and the Etruscans, which, however, cost the life of Quintus Fabius, brother of the Consul, and who had himself been Consul the year before. This ought to make us reflect how well the institutions of that city were calculated to make her great, and what an error other republics commit in deviating from her system. For although the Romans were great lovers of glory, yet they did not esteem it dishonorable to obey those whom they had at a previous time commanded, or to serve in that army of which themselves had been chiefs. This custom is entirely contrary to the opinion, rules, and practice of our times; and in Venice they even yet hold to the error that a citizen who has once held a high post under the state would be dishonored by accepting a lower one; and the city consents to what she cannot change. However honorable this may be for a private citizen, yet for the public it is absolutely useless. A republic can and should have more hope and confidence in that citizen who from a superior grade descends to accept a less important one, than in him who from an inferior employment mounts to the exercise of a superior one; for the latter cannot reasonably be relied upon unless he is surrounded by men of such respectability and virtue that his inexperience may in some measure be compensated for by their counsel and authority. If they had had the same prejudice in Rome as in Venice and the other modern states, so that a man who had once been Consul had refused to return to the army except in the quality of Consul, it would have given rise to infinite inconveniences, greatly to the prejudice of public liberty, because of the errors of the new men in office, as well as of their ambition, which they could indulge the more freely, not having any men around them in whose presence they would be afraid to commit such faults; and thus they would have been more unrestrained, which would have resulted greatly to the public detriment.

Chapter XXXVII

WHAT TROUBLES RESULTED IN ROME FROM THE ENACTMENT OF
THE AGRARIAN LAW, AND HOW VERY WRONG IT IS TO MAKE
LAWS THAT ARE RETROSPECTIVE AND CONTRARY TO OLD ESTAB-
LISHED CUSTOMS

IT was a saying of ancient writers, that men afflict themselves in evil, and become weary of the good, and that both
these dispositions produce the same effects. For when men
are no longer obliged to fight from necessity, they fight from
ambition, which passion is so powerful in the hearts of men
that it never leaves them, no matter to what height they
may rise. The reason of this is that nature has created men
so that they desire everything, but are unable to attain it;
desire being thus always greater than the faculty of acquiring, discontent with what they have and dissatisfaction
with themselves result from it. This causes the changes in
their fortunes; for as some men desire to have more, whilst
others fear to lose what they have, enmities and war are the
consequences; and this brings about the ruin of one province
and the elevation of another. I have made these remarks because the Roman people were not content with having secured themselves against the nobles by the creation of the
Tribunes, to which they had been driven by necessity. Having obtained this, they soon began to fight from ambition,
and wanted to divide with the nobles their honors and possessions, being those things which men value most. Thence
the frenzy that occasioned the contentions about the agrarian law, which finally caused the destruction of the Roman
republic. Now, as in well-regulated republics the state ought

to be rich and the citizens poor, it was evident that the agrarian law was in some respects defective; it was either in the beginning so made that it required constant modifications; or the changes in it had been so long deferred that it became most obnoxious because it was retrospective in its action; or perhaps it had been good in the beginning, and had afterwards become corrupted in its application. But whichever it may have been, this law could never be discussed in Rome without causing the most violent excitement in the city. There were two principal points in this law; one provided that no citizen could possess more than a certain number of acres of land, and the other that all the lands taken from their enemies should be divided amongst the Roman people. This affected the nobles disadvantageously in two ways; for those who had more land than the law allowed (which was the case with the greater part of the nobles) had to be deprived of it; and by dividing amongst the people the lands taken from the enemy, it took from the nobles the chance of enriching themselves thereby, as they had previously done. Now, as it was a powerful class that had been thus affected, and who considered resistance to this law as a defence of the public good, whenever the subject was brought up, it occasioned, as we have said, the most violent disturbances. The nobles used all patience and every means in their power to gain time and delay action upon the subject, either by calling out an army, or by getting one Tribune to oppose another who had proposed the law, or sometimes by yielding in part, or even by sending a colony to any place where lands were to be divided. This was done with the country of Antium, respecting which this law had caused a dispute; and therefore a colony drawn from amongst the citizens of Rome was sent there, to whom that country was assigned. In reference to this, Titus Livius makes the notable remark, that "it was difficult to find any one in Rome willing to inscribe his name to go to that colony; so much more ready were the people to desire possessions in Rome than to go and have them in Antium."

The troubles about this agrarian law continued to disturb Rome for some time, so that the Romans began to send their armies to the extreme ends of Italy, or even beyond; after which matters were seemingly calmed down, owing to the fact that the lands taken from the enemy were at a great distance from Rome, and remote from the eyes of the people, and were situated where it was not easy to cultivate them, and consequently they were less desirable. Besides this, the Romans became less disposed to deprive their vanquished enemies of their lands, as they had done before; and when they did so deprive any of them of their possessions, they sent colonies to occupy them; so that from these several causes the agrarian law lay, as it were, dormant until the time of the Gracchi, who, after having revived it, wholly destroyed the Roman republic. For the power of the adversaries of the law had increased twofold in the mean time, and its revival excited such feelings of hatred between the people and the Senate, that it led to violence and bloodshed beyond all bounds or precedent. So that, the magistrates being unable to check these disturbances, and neither party having any confidence in the public authorities, they both resorted to private expedients, and each of the factions began to look for a chief capable of defending them against the other. In these extreme troubles and disorders the people began to cast their eyes upon Marius, on account of his reputation, which was so great that they had made him Consul four times in succession, and with such short intervals between these several consulates that he was enabled to nominate himself three times more for that office. The nobility, seeing no other remedy against these abuses, gave their favor to Sylla, and made him chief of their party. Thus civil war was provoked, and after much bloodshed and varied fortunes the nobility retained the upper hand. In the time of Cæsar and Pompey these troubles were revived, Cæsar placing himself at the head of the party of Marius, and Pompey upholding that of Sylla; conflicts of arms ensued, and Cæsar remained master and became the first tyrant of Rome, so that that city never afterwards recovered her liberty.

Such was the beginning and the end of the agrarian law. And as I have demonstrated elsewhere that the differences between the Senate and the people had been instrumental in preserving liberty in Rome, because they had given rise to the enactment of laws favorable to liberty, therefore the results of this agrarian law may seem in contradiction with that previous conclusion. But I do not on that account change my opinion, for the ambition of the nobles is so great, that, if it is not repressed by various ways and means in any city, it will quickly bring that city to ruin. So that if the contentions about the agrarian law needed three hundred years to bring Rome to a state of servitude, she would have been brought there much quicker if the people, by these laws and other means, had not for so great a length of time kept the ambition of the nobles in check. This shows us also how much more people value riches than honors; for the Roman nobility always yielded to the people without serious difficulties in the matter of honors, but when it came to a question of property, then they resisted with so much pertinacity that the people, to satisfy their thirst for riches, resorted to the above-described extraordinary proceedings. The chief promoters of these disorders were the Gracchi, whose intentions in this matter were more praiseworthy than their prudence. For to attempt to eradicate an abuse that has grown up in a republic by the enactment of retrospective laws, is a most inconsiderate proceeding, and (as we have amply discussed above) only serves to accelerate the fatal results which the abuse tends to bring about; but by temporizing, the end will either be delayed, or the evil will exhaust itself before it attains that end.

Chapter XXXVIII

FEEBLE REPUBLICS ARE IRRESOLUTE, AND KNOW NOT HOW TO TAKE A DECIDED PART; AND WHENEVER THEY DO, IT IS MORE THE RESULT OF NECESSITY THAN OF CHOICE

THE prevalence of a terrible pestilence in Rome made the Volscians and Equeans think the moment favorable for attacking her. They therefore raised a powerful army, and assailed the Latins and Ernicians, who seeing their country ravaged felt constrained to notify the Romans, so that they might come to their defence; but they, being afflicted by the pestilence, replied to the application of the Latins and Ernicians that they must defend themselves with their own armies, as they were not then in condition to aid them. In this we recognize the sagacity as well as the generosity of the Roman Senate, who, although it was their policy under all circumstances to remain the chief source for directing the resolves and actions of their subjects, yet they were never ashamed when necessity obliged them to adopt a course different from their usual custom, or at variance with previous resolutions. I say this, because on other occasions the same Senate had forbidden those same people to arm and defend themselves; so that to a less sagacious Senate it would have seemed a lowering of their dignity now to concede to these people the privilege of their own defence. But this Senate always judged things as they ought to be judged, and always took the least objectionable course as the best. They well knew the evil of not being able to defend their subjects, and of allowing them to arm and defend themselves without the assistance of the Romans, for the reason given, and for many others that are easily understood; nevertheless, knowing that the Latins and Ernicians would have armed themselves anyhow from necessity, the enemy being upon them, they took the honorable course, and decided that what these people would have been obliged to do anyhow should be done with their sanction; so that, having once disobeyed from necessity, they might not accustom themselves to disobeying from choice.

And although this would seem the proper course for every republic to have pursued under the circumstances, yet feeble and ill-advised republics would never have known how to do it, nor how to gain honor to themselves from an occasion of necessity. The Duke Valentino had taken Faenza, and forced Bologna to submit to his terms; wishing after that to return to Rome by way of Tuscany, he sent a messenger to Florence to ask permission for the passage of himself and his army through their territory. The authorities of Florence held a consultation as to what they should do under the circumstances, but no one advised granting the permission; in which respect they did not follow the Roman policy. For as the Duke had a very strong army, and the Florentines being almost without troops, so that they could not have prevented him from passing, it would have been much more to their credit and honor if the Duke had passed with their permission rather than by force: as it was, they had nothing but shame, which would have been greatly less if they had acted differently. But it is the worst fault of feeble republics to be irresolute, so that whatever part they take is dictated by force; and if any good results from it, it is caused less by their sagacity than by their necessity. I will cite two other instances of this which occurred in our time, and in our own city of Florence.

In the year 1500, when King Louis XII. of France had retaken Milan he was anxious to restore Pisa to the Florentines, so as to receive the fifty thousand ducats that had been promised him for such restitution. He sent his army towards Pisa under command of M. de Beaumont, who, although French, was yet a man in whom the Florentines had great confidence. This general placed his army between Cascina and Pisa, with the view of assailing the walls of the latter city; but after having been a few days engaged in making preparations for the assault, the Pisans sent a deputation to him with offers to give up the city to the French army, on condition that he should pledge himself in the king's name not to hand over the city to the Florentines until four months after the surrender. The Florentines wholly refused to assent to such an arrangement, and the consequence was that, after having commenced the siege, M. de Beaumont was obliged to raise it and retire with shame. This refusal on the part of the Florentines had no other cause than their mistrust of the king of France, into whose hands they had been obliged to place themselves in consequence of their own irresoluteness; and in thus not trusting him, they lost sight of the fact, that it would have been much easier for the king to have restored Pisa to them after once being inside of the city, and had he then not given it up to them, he would openly have exposed his perfidy; but not having the city, he could only make them a promise of it,

which promise they had to purchase of him. It would therefore have been much more to their advantage to have consented to M. de Beaumont's taking Pisa under any pledge,
as was proved by subsequent experience in the year 1502.

When Arezzo revolted, the king of France sent to the aid
of the Florentines the Signor Imbault, with a body of French
troops. Very soon after arriving near Arezzo he began to
negotiate with the Aretines as to terms of surrender; these
were willing to give up the place on certain pledges, similar to those asked by the Pisans. The proposition was rejected in Florence; and when this became known to the
Signor Imbault, he concluded that the Florentines little understood their interests, and took upon himself to conclude
the negotiations of surrender without the participation of
the Florentine commissioners; and accordingly he entered
Arezzo with his troops, giving the Florentines to understand that they were fools and did not understand the ways
of the world, and that, if they wanted Arezzo, they should
let the king know it, who was much better able to give it
to them with his troops inside of that city than when they
were outside of it. There was no end to the abuse heaped
upon the Signor Imbault by the Florentines, until at last
they found out that, if M. de Beaumont had acted in a similar manner, they would have had Pisa as they had Arezzo.

And so, to return to our subject, irresolute republics never
take a wise course except by force; for their weakness never
allows them to resolve upon anything where there is a
doubt; and if that doubt is not overcome by some force, they
remain forever in a state of suspense.

Chapter XXXIX

THE SAME ACCIDENTS OFTEN HAPPEN TO DIFFERENT PEOPLES

WHOEVER considers the past and the present will readily observe that all cities and all peoples are and ever have been animated by the same desires and the same passions; so that it is easy, by diligent study of the past, to foresee what is likely to happen in the future in any republic, and to apply those remedies that were used by the ancients, or, not finding any that were employed by them, to devise new ones from the similarity of the events. But as such considerations are neglected or not understood by most of those who read, or, if understood by these, are unknown by those who govern, it follows that the same troubles generally recur in all republics.

The city of Florence, having after the year 1494 lost a portion of her dominions, such as Pisa and other places, was obliged to make war upon him who held these places; and as he was powerful, they expended great sums of money without any advantage. These large expenditures necessitated heavy taxes, and these caused infinite complaints from the people; and as the war was conducted by a council composed of ten citizens who were called "the Ten of the War," the mass of the people began to hold them in aversion, as being the cause of the war and its expenses, and began to persuade themselves that, if this council were done away with, the war would also be ended. Thus when the time came for reappointing the Ten, they allowed their term to expire without renewing the council, and committed their functions to the Signoria. This course was the more pernicious, as it not only did not relieve them of the war, as the people had persuaded themselves that it would, but it removed the men who had conducted it with prudence, and produced altogether such disorder, that they lost, besides Pisa, Arezzo and many other places; so that the people, perceiving the error they had committed, and that the cause of the evil was the fever and not the physician, re-established the Council of Ten.

A similar ill-feeling had arisen in Rome against the Consuls; for the people, seeing one war growing out of another, and that there was no prospect of repose for them, instead of charging the cause of these wars, as they should have done, upon the ambition of their neighbors who sought to overwhelm them, attributed it to the ambition of the nobles, who, unable to oppress the people within the city of Rome where they were defended by the Tribunes, wished to lead the people outside of Rome, where, being without any support or protection, they could oppress them at will. And therefore they thought that it would be necessary either to remove the Consuls altogether, or to regulate their power in such manner that they should have no authority over the people either at home or abroad. The first who attempted to introduce such a law was one of the Tribunes named Terentillus; he proposed the creation of a Council of Five to examine into the powers of the Consuls and to limit it. This greatly excited the nobles, to whom it seemed as though the very majesty of the empire would thereby be annihilated, and that the nobility would lose all rank in the republic. Nevertheless, such was the obstinacy of the Tribunes that the consular dignity was abolished; and after some other regulations it was finally resolved rather to create Tribunes with consular powers, than to continue the Consuls, so great was their aversion to that office and authority.

And this system was continued for a long time, until they saw the error they had committed, and re-established the Consuls; just as in Florence they returned to the Council of Ten.

Chapter XL

OF THE CREATION OF THE DECEMVIRS IN ROME, AND WHAT IS NOTEWORTHY IN IT; AND WHERE WE SHALL CONSIDER AMONGST MANY OTHER THINGS HOW THE SAME ACCIDENTS MAY SAVE OR RUIN A REPUBLIC

As I wish particularly to discuss the events that followed the creation of the Decemvirs in Rome, it seems to me not superfluous to narrate first all that happened in consequence of this creation, and afterwards to discuss the more notable points; many of which are well worthy of careful reflection by those who wish to maintain the liberty of a republic, as well as those who desire to suppress it. For we shall see in this discussion many errors committed by the Senate, as well as by the people, prejudicial to liberty; and many errors committed by Appius, chief of the Decemvirate detrimental to that tyranny which he intended to have established in Rome. After many contentions between the people and the nobles respecting the adoption of new laws in Rome, by which the liberty of the state should be firmly established, it was agreed to send Spurius Posthumus with two other citizens to Athens for copies of the laws which Solon had given to that city, so that they might model the new Roman laws upon those. After their return to Rome a commission had to be appointed for the examination and preparation of the new laws, and for this purpose ten citizens were chosen for one year, amongst whom was Appius Claudius, a sagacious but turbulent man. And in order that these might make such laws irrespective of any other authority, they suppressed all the other magistracies in Rome, and particularly the Tribunes and the Consuls; the appeal to the people was also suppressed, so that this new magistracy of ten became absolute masters of Rome. Appius very soon absorbed all the authority of his colleagues in himself by reason of his favor with the people; for he had made himself so popular by his manners, that it seemed a wonder how he could in so short a time have acquired, as it were, a new nature and a new spirit, having until then been regarded as a cruel persecutor of the people. The Ten bore themselves very civilly and modestly, having but ten lictors to walk before him whom they had elected to preside over them; and although they had absolute authority, yet, when they had occasion to punish a Roman citizen for homicide, they cited him before the people and made them judge him.

These Decemvirs wrote their laws upon ten tablets, and before finally confirming them exposed them in public, in order that they might be read and discussed by everybody, and that they might learn whether the laws were in any way defective, so that they might be amended before their final confirmation. Hereupon Appius caused a rumor to be circulated throughout Rome, that, if two more tablets were added to the ten, the laws would be still more perfect, so that this opinion, generally accredited, afforded the people the opportunity to reappoint the Ten for another year, of which they readily availed, partly because it relieved them from renominating Consuls, and partly because they hoped also to remain without Tribunes, who were the judges of their causes, as has been said above. When it was resolved, therefore, to reappoint the Ten, the whole nobility strove to obtain these honors, and amongst the foremost was Appius; and such was his urbanity towards the people in asking for it, that it began to excite suspicion amongst his colleagues, "for they could not possibly believe that there could be such spontaneous affability with so much natural arrogance and pride." And as they feared to oppose him openly, they resolved to do it by artifice; and although he was the youngest of them all, they devolved upon him the authority to propose the future Ten to the people, believing that he would observe the practice of others to whom this confidence had been shown, and not propose himself, which was regarded in Rome as an improper and ignominious thing to do. "But he, in fact, converted the impediment into his opportunity," and did not hesitate to nominate himself as the very first, to the astonishment and disgust of all the nobles; and then he nominated nine others to suit himself. This renewal of the Decemvirs for another year began to show to the people and the nobility the mistake they had made. For Appius "quickly put an end to his assumed character" and began to display his innate arrogance; and in the course of a few days he animated his colleagues with his own spirit, and, for the purpose of intimidating the people and the Senate, they employed, instead of twelve lictors, one hundred and twenty. For some days the fear was general, and very soon after they began to disregard the Senate and to beat the people; and if any of them had been maltreated by one Decemvir and appealed for redress to another, he was treated worse on that appeal than he had been in the first instance; so that the people, having become sensible of their error, began, full of affliction, to look for help to the nobles, "there to catch a breath of liberty where before they had feared servitude, to avoid which they had brought the republic to this condition." To the nobles this affliction of the people was welcome, for they hoped that, "wearied of the existing state of things, they would themselves come to desire the re-establishment of the Consuls." The last days of the year now had come, and the additional two tables of the laws were made, but not yet published. The Decemvirs took occasion thence to continue the exercise of their office, and began to use violence in order to retain the government, and to make the young nobles their satellites, upon whom they bestowed the possessions of those whom they condemned; "by which gifts these youths were corrupted, so as to prefer their own license to the general liberty."

It happened at this time that the Sabines and Volscians began a war against the Romans; the apprehension of which made the Decemvirs sensible of the weakness of their government, for without the Senate they could not make war, and to assemble it seemed to them the loss of their authority. Compelled by necessity, however, they resolved upon doing so, and having assembled the Senate, many of the Senators, and particularly Valerius and Horatius, spoke strongly against the arrogance of the Ten; and their authority would have been entirely destroyed had it not been that the Senate, on account of the jealousy of the people, was unwilling to display its authority; thinking that, if the Decemvirs resigned their office voluntarily, the Tribunes of the people might possibly be re-established. They resolved, therefore upon the war, and two armies were put into the field, commanded in part by the Decemvirs. Appius remained in Rome to conduct the government of the city; it was then that he became enamored of Virginia, and on his attempting to carry her off by force, her father Virginius killed her to save her from her ravisher. This provoked violent disturbances in Rome and in the army, who, having been joined by the people of Rome, marched to the Mons Sacer, where they remained until the Decemvirs abdicated their magistracy, and the Consuls and Tribunes were re-established, and Rome was restored to its ancient liberty and form of government.

Here we must note that the necessity of creating the tyranny of the Decemvirs in Rome arose from the same causes that generally produce tyrannies in cities; that is to say, the too great desire of the people to be free, and the equally too great desire of the nobles to dominate. And if the two parties do not agree to secure liberty by law, and either the one or the other throws all its influence in favor of one man, then a tyranny is the natural result. The people and the nobles of Rome agreed to create the Decemvirs, and to endow them with such great powers, from the desire which the one party had to destroy the consular office, and the other that of the Tribunes. Having created the Ten, it seemed to the people that Appius had come over to them and would aid them to keep the nobility down, and therefore they supported him. Now when a people goes so far as to commit the error of giving power to one man so that he may defeat those whom they hate, and if this man be shrewd, it will always end in his becoming their tyrant. For with the support of the people he will be enabled to destroy the nobility, and after these are crushed he will not fail in turn to crush the people; and by the time that they become sensible of their own enslavement, they will have no one to look to for succor. This is the course which all those have followed who have imposed tyrannies upon republics. And if Appius had done the same, his despotism would have had more vitality, and would not have been overthrown so quickly; but he did exactly the reverse, and could not have acted with more imprudence. For to hold his despotic authority he made himself the enemy of those who had given it to him, and who could have maintained him in it; and he equally made himself the friend of those who had in no way contributed to it, and who could do nothing to keep him in it; and he ruined those who were his friends, and sought to make those his friends who never could become so. For although it is the nature of the nobility to desire to dominate, yet those who have no share in such domination are the enemies of the tyrant, who can never win them all over to him, because of their extreme ambition and avarice, which are so great that the tyrant can never have riches and honors enough to bestow to satisfy them all. And thus Appius, in abandoning the people and allying himself with the nobles, committed a manifest error, both for the reasons above stated, and because, to hold a government by violence, it is necessary that the oppressor should be more powerful than the oppressed. Whence it is that those tyrants who have the masses for friends and the nobles for enemies are more secure in the possession of their power, because their despotism is sustained by a greater force than that of those who have the people for their enemies and the nobles for their friends. For with the support of the people his internal forces suffice to sustain him, as was the case with Nabis, the tyrant of Sparta, when he was assailed by all Greece and the Romans; he made sure of the few nobles, and having the people his friends he succeeded in defending himself by their aid, which he never would have been able to do had the people been hostile to him. But the internal forces of the other class, being but few in numbers, are insufficient to maintain him, and therefore it becomes necessary to look for support elsewhere; and this may be of three different kinds. One is to have a body guard composed of foreigners; another is to arm the people of the country, and have them serve in place of the people of the city; and the third is to form an alliance with powerful neighbors able to defend you. By carefully employing these means a tyrant may still be able to maintain himself, notwithstanding that the people are opposed to him. But Appius could not arm the country people for his support, the country and city of Rome being one and the same thing; and what he might have done he knew not how to do, and so his power was lost at the very outset. Both the Senate and the people of Rome committed the greatest errors in the creation of the Decemvirate; and although we have maintained, in speaking of the Dictator, that only self-constituted authorities, and never those created by the people, are dangerous to liberty, yet when the people do create a magistracy, they should do it in such a way that the magistrates should have some hesitation before they abuse their powers. But the people of Rome, instead of establishing checks to prevent the Decemvirs from employing their authority for evil, removed all control, and made the Ten the only magistracy in Rome; abrogating all the others, because of the excessive eagerness of the Senate to get rid of the Tribunes, and that of the people to destroy the consulate. This blinded them so that both contributed to provoke the disorders that resulted from the Decemvirate. "For," as King Ferdinand said, "men often act like certain small birds of prey, who, prompted by their nature, pursue their victims so eagerly that they do not see the larger bird above them, ready to pounce down upon and kill them."

This discourse, as we proposed in the beginning, will have shown the error which the Roman people committed in their efforts to save their liberty, as well as the error of Appius in attempting to seize despotic powers.

Chapter XLI

IT IS IMPRUDENT AND UNPROFITABLE SUDDENLY TO CHANGE FROM HUMILITY TO PRIDE, AND FROM GENTLENESS TO CRUELTY

BESIDES the other errors committed by Appius in attempting to maintain his tyranny, that of changing too suddenly from one quality to the extreme opposite was of no little moment. Although his astuteness in deceiving the people by simulating to be of their party was well employed, and equally so the means he used to bring about the reappointment of the Ten, as well as his audacity in nominating himself, contrary to the expectations of the nobles, and in naming colleagues to suit his own purposes; yet it was very ill-judged in him suddenly to change his character, and from having been a friend of the people, all at once to show himself their enemy,—from being humane to become haughty, and from being easy of access to become difficult,—and to do this so suddenly and without excuse that everybody could see the falseness of his soul. For he who for a time has seemed good, and for purposes of his own wants to become bad, should do it gradually, and should seem to be brought to it by the force of circumstances; so that, before his changed nature deprives him of his former friends, he may have gained new ones, and that his authority may not be diminished by the change. Otherwise his deception will be discovered, and he will lose his friends and be ruined.

Chapter XLII

HOW EASILY MEN MAY BE CORRUPTED

In connection with this matter of the Decemvirate, we should notice also how easily men are corrupted and become wicked, although originally good and well educated. This may be observed in those young nobles whom Appius had chosen for his followers, and who, for the small advantages they derived from it, became supporters of his tyranny; also in Quintus Fabius, one of the second Decemvirate, who, having been one of the best of men, but blinded by a little ambition and seduced by the villany of Appius, changed his good habits into the worst, and became like Appius himself. All this, if carefully studied by the legislators of republics and monarchies, will make them more prompt in restraining the passions of men, and depriving them of all hopes of being able to do wrong with impunity.

Chapter XLIII

THOSE ONLY WHO COMBAT FOR THEIR OWN GLORY ARE GOOD AND LOYAL SOLDIERS

We will consider in this chapter how great a difference there is between an army that is well disposed, and which fights for its own glory, and one that is ill disposed, and has to fight only for the ambition of another; for whilst the Roman armies were habitually victorious under the Consuls, they were invariably beaten under the Decemvirs. This example in part explains the reasons of the uselessness of mercenary troops, who have nothing to make them fight but the small stipend they receive, which is not and cannot be sufficient to make them loyal, or so devoted as to be willing to die for you. For armies that have no such affection towards him for whom they fight as to make them his partisans, will never have bravery enough to resist an enemy who has the least courage. And as this love and devotion can only be found in your own subjects, it is necessary for the purpose of holding a government, or to maintain a republic or kingdom, to have your army composed of your own subjects, as will be seen to have been done by all those whose armies have achieved great successes. The Roman armies under the Decemvirs had the same courage as before, but they had not the same disposition, and therefore did not achieve the customary good results. But so soon as the rule of the Decemvirs had been destroyed, and the armies began again to fight as freemen, they became animated by their ancient spirit, and consequently their enterprises resulted happily, as of old.

Chapter XLIV

A MULTITUDE WITHOUT A CHIEF IS USELESS; AND IT IS NOT WELL TO THREATEN BEFORE HAVING THE POWER TO ACT

THE death of Virginia had caused the Roman people to retire, armed, to the Mons Sacer. The Senate sent ambassadors to them to ask by what authority they had abandoned their captains and retired to the mountains, and so highly was the authority of the Senate respected, that, the people being without a chief, no one dared to answer; as Titus

Livius says, "not for want of plenty to say in reply, but because they lacked some one to make the answer for them"; which is a case in point showing the uselessness of a multitude without a head. Virginius perceived this difficulty, and by his order they appointed twenty military Tribunes to act as their chiefs, to answer for them and to confer with the Senate. They demanded that the Senators Valerius and Horatius should be sent to them, and that they would make known their will to them. But these Senators would not go until after the Ten had resigned their magistracy; after which, having arrived at the Mons Sacer, where the people were, these demanded of them the re-establishment of the Tribunes of the people, and that no magistrates should be appointed without an appeal to the people; and, furthermore, that all the Decemvirs should be delivered up to them, as they wanted to burn them alive. Valerius and Horatius approved of their first demands, but objected to the latter as impious, saying, "You condemn cruelty, and fall into the same crime yourselves"; and advised them to say nothing about the Decemvirs, as they themselves would see that their office and authority should be taken from them, and that the people afterwards would not lack opportunity to satisfy their vengeance. From this we plainly see the folly and imprudence of demanding a thing, and saying beforehand that it is intended to be used for evil; and that one should never show one's intentions, but endeavor to obtain one's desires anyhow. For it is enough to ask a man to give up his arms, without telling him that you intend killing him with them; after you have the arms in hand, then you can do your will with them.

Chapter XLV

IT IS A BAD EXAMPLE NOT TO OBSERVE THE LAWS, ESPECIALLY ON THE PART OF THOSE WHO HAVE MADE THEM; AND IT IS DANGEROUS FOR THOSE WHO GOVERN CITIES TO HARASS THE PEOPLE WITH CONSTANT WRONGS

THE agreement between the Senate and the people having been carried into effect, and Rome restored to her ancient form of government, Virginius cited Appius before the people to defend his cause. He appeared accompanied by many nobles. Virginius insisted upon his being imprisoned, whereupon Appius loudly demanded to appeal to the people. Virginius maintained that he was unworthy of the privilege of that appeal, which he had himself destroyed, and not entitled to have for his defenders the very people whom he had offended. Appius replied that the people had no right to violate that appeal which they themselves had instituted with so much jealousy. But he was nevertheless incarcerated, and before the day of judgment came he committed suicide. And although the crimes of Appius merited the highest degree of punishment, yet it was inconsistent with a proper regard for liberty to violate the law, and especially one so recently made. For I think that there can be no worse example in a republic than to make a law and not to observe it; the more so when it is disregarded by the very parties who made it.

In the year 1494 Florence had reformed its government with the aid of Brother Girolamo Savonarola (whose writings exhibit so much learning, prudence, and courage); and amongst other provisions for the security of the citizens a law had been made which permitted an appeal to the people from the decisions which the Council of Eight and the Signoria might render in cases affecting the state, which had involved great discussions and difficulties in its passage. It happened that shortly after its confirmation five citizens were condemned to death by the Signoria on account of crimes against the state; and when these men wished to appeal to the people, they were not allowed to do so, in manifest disregard of the law. This occurrence did more than anything else to diminish the influence of Savonarola; for if the appeal was useful, then the law should have been observed, and if it was not useful, then it should never have been made. And this circumstance was the more remarked, as Brother Girolamo in his many subsequent preachings never condemned those who had broken the law, and rather excused the act in the manner of one unwilling to condemn what suited his purposes, yet unable to excuse it wholly. Having thus manifested his ambitious and partial spirit, it cost him his reputation and much trouble.

A government also does great wrong constantly to excite the resentment of its subjects by fresh injuries to this or that individual amongst them. This was the case after the Decemvirate, for all the Ten and many other citizens were at different times accused and condemned, so as to create the greatest alarm amongst the nobles, for it seemed as though these condemnations would never cease until the entire nobility should have been destroyed. All this would have produced the worst effects if the Tribune Marcus Duellius had not prevented it by issuing an edict that for the period of one year no one should be allowed to cite or accuse a Roman citizen, and this reassured the whole nobility. These examples show how dangerous it is for a republic or a prince to keep the minds of their subjects in a state of apprehension by pains and penalties constantly suspended over their heads. And certainly no more pernicious course could be pursued; for men who are kept in doubt and uncertainty as to their lives will resort to every kind of measure to secure themselves against danger, and will necessarily become more audacious and inclined to violent changes. It is important, therefore, either never to attack any one, or to inflict punishment by a single act of rigor, and afterwards to reassure the public mind by such acts as will restore calmness and confidence.

Chapter XLVI

MEN RISE FROM ONE AMBITION TO ANOTHER: FIRST, THEY SEEK TO SECURE THEMSELVES AGAINST ATTACK, AND THEN THEY ATTACK OTHERS

THE people of Rome, having recovered their liberty, resumed their original rank in the state, and obtained even more influence than before by means of a number of laws that confirmed their power. It seemed reasonable, therefore, that Rome should now enjoy a period of quiet. But experience proved the contrary, for every day there were new dissensions and disorders. As Titus Livius has most judiciously given the causes that produced these, it seems to me proper to quote his own words, where he says: "The pride of the people or of the nobles always increased as the opposite party was humbled; when the people kept within proper bounds, the young nobles began to insult them, and the Tribunes could do little to prevent it, being themselves outraged. The nobles, on the other hand, although they felt that their young men were too insolent, yet, seeing that the restraints imposed by law could not be observed, preferred that they should be transgressed by their own party rather than by the people. And thus the desire of liberty caused one party to raise themselves in proportion as they oppressed the other. And it is the course of such movements that men, in attempting to avoid fear themselves, give others cause for fear; and the injuries which they ward off from themselves they inflict upon others, as though there were a necessity either to oppress or to be oppressed." In this we see one of the modes in which republics are brought to ruin, and how men rise from one ambition to another; and we recognize the truth of the sentence which Sallust puts into the mouth of Cæsar, "that all evil examples have their origin in good beginnings." The ambitious citizens of a republic seek in the first instance (as we have said above) to make themselves sure against the attacks, not only of individuals, but even of the magistrates. To enable them to do this, they seek to gain friends, either by apparently honest ways, or by assisting men with money, or by defending them against the powerful; and as this seems virtuous, almost everybody is readily deceived by it, and therefore no one opposes it, until the ambitious individual has, without hindrance, grown so powerful that private citizens fear him and the magistrates treat him with consideration. And when he has risen to that point, no one at the beginning having interfered with his greatness, it becomes in the end most dangerous to attempt to put him down, for the reasons I have given above when speaking of the danger of trying to abate an evil that has already attained a considerable growth in a city; so that in the end the matter is reduced to this, that you must endeavor to destroy the evil at the risk of sudden ruin, or, by allowing it to go on, submit to manifest servitude, unless the death of the individual or some other accident intervenes to rid the state of him. For when it has once come to that point that the citizens and the magistrates are afraid to offend him and his adherents, it will afterwards not require much effort on his part to make them render judgments and attack persons according to his will. For this reason republics should make it one of their aims to watch that none of their citizens should be allowed to do harm on pretence of doing good, and that no one should acquire an influence that would injure instead of promoting liberty; of which we shall speak more at length in another place.

Chapter XLVII

ALTHOUGH MEN ARE APT TO DECEIVE THEMSELVES IN GENERAL MATTERS, YET THEY RARELY DO SO IN PARTICULARS

THE people of Rome, as has been related above, having become disgusted with the name of Consul, wanted either to have the Consuls chosen from amongst the plebeians, or that their powers should be limited. The nobility, unwilling to discredit the consular dignity by either of such changes, took a middle course, and consented that four Tribunes should be created, with consular powers, who might be taken either from the nobles or the plebeians. This satisfied the people, as it seemed to destroy the consulate, and to give them a share in the highest magistracy. This gave rise to a remarkable case; for when the election of these Tribunes came on, and the people might have elected all plebeians, they chose, instead, all from the patricians, whence Titus Livius says: "The result of this election teaches us how different minds are during the contentions for liberty and for honors, from what they are when they have to give an im-

partial judgment after the contest is over." In examining
whence this difference arises, I believe that it comes from
this, that men are apt to deceive themselves upon general
matters, but not so much so when they come to particulars.
As a general thing, the Roman people believed themselves
entitled to the consulate, being the majority in the city, and
having to bear more of the dangers of war, and as it was the
vigor of their arms that preserved the liberty of Rome and
established its power. And (as I have said) as their desire
seemed to them reasonable, they were resolved to obtain it
by any means. But when they had to judge of the particular
qualifications of their individual candidates, they discovered
their unfitness, and therefore decided that not one of them
was worthy of that dignity, to which as a body they considered themselves entitled. Thus ashamed of their own candidates, they had recourse to those whom they deemed
worthy of the office. Titus Livius, naturally admiring this
decision, says: "Where will you find nowadays this modesty
and equity, this loftiness of soul, which in those days per-
vaded the whole people?"

In corroboration of this example we may adduce another
notable one which occurred in Capua, after Hannibal had
defeated the Romans at Cannæ. Whilst all Italy rose up in
consequence of this defeat, Capua still remained in a state
of insubordination, because of the hatred that existed between the people and the Senate. Pacovius Calanus being at
that time one of the supreme magistrates, and foreseeing
the dangers that would result from the disorders in that city,
resolved by means of the authority of his office to try and
reconcile the people and the Senate; with this purpose he
caused the Senate to be assembled, and stated to them the
animosity which the people felt towards them, and the
danger to which they were exposed of being massacred by

them if the city were given up to Hannibal in consequence of the defeat of the Romans. He then added, that, if they would leave it to him to manage the matter, he would find means of restoring harmony between the two orders; but that, for this purpose, he would shut them up in their palace, and by seemingly putting them into the power of the people he would save them. The Senators yielded to his suggestion; whereupon Pacovius shut the Senate up in their palace, and then assembled the people and said to them that "the time had arrived when they might subdue the pride of the nobles and revenge themselves for the injuries received at their hands, and that he held the Senate shut up in their palace for this purpose. But believing that they would be unwilling to allow the city to be without a government, it would be necessary, before killing the old Senators, to choose new ones; and that therefore he had put the names of all the Senators into an urn, and would proceed to draw them in their presence, and that one after another those who were drawn should die, after their successors had been elected." And when the first was drawn and his name proclaimed the people raised a great noise, calling him proud, arrogant, and cruel; but when Pacovius asked them to choose another in his place, the whole assembly became quiet, and after a little time one was named by the people; but at the mention of his name some began to whistle, some to laugh, some to speak ill of him in one way, and some in another; and thus, one after another, those that were named were pronounced by them unworthy of the senatorial dignity, so that Pacovius took occasion to speak to them as follows: "Since you are of the opinion that the city would fare ill without a Senate, and as you cannot agree upon the successors of the old Senators, it seems to me it would be well for you to become reconciled with the present Senate, for the fear to which they have been subjected has in great measure humbled them, and you will now find in them that humanity which you in vain look for elsewhere." This suggestion prevailed, and a reconciliation between the two orders followed, and the people, when they came to act upon particulars, discovered the error into which they had fallen in looking at the subject in general.

After the expulsion in 1414 of the principal citizens from Florence, there being no regular government, but rather a certain ambitious license, so that things were going from worse to worse, many of the popular party, seeing the ruin of the city, and not comprehending the cause of it, attributed it to a few powerful citizens, who fomented these disorders so as to enable them to make a government to suit themselves, and to deprive them of their liberty. They went through the Loggia and public places speaking against those prominent citizens, and threatening that, if ever they should themselves become members of the Signoria, they would unveil their deceitful practices, and would punish them for it. It happened in several instances that these citizens did attain to the highest magistracy, and when they had risen to that place, and were enabled to see matters more closely, they discovered the real causes of the disorders, and the dangers that threatened the state, as well as the difficulty of remedying them. And seeing that the times, and not the men, caused the disorders, they promptly changed their opinions and actions, because the knowledge of things in particular had removed from their minds that delusion into which they had fallen by looking at things in general. So that those who at first had heard them speak whilst they were still private citizens, and afterwards saw them remain inactive when they had risen to the supreme magistracy, believed that this was caused, not by the real knowledge of things, but by their having been perverted and corrupted by the great. And as this happened with many, and repeatedly, it gave rise to a saying, "That these people have one mind in the public places, and another mind in the palace." Reflecting now upon all that has been said, we see that the quickest way of opening the eyes of the people is to find the means of making them descend to particulars, seeing that to look at things only in a general way deceives them; as Pacovius did with regard to Capua and the Roman Senate. I believe also that we may conclude from it that no wise man should ever disregard the popular judgment upon particular matters, such as the distribution of honors and dignities; for in these things the people never deceive themselves, or, if they do, it is much less frequently than a small body would do, who had been especially charged with such distributions. Nor does it seem to me superfluous to show in the following chapter the course which the Senate took to deceive the people in the distributions that devolved upon them.

Chapter XLVIII

ONE OF THE MEANS OF PREVENTING AN IMPORTANT MAGISTRACY FROM BEING CONFERRED UPON A VILE AND WICKED INDIVIDUAL IS TO HAVE IT APPLIED FOR BY ONE STILL MORE VILE AND WICKED, OR BY THE MOST NOBLE AND DESERVING IN THE STATE

WHEN the Roman Senate apprehended lest the Tribunes with consular powers should be taken from amongst the plebeians, they adopted one of the two following methods: either they caused the most distinguished and influential men of Rome to become candidates, or by suitable means they bribed some of the most sordid and ignoble to come forward as candidates at the same time with the better quality of plebeians, who usually asked for these offices. This latter course caused the people to be ashamed of bestowing them upon such candidates, and the former course made them ashamed to refuse them to such honorable citizens. All of which corroborates what I have maintained in the preceding chapter, that in general matters the people are apt to deceive themselves, but rarely in particulars.

Chapter XLIX

IF CITIES WHICH FROM THEIR BEGINNING HAVE ENJOYED LIBERTY, LIKE ROME, HAVE FOUND DIFFICULTIES IN DEVISING LAWS THAT WOULD PRESERVE THEIR LIBERTIES, THOSE THAT HAVE HAD THEIR ORIGIN IN SERVITUDE FIND IT IMPOSSIBLE TO SUCCEED IN MAKING SUCH LAWS

THE progress of the Roman republic demonstrates how difficult it is in the constitution of a republic to provide necessary laws for the maintenance of liberty; for notwithstanding the many laws established, first by Romulus, and afterwards by Numa, by Tullus Hostilius, and by Servius, and finally by the Decemvirs created for that purpose, yet fresh necessities constantly developed themselves in the management of the affairs of that city, which made it indispensable to enact new laws. This was the case when they instituted the Censorship, which was one of the most important provisions that helped to preserve the liberties of Rome, so long as liberty existed there. For the Censors being the supreme arbiters of the manners and customs of the Romans, they became the most potent instrument in retarding the progress of corruption in Rome. But it was a serious mistake to create these Censors for a term of five years, although it was corrected after a brief time by the prudence of the Dictator Mamercus, who by a new law reduced the term of office of that new magistracy to eighteen months; which so irritated the Censors then in office that they deprived Mamercus of the right of entrance into the Senate, which act was much blamed by the people as well as by the patricians. And as history does not inform us whether Mamercus had any remedy against this, we must assume either that history is defective upon this point, or that the Roman laws in that respect were not good; for it is not well that a republic should be constituted in such fashion that a citizen can be oppressed without recourse for having promulgated a law for the benefit of liberty.

But to return to our subject, I say that the institution of this new magistracy gives rise to the reflection, that if a city, which from its origin has enjoyed liberty but has of itself become corrupt, has great difficulties in devising good laws for the maintenance of liberty, it is not to be wondered at if a city that had its origin in servitude finds it, not only difficult, but actually impossible, ever to organize a government that will secure its liberty and tranquillity. This, as will be seen, was the case with the city of Florence, which from her first beginning had been subjected to the Roman Empire, and, having always existed under a foreign government, remained for a long time in this subject condition without ever attempting to free herself. And when afterwards the opportunity occurred for her to gain her liberty in a measure, she began by making a constitution that was a mixture of her old and bad institutions with new ones, and consequently could not be good. And thus she has gone on for the two hundred years of which we have any reliable account, without ever having a government that could really be called a republic. The difficulties which Florence experienced have ever been the same in those cities whose origin was similar to hers. And although Florence repeatedly gave ample authority, by public and free suffrage, to a few of her citizens to reform the government, yet these never organized it for the general good, but always with the view of benefiting their own party, which, instead of establishing order in the city, only tended to increase the disorders. And to illustrate my argument by some particular instance, I will observe that one of the most important points to be considered by him who wishes to establish a republic is the question in whose hands he shall place the power over the life and death of its citizens. The constitution of Rome was excellent upon this point, for there an appeal to the people was the ordinary practice, and when an important case occurred, where it would have been perilous to delay execution by such an appeal, they had recourse to the Dictator, who had the right of immediate execution; this, however, was resorted to only in cases of extreme necessity. But in Florence, and in other cities who like her had their origin in servitude, the power of life and death was lodged in the hands of a stranger, sent by the prince to exercise that power. When these cities afterwards became free, they left that power in the hands of a foreigner, whom they called "the Captain." But the facility with which he could be corrupted by the powerful citizens made this a most pernicious system; and in the course of the mutations of their governments that system was changed, and a council of eight citizens was appointed to perform the functions of the Captain; which only made matters worse, for the reason which we have given elsewhere, that a tribunal of a few is always under the control of a few powerful citizens.

Venice knew well how to guard against such an abuse. There the Council of Ten had power to punish any citizen without appeal; but as this number would have been insufficient to punish the powerful, although they had the authority, they established the Council of Forty. Moreover the Council of the Pregadi (which is the highest council) had the power of capital punishment. So that where there was an occasion there was also not wanting a tribunal capable of keeping the most powerful in check. It is no wonder, then,—seeing that even in Rome, where the laws had been made by herself with the aid of her most sagacious citizens, every day fresh occasions arose that made it necessary to have new laws for the protection of liberty,—that in other cities whose beginnings were vicious such difficulties should present themselves as made a proper organization impossible.

Chapter L

NO COUNCIL OR MAGISTRATE SHOULD HAVE IT IN THEIR POWER TO STOP THE PUBLIC BUSINESS OF A CITY

WHEN Quintius Cincinnatus and Julius Mentus were Consuls of Rome, a disagreement arose between them, which caused an interruption of all the public business of the state. When this came to the knowledge of the Senate, they advised the creation of a Dictator, who might do what the discord between the Consuls had prevented them from doing. But the Consuls, disagreeing upon every other matter, agreed only in this one thing,—not to appoint a Dictator. So that the Senate, having no alternative, had recourse to the assistance of the Tribunes, who together with the Senate forced the Consuls to obedience. Whence we should note, in the first instance, the usefulness of the tribunate, which served not only to restrain the violence of the nobles against the people, but also against each other; and, secondly, that the institutions of a city never should place it in the power of a few to interrupt all the important business of the republic. For instance, if you give to a council authority to distribute honors and offices, or devolve upon any magistracy the administration of a certain business, it is proper to impose upon them either the necessity of doing it under all circumstances, or to provide that, in case of their not doing it themselves, it can and shall be done by some one else; otherwise, the constitution would be defective upon this point, and likely to involve the state in great dangers, as we have seen would have been the case in Rome, if they could not have opposed the authority of the Tribunes to the obstinacy of the Consuls.

In the republic of Venice the Grand Council distributed the honors and the offices; it happened several times that this body, from discontent or some erroneous suggestions, did not appoint successors to the magistrates of the city or of the provinces. This caused the greatest possible disorders, for all of a sudden both the city and its subject provinces lacked their legitimate judges; nor could they obtain anything if the majority of the council was not either satisfied or deceived. And this inconvenience would have led to the worst consequences for the city, if the prudent citizens had not provided against it, by availing of the first convenient occasion to make a law that all the public functionaries in the city and in the provinces should never vacate their offices until their successors had been elected and were ready to fill their places. And thus they deprived the Grand Council of the power to expose the republic to great dangers by arresting all public business.

Chapter LI

A REPUBLIC OR A PRINCE MUST FEIGN TO DO OF THEIR OWN LIBERALITY THAT TO WHICH NECESSITY COMPELS THEM

PRUDENT men make the best of circumstances in their actions, and, although constrained by necessity to a certain course, make it appear as if done from their own liberality. This discretion was wisely used by the Roman Senate when they resolved to pay the soldiery out of the public treasury, who before had been obliged to maintain themselves. But as the Senate perceived that war could not be carried on for a length of time in this manner, as they could neither lay siege to places nor move armies to a distance, and judging it necessary to be able to do both, they resolved to pay them from the public funds; yet they did it in such a manner as to gain credit for that to which necessity compelled them; and this favor was so acceptable to the populace that Rome was wild with joy, thinking it a great benefit, which they had never expected and would not have sought themselves. And although the Tribunes endeavored to expose this delusion, showing that it made the burden of the people heavier instead of easier, still they could not prevent its acceptance by the people. This burden was further increased by the manner in which the Senate levied the taxes, imposing the heaviest and largest upon the nobility, and requiring them to pay first of all.

Chapter LII

THERE IS NO SURER AND LESS OBJECTIONABLE MODE OF REPRES-
SING THE INSOLENCE OF AN INDIVIDUAL AMBITIOUS OF POWER,
WHO ARISES IN A REPUBLIC, THAN TO FORESTALL HIM IN THE
WAYS BY WHICH HE EXPECTS TO ARRIVE AT THAT POWER

WE have seen in the preceding chapter how much credit
the patricians gained with the people of Rome by the appar-
ent benefit bestowed upon them, both by the pay granted
to the soldiers as well as by the manner of distributing the
imposts. If the nobility had understood how to maintain this
feeling, all causes for further disturbances would have been
removed, and the Tribunes would have lost the influence
which they had over the people of Rome. For in truth there
is no better nor easier mode in republics, and especially in
such as are corrupt, for successfully opposing the ambition
of any citizen, than to occupy in advance of him those ways
by which he expects to attain the rank he aims at. If this
mode had been employed by the adversaries of Cosimo de'
Medici, it would have been much better than to expel him
from Florence; for if they had adopted his plan of favoring
the people, they would have succeeded without any disturbances or violence in depriving him of the weapons
which he himself employed with so much skill.

Pietro Soderini had obtained great influence in the city of
Florence by no other means than by gaining the good will
of the people, which gave him the reputation of being a
great friend of liberty; it would have been a much easier
and more honest way for those who envied his reputation
and influence, as well as less hazardous for themselves and

less injurious to the city, to have forestalled him in the ways
by which he gained his power, rather than to oppose him in
such manner as to involve in his destruction also the ruin
of the whole republic. For if they had taken from his hands
the weapon that gave him his strength, (which might easily
have been done,) they could have opposed him boldly and
without suspicion in all the councils and public assemblies.
It may be said, perhaps, that if those citizens who hated
Pietro committed an error in leaving him the means of
gaining such influence with the people, Pietro himself erred
in turn in not seizing in advance the means which his adversaries employed to make him feared as a dangerous man;
which was excusable, however, in Soderini, as it would have
been difficult for him to have done so, nor would it have
been honest in him, for the means employed against him
consisted merely in favoring the Medici. It was in that way
that his enemies attacked and finally ruined him. Pietro
could not therefore in honesty have adopted a course by
which through his influence he would have destroyed that
liberty of which he was considered the especial guardian.
Such a change to the side of the Medici on the part of
Soderini could not have been made suddenly, nor could it
have been kept secret. And the very moment that it should
have been discovered that he had become friendly to the
Medici, he would have become suspect and odious to the
people, and would thus have afforded his enemies much
better opportunity for destroying him than they had had
previously.

Before deciding upon any course, therefore, men should
well consider the objections and dangers which it presents;
and if its perils exceed its advantages, they should avoid it,
even though it had been in accordance with their previous
determination; for to do otherwise would expose them to a

similar experience as that of Cicero, who, wishing to destroy
the credit and power of Mark Antony, only increased it.
For Antony, having been declared an enemy of the Senate,
had collected a large army, composed in great part of soldiers who had served under Cæsar; Cicero wishing to withdraw these soldiers from him, advised the Senate to employ
Octavian, and to send him with the army and the Consuls
against Antony, alleging that so soon as the soldiers of Antony should hear the name of Octavian, the nephew of
Cæsar, and who had himself called Cæsar, they would leave
the former and join Octavian; and that Antony, thus bereft
of support, would easily be crushed. But it resulted just the
other way, for Antony managed to win Octavian over to
himself, who, abandoning Cicero and the Senate, allied
himself with the former, which brought about the complete
ruin of the party of the patricians. This might easily have
been foreseen, and therefore they should not have followed
the advice of Cicero, but should have borne in mind the
name and character of him who had vanquished his enemies with so much glory, and seized for himself the sovereignty of Rome; and then they might have known that
they could not expect from his adherents anything favorable
to liberty.

Chapter LIII

HOW BY THE DELUSIONS OF SEEMING GOOD THE PEOPLE ARE
OFTEN MISLED TO DESIRE THEIR OWN RUIN; AND HOW THEY
ARE FREQUENTLY INFLUENCED BY GREAT HOPES AND BRAVE
PROMISES

AFTER the capture of the city of the Veienti, the Roman
people became possessed of the idea that it would be ad-

vantageous for the city of Rome if one half of its inhabitants were to go and settle at Veii; arguing that, inasmuch as that city was rich in lands and houses and near to Rome, one half of the Roman citizens might thus enrich themselves without in any way disturbing by their proximity the public affairs of Rome. This project seemed to the Senate and the most sagacious men of Rome useless, and fraught with danger, so much so that they declared openly that they would rather suffer death than give their consent. When the subject came to be discussed, the people became so much excited against the Senate that it would have led to violence and bloodshed, had not the Senate sheltered itself behind some of the oldest and most esteemed citizens, the reverence for whom restrained the people from carrying their insolence farther. Here we have to note two things; first, that the people often, deceived by an illusive good, desire their own ruin, and, unless they are made sensible of the evil of the one and the benefit of the other course by some one in whom they have confidence, they will expose the republic to infinite peril and damage. And if it happens that the people have no confidence in any one, as sometimes will be the case when they have been deceived before by events or men, then it will inevitably lead to the ruin of the state. Dante says upon this point in his discourse "On Monarchy," that the people often shout, "Life to our death, and death to our life!" It is this want of confidence on the part of the people that causes good measures to be often rejected in republics, as we have related above of the Venetians, who when attacked by so many enemies could not make up their minds to conciliate some of them by giving to them what they had taken from others; it was this that brought the war upon them, and caused the other powers to form a league against them before their final ruin.

If we consider now what is easy and what difficult to persuade a people to, we may make this distinction: either what you wish to persuade them to represents at first sight gain or loss, or it seems brave or cowardly. And if you propose to them anything that upon its face seems profitable and courageous, though there be really a loss concealed under it which may involve the ruin of the republic, the multitude will ever be most easily persuaded to it. But if the measure proposed seems doubtful and likely to cause loss, then it will be difficult to persuade the people to it, even though the benefit and welfare of the republic were concealed under it. All this is supported by numerous examples amongst the Romans as well as strangers, and both in modern and in ancient times.

It was this that produced the unfavorable opinion in Rome of Fabius Maximus, who could not persuade the people of Rome that it would be advantageous for that republic to proceed slowly with the war, and to bear the assaults of Hannibal without engaging in battle with him; because the Roman people considered this course as cowardly, and did not see the advantages that would be gained by it, and Fabius had not the faculty of demonstrating these to them. The people are apt to be so blinded upon questions of courage that, although the Roman people had committed the great error of giving authority to the commander of the cavalry of the army of Fabius to engage in battle contrary to the will of Fabius, so that the Roman camp would have been broken up but for the prudence of Fabius, which remedied the error; yet this experience did not suffice them, for they subsequently made Varro Consul, for no other reason than because he had proclaimed in all the streets and public places of Rome that, if only authority were given to him, he would cut Hannibal to pieces. This occasioned the battle and defeat of Cannæ, and almost caused the ruin of Rome. I will adduce another striking example upon this point. Hannibal had been eight or ten years in Italy, and had drenched the soil of the whole country with the blood of the Romans, when there presented himself before the Senate one M. Centenius Penula, a man of the vilest character, (although he had held some command in the militia,) and offered, if they would give him authority to collect an army of volunteers in whatever place in Italy he pleased, he would in the least possible time deliver Hannibal dead or alive into their hands. This proposition seemed most foolhardy to the Senate; nevertheless, fearing that, if they refused him and the proposition should afterwards become known to the people, it might give rise to disturbances or jealousy and ill feeling against the senatorial order, they acceded to the request of Penula, preferring to expose all who might follow him to the greatest danger, rather than run the risk of causing fresh discontents amongst the people; well knowing how readily they would accept such a proposition, and how difficult it would be to dissuade them from it. Centenius Penula therefore went with an unorganized and undisciplined crowd to find Hannibal, and no sooner did he meet him than himself and all his followers were routed and cut to pieces.

In the city of Athens in Greece, Nicias, one of the most wise and prudent of men, could not persuade the people that it would not be well for them to make war upon Sicily; and the Athenians resolved upon it, contrary to the advice of their wisest men, and the ruin of Athens was the consequence. When Scipio was made Consul, and wished to have the province of Africa, he promised to all the destruction of Carthage; and when the Senate declined to accord him that province, because of the adverse opinion of Fabius

Maximus, he threatened to bring the matter before the people, well knowing that similar propositions always find favor with the people.

We may also cite on this point some examples drawn from the history of our own city of Florence. Messer Ercole Bentivogli, commander of the Florentine troops, and Antonio Giacomini, after having defeated Bartolommeo d' Alviano at San Vincenti, went to lay siege to Pisa, which enterprise was resolved upon by the people in consequence of the brave promises made by Messer Ercole, although many of the most prudent citizens objected, but could not prevent it, being carried away by the general will of the people, who relied upon the commander's brilliant promises.

I say then that there is no easier way to ruin a republic, where the people have power, than to involve them in daring enterprises; for where the people have influence they will always be ready to engage in them, and no contrary opinion will prevent them. But if such enterprises cause the ruin of states, they still more frequently cause the ruin of the particular citizens who are placed at the head to conduct them. For when defeat comes, instead of the successes which the people expected, they charge it neither upon the ill fortune or incompetence of their leaders, but upon their wickedness and ignorance; and generally either kill, imprison, or exile them, as happened to many Carthaginian and Athenian generals. Their previous victories are of no advantage to them, for they are all cancelled by present defeat, as was the case with our Giacomini, who, in consequence of his failure to take Pisa, which the people expected, as he had promised it, fell into such disgrace with the people that, notwithstanding his previous good services, his life was saved only through the humanity of the authorities, who protected him against the people.

Chapter LIV

HOW MUCH INFLUENCE A GREAT MAN HAS IN RESTRAINING AN EXCITED MULTITUDE

THE second thing to note in connection with the subject of the preceding chapter is, that nothing is so apt to restrain an excited multitude as the reverence inspired by some grave and dignified man of authority who opposes them; and therefore it is not without reason that Virgil says:—

> "And when they saw a man of grave aspect
> And full of virtue and of years,
> At once they all were hushed,
> And, listening, stood with eager ears."

Therefore whoever is at the head of an army, or whoever happens to be a magistrate in a city where sedition has broken out, should present himself before the multitude with all possible grace and dignity, and attired with all the insignia of his rank, so as to inspire the more respect. A few years since Florence was divided into two factions, who called themselves the Frateschi and the Arrabiati (madmen). On coming to arms, the Frateschi were beaten; amongst these was Paolantonio Soderini, a citizen then in high repute. During these disturbances the people went armed to his house with the intent of sacking it. Messer Francesco, his brother, then Bishop of Volterra, and now Cardinal, happened by chance to be in the house; and so soon as he heard the noise and saw the crowd, he dressed himself in his best garments, and over them he put his episcopal chasuble, and then went to meet the armed mob, and by the influence of his person and his words he stopped their further violence, which was much talked about and praised in the city for many days.

I conclude, then, that there is no better or safer way of appeasing an excited mob than the presence of some man of imposing appearance and highly respected. And to come back to the preceding text, we see with what obstinacy the Roman people had taken up the plan of going to Veii, because they deemed it advantageous and did not perceive the danger it involved; and how the discontent of the people, which had been excited by the opposition of the Senate to this project, would have led to violence, had not their fury been restrained by the most grave and reverend Senators.

Chapter LV

PUBLIC AFFAIRS ARE EASILY MANAGED IN A CITY WHERE THE
BODY OF THE PEOPLE IS NOT CORRUPT; AND WHERE EQUALITY
EXISTS, THERE NO PRINCIPALITY CAN BE ESTABLISHED; NOR
CAN A REPUBLIC BE ESTABLISHED WHERE THERE IS NO EQUALITY

HAVING sufficiently discussed the subject as to what is to be hoped and feared for states that are corrupt, it seems to me not amiss now to examine a resolution of the Senate of Rome in relation to the vow which Camillus had made, to give the tenth part of the booty taken from the Veienti to Apollo. These spoils having fallen into the hands of the Roman people, and there being no other way of having a correct account of it, the Roman Senate issued an edict that every one should bring to the public treasury one tenth part of the booty he had received. And although this decree was not carried into effect, the Senate having devised other ways and means for satisfying Apollo and the people, nevertheless we can see from that resolution how entirely the Senate trusted in the honesty of the people; and how confident they were that no one would fail to return exactly what had been ordered by that edict. And on the other hand we see how the people never for a moment thought of evading it in any way by giving less than what they ought to give, and how they preferred rather to relieve themselves of this imposition by open demonstrations of indignation. This example, together with the many others heretofore cited, proves how much probity and religion these people had, and how much good there was to be hoped for from them. And truly, where this probity does not exist, no good is to be expected, as in fact it is vain to look for anything good from those countries which we see nowadays so corrupt, as is the case above all others with Italy. France and Spain also have their share of corruption, and if we do not see so many disorders and troubles in those countries as is the case daily in Italy, it is not so much owing to the goodness of their people, in which they are greatly deficient, as to the fact that they have each a king who keeps them united not only by his virtue, but also by the institutions of those kingdoms, which are as yet preserved pure.

In Germany alone do we see that probity and religion still exist largely amongst the people, in consequence of which many republics exist there in the full enjoyment of liberty, observing their laws in such manner that no one from within or without could venture upon an attempt to master them. And in proof that the ancient virtue still prevails there in great part, I will cite an example similar to that given above of the Senate and people of Rome. When these republics have occasion to spend any considerable amount of money for public account, their magistrates or councils, who have authority in these matters, impose upon all the inhabitants a tax of one or two per cent of their possessions. When such a resolution has been passed according to the laws of the country, every citizen presents himself before the collectors of this impost, and, after having taken an oath to pay the just amount, deposits in a strong-box provided for the purpose the sum which according to his conscience he ought to pay, without any one's witnessing what he pays. From this we may judge of the extent of the probity and religion that still exist amongst those people. And we must presume that every one pays the true amount, for if this were not the case the impost would not yield the amount intended according to the estimates based upon former impositions; the fraud would thus be discovered, and other means would be employed to collect the amount required. This honesty is the more to be admired as it is so very rare that it is found only in that country; and this results from two causes. The one is, that the Germans have no great commerce with their neighbors, few strangers coming amongst them, and they rarely visiting foreign countries, but being content to remain at home and to live on what their country produces, and to clothe themselves with the wool from their own flocks, which takes away all occasion for intimate intercourse with strangers and all opportunity of corruption. Thus they have been prevented from adopting either French, Spanish, or Italian customs, and these nations are the great corrupters of the world. The other cause is, that those republics which have thus preserved their political existence uncorrupted do not permit any of their citizens to be or to live in the manner of gentlemen, but rather maintain amongst them a perfect equality, and are the most decided enemies of the lords and gentlemen that exist in the country; so that, if by chance any of them fall into their hands, they kill them, as being the chief promoters of all corruption and troubles.

And to explain more clearly what is meant by the term gentlemen, I say that those are called gentlemen who live idly upon the proceeds of their extensive possessions, without devoting themselves to agriculture or any other useful pursuit to gain a living. Such men are pernicious to any country or republic; but more pernicious even than these are such as have, besides their other possessions, castles which they command, and subjects who obey them. This class of men abound in the kingdom of Naples, in the Roman territory, in the Romagna, and in Lombardy; whence it is that no republic has ever been able to exist in those countries, nor have they been able to preserve any regular political existence, for that class of men are everywhere enemies of all civil government. And to attempt the establishment of a republic in a country so constituted would be impossible. The only way to establish any kind of order there is to found a monarchical government; for where the body of the people is so thoroughly corrupt that the laws are powerless for restraint, it becomes necessary to establish some superior power which, with a royal hand, and with full and absolute powers, may put a curb upon the excessive ambition and corruption of the powerful. This is verified by the example of Tuscany, where in a comparatively small extent of territory there have for a long time existed three republics, Florence, Sienna, and Lucca; and although the other cities of this territory are in a measure subject to these, yet we see that in spirit and by their institutions they maintain, or attempt to maintain their liberty; all of which is due to the fact that there are in that country no lords possessing castles, and exceedingly few or no gentlemen. On the contrary, there is such a general equality that it would be easy for any man of sagacity, well versed in the ancient forms of civil government, to introduce a republic there; but the misfortunes of that country have been so great that up to the present time no man has arisen who has had the power and ability to do so.

We may then draw the following conclusion from what has been said: that if any one should wish to establish a republic in a country where there are many gentlemen, he will not succeed until he has destroyed them all; and whoever desires to establish a kingdom or principality where liberty and equality prevail, will equally fail, unless he withdraws from that general equality a number of the boldest and most ambitious spirits, and makes gentlemen of them, not merely in name but in fact, by giving to them castles and possessions, as well as money and subjects; so that surrounded by these he may be able to maintain his power, and that by his support they may satisfy their ambition, and the others may be constrained to submit to that yoke to which force alone has been able to subject them. And as in this way definite relations will be established between the ruler and his subjects, each will be maintained in their respective ranks. But to establish a republic in a country better adapted to a monarchy, or a monarchy where a republic would be more suitable, requires a man of rare genius and power, and therefore out of the many that have attempted it but few have succeeded; for the greatness of the enterprise frightens men so that they fail even in the very beginning. Perhaps the opinion which I have expressed, that a republic cannot be established where there are gentlemen may seem to be contradicted by the experience of the Venetian republic, in which none but gentlemen could attain to any rank or public employment. And yet this example is in no way opposed to my theory, for the gentlemen of Venice are so more in

name than in fact; for they have no great revenues from
estates, their riches being founded upon commerce and mov-
able property, and moreover none of them have castles or
jurisdiction over subjects, but the name of gentleman is
only a title of dignity and respect, and is in no way based
upon the things that gentlemen enjoy in other countries.
And as all other republics have different classes under different names, so Venice is divided into gentlemen and com-
monalty, and the former have all the offices and honors,
from which the latter are entirely excluded; and this distribution causes no disorders in that republic, for the reasons
elsewhere given. Let republics, then, be established where
equality exists, and, on the contrary, principalities where
great inequality prevails; otherwise the governments will
lack proper proportions and have but little durability.

Chapter LVI

THE OCCURRENCE OF IMPORTANT EVENTS IN ANY CITY OR COUN-
TRY IS GENERALLY PRECEDED BY SIGNS AND PORTENTS, OR BY
MEN WHO PREDICT THEM

WHENCE it comes I know not, but both ancient and modern
instances prove that no great events ever occur in any city
or country that have not been predicted by soothsayers, reve-
lations, or by portents and other celestial signs. And not to
go from home in proof of this, everybody knows how the
descent into Italy of Charles VIII., king of France, was predicted by Brother Girolamo Savonarola; and how, besides
this, it was said throughout Italy that at Arezzo there had
been seen and heard in the air armed men fighting together.
Moreover everybody remembers how, before the death of

Lorenzo de' Medici the elder, the highest pinnacle of the dome of Florence was struck by a bolt from heaven, doing great damage to that building. It is also well known how, before Pietro Soderini, who had been made Gonfaloniere for life, was expelled and deprived of his rank by the people of Florence, the palace itself was struck by lightning. Many more examples might be adduced, which I leave, however, lest I should become tedious. I will relate merely what, according to Titus Livius, happened before the coming of the Gauls to Rome. One Marcius Cædicius, a plebeian, reported to the Senate that, passing through the Via Nuova at midnight, he had heard a voice louder than that of any man which commanded him to notify the Senate that the Gauls were coming to Rome. To explain these things a man should have knowledge of things natural and supernatural, which I have not. It may be, however, as certain philosophers maintain, that the air is peopled with spirits, who by their superior intelligence foresee future events, and out of pity for mankind warn them by such signs, so that they may prepare against the coming evils. Be this as it may, however, the truth of the fact exists, that these portents are invariably followed by the most remarkable events.

Chapter LVII

THE PEOPLE AS A BODY ARE COURAGEOUS, BUT INDIVIDUALLY THEY ARE COWARDLY AND FEEBLE

AFTER the ruin of their country by the invasion of the Gauls, many Romans had gone to live at Veii, contrary to the constitution and the orders of the Senate. To remedy this evil the Senate published an edict commanding every one to return within a given time to inhabit Rome, on pain of certain penalties. At first those against whom this edict was aimed made light of it and derided it, but when the prescribed time approached they all hastened to obey. Titus Livius says on this point, "From being brave and insolent as a body, fear made them individually obedient." And truly nothing can better illustrate the character of a multitude than this example; for they are often audacious and loud in their denunciations of the decisions of their rulers, but when punishment stares them in the face, then, distrustful of each other, they rush to obey. Thus we see that whatever may be said of the good or evil disposition of the people is of little consequence, if you are well prepared to assert and maintain your authority should they be well disposed, and to defend yourself if their disposition be otherwise. This has reference specially to such evil dispositions as arise in the minds of the people from causes other than the loss of liberty, or that of a prince to whom they are much attached and who is still living; in such cases the most powerful remedies are required to restrain them, as these causes are more formidable than any others. But indispositions arising from other causes are easily controlled, especially if the multitude have no chief to whom they can look for support; for whilst on the one hand a loose mob without any leader is most formidable, yet on the other hand it is also most cowardly and feeble; and even if they are armed they will be easily subdued, if you can only shelter yourself against their first fury; for when their spirits are cooled down a little, and they see that they have all to return to their homes, they begin to mistrust themselves, and to think of their individual safety either by flight or submission. An excited multitude, therefore, that wishes to avoid such a result will have promptly to create a chief for itself, who shall direct and keep them united, and provide for their defence; as the Roman people did when, after the death of Virginia, they left Rome and appointed from amongst themselves twenty Tribunes for their protection. And unless they do this they will experience what Titus Livius has said in the above-quoted words, that united in one body they are brave and insolent, but when afterwards each begins to think of his own danger, they become cowardly and feeble.

Chapter LVIII

THE PEOPLE ARE WISER AND MORE CONSTANT THAN PRINCES

TITUS LIVIUS as well as all other historians affirm that nothing is more uncertain and inconstant than the multitude; for it appears from what he relates of the actions of men, that in many instances the multitude, after having condemned a man to death, bitterly lamented it, and most earnestly wished him back. This was the case with the Roman people and Manlius Capitolinus, whom they had condemned to death and afterwards most earnestly desired him back, as our author says in the following words: "No sooner had they found out that they had nothing to fear from him, than they began to regret and to wish him back." And elsewhere, when he relates the events that occurred in Syracuse after the death of Hieronymus, nephew of Hiero, he says: "It is the nature of the multitude either humbly to serve or insolently to dominate." I know not whether, in undertaking to defend a cause against the accusations of all writers, I do not assume a task so hard and so beset with difficulties as to oblige me to abandon it with shame, or to go on with it at the risk of being weighed down by it. Be that as it may, however, I think, and ever shall think, that it cannot be wrong to defend one's opinions with arguments founded upon reason, without employing force or authority.

I say, then, that individual men, and especially princes, may be charged with the same defects of which writers accuse the people; for whoever is not controlled by laws will commit the same errors as an unbridled multitude. This may easily be verified, for there have been and still are plenty of princes, and a few good and wise ones, such, I mean, as needed not the curb that controlled them. Amongst these, however, are not to be counted either the kings that lived in Egypt at that ancient period when that country was governed by laws, or those that arose in Sparta; neither such as are born in our day in France, for that country is more thoroughly regulated by laws than any other of which we have any knowledge in modern times. And those kings that arise under such constitutions are not to be classed amongst the number of those whose individual nature we have to consider, and see whether it resembles that of the people; but they should be compared with a people equally controlled by law as those kings were, and then we shall find in that multitude the same good qualities as in those kings, and we shall see that such a people neither obey with servility nor command with insolence. Such were the people of Rome, who, so long as that republic remained uncorrupted, neither obeyed basely nor ruled insolently, but rather held its rank honorably, supporting the laws and their magistrates. And when the unrighteous ambition of some noble made it necessary for them to rise up in self-defence, they did so, as in the case of Manlius, the Decemvirs, and others who attempted to oppress them; and so when the public good required them to obey the Dictators and Consuls, they promptly yielded obedience. And if the Roman people regretted Manlius Capitolinus after his death, it is not to be wondered at; for they regretted his virtues, which had been such that the remembrance of them filled every one with pity, and would have had the power to produce the same effect upon any prince; for all writers agree that virtue is to be admired and praised, even in one's enemies. And if intense desire could have restored Manlius to life, the Roman people would nevertheless have pronounced the same judgment against him as they did the first time, when they took him from prison and condemned him to death. And so we have seen princes that were esteemed wise, who have caused persons to be put to death and afterwards regretted it deeply; such as Alexander the Great with regard to Clitus and other friends, and Herod with his wife Mariamne. But what our historian says of the character of the multitude does not apply to a people regulated by laws, as the Romans were, but to an unbridled multitude, such as the Syracusans; who committed all the excesses to which infuriated and unbridled men abandon themselves, as did Alexander the Great and Herod in the above-mentioned cases.

Therefore, the character of the people is not to be blamed any more than that of princes, for both alike are liable to err when they are without any control. Besides the examples already given, I could adduce numerous others from amongst the Roman Emperors and other tyrants and princes, who have displayed as much inconstancy and recklessness as any populace ever did. Contrary to the general opinion, then, which maintains that the people, when they govern, are inconsistent, unstable, and ungrateful, I conclude and affirm that these defects are not more natural to the people than they are to princes. To charge the people and princes equally with them may be the truth, but to except princes from them would be a great mistake. For a people that governs and is well regulated by laws will be stable, prudent, and grateful, as much so, and even more, according to my opinion, than a prince, although he be esteemed wise; and, on the other hand, a prince, freed from the restraints of the law, will be more ungrateful, inconstant, and imprudent than a people similarly situated. The difference in their conduct is not due to any difference in their nature (for that is the same, and if there be any difference for good, it is on the side of the people); but to the greater or less respect they have for the laws under which they respectively live. And whoever studies the Roman people will see that for four hundred years they have been haters of royalty, and lovers of the glory and common good of their country; and he will find any number of examples that will prove both the one and the other. And should any one allege the ingratitude which the Roman people displayed towards Scipio, I shall reply the same as I have said in another place on this subject, where I have demonstrated that the people are less ungrateful than princes. But as regards prudence and stability, I say that the people are more prudent and stable, and have better judgment than a prince; and it is not without good reason that it is said, "The voice of the people is the voice of God"; for we see popular opinion prognosticate events in such a wonderful manner that it would almost seem as if the people had some occult virtue, which enables them to foresee the good and the evil. As to the people's capacity of judging of things, it is exceedingly rare that, when they hear two orators of equal talents advocate different measures, they do not decide in favor of the best of the two; which proves their ability to discern the truth of what they hear. And if occasionally they are misled in matters involving questions of courage or seeming utility, (as has been said above,) so is a prince also many times misled by his own passions, which are much greater than those of the people. We also see that in the election of their magistrates they make far better choice than princes; and no people will ever be persuaded to elect a man of infamous character and corrupt habits to any post of dignity, to which a prince is easily influenced in a thousand different ways. When we see a people take an aversion to anything, they persist in it for many centuries, which we never find to be the case with princes. Upon both these points the Roman people shall serve me as a proof, who in the many elections of Consuls and Tribunes had to regret only four times the choice they had made. The Roman people held the name of king in such detestation, as we have said, that no extent of services rendered by any of its citizens who attempted to usurp that title could save him from his merited punishment. We furthermore see the cities where the people are masters make the greatest progress in the least possible time, and much greater than such as have always been governed by princes; as was the case with Rome after the expulsion of the kings, and with Athens after they rid themselves of Pisistratus; and this can be attributed to no other cause than that the governments of the people are better than those of princes.

It would be useless to object to my opinion by referring to what our historian has said in the passages quoted above, and elsewhere; for if we compare the faults of a people with those of princes, as well as their respective good qualities, we shall find the people vastly superior in all that is good and glorious. And if princes show themselves superior in the making of laws, and in the forming of civil institutions and new statutes and ordinances, the people are superior in maintaining those institutions, laws, and ordinances, which certainly places them on a par with those who established them.

And finally to sum up this matter, I sav that both governments of princes and of the people have lasted a long time, but both required to be regulated by laws. For a prince who knows no other control but his own will is like a madman, and a people that can do as it pleases will hardly be wise. If now we compare a prince who is controlled by laws, and a people that is untrammelled by them, we shall find more virtue in the people than in the prince; and if we compare them when both are freed from such control, we shall see that the people are guilty of fewer excesses than the prince, and that the errors of the people are of less importance, and therefore more easily remedied. For a licentious and mutinous people may easily be brought back to good conduct by the influence and persuasion of a good man, but an evil-minded prince is not amenable to such influences, and therefore there is no other remedy against him but cold steel. We may judge then from this of the relative defects of the one and the other; if words suffice to correct those of the people, whilst those of the prince can only be remedied by violence, no one can fail to see that where the greater remedy is required, there also the defects must be greater. The follies which a people commits at the moment of its greatest license are not what is most to be feared; it is not the immediate evil that may result from them that inspires apprehension, but the fact that such general confusion might afford the opportunity for a tyrant to seize the government. But with evil-disposed princes the contrary is the case; it is the immediate present that causes fear, and there is hope only in the future; for men will persuade themselves that the termination of his wicked life may give them a chance of liberty. Thus we see the difference between the one and the other to be, that the one touches the present and the other the future. The excesses of the people are directed against those whom they suspect of interfering with the public good; whilst those of princes are against apprehended interference with their individual interests. The general prejudice against the people results from the fact that everybody can freely and fearlessly speak ill of them in mass, even whilst they are at the height of their power; but a prince can only be spoken of with the greatest circumspection and apprehension. And as the subject leads me to it, I deem it not amiss to examine in the following chapter whether alliances with a republic or with a prince are most to be trusted.

Chapter LIX

LEAGUES AND ALLIANCES WITH REPUBLICS ARE MORE TO BE TRUSTED THAN THOSE WITH PRINCES

As it is of daily occurrence that princes or republics contract leagues or friendships with each other, or that in like manner treaties and alliances are formed between a republic and a prince, it seems to me proper to examine whose faith is most constant and most to be relied upon, that of a republic or that of a prince. In examining the whole subject I believe that in many instances they are equal, but that in others there is a difference; and I believe, moreover, that agreements which are the result of force will no more be observed by a prince than by a republic, and, where either the one or the other is apprehensive of losing their state, that to save it both will break their faith and be guilty of ingratitude. Demetrius, called the Conqueror of Cities, had conferred infinite benefits upon the Athenians. It happened that, having been defeated by his enemies, he took refuge in Athens as a city that was friendly to him, and which he had laid under obligations; but the Athenians refused to receive him, which gave Demetrius more pain than the loss of his men and the destruction of his army. Pompey, after his defeat by Cæsar in Thessaly, took refuge in Egypt with Ptolemy, whom on a former occasion he had reinstated in his kingdom, but was treacherously put to death by him. Both these instances are attributable to the same reasons; yet we see that the republic acted with more humanity and inflicted less injury than the prince. Wherever fear dominates, there we shall find equal want of faith in both, although the same influence may cause either a prince or a republic to keep faith at the risk of ruin. For it may well happen that the prince is the ally of some powerful potentate, who for the moment may not be able to assist him, but who, the prince may hope, will be able to reinstate him in his possessions; or he may believe that, having acted as his partisan, his powerful ally will make no treaties or alliances with his enemies. Such was the fate of those princes of the kingdom of Naples who adhered to the French party. And with regard to republics this occurred with Saguntum in Spain, which hazarded her own safety for the sake of adhering to the Roman party; and with Florence when in the year 1512 she followed the fortune of the French. Taking all things together now, I believe that in such cases which involve imminent peril there will be found somewhat more of stability in republics than in princes. For even if the republics were inspired by the same feelings and intentions as the princes, yet the fact of their movements being slower will make them take more time in forming resolutions, and therefore they will less promptly break their faith.

Alliances are broken from considerations of interest; and in this respect republics are much more careful in the observance of treaties than princes. It would be easy to cite instances where princes for the smallest advantage have broken their faith, and where the greatest advantages have failed to induce republics to disregard theirs; as in the case of the proposal of Themistocles to the Athenians, when in a general assembly he told them that he had something to suggest that would be of greatest advantage to their country; but that it was of such a nature that he could not disclose it publicly without depriving them of the opportunity of availing of it. The people of Athens therefore appointed Aristides to whom Themistocles might communicate his suggestion, upon which they would decide according to the judgment of Aristides. Themistocles thereupon showed him that the fleet of united Greece, relying upon the treaty still in force, was in such position that they could easily make themselves masters of it or destroy it, which would make the Athenians arbiters of all Greece. Whereupon Aristides reported to the people that the proposed plan of Themistocles was highly advantageous but most dishonest, and therefore the people absolutely rejected it; which would not have been done by Philip of Macedon, nor many other princes, who would only have looked to the advantages, and who have gained more by their perfidy than by any other means.

I do not speak of the breaking of treaties because of an occasional non-observance, that being an ordinary matter; but I speak of the breaking of treaties from some extraordinary cause; and here I believe, from what has been said, that the people are less frequently guilty of this than princes, and are therefore more to be trusted.

Chapter LX

HOW THE CONSULATES AND SOME OTHER MAGISTRACIES WERE BESTOWED IN ROME WITHOUT REGARD TO THE AGE OF PERSONS

WE see from the course of history that the Roman republic, after the plebeians became entitled to the consulate, admitted all its citizens to this dignity without distinction of age or birth. In truth, age never formed a necessary qualification for public office; merit was the only consideration, whether found in young or old men. This is evidenced by the case of Valerius Corvinus, who was made Consul at twenty-three years of age; it was he who said to his soldiers that "the consulate was the reward of merit, and not of birth." Upon this subject much may be said. As regards birth, that point was conceded from necessity, and the same necessity that existed in Rome will be felt in every republic that aims to achieve the same success as Rome; for men cannot be made to bear labor and privations without the inducement of a corresponding reward, nor can they be deprived of such hope of reward without danger. It was proper, therefore, that the people should at an early period have had the hope of obtaining the right to the consulate, and that they should nurse that hope for a while, without realizing it; and when after a while that hope no longer sufficed them, the reality had to be conceded to them. The state that does not admit its people to a share of its glory may treat them in its own way, as we have discussed elsewhere; but a state that wishes to undertake what Rome has done cannot make such a distinction.

And admitting that this may be so with regard to birth.

then the question of age is necessarily also disposed of; for in electing a young man to an office which demands the prudence of an old man, it is necessary, if the election rests with the people, that he should have made himself worthy of that distinction by some extraordinary action. And when a young man has so much merit as to have distinguished himself by some notable action, it would be a great loss for the state not to be able to avail of his talents and services; and that he should have to wait until old age has robbed him of that vigor of mind and activity of which the state might have the benefit in his earlier age, as Rome had of Valerius Corvinus, of Scipio, of Pompey, and of many others who had the honors of triumph when very young men.

SECOND BOOK

INTRODUCTION

Men ever praise the olden time, and find fault with the present, though often without reason. They are such partisans of the past that they extol not only the times which they know only by the accounts left of them by historians, but, having grown old, they also laud all they remember to have seen in their youth. Their opinion is generally erroneous in that respect, and I think the reasons which cause this illusion are various. The first I believe to be the fact that we never know the whole truth about the past, and very frequently writers conceal such events as would reflect disgrace upon their century, whilst they magnify and amplify those that lend lustre to it. The majority of authors obey the fortune of conquerors to that degree that, by way of rendering their victories more glorious, they exaggerate not only the valiant deeds of the victor, but also of the vanquished; so that future generations of the countries of both will have cause to wonder at those men and times, and are obliged to praise and admire them to the utmost. Another reason is that men's hatreds generally spring from fear or envy. Now, these two powerful reasons of hatred do not exist for us with regard to the past, which can no longer inspire either apprehension or envy. But it is very different with the affairs of the present, in which we ourselves are either actors or spectators, and of which we have a complete knowledge, nothing being concealed from us; and knowing the good together with many other things that are displeasing to us, we are forced to conclude that the present is inferior to the past, though in reality it may be much more worthy of glory and fame. I do not speak of matters pertaining to the arts, which shine by their intrinsic merits, which time can neither add to nor diminish; but I speak of such things as pertain to the actions and manners of men, of which we do not possess such manifest evidence.

I repeat, then, that this practice of praising and decrying is very general, though it cannot be said that it is always erroneous; for sometimes our judgment is of necessity correct, human affairs being in a state of perpetual movement, always either ascending or declining. We see, for instance, a city or country with a government well organized by some man of superior ability; for a time it progresses and attains a great prosperity through the talents of its lawgiver. Now, if any one living at such a period should praise the past more than the time in which he lives, he would certainly be deceiving himself; and this error will be found due to the reasons above indicated. But should he live in that city or country at the period after it shall have passed the zenith of its glory and in the time of its decline, then he would not be wrong in praising the past. Reflecting now upon the course of human affairs, I think that, as a whole, the world remains very much in the same condition, and the good in it always balances the evil; but the good and the evil change from one country to another, as we learn from the history of those ancient kingdoms that differed from each other in manners, whilst the world at large remained the same. The only difference being, that all the virtues that first found a place in Assyria were thence transferred to Media, and afterwards passed to Persia, and from there they came into

Italy and to Rome. And if after the fall of the Roman Empire none other sprung up that endured for any length of time, and where the aggregate virtues of the world were kept together, we nevertheless see them scattered amongst many nations, as, for instance, in the kingdom of France, the Turkish empire, or that of the Sultan of Egypt, and nowadays the people of Germany, and before them those famous Saracens, who achieved such great things and conquered so great a part of the world, after having destroyed the Roman Empire of the East. The different peoples of these several countries, then, after the fall of the Roman Empire, have possessed and possess still in great part that virtue which is so much lamented and so sincerely praised. And those who live in those countries and praise the past more than the present may deceive themselves; but whoever is born in Italy and Greece, and has not become either an Ultramontane in Italy or a Turk in Greece, has good reason to find fault with his own and to praise the olden times; for in their past there are many things worthy of the highest admiration, whilst the present has nothing that compensates for all the extreme misery, infamy, and degradation of a period where there is neither observance of religion, law, or military discipline, and which is stained by every species of the lowest brutality; and these vices are the more detestable as they exist amongst those who sit in the tribunals as judges, and hold all power in their hands, and claim to be adored.

But to return to our argument, I say that, if men's judgment is at fault upon the point whether the present age be better than the past, of which latter, owing to its antiquity, they cannot have such perfect knowledge as of their own period, the judgment of old men of what they have seen in their youth and in their old age should not be false, inasmuch as they have equally seen both the one and the other. This would be true, if men at the different periods of their lives had the same judgment and the same appetites. But as these vary (though the times do not), things cannot appear the same to men who have other tastes, other delights, and other considerations in age from what they had in youth. For as men when they age lose their strength and energy, whilst their prudence and judgment improve, so the same things that in youth appeared to them supportable and good, will of necessity, when they have grown old, seem to them insupportable and evil; and when they should blame their own judgment they find fault with the times. Moreover, as human desires are insatiable, (because their nature is to have and to do everything whilst fortune limits their possessions and capacity of enjoyment,) this gives rise to a constant discontent in the human mind and a weariness of the things they possess; and it is this which makes them decry the present, praise the past, and desire the future, and all this without any reasonable motive. I know not, then, whether I deserve to be classed with those who deceive themselves, if in these Discourses I shall laud too much the times of ancient Rome and censure those of our own day. And truly, if the virtues that ruled then and the vices that prevail now were not as clear as the sun, I should be more reticent in my expressions, lest I should fall into the very error for which I reproach others. But the matter being so manifest that everybody sees it, I shall boldly and openly say what I think of the former times and of the present, so as to excite in the minds of the young men who may read my writings the desire to avoid the evils of the latter, and to prepare themselves to imitate the virtues of the former, whenever fortune presents them the occasion. For it is the duty of an honest man to teach others that good which the malignity of the times and of fortune has prevented his doing himself; so that amongst the many capable ones whom he has instructed, some one perhaps, more favored by Heaven, may perform it.

Having in the preceding Book treated of the conduct of the Romans in matters relating to their internal affairs, I shall in this Book speak of what the Roman people did in relation to the aggrandizement of their empire.

Chapter I

THE GREATNESS OF THE ROMANS WAS DUE MORE TO THEIR VALOR AND ABILITY THAN TO GOOD FORTUNE

MANY authors, amongst them that most serious writer Plutarch, have held the opinion that the people of Rome were more indebted in the acquisition of their empire to the favors of Fortune than to their own merits. And amongst other reasons adduced by Plutarch is, that by their own confession it appears that the Roman people ascribed all their victories to Fortune, because they built more temples to that goddess than to any other deity. It seems that Livius accepts that opinion, for he rarely makes a Roman speak of valor without coupling fortune with it. Now I do not share that opinion at all, and do not believe that it can be sustained; for if no other republic has ever been known to make such conquests, it is admitted that none other was so well organized for that purpose as Rome. It was the valor of her armies that achieved those conquests, but it was the wisdom of her conduct and the nature of her institutions, as established by her first legislator, that enabled her to preserve these acquisitions, as we shall more fully set forth in the succeeding chapters. But it is said that the fact that the Roman people never had two important wars on hand at the same time was due more to their good fortune than their wisdom; for they did not engage in war with the Latins until they had beaten the Samnites so completely that the Romans themselves had to protect them with their arms; nor did they combat the Tuscans until after they had subjugated the Latins, and had by repeated defeats completely enervated the Samnites. Doubtless if these two powerful nations had united against Rome whilst their strength was yet unbroken, it may readily be supposed that they could have destroyed the Roman republic.

But however this may have been, certain it is that the Romans never had two important wars to sustain at the same time; but it rather appears that the beginning of one caused the termination of the other, or that the ending of one gave rise to the next. This is readily seen by examining the succession of their wars; for, leaving aside the one they were engaged in before the capture of Rome by the Gauls, we see that whilst they fought against the Equeans and the Volscians at a time when these nations were still powerful, no other people rose up to attack them at the same time. But when these were subdued, then occurred the war against the Samnites; and although the Latins revolted before that war was concluded, yet when this revolt broke out the Samnites had already formed a league with the Romans, and it was by the aid of their army that they broke down the pride of the Latins. And when these were subdued, the war with the Samnites was renewed; but the repeated defeats inflicted upon them by the Romans had so enfeebled their forces, that, when the war with the Tuscans occurred, that also was quickly terminated. But the Samnites rose up once more when Pyrrhus came into Italy; and when he was beaten and driven back to Greece, the first war with the Carthaginians was begun, which was hardly terminated before the combined Gauls conspired against Rome, and poured down through the various passes of the Alps in great numbers, but were defeated with terrible carnage between Popolonia and Pisa, where now stands the tower of San Vincenti. After this war was finished, the Romans were not engaged in any other of importance during a period of twenty years; for they only fought the Ligurians and a remnant of Gauls who were in Lombardy. And thus they remained until the second Carthaginian war broke out, and occupied them for sixteen years. When this had been most gloriously concluded, the Macedonian war occurred; and after that the war with Antiochus and Asia. When these had been victoriously terminated, there remained in the whole world neither prince nor republic that could, alone or unitedly, have resisted the Roman power. Considering now the succession of these wars, prior to the last victory, and the manner in which they were conducted, we cannot fail to recognize in them a combination of good fortune with the greatest valor and prudence. And if we examine into the cause of that good fortune we shall readily find it; for it is most certain that when a prince or a people attain that degree of reputation that all the neighboring princes and peoples fear to attack him, none of them will ever venture to do it except under the force of necessity; so that it will be, as it were, at the option of that potent prince or people to make war upon such neighboring powers as may seem advantageous, whilst adroitly keeping the others quiet. And this he can easily do, partly by the respect they have for his power, and partly because they are deceived by the means employed to keep them quiet. And other powers that are more distant and have no immediate intercourse with him, will look upon this as a matter too remote for them to be concerned about, and will continue in this error until the conflagration spreads to their door, when they will have no means for extinguishing it except their own forces, which will no longer suffice when the fire has once gained the upper hand. I will say nothing of how the Samnites re-

mained indifferent spectators when they saw the Volscians
and Equeans defeated by the Romans; and not to be too
prolix I will at once come to the Carthaginians, who had
already acquired great power and reputation when the
Romans were fighting with the Samnites and the Tuscans;
for they were masters of all Africa, they held Sardinia and
Sicily, and had already a foothold in Spain. Their own power, and the fact that they were remote from the confines of
Rome, made them indifferent about attacking the Romans,
or succoring the Samnites and Tuscans, but they did what
men are apt to do with regard to a growing power, they
rather sought by an alliance with the Romans to secure
their friendship. Nor did they become aware of the error
they had committed until after the Romans, having subjugated all the nations situated between them and the Carthaginians, began to contest the dominion of Sicily and
Spain with them. The same thing happened to the Gauls as
to the Carthaginians, and also to King Philip of Macedon
and to Antiochus. Each one of these believed that, whilst
the Romans were occupied with the other, they would be
overcome, and that then it would be time enough either by
peace or war to secure themselves against the Romans. So
that I believe that the good fortune which followed the
Romans in these parts would have equally attended other
princes who had acted as the Romans did, and had displayed the same courage and sagacity.

It would be proper and interesting here to show the course
which the Romans adopted when they entered the territory
of an enemy, but that we have already explained this at
length in our treatise of "The Prince." I will only say in a
few words that they always endeavored to have some friend
in these new countries who could aid them by opening the
way for them to enter, and also serve as a means for re-

taining their possession. Thus we see that by the aid of the Capuans they entered Samnium, and through the Camertini they got into Tuscany; the Mamertini helped them into Sicily, the Saguntines into Spain, Masinissa into Africa, and the Massilians and Eduans into Gaul. And thus they never lacked similar support to facilitate their enterprises, both in the acquisition and preservation of new provinces. And those people who will observe the same mode of proceeding will find that they have less need of fortune than those who do not. And to enable everybody to know how much more the valor and ability of the Romans served them in the conquest of their empire than Fortune, we will discuss in the following chapter the characters of the different peoples whom the Romans had to encounter, and with what obstinate courage they defended their liberty.

Chapter II

WHAT NATIONS THE ROMANS HAD TO CONTEND AGAINST, AND WITH WHAT OBSTINACY THEY DEFENDED THEIR LIBERTY

NOTHING required so much effort on the part of the Romans to subdue the nations around them, as well as those of more distant countries, as the love of liberty which these people cherished in those days; and which they defended with so much obstinacy, that nothing but the exceeding valor of the Romans could ever have subjugated them. For we know from many instances to what danger they exposed themselves to preserve or recover their liberty, and what vengeance they practised upon those who had deprived them of it. The lessons of history teach us also, on the other hand, the injuries people suffer from servitude. And whilst in our own times there is only one country in which we can say that free communities exist, in those ancient times all countries contained numerous cities that enjoyed entire liberty. In the times of which we are now speaking, there were in Italy from the mountains that divide the present Tuscany from Lombardy, down to the extreme point, a number of independent nations, such as the Tuscans, the Romans, the Samnites, and many others, that inhabited the rest of Italy. Nor is there ever any mention of there having been other kings besides those that reigned in Rome, and Porsenna, king of the Tuscans, whose line became extinct in a manner not mentioned in history. But we do see that, at the time when the Romans went to besiege Veii, Tuscany was free, and so prized her liberty and hated the very name of king, that when the Veienti had created a king in their city for its defence, and applied to the Tuscans for help against the Romans, it was resolved, after repeated deliberations, not to grant such assistance to the Veienti so long as they lived under that king; for the Tuscans deemed it not well to engage in the defence of those who had voluntarily subjected themselves to the rule of one man. And it is easy to understand whence that affection for liberty arose in the people, for they had seen that cities never increased in dominion or wealth unless they were free. And certainly it is wonderful to think of the greatness which Athens attained within the space of a hundred years after having freed herself from the tyranny of Pisistratus; and still more wonderful is it to reflect upon the greatness which Rome achieved after she was rid of her kings. The cause of this is manifest, for it is not individual prosperity, but the general good, that makes cities great; and certainly the general good is regarded nowhere but in republics, because whatever they do is for the common benefit, and should it happen to prove an injury to one or more individuals, those for whose benefit the thing is done are so numerous that they can always carry the measure against the few that are injured by it. But the very reverse happens where there is a prince whose private interests are generally in opposition to those of the city, whilst the measures taken for the benefit of the city are seldom deemed personally advantageous by the prince. This state of things soon leads to a tyranny, the least evil of which is to check the advance of the city in its career of prosperity, so that it grows neither in power nor wealth, but on the contrary rather retrogrades. And if fate should have it that the tyrant is enterprising, and by his courage and valor extends his dominions, it will never be for the benefit of the city, but only for his own; for he will never bestow honors and office upon the good and brave citizens over whom he tyrannizes, so that he may not have occasion to suspect and fear them. Nor will he make the states which he conquers subject or tributary to the city of which he is the despot, because it would not be to his advantage to make that city powerful, but it will always be for his interest to keep the state disunited, so that each place and country shall recognize him only as master; thus he alone, and not his country, profits by his conquests. Those who desire to have this opinion confirmed by many other arguments, need but read Xenophon's treatise "On Tyranny."

It is no wonder, then, that the ancients hated tyranny and loved freedom, and that the very name of Liberty should have been held in such esteem by them; as was shown by the Syracusans when Hieronymus, the nephew of Hiero, was killed. When his death became known to his army, which was near Syracuse, it caused at first some disturbances, and they were about committing violence upon his murderers; but when they learnt that the cry of Liberty had been raised in Syracuse, they were delighted, and instantly returned to 'order. Their fury against the tyrannicides was quelled, and they thought only of how a free government might be established in Syracuse. Nor can we wonder that the people indulge in extraordinary revenge against those who have robbed them of their liberty; of which we could cite many instances, but will quote only one that occurred in Corcyra, a city of Greece, during the Peloponnesian war. Greece was at that time divided into two parties, one of which adhered to the Athenians, and the other to the Spartans, and a similar division of parties existed in most of the Greek cities. It happened that in Corcyra the nobles, being the stronger party, seized upon the liberties of the people; but with the assistance of the Athenians the popular party recovered its power, and, having seized the nobles, they tied their hands behind their backs, and threw them into a prison large enough to hold them all. They thence took eight or ten at a time, under pretence of sending them into exile in different directions; but instead of that they killed them with many cruelties. When the remainder became aware of this, they resolved if possible to escape such an ignominious death; and having armed themselves as well as they could, they resisted those who attempted to enter the prison; but when the people heard this disturbance, they pulled down the roof and upper portion of the prison, and suffocated the nobles within under its ruins. Many such notable and horrible cases occurred in that country, which shows that the people will avenge their lost liberty with more energy than when it is merely threatened.

Reflecting now as to whence it came that in ancient times the people were more devoted to liberty than in the present, I believe that it resulted from this, that men were stronger in those days, which I believe to be attributable to the differ-

Christianity vs. Ancients

ence of education, founded upon the difference of their religion and ours. For, as our religion teaches us the truth and the true way of life, it causes us to attach less value to the honors and possessions of this world; whilst the Pagans, esteeming those things as the highest good, were more energetic and ferocious in their actions. We may observe this also in most of their institutions, beginning with the magnificence of their sacrifices as compared with the humility of ours, which are gentle solemnities rather than magnificent ones, and have nothing of energy or ferocity in them, whilst in theirs there was no lack of pomp and show, to which was superadded the ferocious and bloody nature of the sacrifice by the slaughter of many animals, and the familiarity with this terrible sight assimilated the nature of men to their sacrificial ceremonies. Besides this, the Pagan religion deified only men who had achieved great glory, such as commanders of armies and chiefs of republics, whilst ours glorifies more the humble and contemplative men than the men of action. Our religion, moreover, places the supreme happiness in humility, lowliness, and a contempt for worldly objects, whilst the other, on the contrary, places the supreme good in grandeur of soul, strength of body, and all such other qualities as render men formidable; and if our religion claims of us fortitude of soul, it is more to enable us to suffer than to achieve great deeds.

These principles seem to me to have made men feeble, and caused them to become an easy prey to evil-minded men, who can control them more securely, seeing that the great body of men, for the sake of gaining Paradise, are more disposed to endure injuries than to avenge them. And although it would seem that the world has become effeminate and Heaven disarmed, yet this arises unquestionably from the baseness of men, who have interpreted our religion according to the promptings of indolence rather than those of virtue. For if we were to reflect that our religion permits us to exalt and defend our country, we should see that according to it we ought also to love and honor our country, and prepare ourselves so as to be capable of defending her. It is this education, then, and this false interpretation of our religion, that is the cause of there not being so many republics nowadays as there were anciently; and that there is no longer the same love of liberty amongst the people now as there was then. I believe, however, that another reason for this will be found in the fact that the Roman Empire, by force of arms, destroyed all the republics and free cities; and although that empire was afterwards itself dissolved, yet these cities could not reunite themselves nor reorganize their civil institutions, except in a very few instances.

Be that, however, as it may, the Romans found everywhere a league of republics, well armed for the most obstinate defence of their liberties, showing that it required the rare ability and extreme valor of the Romans to subjugate them. And to give but one example of this, we will confine ourselves to the case of the Samnites, which really seems marvelous. This people Titus Livius himself admits to have been so powerful and valiant in arms that, until the time of the Consul Papirius Cursor, grandson of the first Papirius, a period of forty years, they were able to resist the Romans, notwithstanding their many defeats, the destruction of their cities, and much slaughter. That country, which was then so thickly inhabited and contained so many cities, is now almost a desert; and yet it was originally so powerful and well governed that it would have been unconquerable by any other than Roman valor. It is easy to discover the cause of this different state of things, for it all comes from this, that formerly that people enjoyed freedom, and now they live in servitude; for, as I have already said above, only those cities and countries that are free can achieve greatness. Population is greater there because marriages are more free and offer more advantages to the citizen; for people will gladly have children when they know that they can support them, and that they will not be deprived of their patrimony, and where they know that their children not only are born free and not slaves, but, if they possess talents and virtue, can arrive at the highest dignities of the state. In free countries we also see wealth increase more rapidly, both that which results from the culture of the soil and that which is produced by industry and art; for everybody gladly multiplies those things, and seeks to acquire those goods the possession of which he can tranquilly enjoy. Thence men vie with each other to increase both private and public wealth, which consequently increase in an extraordinary manner. But the contrary of all this takes place in countries that are subject to another; and the more rigorous the subjection of the people, the more will they be deprived of all the good to which they had previously been accustomed. And the hardest of all servitudes is to be subject to a republic, and this for these reasons: first, because it is more enduring, and there is no hope of escaping from it; and secondly, because republics aim to enervate and weaken all other states so as to increase their own power. This is not the case with a prince who holds another country in subjection, unless indeed he should be a barbarous devastator of countries and a destroyer of all human civilization, such as the princes of the Orient. But if he be possessed of only ordinary humanity, he will treat all cities that are subject to him equally well, and will leave them in the enjoyment of their arts and industries, and measurably all their ancient institutions. So that if they cannot grow the same as if they were free, they

will at least not be ruined whilst in bondage; and by this is
understood that bondage into which cities fall that become
subject to a stranger, for of that to one of their own citizens
we have already spoken above.

Considering now all that has been said, we need not wonder at the power which the Samnites possessed, so long as
they were free, nor at the feeble condition to which they
afterwards became reduced when they were subjugated.
Titus Livius testifies to this in several instances, and mainly
in speaking of the war with Hannibal, where he states that
the Samnites, pressed by a legion of Romans which was at
Nola, sent messengers to Hannibal to implore his assistance.
These said in their address that for a hundred years they had
combated the Romans with their own soldiers and generals,
and had many times sustained the contest against two consular armies and two Consuls at once; but that now they
had been reduced so low that they were hardly able to defend themselves against the one small Roman legion that
was stationed at Nola.

Chapter III

ROME BECAME GREAT BY RUINING HER NEIGHBORING CITIES, AND BY FREELY ADMITTING STRANGERS TO HER PRIVILEGES AND HONORS

"Crescit interea Roma, Albæ ruinis." Those who desire a
city to achieve great empire must endeavor by all possible
means to make her populous; for without an abundance of
inhabitants it is impossible ever to make a city powerful.
This may be done in two ways; either by attracting population by the advantages offered, or by compulsion. The first

is to make it easy and secure for strangers to come and establish themselves there, and the second is to destroy the neighboring cities, and to compel their inhabitants to come and dwell in yours. These principles were so strictly observed by the Romans, that, in the time of the sixth king, Rome had already eighty thousand inhabitants capable of bearing arms. The Romans acted like a good husbandman, who for the purpose of strengthening a tree and making it produce more fruit and to mature it better, cuts off the first shoots it puts out, so that by retaining the sap and vigor in the trunk the tree may afterwards put forth more abundant branches and fruit. And that this is a good plan for aggrandizing a city and extending its empire, is proved by the example of Sparta and Athens, both most warlike republics, and regulated by most excellent laws; and yet they did not attain the same greatness as Rome, which was far less well regulated. No other reason can be assigned for this than the above; for Rome, from having by the above two methods increased its population, was enabled to put two hundred thousand men into the field, whilst Sparta and Athens could not raise more than twenty thousand each. And this resulted not from Rome's being more favorably situated, but solely from the difference in their mode of proceeding. For Lycurgus, the founder of the Spartan republic, believing that nothing would more readily destroy his laws than the admixture of new inhabitants, did everything possible to prevent strangers from coming into the city. Besides prohibiting their obtaining citizenship by marriage, and all other intercourse and commerce that bring men together, he ordered that in his republic only leather money should be used, so as to indispose all strangers from bringing merchandise into Sparta, or exercising any kind of art or industry there, so that the city never could increase in population.

Now, as all the actions of men resemble those of nature, it is neither natural nor possible that a slender trunk should support great branches; and thus a small republic cannot conquer and hold cities and kingdoms that are larger and more powerful than herself, and if she does conquer them, she will experience the same fate as a tree whose branches are larger than the trunk, which will not be able to support them, and will be bent by every little breeze that blows. Such was the case with Sparta when she had conquered all the cities of Greece; but no sooner did Thebes revolt, than all the other cities revolted likewise, and the trunk was quickly left without any branches. This could not have happened to Rome, whose trunk was so strong that it could easily support all its branches. The above modes of proceeding, then, together with others of which we shall speak hereafter, made Rome great and most powerful, which Titus Livius points out in these few words: "Rome grew, whilst Alba was ruined."

Chapter IV

THE ANCIENT REPUBLICS EMPLOYED THREE DIFFERENT METHODS FOR AGGRANDIZING THEMSELVES

WHOEVER has studied ancient history will have found that the republics had three methods of aggrandizement. One of these was that observed by the ancient Tuscans, namely, to form a confederation of several republics, neither of which had any eminence over the other in rank or authority; and in their conquests of other cities they associated these with themselves, in a similar manner to that practised by the Swiss nowadays, and as was done anciently in Greece by the

Achaians and the Ætolians. But as the Romans had many wars with the Tuscans, I will (by way of illustrating the first method) give a more particular account of these people. Before the establishment of the Roman empire, the Tuscans were very powerful in Italy, both by land and by sea; and although we have no particular history of them, yet there are some traditions and vestiges of their greatness; and it is known that they sent a colony to the shores of the sea north of them, which they called Adria, and which became so important that it gave its name to that sea, which is still called the "Adriatic." It is also known that they subjected to their authority the entire country stretching from the Tiber to the foot of the Alps, comprising the main body of Italy; although two hundred years before the Romans became so powerful the Tuscans lost their dominion over that part of the country which is now called Lombardy. This province had been seized and occupied by the Gauls, who either from necessity, or attracted by the soft climate and the fruits of Italy, and especially the wine, came there led by their chief Bellovesus; and having routed and driven out its inhabitants, they established themselves there and built numerous cities, and gave that country their own name of Gallia, which it bore until subjugated by the Romans. The Tuscans then lived in perfect equality, and employed for their aggrandizement the first method mentioned above. Their confederation consisted of twelve cities, amongst which were Clusium, Veii, Fiesole, Volterra, and others, who governed their empire; their conquests, however, could not extend beyond Italy, a considerable part of which remained still independent of them for reasons which we will state further on.

The second method employed by the ancient republics for their aggrandizement was to make associates of other states;

reserving to themselves, however, the rights of sovereignty, the seat of empire, and the glory of their enterprises. This was the method observed by the Romans. The third method was to make the conquered people immediately subjects, and not associates, and was practised by the Spartans and Athenians. Of these three methods the latter is perfectly useless, as was proved by these two republics, who perished from no other cause than from having made conquests which they could not maihtain. For to undertake the government of conquered cities by violence, especially when they have been accustomed to the enjoyment of liberty, is a most difficult and troublesome task; and unless you are powerfully armed, you will never secure their obedience nor be able to govern them. And to enable you to be thus powerful it becomes necessary to have associates, by whose aid you can increase the population of your own city; and as neither Sparta nor Athens did either of these things, their conquests proved perfectly useless. Rome, on the contrary, followed the second plan, and did both things, and consequently rose to such exceeding power; and as she was the only state that persistently adhered to this system, so she was also the only one that attained such great power. Having created for herself many associates throughout Italy, she granted to them in many respects an almost entire equality, always, however, reserving to herself the seat of empire and the right of command; so that these associates (without being themselves aware of it) devoted their own efforts and blood to their own subjugation. For so soon as the Romans began to lead their armies beyond the limits of Italy, they reduced other kingdoms to provinces, and made subjects of those who, having been accustomed to live under kings, were indifferent to becoming subjects of another; and from having Roman governors, and having been conquered by Roman arms, they recognized no superior to the Romans. Thus the associates of Rome in Italy found themselves all at once surrounded by Roman subjects, and at the same time pressed by a powerful city like Rome; and when they became aware of the trap into which.they had been led, it was too late to remedy the evil, for Rome had become too powerful by the acquisition of foreign provinces, as also within herself by the increased population which she had armed. And although these associates conspired together to revenge the wrongs inflicted upon them by Rome, yet they were quickly subdued, and their condition made even worse; for from associates they were degraded to subjects. This mode of proceeding (as has been said) was practised only by the Romans; and a republic desirous of aggrandizement should adopt no other plan, for experience has proved that there is none better or more sure.

The first method of which we have spoken, that of form-ing confederations like those of the Tuscans, Achaians, and Ætolians, or the Swiss of the present day, is next best after that practised by the Romans; for if it does not admit of extensive conquests, it has at least two other advantages: the one, not to become easily involved in war, and the other, that whatever conquests are made are easily preserved. The reason why a confederation of republics cannot well make extensive conquests is, that they are not a compact body, and do not have a central seat of power, which embarrasses consultation and concentrated action. It also makes them less desirous of dominion, for, being composed of numerous communities that are to share in this dominion, they do not value conquests as much as a single republic that expects to enjoy the exclusive benefit of them herself. Furthermore, they are governed by a council, which naturally causes their resolutions to be more tardy than those that emanate from a single centre. Experience has also shown that this system of confederation has certain limits, which they have in no instance transgressed; being composed of twelve or fourteen states at most, they cannot well extend beyond that number, as their mutual defence would become difficult, and therefore they seek no further extension of their dominion,—either because necessity does not push them to it, or because they see no advantage in further conquests, for the reason given above. For in such case they would have to do one of two things: either to continue adding other states to their confederation, which would then become so numerous as to create confusion, or they would have to make the conquered people subjects. And as they see the difficulties of this, and the little advantage that would result from it, they attach no value to an extension of their dominion. When therefore these confederations have become sufficiently strong by their number, so that they consider themselves secure, they are apt to do two things: one, to take smaller states under their protection, and thus to obtain money from them which they can easily divide amongst themselves; and the other is to engage in the military service and pay of one prince or another, as the Swiss do nowadays, and as we read in history was done by those mentioned above. Titus Livius gives us proof of this when he relates how Philip, king of Macedon, being engaged in negotiations with Titus Quintius Flaminius in presence of one of the prætors of the Ætolians, addressed that prætor and reproached him with the avarice and lack of good faith of the Ætolians; saying that "they were not ashamed to take military service under any one, and at the same time supply troops to his enemy, so that the Ætolian colors were often seen in both opposing armies." We see therefore that this system of confederations has always been the same, and has ever produced the same results. We also see that to make conquered people subjects has ever been a source of weakness and of little profit, and that when carried too far it has quickly proved ruinous to the conqueror. And if this system of making subjects is disadvantageous to warlike republics, how much more pernicious must it be for such as have no armies, as is the case with the Italian republics of our day?

All this proves, therefore, the excellence of the plan adopted by the Romans, which is the more to be admired as they had no previous example to guide them, and which has not been followed by any other state since Rome. As to the system of confederations, that has been followed only by the Swiss, and by the Suabian league. In conclusion, we will state that many wise institutions of the Romans, both as regards the government of their internal and external affairs, have not only not been imitated in our times, but have not even been taken into account by any one, being deemed by some not to have been founded in truth, by some to be impossible, and by others inapplicable and useless; so that by remaining in this ignorance Italy has become the prey of whoever has chosen to attack her. But if it has seemed too difficult to imitate the example of the Romans, certainly that of the ancient Tuscans should not be deemed so, especially by the Tuscans of the present day. For if they failed to acquire that power in Italy which the Roman method of proceeding would have given them, they at least lived for a long time in security, with much glory of dominion and of arms, and high praise for their manners and religion. This power and glory of the ancient Tuscans was first checked by the Gauls, and afterwards crushed by the Romans; and was so completely annihilated, that, although two thousand years ago the power of the Tuscans was very great, yet now there is scarcely any memento or vestige of it. And this has caused me to consider as to whence this oblivion of things arises, which I propose to discuss in the following chapter.

Chapter V

THE CHANGES OF RELIGION AND OF LANGUAGES, TOGETHER WITH
THE OCCURRENCE OF DELUGES AND PESTILENCES, DESTROY THE
RECORD OF THINGS

To those philosophers who maintain that the world has existed from eternity, we might reply, that, if it were really of such antiquity, there would reasonably be some record beyond five thousand years, were it not that we see how the records of time are destroyed by various causes, some being the acts of men and some of Heaven. Those that are the acts of men are the changes of religion and of language; for when a new sect springs up, that is to say a new religion, the first effort is (by way of asserting itself and gaining influence) to destroy the old or existing one; and when it happens that the founders of the new religion speak a different language, then the destruction of the old religion is easily effected. This we know from observing the proceedings of the Christians against the heathen religion; for they destroyed all its institutions and all its ceremonies, and effaced all record of the ancient theology. It is true that they did not succeed in destroying entirely the record of the glorious deeds of the illustrious men of the ancient creed, for they were forced to keep up the Latin language by the necessity of writing their new laws in that tongue; but if they could have written them in a new language (bearing in mind their other persecutions), there would have been no record whatever left of preceding events. Whoever reads the proceedings of St. Gregory, and of the other heads of the Christian religion, will see with what obstinacy they persecuted all ancient memorials, burning the works of the historians and of the poets, destroying the statues and images and despoiling everything else that gave but an indication of antiquity. So that, if they had added a new language to this persecution, everything relating to previous events would in a very short time have been sunk in oblivion.

It is reasonable to suppose that what the Christians practised towards the Pagans, these practised in like manner upon their predecessors. And as the religions changed two or three times in six thousand years, all memory of the things done before that time was lost; and if nevertheless some vestiges of it remain, they are regarded as fabulous, and are believed by no one; as is the case with the history of Diodorus Siculus, who gives an account of some forty or fifty thousand years, yet is generally looked upon as being mendacious, and I believe with justice.

As to causes produced by Heaven, they are such as destroy the human race, and reduce the inhabitants of some parts of the world to a very few in number; such as pestilence, famine, or inundations. Of this the latter are the most important, partly because they are most universal, and partly because the few that escape are chiefly ignorant mountaineers, who, having no knowledge of antiquity themselves, cannot transmit any to posterity. And should there be amongst those who escape any that have such knowledge, they conceal or pervert it in their own fashion, for the purpose of gaining influence and reputation; so that there remains to their successors only just so much as they were disposed to write, and no more. And that such inundations, pestilences, and famines occur cannot be doubted, both because all history is full of accounts of them, and because we see the effects of them in the oblivion of things, and also because it seems reasonable that they should occur. For in nature as in simple bodies, when there is an accumulation of superfluous matter, a spontaneous purgation takes place, which preserves the health of that body. And so it is with that compound body, the human race; when countries become overpopulated and there is no longer any room for all the inhabitants to live, nor any other places for them to go to, these being likewise all fully occupied,—and when human cunning and wickedness have gone as far as they can go,—then of necessity the world must relieve itself of this excess of population by one of those three causes; so that mankind, having been chastised and reduced in numbers, may become better and live with more convenience. Tuscany then, as I have said above, was once powerful, religious, and virtuous; it had its own customs and language; but all this was destroyed by the Roman power, so that there remained nothing of it but the memory of its name.

Chapter VI

OF THE MANNER IN WHICH THE ROMANS CONDUCTED THEIR WARS

HAVING explained the means which the Romans employed for their aggrandizement, we will now show how they conducted their wars; and we shall see with how much prudence they deviated in all their actions from the methods universally adopted by other nations, so as to make their road to supreme power easy. The object of those who make war, either from choice or ambition, is to conquer and to maintain their conquests, and to do this in such a manner as to enrich themselves and not to impoverish the conquered country. To do this, then, the conqueror should take care not to spend too much, and in all things mainly to look to the public benefit; and therefore he should imitate the manner and conduct of the Romans, which was first of all to "make the war short and sharp," as the French say; for as they always put powerful armies into the field, they brought all the wars which they had with the Latins, the Samnites, and the Tuscans to a very speedy conclusion. And if we note all they did from the foundation of Rome until the siege of Veii, we shall observe that all their expeditions were completed in six, ten, or at most twenty days. For it was their custom so soon as war was declared to take the field immediately with their armies, and promptly to meet the enemy and give him battle; and when they had gained it, the enemy (to save his country from being devastated) came to terms, and the Romans condemned him to cede a portion of his territory, which they converted into private possessions, or established colonies upon it, and which, from being situated upon their confines, served as a guard to the Roman frontier, with equal benefit to the colonists who received these possessions and to Rome, which was thus guarded without expense. Nor can any plan be more effectual, secure, or more beneficial; for so long as the enemy remained quiet, so long did that guard suffice; and if he came out in force to threaten the colony, the Romans also took the field in force and quickly engaged him in battle and defeated him, and, having imposed upon him heavier conditions than before, they returned home. And thus they increased from day to day their reputation with their enemies, as well as their strength within their own state. They adhered closely to this system until after the siege of Veii, when they changed it. And to enable them to carry on longer wars, and at greater distances, they began to pay their soldiers, which until then they had not done, not deeming it necessary for short wars. But notwithstanding their paying their troops so as to enable them to keep the field longer, yet they never varied from their original system of finishing the wars as quickly as possible, according to time and place; nor did they ever omit the establishment of colonies. For apart from their usual custom, the ambition of the Consuls also contributed to make the wars short, for being elected only for one year, the half of which they were obliged to remain in quarters, they naturally wanted to finish the wars quickly, so as to enable them to have the honors of triumph; and the establishment of colonies proved of the greatest public advantage and convenience. In the distribution of the booty the Romans, however, made some changes. In this they were not so liberal as they had been at first, partly because it did not seem to them so necessary since the soldiers received regular pay, and partly because the booty was so much larger that they applied it to the enriching of the public treasury, so that they might be able to carry on their enterprises without subjecting the city to any contributions; and in this way the public treasury became in a short time very rich. These two ways, then, of disposing of the booty and of establishing colonies caused the Romans to become enriched by their wars, whilst less wise states were impoverished by theirs; and this at last came to such a point that a Consul was not considered as having merited the honors of triumph if he did not bring home to the treasury large quantities of gold and silver, and all sorts of other booty.

And by their above-described conduct in terminating each war promptly, but exhausting at the same time their enemies by the constant renewal of the wars, and by defeating their armies and devastating their territories, and imposing conditions that were most advantageous to themselves, the Romans steadily increased their wealth and power.

Chapter VII

HOW MUCH LAND THE ROMANS ALLOWED TO EACH COLONIST

IT is difficult to find out the truth as to the precise extent of land which the Romans conceded to each colonist. I believe they gave them more or less, according to the locality where they established the colony; but I judge that, under all circumstances and in all localities, the quantity of land bestowed was small. For the reasons, first, that they might send a greater number of men to the colonies, who were to serve as a guard to the country; and, secondly, because the Romans were poor at home, and it would not have been reasonable that they should have wished their colonists to become accustomed to too much abundance.

Titus Livius tells us that, after the taking of Veii, the Romans established a colony there, and distributed to each man three and seven twelfths *jugers,* equal to two and two thirds acres English measure. For besides the above considerations, they judged that it was not the extent of land, but its good cultivation, that made wealth. It is necessary also that each colony should have public pastures for their cattle, and forests to supply wood for fuel, without which no colony could exist.

Chapter VIII

THE REASONS WHY PEOPLE LEAVE THEIR OWN COUNTRY TO SPREAD OVER OTHERS

SINCE we have discussed above the manner in which the Romans conducted their wars, and how the Tuscans were attacked by the Gauls, it seems to me not foreign to the subject to point out that there are two different kinds of war. The one springs from the ambition of princes or republics that seek to extend their empire; such were the wars of Alexander the Great, and those of the Romans, and those which two hostile powers carry on against each other. These wars are dangerous, but never go so far as to drive all its inhabitants out of a province, because the conqueror is satisfied with the submission of the people, and generally leaves them their dwellings and possessions, and even the enjoyment of their own institutions. The other kind of war is when an entire people, constrained by famine or war, leave their country with their families for the purpose of seeking a new home in a new country, not for the purpose of subjecting it to their dominion as in the first case, but with the intention of taking absolute possession of it themselves and driving out or killing its original inhabitants. This kind of war is most frightful and cruel; and it is of this kind of war that Sallust speaks at the end of the history of Jugurtha, when he says that, after Jugurtha was vanquished, they heard of the movements of the Gauls, who were coming into Italy. He then tells us that the Romans had combated all the other nations only for the purpose of subjecting them to their empire, but that in their contest with the Gauls each side fought for its very existence. A prince or a republic that assails another country is satisfied merely to kill its chiefs, but when an entire people aims to possess itself of a country and to live upon that which gives support to its original inhabitants, it must necessarily destroy them all.

The Romans had three such most dangerous wars to sustain. The first was when Rome itself was taken by the same Gauls, who, as we have said, had taken Lombardy from the Tuscans, and established themselves in that country. Titus Livius assigns two causes for this invasion: the first, which I have already mentioned, was that the Gauls were tempted by the delicious fruits, and especially the wine of Italy, which they had not in their own country; the second was that Gaul was so overpopulated that the country could not support all its inhabitants, and therefore its chiefs deemed it necessary that a portion of them should go in search of a new country for their dwelling-place. Having formed that resolution they chose as captains of those who were to leave Bellovesus and Sicovesus, two of their princes, of whom the first came into Italy and the other went to Spain. It was this descent of Bellovesus into Italy that led to the occupation of Lombardy, and afterwards to the first attack of the Gauls upon Rome. The second war with the Gauls occurred soon after the first Carthaginian war, and it was then that the Romans slaughtered over two hundred thousand Gauls between Piombino and Pisa. The third war of this kind was when the Teutons and the Cimbrians came into Italy, who, after having defeated several Roman armies, were themselves utterly vanquished by Marius. The Romans then were victorious in these three most perilous wars; and it required all their energy to enable them to be successful; for we see that when their armies afterwards lost their ancient valor, the Roman Empire was destroyed by similar hordes, such as the Goths,

Vandals, and others, who made themselves masters of the whole Western Empire.

These tribes migrated from their own countries, as we have said above, driven by hunger, or war, or some other scourge, which they had experienced at home and which obliged them to seek new dwelling-places elsewhere. Sometimes they came in overwhelming numbers, making violent irruptions into other countries, killing the inhabitants and taking possession of their goods, establishing new kingdoms and changing the very names of the countries. This was done by Moses, and equally by those Barbarian tribes that took possession of the Roman Empire. In fact, the new names which we find in Italy and in other countries have no other origin than in the fact of being so called by their new occupants; such for instance as Lombardy, which was called Cisalpine Gaul, whilst France was called Transalpine Gaul, and now it is called after the Franks who conquered it. Slavonia was called Illyria, Hungary Pannonia, England Britannia; and thus many other countries have changed names, to enumerate which would be tedious. Moses also changed the name of that part of Syria which he occupied into Judæa. And as I have said above that peoples are sometimes driven from their own countries by war, which obliges them to seek new dwelling-places, I will cite the example of the Maurusians, originally inhabiting Syria, who, when they heard of the coming of the Hebrews, considered themselves not strong enough to resist them, and therefore deemed it best to leave their country and save themselves, rather than to attempt to save the former and be themselves destroyed. They therefore left Syria with their families and went into Africa, where they established themselves, after driving away the original inhabitants whom they found there. And thus the same people, who were incapable of defending their own country, yet could seize and occupy that of others. Procopius, who wrote an account of the war which Belisarius carried on against the Vandals who had taken possession of Africa, relates that he himself had seen inscriptions on certain columns in the places that were inhabited by these Maurusians, in these words: "We Maurusians who fled from before Jesus the Robber, son of Nava,"—whence we see the reason of their having left Syria. Those people, therefore, who are driven from their own country by the extremest necessity are the most dangerous, and can be resisted only when opposed by formidable armies. But when such as are obliged to leave their own country are not numerous, then of course they are less dangerous than a whole people such as we have spoken of; for they cannot then effect anything by force, but must employ cunning and address to obtain possession of some abiding-place; and having succeeded in this, they must seek to maintain themselves there by friendships and alliances. It was thus that Æneas did, and Dido and the Massilians and others, who all maintained themselves in the places where they had established themselves with the consent of the inhabitants of those countries.

The great hordes of Barbarians that have overrun other countries have nearly all come from Scythia, a cold and sterile country, whence they were compelled to migrate, the population being very great and the country too poor to support it; there being many causes that drove them away, and none to retain them. And if there have been no similar irruptions of Barbarians during the past few hundred years, it is owing to a variety of reasons. The first was the great migration that occurred at the time of the decline of the Roman Empire, when more than thirty entire tribes left Scythia. The second was that Germany and Hungary, whence also similar swarms of people had issued, have so improved their countries that their population can exist there with comfort, and therefore have no occasion for migrating. And furthermore the men of these two nations are most warlike, and thus serve as a dike and bulwark to keep the Scythians, whose country joins theirs, from presuming to pass them. There have been also at times great movements amongst the Tartar hordes, but these have been checked by the Hungarians and the Poles, who have often boasted that had it not been for their armies both Italy and the Church would many a time have felt the pressure of these Tartar hordes. Let this suffice of those people.

Chapter IX

WHAT THE CAUSES ARE THAT MOST FREQUENTLY PROVOKE WAR BETWEEN SOVEREIGNS

THE cause of the war between the Romans and the Samnites, who had for a long time been allies, was that which generally produces ruptures between great powers. This cause is sometimes due to accident, or it results from the policy of the party that desires to make the war. Between the Romans and the Samnites the cause of war was accidental; for the intention of the Samnites in attacking the Sidicians, and afterwards the Campanians, was not to provoke war with the Romans. But the Campanians, being hard pressed, appealed for help to Rome, against the wishes both of the Romans and the Samnites, and gave themselves entirely to the Romans, who for their defence had to take the war upon themselves, believing that they could not with honor avoid it. For although they felt that it was not reasonable that they should defend the Campanians against the Samnites, who were their own allies, yet it seemed to them that it would be disgraceful in them not to defend them as voluntary subjects; persuaded that, if they did not undertake their defence, it would have the effect of alienating forever all those who might desire to come voluntarily under their dominion. And as the aim of Rome was empire and glory, and not repose, they could not decline this opportunity.

A similar occasion gave rise to the first war against the Carthaginians, when the Romans undertook the defence of the Messenians in Sicily, which may also be attributed to accident. But the second war between the Romans and Carthaginians was not accidental; for Hannibal, the Carthaginian general, assailed the Saguntines, who were the allies of the Romans in Spain, not so much for the purpose of injuring the Saguntines as to provoke the Romans to arms, so as to have occasion to combat them and pass into Italy. This mode of provoking new wars has always been common amongst potentates, who want at least to make a show of respect for treaties. For if I desire to make war upon any prince with whom I have concluded treaties that have been faithfully observed for a length of time, I shall attack some friend or ally of his under some color of justification, well knowing that, in thus attacking his friend, he will resent it, and I shall then have grounds for declaring war against him; or, if he does not resent it, he will thereby manifest his weakness and lack of fidelity in not defending an ally entitled to his protection. And one or the other of these means will make him lose his reputation, and facilitate the execution of my designs.

We must note, in relation to the course of the Campanians in giving themselves as voluntary subjects to the Romans by way of inducing these to assume the war against the Samnites, that the best remedy which a city has, that is unable to defend herself alone, and is yet resolved anyhow to resist her aggressor, is to give herself freely to whomever she desires for her defender; as the Campanians did to the Romans, and the Florentines to King Robert of Naples, who, though unwilling to defend them as friends, yet defended them afterwards as subjects against the power of Castruccio of Lucca, when he pressed them hard.

Chapter X

MONEY IS NOT THE SINEWS OF WAR, ALTHOUGH IT IS GENERALLY SO CONSIDERED

EVERY one may begin a war at his pleasure, but cannot so finish it. A prince, therefore, before engaging in any enterprise should well measure his strength, and govern himself accordingly; and he must be very careful not to deceive himself in the estimate of his strength, which he will assuredly do if he measures it by his money, or by the situation of his country, or the good disposition of his people, unless he has at the same time an armed force of his own. For although the above things will increase his strength, yet they will not give it to him, and of themselves are nothing, and will be of no use without a devoted army. Neither abundance of money nor natural strength of the country will suffice, nor will the loyalty and good will of his subjects endure, for these cannot remain faithful to a prince who is incapable of defending them. Neither mountains nor lakes nor inaccessible places will present any difficulties to an enemy where there is a lack of brave defenders. And money alone, so far from being a means of defence, will only render a prince the more liable to being plundered. There cannot, therefore, be a more erroneous opinion than that money is the sinews of war. This was said by Quintus Curtius in the war between Antipater of Macedon and the king of Sparta, when he tells that want of money obliged the king of Sparta to come to battle, and that he was routed; whilst, if he could have delayed the battle a few days, the news of the death of Alexander would have reached Greece, and in that case he would have remained victor without fighting. But lacking money, and fearing the defection of his army, who were unpaid, he was obliged to try the fortune of battle, and was defeated; and in consequence of this, Quintus Curtius affirms money to be the sinews of war. This opinion is constantly quoted, and is acted upon by princes who are unwise enough to follow it; for relying upon it, they believe that plenty of money is all they require for their defence, never thinking that, if treasure were sufficient to insure victory, Darius would have vanquished Alexander, and the Greeks would have triumphed over the Romans; and, in our day, Duke Charles the Bold would have beaten the Swiss; and, quite recently, the Pope and the Florentines together would have had no difficulty in defeating Francesco Maria, nephew of Pope Julius II., in the war of Urbino. All that we have named were vanquished by those who regarded good troops, and not money, as the sinews of war. Amongst other objects of interest which Crœsus, king of Lydia, showed to Solon of Athens, was his countless treasure; and to the question as to what he thought of his power, Solon replied, "that he did not consider him powerful on that account, because war was made with iron, and not with gold, and that some one might come who had more iron than he, and would take his gold from him." When after the death of Alexander the Great an immense swarm of Gauls descended into Greece, and thence into Asia, they sent ambassadors to the

king of Macedon to treat with him for peace. The king, by
way of showing his power, and to dazzle them, displayed
before them great quantities of gold and silver; whereupon
the ambassadors of the Gauls, who had already as good as
signed the treaty, broke off all further negotiations, excited
by the intense desire to possess themselves of all this gold;
and thus the very treasure which the king had accumulated
for his defence brought about his spoliation. The Venetians,
a few years ago, having also their treasury full, lost their
entire state without their money availing them in the least
in their defence.

I maintain, then, contrary to the general opinion, that the
sinews of war are not gold, but good soldiers; for gold alone
will not procure good soldiers, but good soldiers will always
procure gold. Had the Romans attempted to make their
wars with gold instead of with iron, all the treasure of the
world would not have sufficed them, considering the great
enterprises they were engaged in, and the difficulties they
had to encounter. But by making their wars with iron, they
never suffered for the want of gold; for it was brought to
them, even into their camp, by those who feared them. And
if want of money forced the king of Sparta to try the fortune
of battle, it was no more than what often happened from
other causes; for we have seen that armies short of provisions, and having to starve or hazard a battle, will always
prefer the latter as the more honorable course, and where fortune may yet in some way favor them. It has also often happened that a general, seeing that his opposing enemy is about
to receive reinforcements, has preferred to run the risk of a
battle at once, rather than wait until his enemy is reinforced
and fight him then under greater disadvantage. We have
seen also in the case of Asdrubal, when he was attacked
upon the river Metaurus by Claudius Nero, together with an-

other Roman Consul, that a general who has to choose between battle or flight will always prefer to fight, as then,
even in the most doubtful case, there is still a chance of victory, whilst in flight his loss is certain anyhow.

There are, then, an infinity of reasons that may induce a
general to give battle against his will, and the want of money
may in some instances be one of them; but that is no reason
why money should be deemed the sinews of war, which
more than anything else will influence him to that course.
I repeat it again, then, that it is not gold, but good soldiers,
that insure success in war. Certainly money is a necessity, but
a secondary one, which good soldiers will overcome; for it
is as impossible that good soldiers should not be able to
procure gold, as it is impossible for gold to procure good
soldiers. History proves in a thousand cases what I maintain, notwithstanding that Pericles counselled the Athenians
to make war with the entire Peloponnesus, demonstrating
to them that by perseverance and the power of money they
would be successful. And although it is true that the Athenians obtained some successes in that war, yet they succumbed
in the end; and good counsels and the good soldiers of
Sparta prevailed over the perseverance and money of the
Athenians. But the testimony of Titus Livius upon this
question is more direct than any other, where, in discussing
whether Alexander the Great, had he come into Italy, would
have vanquished the Romans, he points out that there are
three things pre-eminently necessary to success in war,—
plenty of good troops, sagacious commanders, and good fortune; and in examining afterwards whether the Romans or
Alexander excelled most in these three points, he draws his
conclusion without ever mentioning the subject of money.
The Campanians, when requested by the Sidicians to take
up arms in their behalf against the Samnites, may have

measured their strength by their money, and not by their soldiers; for having resolved to grant the required assistance, they were constrained after two defeats to become tributary to the Romans to save themselves.

Chapter XI

IT IS NOT WISE TO FORM AN ALLIANCE WITH A PRINCE THAT HAS MORE REPUTATION THAN POWER

TITUS LIVIUS, wishing to show the error of the Sidicians in trusting to the aid of the Campanians, and the mistake of the latter in thinking themselves able to help them, could not have expressed this idea more forcibly than in these words: "The Campanians brought a greater name in aid of the Sidicians than forces for their protection." Whence we should conclude that the alliances made with princes who on account of their remoteness cannot conveniently come to your assistance, or who lack the power to do so from internal dissensions or from any other cause, bring more reputation than substantial help to those who rely upon them. This happened in our day to the Florentines, when they were assailed in 1479 by the Pope and the king of Naples, and when they derived from their alliance with the king of France "more reputation than protection." The same thing would also happen to any one who should engage in any enterprise relying upon the friendship of the Emperor Maximilian; for that would be one of those alliances that would bring to him who made it "more reputation than protection," like what we have said of the Campanians and the Sidicians.

The Campanians, then, made a mistake in imagining

themselves more powerful than they were in reality; and thus a want of proper judgment sometimes causes men, who are incompetent to defend themselves, to engage in war for the defence of others. This was done also by the Tarentines, who, when the Roman army was opposing that of the Samnites, sent ambassadors to the Roman Consul to let him know that they wanted peace between the two nations, and that they were ready to make war upon the one that should refuse peace. Whereupon the Consul, laughing at their proposition, caused his bugles to sound to battle in presence of the ambassadors, and commanded his army to attack the enemy; thus showing to the Tarentines by act and not by words of what answer he deemed their proposal worthy.

Having discussed in the present chapter the wrong course which princes sometimes take for the defence of others, I will in the next speak of the means they should employ for their own defence.

Chapter XII

WHETHER IT IS BETTER, WHEN APPREHENDING AN ATTACK, TO AWAIT IT AT HOME, OR TO CARRY THE WAR INTO THE ENEMY'S COUNTRY

I HAVE heard men of much practical experience in the art of war discuss the question whether, supposing there to be two princes of nearly equal power, one of whom, being the most spirited, has declared war against the other, it be better for the latter to await the attack within his own territory, or to march directly into the country of the former and attack him; and I have heard them give good reasons in favor of either proceeding. Those favoring the latter course cited

the advice given by Crœsus to Cyrus, to whom, upon arriving at the confines of the Messagetes, their queen, Tamiris,
sent to ask which course he preferred, whether to come into
her kingdom and attack her there, in which case she would
await him, or that she should come out to meet him beyond
her confines. When the matter was under discussion, Crœsus, contrary to the opinion of the others, advised Cyrus to
attack Tamiris within her own possessions, alleging that,
if he were to defeat her away from her country, he would
not be able to take her kingdom from her, as she would in
that case have time to recover; but if he vanquished her
within her dominions, he would be able to follow her in
her flight, and thus, without giving her time to recover, he
could deprive her of her state. They cited also the advice
which Hannibal gave to Antiochus, when that king contemplated war against the Romans, on which occasion that general pointed out to him that the Romans could never be
beaten except in Italy, for there he could turn against them
their arms, their allies, and their wealth; but if he combated
them away from Italy, leaving them that country undisturbed, he would leave them a never-failing source of sup-
ply·of forces whenever they might need them; and he concluded that it would be easier to take the city of Rome from
the Romans than their empire, and all Italy sooner than
her provinces. They furthermore adduced the case of Agathocles, who, not being able to sustain the attacks of the
Carthaginians at home, became the assailant himself, and
reduced them to the necessity of suing for peace. They also
cited Scipio, who, to relieve Italy, carried the war into Africa.

Those of the opposite opinion maintained that the greatest evil that can be inflicted upon an enemy is to draw him
away from his own country; and, in support of that opinion,
quoted the Athenians, who, so long as they made war at

their convenience at home, were always victorious, but when they sent their army to a distance from home into Sicily, lost their liberty. They cited the poetic fable, according to which Antæus, king of Libya, being attacked by Hercules the Egyptian, proved unconquerable so long as he remained within the limits of his own kingdom, but when he was drawn away from home by the artfulness of Hercules lost his state and his life. This gave rise to the fable that the giant Antæus, in his contest with Hercules, recovered his strength whenever thrown to the ground, the earth being his mother; and therefore Hercules, upon observing this, lifted him high in the air and crushed him. Amongst modern instances they cited the well-known case of King Ferdinand of Naples, esteemed one of the wisest princes of his time. When, two years before his death, the report came to him that Charles VIII., king of France, intended to attack him, he at once set to work to prepare for the war; but falling sick and about to die, he left, amongst other instructions to his son Alfonso, the advice to await the enemy within his kingdom, and on no account to move his forces outside of his own dominions. Alfonso, however, did not heed this advice, but sent his army into the Romagna, and, without fighting, lost it and his state. Besides the instances quoted, the reasons brought forward in favor of one or the other opinion were, that he who attacks acts with more spirit than he who awaits the attack, and so inspires the troops with greater confidence; by attacking the enemy in his own country, you deprive him also of many advantages in availing of his resources; his subjects, who are plundered, can afford him no assistance, and the presence of the enemy constrains the prince to be more considerate in exacting money or too many other services from them; so that, as Alexander said, the very sources that enable him to sustain the war will be dried up. Besides, the attacking troops, being in a strange country, feel the necessity of fighting, which very necessity inspires them with greater courage.

On the other hand, it is said that by awaiting the enemy many advantages are gained, for without inconveniencing your own people you may cause great inconvenience to the enemy in the supply of provisions and all the other things that an army requires. By the better knowledge of the country you can impede the enemy's designs; and the facility of uniting all your troops enables you to oppose him with greater numbers, whilst he has not been able to withdraw all his forces from his own country. And then in case of defeat you can more readily reorganize your army, because many of your soldiers will escape, finding ready places of refuge near at hand. Nor have you to send to a distance for reinforcements, so that you are enabled to employ all your forces without risking all your fortune, whilst in a distant war you risk all your fortune without being able to employ all your forces. Some by way of more effectually weakening the enemy permit him to enter some days' march into their country, and allow him to take a number of places, so that his army may be weakened by his having to garrison those places, and then they may be able to combat him the more easily.

But to say now what I think on the subject, I believe that we must make this distinction. A country is either well armed, as that of the Romans was, or as that of the Swiss is nowadays; or it is not well armed, as was the case with the Carthaginians, and is at present with France and Italy. In the latter case you must keep the enemy at a distance; for as your strength consists in your money, and not in soldiers, you are lost whenever you are prevented from availing of your financial resources, and nothing interferes so much with that as war within your own territory. The Carthaginians are an instance of this: so long as they were undisturbed at home, their revenues enabled them to carry on the war against the Romans; but when they were attacked in their own country, they were not able even to resist Agathocles. The Florentines could not defend themselves against Castruccio, lord of Lucca, who had attacked them at home, so that they were obliged to give themselves to Robert of Naples to obtain his protection. But after the death of Castruccio these same Florentines had the courage to attack the Duke of Milan within his own dominions, and to deprive him of his state. As much courage as they displayed in the war at a distance, just so much weakness did they exhibit in the war at home. But when nations are armed as the Romans were and the Swiss are, then it becomes the more difficult to overcome them the nearer home they are attacked; for then these states can unite more forces to resist an invasion than to attack an enemy at a distance. Nor does the authority of Hannibal affect my opinion upon that point; for his passions and his interests dictated the counsel he had given to Antiochus. For if the Romans had experienced in Gaul three such defeats as they suffered at the hands of Hannibal in Italy, they would certainly have been ruined; for they could not have availed of the fragments of their armies as they did in Italy, and could not have reorganized them with the same ease; nor could they have resisted the enemy so well with the same forces. They never sent more than fifty thousand men to invade any province; but to defend themselves at home against the Gauls after the first Punic war, they put eighteen hundred thousand men under arms. Nor could they have vanquished the Gauls in Lombardy as they did in Tuscany, for they could not have moved so large a force against that numerous enemy at so great a distance, nor carried on the war there with the same advantages. The Cimbrians routed a Roman army in Germany, and the Romans could not repair the disaster; but when the Cimbrians came into Italy, the Romans were able to unite all their forces and destroyed the Cimbrians. The Swiss are easily beaten when away from home, where they cannot send more than thirty or forty thousand men; but it is most difficult to overcome them at home, where they are able to gather together a hundred thousand men.

I conclude then, again, that a prince who has his people well armed and disciplined for war should always await a powerful and dangerous enemy at home, and should not go to meet him at a distance. But a prince whose subjects are unarmed, and the country unaccustomed to war, should always keep it as far away from home as possible; and thus both one and the other will best defend themselves, each in his own way.

Chapter XIII

CUNNING AND DECEIT WILL SERVE A MAN BETTER THAN FORCE TO RISE FROM A BASE CONDITION TO GREAT FORTUNE

I BELIEVE it to be most true that it seldom happens that men rise from low condition to high rank without employing either force or fraud, unless that rank should be attained either by gift or inheritance. Nor do I believe that force alone will ever be found to suffice, whilst it will often be the case that cunning alone serves the purpose; as is clearly seen by whoever reads the life of Philip of Macedon, or that of Agathocles the Sicilian, and many others, who from the lowest or most moderate condition have achieved thrones and great empires. Xenophon shows in his Life of Cyrus the necessity of deception to success: the first expedition of Cyrus against the king of Armenia is replete with fraud, and it was deceit alone, and not force, that enabled him to seize that kingdom. And Xenophon draws no other conclusion from it than that a prince who wishes to achieve great things must learn to deceive. Cyrus also practised a variety of deceptions upon Cyaxares, king of the Medes, his maternal uncle; and Xenophon shows that without these frauds Cyrus would never have achieved the greatness which he did attain. Nor do I believe that there was ever a man who from obscure condition arrived at great power by merely employing open force; but there are many who have succeeded by fraud alone, as, for instance, Giovanni Galeazzo Visconti in taking the state and sovereignty of Lombardy from his uncle, Messer Bernabo. And that which princes are obliged to do in the beginning of their rise, republics are equally obliged to practise until they have become powerful enough so that force alone suffices them. And as Rome employed every means, by chance or choice, to promote her aggrandizement, so she also did not hesitate to employ fraud; nor could she have practised a greater fraud than by taking the course we have explained above of making other peoples her allies and associates, and under that title making them slaves, as she did with the Latins and other neighboring nations. For first she availed of their arms to subdue their mutual neighbors, and thus to increase her state and reputation; and after having subdued these, her power increased to that degree that she could subjugate each people separately in turn. The Latins never became aware that they were wholly slaves until they had witnessed two defeats of the Samnites, and saw them obliged to accept the terms of peace dictated to them. As this victory greatly increased the reputation of the Romans with the more distant princes, who felt the weight of their name before experiencing that of their arms, so it excited envy and apprehension in those who had seen and felt their arms, amongst whom were the Latins. And this jealousy and fear were so powerful that not only the Latins, but also the colonies which the Romans had established in Latium, together with the Campanians, whose defence the Romans had but a short time previously undertaken, conspired together against the Romans. The Latins began the war in the way we have shown that most wars are begun, not by attacking the Romans, but by defending the Sidicians from the Samnites, against whom the latter were making war with the permission of the Romans. And that it is true that the Latins began the war because they had at last become aware of the bad faith of the Romans is demonstrated by Titus Livius, when at an assembly of the Latin people he puts the following words into the mouth of Annius Setinus, a Latin Prætor: "For if now we can bear servitude under the specious name of equal confederates," &c.

We see therefore that the Romans in the early beginning of their power already employed fraud, which it has ever been necessary for those to practise who from small beginnings wish to rise to the highest degree of power; and then it is the less censurable the more it is concealed, as was that practised by the Romans.

Chapter XIV

MEN OFTEN DECEIVE THEMSELVES IN BELIEVING THAT BY HUMIL-ITY THEY CAN OVERCOME INSOLENCE

WE often see that humility not only is of no service, but is actually hurtful, especially when employed towards insolent men, who from jealousy or some other motive have conceived a hatred against you. Of this our historian gives proof on the occasion of the war between the Romans and Latins. For when the Samnites complained to the Romans that the Latins had attacked them, the Romans, unwilling to irritate the Latins, declined to forbid them to continue that war: this not only had the desired effect of not irritating them, but actually encouraged them to that degree that they almost immediately displayed open enmity towards the Romans. This appears from the words employed by the same Latin Prætor Annius, at the same assembly·mentioned above, when he said: "You have put their patience to the proof in refusing them troops; who can doubt that this would have excited their resentment, and yet they have quietly borne this vexation. They have heard that we are arming against their allies the Samnites, and yet have not stirred from their city. Whence then comes their great modesty, but from their knowledge of our power and their own?" These words show in the clearest manner to what degree the patience of the Romans increased the insolence of the Latins. And therefore no prince should ever forego his rank, nor should he ever voluntarily give up anything (wishing to do so honorably) unless he is able or believes himself able to hold it. For it is almost always better (matters having come to the point that he cannot give it up in the above manner) to allow it to be taken from him by force, rather than by the apprehension of force. For if he yields it from fear, it is for the purpose of avoiding war, and he will rarely escape from that; for he to whom he has from cowardice conceded the one thing will not be satisfied, but will want to take other things from him, and his arrogance will increase as his esteem for the prince is lessened. And, on the other hand, the zeal of the prince's friends will be chilled on seeing him appear feeble or cowardly. But if, so soon as he discerns his adversary's intention, he prepares his forces, even though they be inferior, the enemy will begin to respect him, and the other neighboring princes will appreciate him the more; and seeing him armed for defence, those even will come to his aid who, seeing him give up himself, would never have assisted him.

This reasoning applies to the case when there is only one enemy; but when there are several, it will always be a wise plan for the prince to yield something of his possessions to some one of them, either for the purpose of gaining him over if war has already been declared, or to detach him from the enemies that are leagued against him.

Chapter XV

FEEBLE STATES ARE ALWAYS UNDECIDED IN THEIR RESOLVES; AND SLOW RESOLVES ARE INVARIABLY INJURIOUS

In connection with this war between the Latins and the Romans, and its origin, we should observe that it is well in all deliberations to come at once to the essential point, and not always to remain in a state of indecision and uncertainty.

This was evidenced in the council which the Latins held on the occasion when they contemplated detaching themselves from the Romans. For the Romans, being apprised of the evil disposition of the Latin people, wished to assure themselves upon that point, and to see whether they might regain their friendship without resorting to arms, and therefore requested the Latins to send eight of their citizens to Rome for a conference. When the Latins were informed of this, conscious of having done many things that were displeasing to the Romans, they convoked a council to decide as to who should go to Rome, and to instruct them as to what they should say. And whilst discussing the matter, their Prætor Annius said these words: "I hold it to be of the highest importance for our interests that we should think rather of what we shall do than what we shall say; when we have decided upon that, it will be easy to accommodate our words to our acts." Certainly a most correct maxim, and one that should be borne in mind by all princes and republics; for it is impossible to explain one's self properly when in doubt and indecision as to what is to be done; but once resolved and decided, it is easy to find suitable words. I have the more willingly remarked upon this point as I have often known such indecision to interfere with proper public action, to the detriment and shame of our republic. And it will always happen that in doubtful cases, where prompt resolution is required, there will be this indecision when weak men have to deliberate and resolve. Slow and dilatory deliberations are not less injurious than indecision, especially when you have to decide in favor of an ally; for tardiness helps no one, and generally injures yourself. It ordinarily arises from lack of courage or force, or from the evil disposition of those who have to deliberate, being influenced by passion to ruin the state or to serve some personal interests, and who therefore do not allow the deliberations to proceed, but thwart and impede them in every way. Good citizens therefore never impede deliberations, especially in matters that admit of no delay, even if they see the popular impulse tending to a dangerous course.

After the death of Hieronymus, tyrant of Syracuse, and whilst the war between the Carthaginians and Romans was at its height, a difference arose amongst the Syracusans whether they should declare in favor of the Romans or the Carthaginians. And party feeling ran so high that the matter remained undecided, and they came to no conclusion until finally Apollonides, one of the first men of Syracuse, in a speech full of good sense, showed them "that those were to blame who were of the opinion that they should adhere to the cause of the Romans, and not those who wanted them to support the Carthaginians; but that their indecision and tardiness in determining either one way or the other was greatly to be deprecated, because that indecision would assuredly lead to the ruin of the republic; but when they once had decided upon a course, whatever it might be, they might then hope to derive some advantage from it." Titus Livius could not have shown the disadvantages of indecision more strikingly than by this example. He shows it also in the case of the Latins, when they had asked the Lavinians for help against the Romans. These delayed so long before determining upon it, that, when they had finally just marched out of the city to render the wished for succor, the news came that the Latins were routed; this caused their Prætor Milonius to say, "that this short march would cost them dear with the Romans; for if they had decided at once either to assist the Latins or not, they would in the latter case not have irritated the Romans; and in the former case, their help, having come in time, might by the junction of their forces have enabled the Latins to be victorious; but that, by delaying their decision, they could but lose in either case,"—as indeed it happened.

If the Florentines had acted upon this principle they would not have suffered so much trouble and injury from the French, when King Louis XII of France came into Italy to attack Lodovico, Duke of Milan. For when that king meditated this descent, he sought the alliance of the Florentines; and their ambassadors to the king agreed with him that Florence should remain neutral, on condition that the king after arriving in Italy should take their state under his protection, and that the republic should have one month's time to ratify this treaty. But this ratification was protracted so long by those who most imprudently favored the cause of Duke Lodovico, that before it was done the king had already been victorious; and when finally the Florentines wished to ratify the treaty, he declined it, seeing that the friendship of the Florentines was not a voluntary but a forced one. This cost the Florentines a great deal of money, and came near losing them their state, as happened to them another time afterwards from a similar cause. And this course was the more reprehensible as it was not even of service to Duke Lodovico, who, had he been victorious, would have shown even more resentment against the Florentines than King Louis did.

Although I have already in another chapter treated of the evils resulting to republics from such weakness, yet, as the opportunity presented itself anew, I wished to repeat it, because it seems to me one of the things which republics similar to ours should note especially.

Chapter XVI

WHEREIN THE MILITARY SYSTEM DIFFERS FROM THAT OF THE ANCIENTS

THE most important battle ever fought by the Romans in any war was that with the Latins during the consulate of Torquatus and Decius. As by the loss of this battle the Latins, as a matter of course, became slaves to the Romans, so would the latter have become slaves to the Latins if these had been victorious. Titus Livius is also of the same opinion; and represents the two armies to have been in all respects equal as regards numbers, discipline, bravery, and obstinacy, the only difference having been in the commanders, those of the Roman army having displayed more skill and heroism than those of the Latins. We also observe, in the course of this battle, two unprecedented occurrences, the like of which have hardly ever been known since; for to sustain the courage of their soldiers, and render them obedient to command and more determined in action, one of the two Consuls killed himself, and the other slew his son. The equality which Titus Livius says existed between the two armies resulted from the fact that they had for a long time combated together, spoke the same language, had the same discipline and the same arms; and therefore their order of battle was the same, and the very names of the divisions of their armies and their officers were identical. Being then of equal strength and courage, it was necessary that something extraordinary should occur to give greater steadiness and obstinacy to the courage of the one than the other; for, as we have said elsewhere, victory depends upon this stubbornness, for so long as that endures in the combatants, no army will ever turn its back. And to make that spirit more enduring in the hearts of the Romans than with the Latins, partly chance and partly the heroism of the Consuls gave occasion to Torquatus to sacrifice his son, and Decius to kill himself.

In demonstrating this equality of the two contending armies, Titus Livius gives the whole organization of the Roman armies, and their order of battle; as he has explained this very fully, I shall not repeat it here, but will only remark upon such points as seem to me especially noteworthy, and the neglect of which by all the commanders of our times has given rise to great disorders in the armies during battle. I say, then, that from the evidence of Titus Livius we gather that the Roman armies were composed of three main divisions; the first was called "Hastati," the second "Principi," and the third "Triarii," and each of these divisions had its cavalry. In the ordering of a battle they placed the Hastati in front, directly behind came the Principi, and the third rank was formed of the Triarii. The cavalry of all of them were placed to the right and left of each line, and these squadrons, from their form and the place they occupied, were called "Alæ," or wings, because they seemed like two wings of the body of the army. The division of the Hastati, which was in front, was closely serried, so that they might more effectually strike the enemy, or sustain the shock of his attack. The line of the Principi (not being the first to engage in the fight, and bound to support the first line when it was struck or in danger of being overcome) was not closely serried like the first, but kept its ranks open so as to receive within them the first, without being thrown into confusion by it, whenever the pressure of the enemy obliged them to retreat. The third line, or the

Triarii, had to keep its ranks even more open than the second, so that in case of need it might receive within them the lines of both the Hastati and the Principi. These three lines thus deployed began the battle, and if the line of the Hastati was forced or beaten, they retreated within the open ranks of the Principi, and the two lines thus united into one renewed the fight; and if these were also forced and repulsed, they all fell back within the open ranks of the Triarii, and all three lines, now forming but one body, again resumed the battle; and if they were overpowered (having no further reserve to fall back upon) the day was lost. And as every time that the line of the Triarii became engaged, the army was considered in danger, it gave rise to the saying, "The matter has come to the Triarii," which was as much as to say, "We have come to our last resource."

The commanders of our day, having entirely abandoned the ancient military organization and discipline, have also abandoned this plan of order of battle, which is none the less a most important one. For a general who disposes his army in such manner that it can rally three several times in the course of a battle, must have fortune against him three times before being defeated, and must have an enemy opposed to him sufficiently superior to overcome him three times. But if an army can resist only a single shock, as is the case nowadays with the Christian armies, it may easily lose the battle; for with the slightest disorder even the most mediocre courage may carry off the victory. And what prevents our armies from being able to rally three times is the abandonment of the old Roman method of receiving one rank within another; and this has arisen from the present system of order of battle, which has one of these two defects: either the troops are formed shoulder to shoulder in one line, so as to present a very wide front and very little depth, which makes the order of battle very weak, being so thin; or, by way of making it stronger, they reduce the width of front, and form their troops according to the Roman fashion. In the latter case, if the first rank is broken, it will be unable to fall back into the second rank, which has no open spaces to receive it, and they will fall into utter confusion, and be disorganized; for if the front rank be struck, it will recoil upon the second line, and if the second line wishes to come to the front, it is impeded by the first. Thus the first line pushing upon the second, and the second upon the third, there ensues such confusion that the slightest accident may cause the loss of the whole army.

At the battle of Ravenna, which according to our modern ideas was a well-contested battle, in which the French commander, Gaston de Foix, was killed, the French and Spanish troops formed in the manner first above described, that is to say, the two armies were placed side by side, so as to present a very wide front and but little depth. And this is the order generally adopted by modern commanders when they have a large plain for their battle-ground, as at Ravenna; for they are so convinced of the disorder produced by the falling back of the first line upon the second, that they avoid as much as possible the system of several successive lines, and form a wide front, as we have explained. But when the nature of the country restricts them in this, they are obliged to adopt the other system, without thinking of preventing its disadvantages. In similar disorder their cavalry rides through the enemy's country for the purpose of plunder, or some other hostile purpose. At Santo Regolo and elsewhere, in the war which the Florentines carried on against the Pisans on account of their rebellion, after the coming into Italy of Charles VIII., king of France, the Florentines owed their defeat to nothing but their own cavalry, which being in front was repulsed by the enemy, and, being thrown back upon the Florentine infantry, broke through their lines; whereupon all the rest of the army turned their backs and took to flight. Messer Criaco del Borgo, general of the Florentine infantry, has repeatedly assured me himself that he would never have been routed but for his own cavalry. The Swiss, who are masters in the modern art of war, whenever they serve with the French, are above all careful to place themselves at the wings, so that, in case the cavalry of their allies is repulsed, it may not be thrown back upon them.

Although this would seem easy to understand, and even more easy to do, yet there has been thus far not one of our modern commanders who has imitated the method of the ancient Romans, and corrected the faults of the modern system. They divide their armies also into three corps, calling the first the "Vanguard," the second the "Corps of Battle," and the third the "Rear-guard"; but this division is of little use to them, except in providing quarters for them separately; for in active service it is rare that they do not unite them all into one body, so that all share the same fortune of battle. And generally, by way of excusing their ignorance, they allege that the force of the artillery will not allow them in the present day to follow the ancient practices; but this point we will discuss in the following chapter, where we shall examine the question whether the use of artillery really prevents the adoption of the ancient method.

Chapter XVII

**OF THE VALUE OF ARTILLERY TO MODERN ARMIES, AND WHETHER
THE GENERAL OPINION RESPECTING IT IS CORRECT**

CONSIDERING the many open field fights, or pitched battles
as they are called in our day, that were fought by the Romans
at various times, I have reflected upon the opinion so universally entertained, that, if artillery had existed in ancient
times, the Romans would not have been allowed so easily to
conquer provinces and make other peoples tributary to
themselves; nor would they in any way have been able to
extend their dominions so largely. It is further said, that
the use of these fire-arms prevents men from displaying the
same personal valor as they could in ancient times; that it
is more difficult to join battle than formerly, and that the
same organization and discipline of armies cannot be preserved; and that henceforth the battles will be fought mainly
by artillery. I deem it, therefore, not from our purpose to
examine whether these opinions are correct, and in how far
the introduction of artillery has increased or diminished the
strength of armies, and whether it gives or takes away from
good commanders the opportunity of acting valiantly.

I shall begin by examining the first proposition, that the
Romans never could have carried their conquests so far if
artillery had been in use in their time. To this I reply, that
wars are either defensive or aggressive, and thus we must
inquire first whether artillery be most useful for attack or
for defence. Whatever may be said on either side of the
question, I believe that it is beyond comparison more damaging to him who has to defend himself than to him who at-

tacks. My reason for saying this is, that he who is on the defensive is either within some fortified place, or he is in camp protected by intrenchments. If he is within a fortified place, it is either a small one, such as they generally are, or it is a large one. In the first case he is certainly lost, for the power of artillery is such that even the strongest walls will in a few days be battered down by it; and if he who is within has not a considerable space for retreat, and cannot protect himself by new ditches and earthworks, he is lost, and will not be able to resist the enemy, who will rush in through the breach in the wall, and whatever artillery he may have will in that case be of no use to him, for it is a maxim that artillery cannot resist an assault of troops in mass; and thus the fury of the Ultramontanes has never been resisted by those defending fortified places. The assaults of the Italians in battle are easily resisted when made, not in serried masses, but in small detachments, which assaults they very properly call skirmishes; and when they deliberately attempt in this disorderly manner to enter a breach where there is artillery, they go to manifest destruction, for in such case the artillery within is effective. But when a breach is assaulted by troops in dense masses, where one pushes upon the other, unless impeded by ditches and earthworks, they will succeed in entering any place; and although some will be killed, yet not so many as to prevent the victory. The truth of this has been demonstrated by many captures of strong places by the Ultramontanes in Italy, and especially that of Brescia; for when that city had revolted against the French, the citadel being still held by the king of France, the Venetians, by way of resisting the attacks of those who might enter the place, had mounted artillery in every convenient place, in front and flank, along the streets that lead from the citadel to the city. The French commander, Gaston de Foix, however, paid no attention to this, but marched down on foot with his troops, through the midst of the artillery, and took the city; and according to report his troops did not suffer seriously. Thus, whoever is besieged in a small place, having no space to enable him to retreat behind ditches and earthworks, after the walls are breached, and having to rely for his further defence solely upon his artillery, will quickly be lost. But supposing that you have to defend a large place, with ample space for convenient retreat, even then I maintain that the employment of artillery is without comparison more advantageous for the besiegers than the besieged. For to make artillery damage the besieger it must necessarily be placed higher than the level of the surrounding country, otherwise every little earthwork that the enemy may throw up will secure him against all your efforts to injure him; so that being obliged to raise your artillery upon your walls, or to elevate it in some other way above the level of the country, you expose yourself to two difficulties: the first, that you cannot thus place artillery of the same caliber and power as the besieger's, as that requires considerable space; the second is, that even if you should be able thus to place your guns, you cannot make your batteries secure against the artillery of the assailant, who has the advantage of being able to place his on higher ground, having all the convenience of space for manœuvring his guns which the besieged lacks. So that it is impossible for him who defends the place to keep his guns in an elevated position if the besieger has plenty and powerful artillery; and if his batteries are too low, then they are to a great extent useless, as we have said above. Thus the defence of fortified cities depends upon the arms and valor of the garrison, the same as in ancient times, and upon artillery of small caliber, and the little advantage derived from that is almost entirely counterbalanced by disad-

vantages; for it obliges you to give but little elevation to
your walls and to bury them, as it were, in the ditches; so
that when you come to a hand-to-hand fight after the walls
are breached or the ditches filled up, you will be at greater
disadvantage than before; and therefore, as we have said
above, the use of artillery is of greater advantage to the besieger than to the besieged.

In the third case, when you intrench yourself in camp, so
as not to be forced to deliver battle except at your convenience or advantage, I maintain that under those circumstances
you have generally no better means for defence or combat
than what the ancients had; and often even your artillery
operates to your disadvantage, for if the enemy turns your
intrenchments so as to get into your rear, and has but slightly the advantage of you in the ground, which may easily
happen, so as to place him but a little higher than you are,
or should he attack you before your intrenchments are sufficiently completed to cover you effectually, he may quickly
dislodge you, and thus there is nothing left you but to issue
from your intrenchments and come to battle. This happened
to the Spaniards at the battle of Ravenna, who, being posted
between the river Ronco and an earthwork which had not
been raised high enough, and the French having slightly
the advantage of the ground, were forced by the latter to
leave their intrenchments and come to open battle. But supposing, as must often happen, that you have chosen the
highest ground in the neighborhood for your camp, and that
your intrenchments are good and sufficient, so that owing
to your position and your other preparations the enemy does
not venture to attack you, in that case he will resort to the
same means as the ancients did when the adversary had
placed himself in an impregnable position; that is, he will
scour the country, plunder the towns and villages of your

allies, and cut off your supplies of provisions, so that you will be forced to abandon your intrenchments and come to battle, where your artillery will avail you but little, as we shall show further on. If now we recall to mind the manner in which the Romans made war, and remember that all their wars were aggressive and not defensive, we must see (from all that has been said above) that they would have had even greater advantages if they had had the use of artillery, and that their conquests would have been even more rapid than they were.

Now, as to the second proposition, that, since the introduction of artillery men cannot display the same personal bravery as anciently, I maintain that, where men have to present themselves to the fire in small and scattered numbers, they are exposed to greater danger than when in ancient times they had to escalade a place, or make similar assaults, in which they had to act, not in a compact body, but singly and one after the other. It is also true that the lives of the commanders and principal officers of the armies are more exposed now than formerly; for as they can be reached everywhere by the artillery, it is of no use for them to place themselves in the rear ranks, protected by their best men. Nevertheless, we see that these dangers rarely cause any extraordinary losses; for places that are well supplied with artillery are not taken by escalade, nor are they attempted to be taken by feeble assaults, but are regularly besieged, as was done in ancient days. And even with such places as can be taken by assault, the danger is not much greater now than then; for even in those days the ancients did not lack means of defending their places by throwing projectiles upon the enemy, which, although not so noisy as cannon, yet were equally effective in the killing of men. As to the danger of death to which commanders and leaders of bands are said to be more exposed nowadays, the twenty-four years during which the last war in Italy was protracted furnish fewer examples of generals killed than any ten years of war of the ancients. For with the exception of the Count Louis de Mirandola, who was killed at Ferrara when the Venetians besieged that city a few years ago, and the Duke of Nemours, who was killed at Cirignuola, none were killed by artillery; for Gaston de Foix was killed by the sword, and not by a bullet. So that if men nowadays give less proof of valor than formerly, it is not chargeable to the introduction of artillery, but to bad discipline and the feebleness of the armies, which being in the aggregate deficient in courage and vigor, cannot show it in their individual parts.

As to the other proposition advanced, that there are nowadays no more hand-to-hand fights, and that hereafter war will be made altogether with artillery, I maintain that this opinion is wholly erroneous, and will be so regarded by all those generals who desire to manage their armies in the manner of the ancients. For whoever wishes to form a good army must, by real or sham fights, train his troops to attack the enemy sword in hand, and to seize hold of him bodily; and he must rely more upon infantry than upon cavalry, for reasons which I will explain further on. And by thus relying upon the infantry, and upon the above-indicated mode of training them, artillery will prove entirely useless. For the infantry, in engaging the enemy hand to hand, can more easily escape the effects of the artillery than it could in ancient times the rush of the elephants and the scythe chariots, and other now obsolete means of attack which the Roman infantry had to encounter, and against which they knew how to defend themselves. And they would most probably have found also the means of escaping the effects of the artillery, as the time during which its fire is most damaging is so much less than that during which the elephants and the scythe chariots were dangerous. For whilst these carried disorder into the ranks in the very midst of the fight, the artillery interferes with you only at the beginning of the battle, and then it is easily avoided by the infantry, either by availing of the natural cover of the ground, or by lying down during the fire. And experience has shown even this to be hardly necessary, especially with regard to heavy artillery, which cannot be so accurately directed; for when aimed too high the balls pass over you, and when too low they do not reach you. And when you have engaged the enemy hand to hand, then it is perfectly evident that neither light nor heavy artillery can do you any more damage; for if the enemy has planted his guns in the front, they will fall into your hands, and if in the rear, then they will damage his own troops sooner than yours; and if he places his guns on the flank, they cannot injure you to that degree but that you can rush up and capture them, the same as in the first case. All this cannot be gainsaid, for we have seen how the Swiss at Novara, in 1513, without cavalry or artillery, went to encounter the French, who were well provided in their intrenchments with artillery, and routed them without suffering much from the effect of the guns. And the reason of this is, that, besides the other things mentioned above, the artillery, to be well served, needs to be protected by walls, ditches, or earthworks; and if it lacks this protection it is either captured or becomes useless, as generally happens in open field battles, when it is protected only by men. On the flank the artillery cannot be employed differently from what the ancients did their catapults and other engines of war, which were always placed outside of the squadrons, so that they should not break the ranks; and whenever they were hard pushed by cavalry or other troops, they promptly took shelter behind the legions. And whoever employs artillery differently does not understand the matter well, and relies upon that which may easily disappoint him. And if the Turks by means of their artillery gained the victory over the Persians and the Egyptians, it resulted from no other merit than the unusual noise, which frightened the cavalry. I will conclude this chapter, therefore, by saying that artillery is useful in an army when the soldiers are animated by the same valor as that of the ancient Romans, but without that it is perfectly inefficient, especially against courageous troops.

Chapter XVIII

ACCORDING TO THE AUTHORITY OF THE ROMANS AND THE EXAMPLE OF ANCIENT ARMIES WE SHOULD VALUE INFANTRY MORE THAN CAVALRY

IT can be clearly demonstrated by many arguments and facts, that in all their military operations the Romans valued foot soldiers more than cavalry, and that they based all their plans upon the former. This is proved by many instances, one of the most striking of which occurred at the battle with the Latins near the Lake Regillus; when the Roman army had already begun to give way, they made their cavalry dismount to assist the infantry, and, thus supported, they renewed the fight and carried off the victory. This shows clearly that the Romans relied more upon the same men when on foot than on horseback. They employed the same expedient in several other combats, and found it always of greatest value in moments of danger. I care not for the opinion of Hannibal upon this point, who, on seeing at the battle of Cannæ that the Roman Consul made the cavalry dismount, by way of deriding this manœuvre, said, "I would rather they should deliver them to me bound." Although this was the opinion of a most distinguished soldier, yet, if we have to decide the question upon authority, I would rather trust to that of the Roman republic, and the many eminent commanders which she produced, than to the single opinion of Hannibal; although even without referring to authorities there are plenty of manifest reasons. For a man on foot can go into many places where he could not penetrate on horseback; infantry can be made to preserve their ranks, and can be taught to reform them when broken; whilst it is difficult to make horses keep their ranks, and impossible to reform them when once broken. Besides this we find amongst horses (the same as amongst men) some that lack spirit and some that have too much. And it often happens that a spirited horse is ridden by a coward, or a timid horse by a man of courage; however this disparity may arise, it renders both useless, and invariably causes disorder. Well-disciplined infantry can easily break a squadron of cavalry, but it is with the greatest difficulty that cavalry can break the ranks of infantry. This opinion is corroborated not only by many examples of ancient and modern times, but is also sustained by the authority of those who study and direct the affairs of civilized societies; from which it appears that at first war was made exclusively with cavalry, because disciplined infantry had not yet been organized; but no sooner was this done than it was at once found to be more useful than cavalry, which, however, is also very necessary in armies, for the purposes of reconnaissance, to secure and ravage the country, to pursue a flying enemy, and to oppose the adversary's cavalry. But the infantry must ever be regarded and valued as the very foundation and nerve of an army.

And thus amongst the greatest faults of the Italian princes, which have made Italy slave to the foreigner, is that they have made too little account of infantry, having given all their care and attention to mounted troops. This error has been caused by the evil disposition of the commanders and the ignorance of the rulers; for during the past twenty-five years the Italian armed forces have been entirely under the control of men who held no government or state, who were in a measure mere soldiers of fortune, whose chief thought was to promote their own influence and reputation by their arms, whilst the princes themselves were wholly without any armed force of their own. And as these adventurers could not keep a large force of foot soldiers in their pay, having no subjects of whom they could avail for that purpose, and as a small number would not have had the effect of making them formidable, they employed mounted men; for the pay of two or three hundred horse kept a condottiere in credit, and this payment was not so large but what princes possessing states could conveniently meet it. And to facilitate this and maintain their own credit, they did all they could to destroy all affection for and reputation of the infantry, and to transfer it to their mounted men; and so increased this disorder, that the infantry constituted the smallest part of some of the largest armies. This practice, together with other disorders which occurred at the same time, so enfeebled our armies that Italy has remained ever since an easy victim of the Ultramontanes. This error of preferring cavalry to infantry is proved still more palpably by another Roman example. The Romans were besieging Sora, and a squadron of cavalry having issued from the city for the purpose of harassing the Roman camp, the master of the Roman horse went to meet it with his cavalry, and came to a hand-to-hand fight with them. Chance would have it that at the first shock both captains were killed; the combat continued nevertheless, though both parties were left without any one to direct them, when the Romans, the more easily to overcome the enemy, dismounted, thus forcing the others to do the same in self-defence; the Romans, however, carried off the victory.

Nothing could more conclusively prove the superiority of infantry over cavalry than this instance; for in the other cases cited, the Consuls caused the cavalry to dismount for the purpose of assisting the infantry, which was suffering and needed support, but here it was neither to help their own nor to combat the enemy's infantry, but it was a combat of cavalry against cavalry, and despairing of success the Romans judged that by dismounting victory would be more easy, and the result proved their judgment correct. I maintain further that a well-disciplined body of infantry can only be overcome with greatest difficulty, and then only by another body of infantry. Crassus and Mark Anthony invaded Parthia, and advanced many days' journey into the interior with a Roman army composed of a large body of infantry and but few horse. They had to encounter the innumerable cavalry of the Parthians, and Crassus with a portion of the army was slain; but Mark Antony saved himself and the remainder of the army in the most gallant manner. But even in this mishap of the Romans we see how greatly superior infantry is to cavalry; for although being in a wide and open country, where there are but few mountains and still fewer rivers, remote from the sea and far from all conveniences, yet Mark Antony saved himself most skilfully, according to the judgment of the Parthians themselves; and the entire Parthian cavalry never ventured to attack his ranks. And the loss of Crassus is shown by a careful examination of the history of this expedition to have been more the result of deception than because he was overpowered, for even in his greatest straits the Parthians never dared to attack him in front, but hovered upon his flank, and by interrupting his supplies and deluding him by false promises of provisions they reduced him to the last extremity.

I believe I should have greater difficulty in proving the superiority of infantry over cavalry, were it not that there are plenty of modern examples which bear amplest testimony upon this point. We have seen nine thousand Swiss at Novara attack and defeat ten thousand horse and as many infantry, for the cavalry could do them no harm, and, the infantry being for the most part Gascons and ill-disciplined, the Swiss made no account of them. We have subsequently seen twenty-six thousand Swiss at Marignan attack Francis I, king of France, whose army consisted of twenty thousand horse and forty thousand infantry, and one hundred pieces of artillery; and if they were not victorious, as at Novara, they nevertheless fought most bravely during two entire days, and though defeated in the end, yet they saved the half of their army. Marcus Attilius Regulus risked with his infantry not only the attack of the Numidian cavalry, but also the charge of the elephants; and although unsuccessful in carrying out his designs, yet it was not because his infantry was not such but what he believed it capable of overcoming those difficulties. I repeat, therefore, that to be able to overcome a well-ordered infantry, it is necessary to oppose to them one even better organized and disciplined, otherwise defeat is certain.

In the time of Filippo Visconti, Duke of Milan, some sixteen thousand Swiss descended into Lombardy. The Duke, having at that time Carmignuola in his service as captain, sent him with about five thousand horse and a small body of infantry to meet the Swiss. This commander, not knowing the Swiss method of fighting, went to meet them with his mounted men, presuming that he would be able to rout them at the first shock; but he found them immovable, and, having lost a large number of his men, he retreated. Being however a most able and courageous soldier, and full of resources in every emergency, he reformed his men and renewed the attack, after having first made all his men-at-arms dismount, whom he placed in front of his infantry, and thus assailed the Swiss, who were unable to defend themselves against them. The men-at-arms of Carmignuola being now on foot and well armed, and protected by armor, easily penetrated the ranks of the Swiss, without themselves suffering much harm; and having once broken the ranks of the adversary they did them great damage, so that of all the Swiss none escaped except such as were spared by the humanity of Carmignuola.

I believe that many recognize the superiority of infantry over cavalry, but the times are unhappily such that neither the example of the ancients or the moderns, nor the admission of their having been in error, will suffice to induce the princes of the present day to alter their minds, or to make them think that to give reputation to the army of any state it is necessary to revive the discipline of the ancients, cherish and honor it, and give it life, so that in return it may give life and reputation to the state. And as they deviate from this, so they deviate from the other matters referred to above; and thus it is that their conquests become a burden to the state, instead of contributing to its greatness, as we shall show further on.

Chapter XIX

CONQUESTS MADE BY REPUBLICS THAT ARE NOT WELL CONSTI-
TUTED, AND DO NOT FOLLOW IN THEIR CONDUCT THE EXAMPLE
OF THE ROMANS, ARE MORE CONDUCIVE TO THEIR RUIN THAN
TO THEIR ADVANCEMENT

THE false opinions, founded upon bad examples, that have
been introduced amongst us in this corrupt century, prevent men from liberating themselves from the force of their
accustomed habits. Would it have been possible thirty years
ago to have persuaded an Italian that ten thousand infantry
could have attacked, in an open plain, ten thousand cavalry
and as many infantry? and not only to have fought, but actually to have defeated them, as we have seen that the Swiss
did at the battle of Novara, already referred to? And although history is full of such examples, yet they would not
have believed it; and if they had, they would have said that
nowadays the troops are better armed, and that a squadron
of mounted men would be able to charge a solid wall of
rock, and therefore could not be resisted by mere infantry.
And with such erroneous arguments their judgments are
corrupted, forgetting that Lucullus, with a comparatively
small body of infantry, routed one hundred and fifty thousand cavalry of King Tigranes, amongst which there was a
corps perfectly similar to the men-at-arms of the present
day. The fallacy of these opinions had to be demonstrated by
the example of the troops of the Ultramontanes. And as we
have to admit the truth of what history tells us in regard to
the infantry of the ancients, so we ought also to believe in
the truth and utility of their other institutions; thus repub-

lics and princes would have committed fewer errors, and would have been stronger in resisting the assaults of any enemy that might unawares have come upon them. They would not have put their hope in flight, and those who had the direction of the government of states would have been better able to point out the means of aggrandizement, or the means of preservation. They would have believed that to increase the number of their citizens, to gain allies instead of subjects, to establish colonies to guard the conquered territories, to turn all booty over to the public treasury, to subdue the enemy by incursions and battles and by sieges, to keep the state rich and the individual citizen poor, and above all to maintain a well-disciplined army,—that all these are the true means of aggrandizing a republic and founding a great empire. And if these means had not suited them, they would at least have been convinced that acquisitions by any other means would lead to the ruin of a state; they would have put a curb upon all ambition by regulating the internal affairs of their city by good laws and customs, prohibiting all conquests and confining themselves merely to providing for their security and defence; as is done by the republics of Germany, who live in that manner, and have thus enjoyed their liberty for a long time.

Nevertheless (as I have said when discussing the difference between a state organized for conquest and one that aims only at its own preservation) it is impossible for a republic to remain long in the quiet enjoyment of her freedom within her limited confines; for even if she does not molest others, others will molest her, and from being thus molested will spring the desire and necessity of conquests, and even if she has no foreign foes, she will find domestic enemies amongst her own citizens, for such seems to be the inevitable fate of all large cities. The fact that the free cities of Germany have been able to exist in this fashion for a length of time, is owing to certain conditions prevailing in that country, such as are not found elsewhere, and without which they could not have maintained their institutions and existence. That part of Germany of which I speak was formerly subject to the Roman Empire, the same as France and Spain; but during the decadence of that empire, when its dominion was reduced to Germany, the more powerful cities of that country began to free themselves by purchase, according to the weakness or necessity of the Emperors, by the payment of a small annual quit-rent. And gradually all the cities that held directly from the Emperor, and were not subject to any prince, purchased their liberty in like manner. It happened at about the same time when these cities bought their freedom, that certain communities subject to the Duke of Austria revolted against him; amongst these were Fribourg, the Swiss, and others, who, prospering from the start, gradually became formidable to their neighbors; and this was particularly the case with the Swiss communities. And thus Germany is now divided between the Emperor, certain princes, the republics called free or imperial cities, and the Swiss communities; and the reason why amongst these states with such a diversity of forms of government we see no wars, or only wars of short duration, is that this shadow of an Emperor, although having no direct power, yet has so much influence over them that, by interposing his authority as a conciliator and mediator, he quickly puts an end to any differences that occur between them. The most important wars, and those that have lasted longest, were those between the Swiss and the Duke of Austria; and although for a long while past the Emperor and the Duke of Austria have been one and the same person, yet he has never been able to overcome the courage of the Swiss, and force alone has been able to bring about treaties of peace between them. Nor has the rest of Germany afforded him much help against the Swiss, partly because the free cities do not wish to interfere with those who desire to live in freedom like themselves, and partly because the princes are unable to assist him from poverty, or unwilling, from jealousy of his power. The free cities of Germany, then, can live in the tranquil enjoyment of their small domain, having no occasion for wishing to increase it, because of the protection of the Imperial authority; and they live united within their walls because they have an enemy near who would quickly avail himself of any internal dissension to seize and occupy their cities. But if Germany were differently constituted, they would have to seek to aggrandize themselves, and would have to abandon their quiet life.

As the same conditions do not exist in other countries they cannot adopt the same system as these free imperial cities, but must seek to increase their power by leagues and alliances, or to extend it like the Romans. And whoever attempts any other mode will quickly come to ruin, for in a thousand ways, and for many reasons, acquisitions of territory may prove injurious; for one may well extend one's dominion without increasing one's power, but the acquisition of dominion without power is sure to bring with it ruin. Whoever impoverishes himself by war acquires no power, even though he be victorious, for his conquests cost him more than they are worth. This the Venetians did, and the Florentines, who were much weaker when they held, the one Lombardy, and the other Tuscany, than they were when the one was satisfied with the dominion of the sea, and the other with her six miles of territory. All of which resulted from their desire of aggrandizement, without the knowledge of the proper means. And they deserve the more blame, as they had less excuse, having before their eyes the method practised by the Romans, which they might have followed, whilst the Romans, having no precedents to guide them, had to develop the system exclusively by their own sagacity. Moreover acquisitions sometimes prove most injurious even to a well-regulated republic, when they consist either in a city or province that has been enervated by pleasures and luxury; for these indulgences and habits become contagious by intercourse with the inhabitants. This happened to the Romans when they took Capua, and afterwards also to Hannibal; and if this city had been at a greater distance from Rome, and if the excesses of the soldiers had not been so promptly corrected, or if Rome herself had at that time been in the least degree corrupted, the acquisition of Capua would undoubtedly have proved the ruin of the Roman republic. Titus Livius bears witness to this in the following words: "Capua, the seat of all sensual pleasures and least conducive to military discipline, had already turned the captivated spirits of the soldiers from the remembrance of their own country." And truly cities or provinces of similar character revenge themselves upon their conquerors without battles and without blood; for by communicating to them their own corrupt habits and manners, they expose them to being vanquished by whoever chooses to attack them. Juvenal well understood this when he says in one of his satires that the conquest of foreign countries had caused the Romans to adopt foreign manners and customs, and that, in exchange for their accustomed frugality and other most admirable virtues, "Gluttony and luxury dwell there, and will avenge the conquered universe." If then conquests proved so very nearly pernicious to Rome, in the days when she displayed so much wisdom and virtue in her conduct, what would the consequence be to those who deviate so far from that example? And what would it be, if to the other errors (which we have discussed so fully above) they add the employment of mercenaries or auxiliary troops? The dangers so frequently resulting from that we will point out in the next chapter.

Chapter XX

OF THE DANGERS TO WHICH PRINCES AND REPUBLICS ARE EXPOSED THAT EMPLOY AUXILIARY OR MERCENARY TROOPS

WERE it not that I have in another work of mine treated at length of the uselessness of mercenaries and auxiliaries, and of the advantage of having national troops, I should discuss that subject more fully here; as it is, however, I shall refer to it but briefly, for I do not think that I ought to pass it over entirely, having found a most striking example of it related by Titus Livius. I understand by auxiliary troops such as a prince or republic sends to your aid, but which are paid, and the commander of which is appointed by the prince or republic. Titus Livius relates the following. The Romans had on different occasions defeated the Samnites with the troops which had been sent from Rome to aid the Capuans; and having relieved these of the war of the Samnites, they returned to Rome, leaving, however, two legions in the country for the protection of the Capuans, who had been deprived of their garrison, so as to save their city from falling again a prey to the Samnites. These legions, plunged in idleness, became so fond of Capua that, forgetful of their own country and of the respect due to the Senate, they conspired to make themselves masters of that country, which they had defended with their valor, deeming the inhabitants, who were incapable of protecting themselves, unworthy of its possession. When this plot became known to the Romans, they suppressed and punished it, as we shall more fully relate when we come to speak of conspiracies.

I repeat, then, that of all kinds of troops, auxiliaries are the most dangerous; for the prince or republic that calls them to their assistance has no control or authority whatever over them, as that remains entirely with him who sends them; for, as I have said, auxiliary troops that are sent you by any prince are under officers appointed by him, under his banner, and are paid by him, as was the case with the army sent by the Romans to Capua. Such troops, when victorious, generally plunder as well him to whose assistance they were sent as the enemy against whom they have been employed; and this they do either from the perfidy of the prince who sends them, or from their own ambition. And although it was not the intention of the Romans to break the treaty and convention they had made with the Capuans, yet the opportunity and facility of taking the country from the Capuans seemed so great to the soldiers that it suggested the thought and prompted the attempt. We might cite many more examples, but this one suffices, together with that of the people of Rhegium, who lost their city and their lives by a legion which the Romans had sent there to garrison the place. A prince or republic, then, should adopt any other course rather than bring auxiliaries into their state for its defence, especially when their reliance is wholly upon them; for any treaty or convention with the enemy, however hard the conditions, will be less hard to bear than the danger from auxiliaries. And if we read carefully the history of the past, and observe the course of present events, we shall find that for one who derived benefit from auxiliaries there are an endless number who have been disappointed. And in truth no more favorable opportunity could be presented to an ambitious prince or republic for seizing a city or a province, than to be asked to send troops there to assist in its defence. And therefore any one whose ambition so far misleads him as to call in strangers to aid in his defence, or in an attack upon others, seeks to acquire that which he will not be able to hold, and which after acquiring will be easily taken from him. But the ambition of men is such that, to gratify a present desire, they think not of the evils which will in a short time result from it. Nor will they be influenced by the examples of antiquity, which I have cited upon this and other points; for if they were, they would see that the more liberality they show to their neighbors, and the less desire they manifest to rob them of their territory, the more readily will those neighbors throw themselves into their arms, as we shall see further on from the conduct of the Capuans.

Chapter XXI

THE FIRST PRÆTOR SENT BY THE ROMANS ANYWHERE WAS TO CAPUA, FOUR HUNDRED YEARS AFTER THEY BEGAN TO MAKE WAR UPON THAT CITY

WE have shown very fully in preceding chapters how differently the Romans proceeded towards the peoples they conquered from what is done in the present day by those who extend their jurisdiction; and how they left the people of those places which they did not destroy in the enjoyment of their own laws and institutions, even when they made subjects of them, and not mere allies; and how they avoided leaving any evidence of the Roman authority there, but simply imposed upon the people certain conditions, and so long as these were faithfully complied with, so long did they maintain those people in their dignity and state. And we know that this system was practised by them until they carried their conquests beyond the confines of Italy, and began to reduce the conquered kingdoms and states to the condition of provinces. The most striking illustration of this was that the first Prætor whom they sent to any place was to Capua; and this was done not from any ambitious views of their own, but because they had been requested to do it by the Capuans themselves. For dissensions having arisen between them, they deemed it necessary to have some Roman citizen reside in their city who should restore order and union amongst them. Influenced by this example and impelled by a similar necessity, the people of Antium asked the Romans to send them also a Prætor. So that Titus Livius says, in relation to this incident, "that the Romans conquered as much by their justice as by their arms." We see, therefore, how much this mode of proceeding facilitated the aggrandizement of the Roman Empire; for those cities mainly that are accustomed to enjoy liberty, and to be governed by their own citizens, remain more quiet and content under a government which they do not see (even should it involve some inconvenience) than under one which they have daily before their eyes, and which would seem constantly to remind them of their servitude. Another advantage resulting to a prince from being thus at a distance is his not having under his immediate control the judges and magistrates that decide civil and criminal causes, as no sentence pronounced by them will bring censure or odium upon him, and thus he escapes many occasions for calumny and hatred.

I might cite many examples of ancient times in support of the truth of what I say, but will only adduce one recent one in Italy. It is well known that Genoa has several times been taken by the French, and the king has always (with the exception of the present time) sent French governors there to administer it in his name. Only at the present time he has allowed the city to govern itself by a Genoese governor, not because the king preferred it, but from the force of circumstances. And most assuredly, if we examine which of these two modes gives most security to the king and satisfaction to the Genoese, we shall find it to be the latter. Besides this the people will the more readily throw themselves into your arms, the less disposition you manifest to subjugate them; and they will be the less apprehensive of any attempt on your part upon their liberties, the more humane and affable you show yourself towards them. It was this affability and liberality that caused the Capuans to apply to the Romans for a Prætor. If, on the other hand, the Romans had manifested the slightest desire to send one there, it would at once have excited jealousy in the minds of the Capuans, and would have alienated them from the Romans.

But why need we go to Capua and to Rome for examples, when we have plenty in Florence and in Tuscany? Every one knows how the city of Pistoja long since placed herself voluntarily under the dominion of the Florentines; and it is equally well known what bitter enmity exists between the Florentines, the Pisans, the Lucchese, and the Siennese. This diversity of affection has not arisen because the Pistojans do not value their liberty as highly as the others do theirs, or do not esteem themselves as much as the others do; but because the Florentines have always borne themselves like brothers towards the Pistojans, and like enemies towards the others. It was this that induced the Pistojans to place themselves voluntarily under the government of Florence, whilst the others always have made, and continue to make, the most strenuous efforts to avoid becoming subject to the Florentines. And doubtless, if the Florentines had attached their neighbors to themselves by treaties of amity, or by rendering them assistance, instead of frightening them off, they would now be the undisputed masters of Tuscany. I do not mean to say by this, however, that arms and force are never to be employed, but that they should be reserved as the last resort when other means fail.

Chapter XXII

HOW OFTEN THE JUDGMENTS OF MEN IN IMPORTANT MATTERS ARE ERRONEOUS

THOSE who have been present at any deliberative assemblies of men will have observed how erroneous their opinions often are; and in fact, unless they are directed by superior men, they are apt to be contrary to all reason. But as superior men in corrupt republics (especially in periods of peace and quiet) are generally hated, either from jealousy or the ambition of others, it follows that the preference is given to what common error approves, or to what is suggested by men who are more desirous of pleasing the masses than of promoting the general good. When, however, adversity comes, then the error is discovered, and then the people fly for safety to those whom in prosperity they had neglected, as we shall show at length in its proper place. Certain events also easily mislead men who have not a great deal of experience, for they have in them so much that resembles truth that men easily persuade themselves that they are correct in the judgment they have formed upon the subject. Such was the error committed by the Latins when they followed the advice of the Prætor Numicius, after they had been defeated by the Romans; and such also was the error, so generally believed in a few years ago, when Francis I, king of France, attempted the conquest of Milan, which was defended by the Swiss.

When, after the death of Louis XII, Francis, Duke of Angoulême, succeeded to the throne of France, he desired to recover for his kingdom the Duchy of Milan, which a few years previously had been taken by the Swiss, with the aid of Pope Julius II. For this purpose he wanted to have allies in Italy to facilitate his enterprise; and besides the Venetians, whom King Louis had already gained over, he tried to secure the support of the Florentines and of Pope Leo X, deeming their alliance most important to his success, inasmuch as the king of Spain had troops in Lombardy, and the forces of the Emperor of Germany held Verona. The Pope, however, did not yield to the solicitations of the French king, but was persuaded by his counsellors (according to report) to remain neutral. These had demonstrated to him that the surest means of victory for the Church would be to have neither the king of France nor the Swiss too powerful in Italy, and that, if he wished to restore the Church to her former liberty, it was necessary to free her from the yoke of both the one and the other of these powers. And as it would be impossible to overcome either of them separately, and still less both of them together, it would be best to allow either of them to defeat the other, and that then the Church, with the aid of her friends, could with safety assail the one that had remained victorious. And certainly a more favorable opportunity than the present could not offer for the execution of this plan, as both parties were in the field face to face, and the Pope had his forces well organized, and might show himself on the confines of Lombardy, near to both armies, under color of wishing merely to protect his own possessions, where he could remain quietly until a battle should take place, which it was reasonable to suppose would be a bloody one, both armies being equally strong and brave; and that this would leave the victor so weakened that it would be easy for the Pope to attack and defeat him; and that thus he would, with great glory to himself, remain master of Lombardy and arbiter of all Italy. The result, however, proved how completely erroneous this judgment was. The Swiss were defeated after a most bloody fight; but the Spanish and Papal troops, so far from presuming to attack the victorious French, took to flight. Nor would that have availed for their safety, had it not been for the humanity or indifference of the French king, who cared not for a second victory, but was satisfied to conclude a treaty of peace with the Church.

The advice under which the Pope had acted in this matter was founded upon reasons which, taken separately, were sound enough, but viewed as a whole were entirely false. For it rarely happens that the victor in a battle loses many of his men; he loses only those that are killed in the fight, and none by flight; and in the heat of the action, when men are contending hand to hand, few are actually killed, because such a combat lasts but a short time. But even if it were continued longer, and many of the victorious army were slain, the prestige which follows victory and the terror which it brings with it are such that it greatly outweighs the loss which the conqueror suffers by the death of his men. So that an army that attacks him in the belief that he has been weakened, would find itself greatly mistaken, unless

it should be sufficiently powerful to be able to have con-
tended with him at any time even before the victory. In such
case it may, according to its valor and fortune, either win
or lose; but even then, the army that has already fought a
battle and been victorious will have rather the advantage
over the other. This was conclusively proved by the experience of the Latins, both because of the error committed
by the Prætor Numicius and by the ills which those people suffered who believed him when, after the defeat of the
Latins by the Romans, he went through all Latium crying
that now was the time for attacking the Romans, because
they had been so weakened by the battle which they had
fought with the Latins, and because the victory which they
had gained was really only such in name, inasmuch as their
losses had been quite as great as though they had been defeated, and that the smallest force that were now to oppose
them would completely destroy them. In consequence of
which the people who accepted the advice of Numicius
raised a new army, but were quickly beaten by the Romans,
and suffered all the evils that will ever befall those who hold
similar erroneous opinions.

Chapter XXIII

HOW MUCH THE ROMANS AVOIDED HALF-WAY MEASURES WHEN THEY HAD TO DECIDE UPON THE FATE OF THEIR SUBJECTS

"Such was the state of things in Latium that they could
neither bear peace nor war." Of all the unhappy conditions
to which princes or republics can be reduced, the most unhappy is that when they are unwilling to accept peace and
incapable of sustaining war; and to this condition those are

reduced who consider themselves oppressed by the terms of peace, and who, if they wished to make war, would have to yield themselves a prey to their allies, or victims to their enemies. And all this results from following evil counsels, and from taking a wrong course because of not having estimated their forces correctly, as has been shown above. Princes or republics who form a proper estimate of their forces will hardly ever be reduced to a condition similar to that of the Latins, who made terms with the Romans when they ought not to have done it, and declared war when they should not have done it; and so managed that both the friendship and the enmity of Rome proved equally injurious to them. The Latins were defeated and reduced to the greatest extremities, first by Manlius Torquatus, and afterwards by Camillus, who after having compelled them to surrender at discretion, and having placed Roman garrisons in all their towns and taken hostages from each, returned to Rome and reported to the Senate that all Latium was in the hands of the Roman people. And as the action of the Roman Senate on this occasion was very remarkable and worthy of being noted, so that it may serve as an example to any prince to whom a similar occasion may be presented, I shall quote the very words which Livius puts into the mouth of Camillus, which show both the manner in which the Romans proceeded in their aggrandizement, and how in all decisions of state they avoided half-way measures and always went to extremes. For government consists mainly in so keeping your subjects that they shall be neither able nor disposed to injure you; and this is done by depriving them of all means of injuring you, or by bestowing such benefits upon them that it would not be reasonable for them to desire any change of fortune. This will be best understood, first from the proposition of Camillus, and then from the decision of the Senate upon the subject. "The immortal gods thus leave you masters of the course you have to take, and have placed it in your hands to decide whether Latium shall exist or not. You can secure a perpetual peace with Latium by employing, according to your choice, either severity or clemency. Will you proceed with cruel severity against the vanquished who have surrendered to you at discretion? If so, you are at liberty to destroy all Latium; or will you rather, in accordance with the example of your ancestors, increase the power of the Roman republic by granting to the vanquished the rights of citizenship? If so, you have now the opportunity for most glorious increase. Certainly that empire is the most firm and assured where obedience is cheerfully rendered; whilst, therefore, the minds of these people are in a state of stupor and suspense between hope and fear; it behooves you to assure yourselves either by severity or by bestowing benefits upon them." This proposition of Camillus was followed by the resolve of the Senate in conformity with the address of the Consul; so that they sought town after town of any importance in Latium, and either heaped benefits upon them or destroyed them; granting to some exemptions and privileges, giving them the rights of citizenship, and making in every way sure of them. The others were destroyed; colonies were sent there, and the inhabitants were transferred to Rome, or so entirely dispersed that they could neither by arms nor in any other way do any injury to Rome.

And it was thus that the Romans never took any undecided middle course in important affairs, as I have stated above. All princes and republics should imitate this example, and this is the course which the Florentines ought to have adopted when in 1502 Arêzzo and the entire Val di Chiana revolted. Had they done so, they would have fairly established their dominion over them, and have greatly increased the city of Florence, and given her those fields which she lacked for her subsistence. But they took that middle course which is pernicious in the extreme, when the question to be decided affects the fate of men. They exiled a portion of the Aretines, and a portion of them they condemned to death; and all of them were deprived of their ancient rank and honors, which they had enjoyed in their city, and yet the city itself was left entire. And when some one in the public councils advised the destruction of Arezzo, those who were deemed the most prudent replied, that it would be but little honor for the republic to destroy that city, inasmuch as it would have the appearance of their having done it because Florence lacked the power to hold it. This was one of those specious reasons that seem true, but are not; on the same principle we should not be able to kill a parricide, or any other criminal or infamous person, lest it should be deemed dishonorable to the prince to show that he lacked force to restrain a single person. And those who reason thus do not see that often individual men, and sometimes a whole city, will act so culpably against the state that as an example to others and for his own security the prince has no other remedy but to destroy it entirely. Honor consists in being able, and knowing when and how, to chastise evil-doers; and a prince who fails to punish them, so that they shall not be able to do any more harm, will be regarded as either ignorant or cowardly. The propriety of the decisions of the Romans, when required to make any, is proved also by the judgment given against the Privernati. And here we must remark two things from the text of Livius; the one where he says, above, that rebellious subjects must either be conciliated by benefits or destroyed; and the other, where he points out the advantage of frankness and courage, especially when exhibited in the presence of judicious men. The Roman Senate was assembled to judge the inhabitants of Privernum, who had revolted, but had by force been brought back to obedience to the Romans. The Privernati had sent a number of their citizens to implore the clemency of the Roman Senate, and having been brought into the presence of that body, one of them was asked by a Senator, "What punishment he thought that his people had deserved?" To which the Privernate answered, "That punishment which men merit who believe themselves worthy of liberty." Whereupon the Consul replied, "If we remit your punishment, what sort of a peace may we hope to conclude with you?" To which the other responded, "An eternal and sincere peace, if you grant us good conditions; but if otherwise it will be but of short duration." And although this reply displeased some, yet the wiser part of the Senate said, "that this was the answer of a free and brave man, and that they could not believe that either a people or an individual would otherwise than from necessity remain in a condition that was painful to them; and that there could be no reliance upon any peace unless it was voluntary, and that it was hopeless to look for good faith from those who were treated as slaves." After these words the Senate resolved that the Privernati should be admitted to the citizenship of Rome, and in conferring the honor of these privileges upon them, said, "that men who hold their liberty above everything else were worthy of being Roman citizens." So much did the frank and high-minded reply of the Privernati please the magnanimous Romans; in fact, any other would have been false and cowardly. And those who believe men to be otherwise, especially such as are or consider themselves free, deceive themselves; and under this illusion they are apt to take a course that is neither good in itself nor satisfactory to those who are affected by it. And this occasions the frequent rebellions and the ruin of states.

But to come back to my proposition, I conclude from the two examples given that, when a decision has to be made involving the fate of powerful cities that are accustomed to free institutions, they must either be destroyed, or conciliated by benefits. Any other course will be useless; and, above all, half measures should be avoided, these being most dangerous, as was proved by the Samnites, who, when they had hemmed the Romans in between the Caudine forks, disregarded the advice of an old man, who counselled them either to let the Romans depart honorably, or to kill them all. And by taking the middle course of disarming them and obliging them to pass under a yoke, they let them depart with shame and rage in their hearts. So that the Samnites soon after found, to their cost, how salutary the old man's advice had been, and how injurious the course which they had adopted, as we shall more fully show in another place.

Chapter XXIV

FORTRESSES ARE GENERALLY MORE INJURIOUS THAN USEFUL

It may perhaps seem to the learned men of our time that the Romans acted without proper consideration when, in their desire to make sure of the people of Latium and of the city of Privernum, they did not build some fortresses there to serve as a check, and as a guaranty of their fidelity; especially as it is a general saying of our wiseacres in Florence that Pisa and other similar cities should be held by citadels. Doubtless, if the Romans had been of the same composition, they would have constructed fortresses; but as they were men of very different courage, judgment, and power, they did not build them. And so long as Rome was free, and adnered to her old customs and admirable constitution, they never built fortresses to hold either cities or countries which they had conquered, although they preserved some of the strong places which they found already existing. Seeing, then, the mode of proceeding of the Romans in this respect, and that of the princes of our present time, it seems to me proper to examine whether it is well to build fortresses, and whether they are of benefit or injury to him who builds them. We must consider, then, the object of fortresses, with reference to their serving as a means of defence against a foreign enemy as well as against one's own subjects.

In the first case, I maintain they are unnecessary, and in the second decidedly injurious. I will begin by explaining why they are injurious in the second case, and therefore say that whenever either princes or republics are afraid lest their subjects should revolt, it results mainly from the hatred of the subjects on account of the bad treatment experienced from those who govern them; and this comes either from the belief that they can best be controlled by force, or from lack of sound judgment in governing them. And one of the things that induce the belief that they can be controlled by force is the possession of fortresses with which to menace them; and thus the ill treatment that engenders hatred in the subjects arises in great measure from the fact that the prince or republic hold the fortresses, which (if this be true) are therefore by far more injurious than useful. For in the first instance (as has been said) they cause you to be more violent and audacious towards your subjects; and next, they do not afford the security which you imagine; for all the measures of force and violence that you employ to hold a people amount to nothing, except these two: either you must keep a good army always ready to take the field, as the Romans did; or you must scatter, disorganize, and destroy the people so completely that they can in no way injure you; for, were you merely to impoverish them, "the spoliated still have their arms"; if you disarm them, "their fury will serve them instead of arms"; if you kill the chiefs and continue to oppress the others, new chiefs will spring up like the heads of the Hydra. If you build fortresses they may serve in time of peace to encourage you to oppress your subjects; but in time of war they are most useless, because they will be assailed by the enemy as well as by your subjects, and cannot possibly resist both. And if ever they were useless, it is now in our day, on account of the power of artillery, in consequence of which small places, where you cannot retreat behind second intrenchments, cannot possibly be defended, as has been explained above.

I will discuss this subject in a more familiar manner. Prince or republic, you would either keep the people of your own city in check by means of fortresses, or you wish to hold a city that has been taken in war. I shall turn to the prince, and say to him that "nothing can be more useless than such a fortress for keeping your own citizens in check, for the reasons given above; for it will make you more prompt and regardless in oppressing them, which will expose you to ruin by exciting your subjects against you to that degree that you will not be able to defend the very citadel that has provoked it." A good and wise prince, desirous of maintaining that character, and to avoid giving the opportunity to his sons to become oppressive, will never build fortresses, so that they may place their reliance upon the good will of their subjects, and not upon the strength of citadels. And although Count Francesco Sforza, who had become Duke of Milan, and was reputed a sagacious man, caused a citadel to be built at Milan, yet I maintain that in that respect he did not prove himself wise, for the result demonstrated that that citadel, so far from giving security to his heirs, proved their ruin; for in the belief that, being perfectly secure by the protection which this citadel afforded, they might with impunity outrage and oppress their citizens, they indulged in all sorts of violence, which made them so odious that they lost their state at the first attack of an enemy; and the citadel, which during peace had done them so much harm, was of no service in defending them in war. For if they had not had it, and had not unwisely treated their citizens so harshly, they would sooner have discovered their danger, and would have retreated; and would then have been able to resist the impetuous assault of the French more bravely without the citadel, but supported by the good will of their people, than with the citadel and the hostility of their people.

In truth, fortresses are of no advantage to you in any way, for they are lost either by the treachery of those who are put to guard them, or by the violence of the assailants, or by famine. And if you want to have any benefit from fortresses, and have them serve you in recovering the state that you may have lost, when the only thing that remains to you is the citadel, you must have an army with which you can attack the enemy that has dispossessed you of your state; and if you have such an army you would recover your state anyhow, even if there were no such citadel,—in fact, even more easily, for the people would be more friendly to you, because they would not have received bad treatment at your hands when you were relying upon your fortress. And experience has shown that the citadel of Milan was of no use, either to the Sforzas or to the French, in times of adversity for either the one or the other; but that it rather wrought harm and ruin to both, because in consequence of their reliance upon it they gave no thought to holding that state by means of more just and proper government. Guidobaldo, Duke of Urbino, son of Frederick, who in his day was esteemed one of the most distinguished captains, was driven from his state by Cesar Borgia, son of Pope-Alexander VI. When afterwards in the course of events he regained his possessions, he caused all the fortresses in the state to be destroyed, because he believed them to be injurious. For, being beloved by his subjects, he did not need them on their account, and with regard to his enemies, he had seen that he could not hold them without an army in the field, and therefore he resolved to destroy them. Pope Julius II., after having driven the Bentivogli out of Bologna, built a citadel there, and then caused one of his governors to have some of the people assassinated. This caused a revolt, and the Pope quickly lost the citadel; so that it proved to have been of no use to him, but rather an injury, the more so as it might have been of some service had he borne himself differently towards the people. Niccolo da Castello, father of the Vitelli, having returned to his country whence he had been exiled, promptly razed two fortresses that had been built by Sixtus IV., deeming that it was only the good will of the people, and not the fortresses, that could maintain him in that state. But the most recent and most notable instance, and the one most fit to prove the futility of building and the advantage of destroying fortresses, is that which occurred at Genoa in our immediate time. It is well known that in 1507 Genoa revolted against Louis XII., king of France, who came with all his forces to recover that city, and, having succeeded in this, he caused the construction of the most formidable citadel that had ever been built; for owing to its situation and other circumstances, it seemed actually impregnable, being placed upon the point of a high hill that extended into the sea, called by the Genoese Codefa, and thus commanding the entire port of Genoa, and a considerable portion of the surrounding country. It happened afterwards, in the year 1512, that the French, being driven out of Italy, Genoa revolted in spite of the citadel (which remained in the hands of the French). The government was seized by Ottaviano Fregoso, who, after sixteen months of great effort, took the city by famine. Every one believed, and many advised, that he would preserve the citadel as a refuge in any event; but being a very sagacious man, and knowing that it was the good will of the people, and not fortresses, that maintain princes in their states, he had the citadel destroyed. And thus, instead of founding his state upon the strength of the fortress, but upon his valor and prudence, he has held it ever since to this day. And where formerly a thousand foot soldiers sufficed to overturn the government of Genoa, more than ten thousand could not now injure him; which shows that the destruction of the citadel did no more injure Ottaviano than the building of it protected the king of France; for when the latter was able to come into Italy at the head of an army, he recovered Genoa without the aid of a citadel; but without such an army he could not hold Genoa, although he had the support of a citadel, the building of which caused him great expense and its loss much disgrace, whilst to Ottaviano the taking of it brought much glory and its destruction great advantage.

But let us come now to republics that build fortresses, not within their own territory, but in that which they conquer. And if the example of France and Genoa does not suffice to expose the fallacy of this, the case of Florence and Pisa certainly will; for the Florentines built a citadel to hold that city, ignorant of the principle that to hold a city that had always hated everything that bore the name of Florentine, that had enjoyed free institutions, and that had resorted to rebellion as a refuge for liberty, it was necessary to follow the practice of the old Romans, either to convert her into an ally and associate, or to destroy her entirely. How much reliance can be placed upon fortresses was shown when King Charles came into Italy, to whom they all surrendered, either through the treachery of their governors, or from fear of a worse fate. If there had been no citadel the Florentines would not have based their hopes of holding Pisa upon this means, and the king of France never would have been able in that way to deprive the Florentines of that city. The means which they in that case would have employed to hold Pisa until then, would perhaps have sufficed to preserve it altogether, and certainly would have stood the test better than the citadel.

I conclude, then, that to hold one's own country fortresses are injurious, and to hold conquered territory they are useless. The authority of the Romans is enough for me: they razed the strong places in the countries which they wished to hold, and never built any new ones. And if the example of Tarentum in ancient times, and that of Brescia in modern times, be quoted in opposition to my opinion, both of which places were recovered from their revolted inhabitants by means of their citadels, I reply, that for the recovery of Tarentum Fabius Maximus was sent at the beginning of the year with the entire army, and he would have succeeded in retaking that city independent of the citadel, although he made use of it; for if the citadel had not existed, he would have found other means of accomplishing the same end. And truly I do not see of what sort of advantage a fortress can be, if to recover possession of your country it is necessary to send a consular army with a Fabius Maximus to command it. That the Romans would have retaken Tarentum anyhow is proved by the example of Capua, where there was no cita-

del, and which they recovered by the mere valor of their
army. But let us come to Brescia. I say that it rarely happens,
as it did in this case, that when a city revolts, and whilst the
citadel remains in your hands, you should have a powerful
army near at hand, like that of the French; for Gaston de
Foix was with his army at Bologna, and the moment he
heard of the loss of Brescia he marched his army there, and,
having arrived, recovered the place by means of the citadel.
But the citadel of Brescia to be thus of service needed a Gaston de Foix with the French army to come to its support
within three days. Thus this example does not suffice to con-
trovert the instances I have adduced; for a number of fortresses have been taken and retaken in the wars of our times,
according as the one or the other party were the stronger or
the weaker in the field; not only in Lombardy, but also in
the Romagna, in the kingdom of Naples, and in fact
throughout all Italy. But as to the building of fortresses for
defence against foreign enemies, I say that they are not
needed by those peoples or kingdoms that have good armies;
for good armies suffice for their defence without fortresses,
but fortresses without good armies are incompetent for defence. Experience proves this to be the case with those who
manage their government and other affairs well, as was the
case with the Romans and Spartans; for whilst the Romans
built no fortresses, the Spartans not only refrained from
doing so, but even did not permit their city to be protected
by walls, for they wanted to rely solely upon the valor of
their men for their defence, and upon no other means. And
therefore when a Spartan was asked by an Athenian whether
he did not think the walls of Athens admirable, he replied,
"Yes, if the city were inhabited by women."

The prince, then, who has a good army, may have upon
his frontiers, or on the sea, some fortresses that may for

some days hold an enemy in check, to enable the prince to gather his forces; such fortresses may occasionally be useful to him, but not necessary. But when the prince has not a good army, then fortresses whether within his territory or upon the frontiers are either injurious or useless to him; injurious, because they are easily lost, and when lost are turned against him; and even if they are so strong that the enemy cannot take them, he will march by with his army and leave them in the rear; and thus they are of no benefit, for good armies, unless opposed by equally powerful ones, march into the enemy's country regardless of cities or fortresses, which they leave in their rear. We have many instances of this in ancient history; and Francesco Maria did the same thing quite recently, when, marching to attack Urbino, he left ten hostile cities behind him without paying the least attention to them. A prince then, who can raise a good army, need not build any fortresses; and one who cannot should not build any. It is proper enough that he should fortify the city in which he resides, so as to be able to resist the first shock of an enemy, and to afford himself the time to negotiate, or to obtain aid from without for his relief; but anything more is mere waste of money in time of peace, and useless in time of war. And thus whoever reflects upon all I have said upon the subject will see that the same wisdom which inspired the Romans in all other matters equally guided them in their decisions respecting the Latins and the Privernati, when, instead of relying upon fortresses, they secured the allegiance of these people by wiser and more magnanimous means.

Chapter XXV

IT IS AN ERROR TO TAKE ADVANTAGE OF THE INTERNAL DISSEN-
SIONS OF A CITY, AND TO ATTEMPT TO TAKE POSSESSION OF IT
WHILST IN THAT CONDITION

THE dissensions between the people and the nobility in the Roman republic were so great, that the Veienti together with the Tuscans, thought the opportunity favorable for crushing out the name of Rome entirely; and having formed an army and made incursions into the Roman territory, the Senate sent Cn. Manlius and M. Fabius against them; and when they had moved their army near to that of the Veienti, these began with insults and attacks to abuse and offend the Romans, with such a degree of temerity and insolence that it caused the Romans to forget their dissensions and to become united; so that when it came to a regular battle between them and the Veienti and Tuscans, the Romans completely defeated and routed them. This shows how apt men are to deceive themselves (as we have shown above) in deciding upon what course they are to take, and how frequently they lose where they had confidently hoped to win. The Veienti thought that, by assailing the Romans at a moment when they were divided by internal dissensions, they would have an easy victory over them; but their very attack restored union amongst the Romans, and that caused the defeat of the Veienti. These dissensions in republics are generally the result of idleness and peace, whilst apprehension and war are productive of union; and therefore if the Veienti had been wise, the more they had seen the Romans divided amongst themselves, the more they would have kept war away from them, and should have tried to subjugate them by the arts of peace. The way to do this is to try and win the confidence of the citizens that are divided amongst themselves, and to manage to become the arbiter between them, unless they should have come to arms; but having come to arms, then sparingly to favor the weaker party, so as to keep up the war and make them exhaust themselves, and not to give them occasion for the apprehension, by a display of your forces, that you intend to subjugate them and make yourself their prince. And if this course be well carried out, it will generally end in your obtaining the object you aim at. The city of Pistoja (as I have said in another chapter) did not come to the republic of Florence by any other than the above means; for its people being divided amongst themselves, the Florentines favored first one party and then the other, and brought them to that point that, wearied of their disturbed existence, they threw themselves spontaneously into the arms of Florence. The city of Sienna changed her government through the influence of the Florentines only when these aided her with small and unimportant favors; for had these favors been large and of importance, the Siennese would immediately have united in defence of the existing government. I will add one more example to the above. Filippo Visconti, Duke of Milan, often made war upon Florence, relying upon her internal dissensions, but was always the loser; so that he said, in lamenting his unsuccessful attempts, that "the follies of the Florentines have cost him two millions in gold."

The Veienti and the Tuscans then (as I have said above) were deluded by the hope of being able to take advantage of the dissensions of the Romans, and were in the end defeated by them in battle. And in the same way will all those be deceived who in a similar manner and for similar reasons believe that they can subjugate a people.

Chapter XXVI

CONTEMPT AND INSULTS ENGENDER HATRED AGAINST THOSE WHO INDULGE IN THEM, WITHOUT BEING OF ANY ADVANTAGE TO THEM

I HOLD it to be a proof of great prudence for men to abstain from threats and insulting words towards any one, for neither the one nor the other in any way diminishes the strength of the enemy; but the one makes him more cautious, and the other increases his hatred of you, and makes him more persevering in his efforts to injure you. This was seen in the case of the Veienti, of whom we have spoken in the preceding chapter, who added insulting words against the Romans to the injuries of war, which no prudent captain should permit his soldiers to indulge in, for they inflame and excite the enemy to revenge, and in no way impede his attacking you (as has been said), so that they are in fact so many weapons that will be turned against you. A striking instance of this occurred in Asia, when Gabades, commander of the Persians, having for a long time besieged Amida and becoming weary of the siege, resolved to abandon it; and having already broken up his camp, the inhabitants of the place came upon the walls, and, inflated with the thought of victory, assailed his army with every kind of insult, vilifying them and accusing and reproaching them for their cowardice and poltroonery. Babades, irritated by this, changed his mind and resumed the siege, and his indignation at these insults so stimulated his efforts, that he took the city in a few days, and gave it up to sack and pillage. The same thing happened to the Veienti, who, not content with making war upon the Romans, outraged them with insulting words, advancing up to the very stockade of their camp to fling insults at them, thus irritating the Romans more by their words than their arms; so that the soldiers, who at first had fought unwillingly, now constrained the Consuls to bring on a battle, in which they made the Veienti suffer the penalties of their insolence. It is the duty, therefore, of every good general of an army, or chief of a republic, to use all proper means to prevent such insults and reproaches from being indulged in by citizens or soldiers, either amongst themselves or against the enemy; for if used against an enemy they give rise to the above-described inconveniences, and between the soldiers and the citizens it is even worse, unless they are promptly put a stop to, as has ever been done by prudent rulers. The Roman legion that had been left at Capua, having conspired against the Capuans, (as we shall relate in its place,) and this conspiracy having given rise to a sedition which was quelled by Valerius Corvinus, one of the stipulations of the convention that was concluded with them provided the severest penalties against whoever should at any time reproach the soldiers with this selection. Tiberius Gracchus, who in the war with Hannibal had been called to the command of a certain number of slaves, who had been armed because of the scarcity of freemen, ordered amongst the first things that the penalty of death should be inflicted upon whoever reproached any of them with their former servitude; so dangerous did the Romans esteem it to treat men with contempt, or to reproach them with any previous disgrace, because nothing is more irritating and calculated to excite greater indignation than such reproaches, whether founded upon truth or not; "for harsh sarcasms, even if they have but the least truth in them, leave their bitterness rankling in the memory."

Chapter XXVII

WISE PRINCES AND REPUBLICS SHOULD CONTENT THEMSELVES WITH VICTORY; FOR WHEN THEY AIM AT MORE, THEY GENERALLY LOSE

THE use of insulting language towards an enemy arises generally from the insolence of victory, or from the false hope of victory, which latter misleads men as often in their actions as in their words; for when this false hope takes possession of the mind, it makes men go beyond the mark, and causes them often to sacrifice a certain good for an uncertain better. And as this matter well merits consideration, it seems to me better to demonstrate it by ancient and modern examples, rather than attempt to do so by arguments, which will not do as well. After Hannibal had defeated the Romans at Cannæ, he sent messengers to Carthage to announce his victory and to ask for support. The question as to what should be done was warmly discussed in the Senate of Carthage. Hanno, an old and sagacious citizen, advised that they should prudently avail of the victory to make peace with the Romans, which, he argued, they could do now with much more favorable conditions, having been victorious, than they could possibly have expected if they had been defeated; and that the object of the Carthaginians should be to show to the Romans that, whilst they were able to combat them, yet having won a victory they were not disposed to risk losing the fruits of it by the hope of still further successes. The Carthaginian Senate did not adopt this course, though they recognized the wisdom of it after the opportunity was lost. After Alexander the Great had conquered the entire Orient, the republic of Tyre, (most eminent and powerful in those days, the city being situated upon the water like that of the Venetians,) seeing the success and power of Alexander, sent ambassadors to him to assure him of their friendly disposition, and of their readiness to render him obedience, but that they could not consent to receive him or his forces within their city. Whereupon Alexander became indignant that a city should attempt to close her gates to him when all the rest of the world had thrown open theirs; he declined to receive the ambassadors, and, refusing the terms offered to him, he began to lay siege to the city. Tyre being surrounded by water, and abundantly supplied with provisions and all munitions necessary for her defence, Alexander found after four months of siege that the taking of the city would require more of his time and glory than most of his other conquests had done, and therefore resolved to try negotiations and to concede to the Tyrians all they themselves had asked. But the Tyrians on their part, having become elated, now refused to make terms, and killed the messengers whom Alexander had sent to them. This so enraged Alexander that he assaulted the city with such vigor that he captured and destroyed her, and made slaves of her men. In the year 1502 a Spanish army came into the Florentine dominions for the purpose of reinstating the Medici in the government of Florence, and to levy contributions from the city; the Spaniards had been called there by the citizens themselves, who had encouraged them with the hope that they would take up arms in their favor so soon as they should have entered the Florentine territory. But when the Spaniards had arrived in the plains of Florence, they found no one coming to their support, and having run out of provisions they attempted to open negotiations; but the citizens of Florence had become insolent, and declined all terms.

The loss of Prato and the ruin of their own state were the consequence of this conduct. Princes that are attacked cannot then commit a greater error, especially when their assailant greatly exceeds them in power, than to refuse all accommodation, and more particularly when it has been offered; for no terms will ever be so hard but what they will afford some advantage to him who accepts them, so that he really obtains thereby a share of the victory. And therefore the people of Tyre should have been satisfied to have Alexander accept the propositions which he had at first refused; for it would have been victory enough for them to have made so great a conqueror, with arms in hand, come to their own terms. And so it should also have sufficed the Florentines, and it would have been a great victory for them, if the Spaniards had yielded in something to their will, without accomplishing all their own designs, which had for their object to change the government of Florence, to detach it from France, and to levy contributions from it. If out of these three objects the Spaniards had gained two, leaving to the people of Florence the first, namely its government, it would have been to some extent an honorable and satisfactory arrangement for both parties, and the people ought not to have cared about the two last points provided they preserved their liberty; nor should they (even if they had seen a chance of a greater and almost certain victory) have exposed their independence to the hazards of fortune, because that was their last stake, which no prudent man will ever risk except from extreme necessity.

Hannibal left Italy after sixteen years of triumphs, having been recalled by the Carthaginians to come to the rescue of his own country; he found Asdrubal and Syphax utterly beaten, the kingdom of Numidia lost, Carthage confined to the limits of her walls, and having no other resources to look to but him and his army. Knowing that this was the last resource of his country, Hannibal did not want to risk it without having first tried all other means, and was not ashamed to ask for peace, convinced that peace and not war was the only means of saving his country. The Romans having refused his request, he resolved to fight, though almost certain of defeat, judging that there might possibly be a chance of his being victorious, and that at least he should lose gloriously. And if so great and valiant a general as Hannibal, with his entire army, sought peace rather than risk a battle, seeing that his defeat would expose his country to enslavement, what should any less valiant and experienced generals do? But men always commit the error of not knowing where to limit their hopes, and by trusting to these rather than to a just measure of their resources, they are generally ruined.

Chapter XXVIII

HOW DANGEROUS IT IS FOR A REPUBLIC OR A PRINCE NOT TO AVENGE A PUBLIC OR A PRIVATE INJURY

WHAT men will do from indignation and resentment is clearly seen from what happened to the Romans when they had sent the three Fabii as ambassadors to the Gauls, who had come to attack the Tuscans, and more especially the city of Clusium. The inhabitants having sent to Rome for assistance, the Romans sent ambassadors to the Gauls to notify them to abstain from making war upon their allies, the Tuscans. These ambassadors being more accustomed to act than to speak, and having arrived at the place at the very moment when the Tuscans and Gauls were engaged in battle, threw themselves upon the latter to combat them.

Having been recognized by these, all the resentment which before they had felt towards the Tuscans was now turned against the Romans; and was increased even, because the Gauls complained through their ambassadors to the Romans of this wrong, and having demanded as a reparation therefor that the three Fabii should be delivered up to them, the Romans not only did not surrender or punish them in any way, but at the next assembling of the Comitii they were made Tribunes, with consular powers. When the Gauls saw the very men who should have been chastised thus rewarded with honors, they regarded it as an intentional insult and disgrace to themselves; and, exasperated by anger and indignation, they attacked Rome and captured the whole city, excepting only the Capitol. This misfortune was brought upon themselves by the Romans, through nothing but their disregard of justice, and because their ambassadors, who had violated the laws of nations, instead of being punished, had been rewarded with high honors.

This shows how careful republics and princes should be to avoid similar wrongs, either to an entire people or to an individual; for if any man be grievously wronged, either by a state or by another individual, and satisfactory reparation be not made to him, if he lives in a republic he will revenge himself, even if it involves the ruin of the state, and if he lives under a prince, and be at all high-spirited, he will never rest until he have revenged himself upon him in some way, though he may see that it will cause his own ruin. To prove the truth of this, we have a most flagrant and authentic instance in the case of Philip of Macedon, father of Alexander the Great. Amongst the followers of his court was Pausanias, a noble youth of rare beauty, of whom Attalus, one of the chief officers of Philip, had become greatly enamored; and having several times pressed Pausanias to yield to his unnatural desires, which the youth had indignantly repelled, Attalus resolved by perfidy and force to obtain what he could not have otherwise. He therefore gave a grand banquet, to which he invited Pausanias, amongst a number of other nobles. After all had feasted and were filled with wine, he had Pausanias seized and carried to a retired place; and after having vented his own unnatural lust upon him, by way of subjecting him to still greater shame he caused a number of his other guests to subject him to a similar abuse. Pausanias repeatedly complained to Philip of this outrage, who for a while indulged him with the promise of revenge; but he not only failed to perform it, but promoted Attalus to the governorship of one of the Greek provinces. Whereupon Pausanias, seeing his enemy honored instead of being chastised, turned his whole resentment from him who had wronged him against Philip, for not having avenged him; and one morning, on the solemn occasion of the nuptials of the daughter of Philip with Alexander of Epirus, whilst Philip, accompanied by the two Alexanders, his son and son-in-law, was on his way to the temple to celebrate the marriage of his daughter, Pausanias slew him. This example, very similar to that of the Romans, should make all rulers remember never to esteem a man so lightly as to believe that, having heaped injuries and insults upon him, he will not seek to revenge himself, even at the risk of his own life.

Chapter XXIX

FORTUNE BLINDS THE MINDS OF MEN WHEN SHE DOES NOT WISH THEM TO OPPOSE HER DESIGNS

IF we observe carefully the course of human affairs, we shall often notice accidents and occurrences against which it seems to be the will of Heaven that we should not have provided. And if the events to which I refer occurred at Rome, where there was so much virtue, so much religion, and such order, it is no wonder that similar circumstances occur even much more frequently in a city or province deficient in the above advantages. As the case in point is most remarkable in proving the power of Heaven over human affairs, Titus Livius relates it at length in the most effective language, saying that "Heaven, wishing to make the Romans feel its power, first caused the Fabii, who had been sent as ambassadors to the Gauls, to commit a grave error; and then, in consequence of this act, it excited the Gauls to make war upon Rome. Afterwards, Heaven ordained that nothing worthy of the Roman people should be done to meet this war, having first caused Camillus, the only citizen capable of averting so great an evil, to be exiled to Ardea; and afterwards, the same people who had repeatedly created a Dictator to check the impetuous attacks of the Volscians and other neighboring enemies, failed to do so when the Gauls were marching upon Rome." They also displayed great lack of zeal and diligence in their levies of troops, which were very insufficient; and altogether they were so slow in taking up arms, that they were barely in time to encounter the Gauls upon the river Allia, ten miles from Rome. Here the Tribunes established their camp, without any sign of their customary diligence, without proper examination of the ground, without surrounding the camp with either ditch or stockade, and without any of those precautions which divine or human reason would prompt. And in their order of battle they formed their ranks open and feeble, so that neither the soldiers nor the captains did anything worthy of the Roman discipline; for they fought without bloodshed, and fled even before they were fairly attacked. The greater part of the army went off to Veii, and

the rest retreated to Rome, where they went direct to the
Capitol, without entering even their own houses. And the
Senate, so far from defending Rome (any more than the
others), did not even close its gates; a portion sought safety
in flight, and a portion took refuge in the Capitol with the
remnant of the army. It is true that in the defence of this
citadel they employed some method and prudence; they did
not encumber it with useless men; they supplied it with all
the provisions possible, so as to be able to support a long
siege; and the crowd of useless old men, women, and children fled and dispersed in great part to the neighboring
places, and the others remained in Rome, a prey to the
Gauls; so that any one who had read of the deeds done by
this people so many years before, and had then witnessed
their conduct on that occasion, could not possibly have believed them to be the same people. And Titus Livius, who
has given an account of all the above troubles, concludes by
saying, "Fortune thus blinds the minds of men when she
does not wish them to resist her power."

Nothing could be more true than this conclusion; and
therefore men who habitually live in great adversity or prosperity deserve less praise or less blame. For it will generally
be found that they have been brought to their ruin or their
greatness by some great occasion offered by Heaven, which
gives them the opportunity, or deprives them of the power,
to conduct themselves with courage and wisdom. It certainly
is the course of Fortune, when she wishes to effect some
great result, to select for her instrument a man of such spirit
and ability that he will recognize the opportunity which is
afforded him. And thus, in the same way, when she wishes
to effect the ruin and destruction of states, she places men at
the head who contribute to and hasten such ruin; and if

there be any one powerful enough to resist her, she has him killed, or deprives him of all means of doing any good. The instances cited show clearly how Fortune, by way of strengthening Rome and carrying her to that greatness to which she attained, deemed it necessary to subject her to defeat, (as we shall show in the beginning of the following Book,) but did not wish to ruin her entirely. And therefore we see how she caused Camillus to be exiled, but not killed; how she caused the city of Rome to be taken by the Gauls, but not the citadel; and in the same way she caused the Romans to do nothing well for the protection of the city, whilst in their preparations for the defence of the Capitol they omitted nothing. To permit Rome to be taken, Fortune caused the greater part of the troops who were beaten on the river Allia to go to Veii, and thus seemingly cut off all means for saving the city; and yet, at the same time whilst doing all this, she prepared everything for the recovery of Rome. She caused almost an entire army to go to Veii, and Camillus to be exiled to Ardea, so that, under the command of a general with a reputation untarnished by the disgrace of defeat, a sufficient body of troops might be brought together for the recapture of the city.

I might cite some modern examples in confirmation of the views I have advanced, but do not deem it necessary, as that of the Romans suffices. I repeat, then, as an incontrovertible truth, proved by all history, that men may second Fortune, but cannot oppose her; they may develop her designs, but cannot defeat them. But men should never despair on that account; for, not knowing the aims of Fortune, which she pursues by dark and devious ways, men should always be hopeful, and never yield to despair, whatever troubles or ill fortune may befall them.

Chapter XXX

REPUBLICS AND PRINCES THAT ARE REALLY POWERFUL DO NOT PURCHASE ALLIANCES BY MONEY, BUT BY THEIR VALOR AND THE REPUTATION OF THEIR ARMIES

THE Romans were besieged in the Capitol, and although in expectation of succor from Veii and from Camillus, yet, driven by hunger, they came to terms with the Gauls, according to which they were to pay them a certain amount of gold; but whilst in the act of concluding this arrangement, the gold being already in the scales, Camillus arrived with his army, which according to Livius was caused by Fortune, "who did not want that the Romans should live as having purchased their freedom with gold." It is noteworthy that not only in this instance, but also in the whole course of the existence of the Roman republic, the Romans never made any acquisitions by means of money; nor did they ever purchase a peace, but secured it always by the valor of their arms, which I do not believe can be said of any other republic.

Amongst the other indications by which the power of a republic may be recognized is the relation in which they live with their neighbors; if these are tributary to her by way of securing her friendship and protection, then it is a sure sign that that republic is powerful. But if these neighboring states, though they may be more feeble than herself, draw money from her, then it is a sure indication of great weakness on the part of the republic. Let any one read the whole history of Rome, and he will see that the Massilians, the Eduans, the isle of Rhodes, Hiero of Syracuse, the kings

Eumenes and Masinissa, all living near the confines of the Roman Empire, for no other reason than to secure to themselves its friendship and protection, contributed materially to its needs and expenses by large tributes. On the other hand, we see in the case of feeble states, and to begin with our own Florence in the past century and at the period of her greatest glory, that there was not a petty lord in the Romagna that did not draw a pension from her, besides also allowing pensions to Perugia, Castello, and other neighboring cities. But the very reverse would have been the case if Florence had been warlike and powerful; for then they would have paid tribute to her for the advantage of having her protection, and instead of selling their friendship to Florence they would have had to purchase hers. The Florentines, however, are not the only ones that can be reproached with this habitual cowardice; the Venetians acted in the same way, and even the king of France, who with so great a kingdom became tributary to the Swiss and to the king of England; and this resulted solely from their having disarmed their peoples, and because the king of France and the other states mentioned preferred the immediate advantage of being able to oppress their subjects, and to avoid an imaginary rather than a real evil, to doing that which would have assured their own tranquillity and the permanent happiness of their states. Such a cowardly policy may for a time insure quiet, but will inevitably lead in the end to irretrievable injury and ruin.

It would be tedious to relate how many times the Florentines, the Venetians, and the kingdom of France have bought off wars with money; and how many times they subjected themselves to an ignominy to which the Romans submitted once only. It would be equally tedious to relate how many places the Florentines and the Venetians have purchased with money, which afterwards caused great disorders; showing that what has been purchased with gold cannot be defended with iron. The Romans continued their high-minded course so long as they enjoyed liberty, but when they submitted to the rule of Emperors, and these Emperors began to be corrupted, preferring the shade of the palace to the sun of the camp, then they also began to buy off the Parthians, the Germans, and other neighboring peoples, which was the beginning of the ruin of this great empire. These are some of the unhappy consequences of disarming the people; whence also results another and even greater evil, namely, that the more the enemy penetrates into your country, the more will he discover your weakness. For princes and republics who act thus will oppress the people of the interior of their states so as to procure men whom they can send to the frontiers to keep off the enemy. It gives rise also to the practice of giving subsidies to the princes and peoples that are near the confines of the state, to serve as a bulwark and keep the enemy at a distance. This enables the states that practise this system to make some resistance at their frontiers, yet when the enemy has once passed these, they can present no further obstacle to him. And yet they do not see how much their mode of proceeding is opposed to all good principles; for it is the heart and vital parts of the body that should be protected and defended, and not the extremities, for without the latter life is possible, but without the former death is certain; and states like those described above keep their hands and feet armed, but leave their heart unprotected. The evils which Florence has suffered from this system have often been seen, and may be seen any day; for whenever a hostile army passed the frontiers of the republic and approached the centre, all further resistance was vain. It is but a few years since that the Venetians afforded similar proof of the truth of what I say; and if their city were not surrounded by water, we should have seen the end of it. The same results have not been so often experienced in France, because that kingdom is so great that it has few enemies that are her superiors. Nevertheless, when the English attacked France in the year 1513, the whole country trembled, and the king, as well as everybody else, was of the opinion that the loss of a single battle would deprive him of his state.

With the Romans the very opposite was the case, for the nearer the enemy approached the city of Rome the more powerful he found the resistance. The coming of Hannibal into Italy shows that after three defeats, and after the loss of so many officers and men, the Romans not only were able to sustain the war, but actually proved victorious. All of which was the consequence of having the heart of the state well armed, and making little account of the extremities; for the foundation of the power of Rome consisted in the people of Rome itself, the Latin people, and the other allies and colonies of Rome in Italy, whence they drew soldiers enough to enable them to conquer and hold the world. The truth of this is shown by the question asked by Hanno, the Carthaginian, of the messengers whom Hannibal had sent to Carthage after the battle of Cannæ. These, having magnified the deeds of Hannibal, were asked by Hanno "whether any of the Roman people had come to sue for peace, and whether any of the cities of Latium or any of the colonies had revolted against Rome." And when they replied in the negative to both these questions, Hanno said, "In that case the war is but begun."

From what I have said in this and in preceding chapters, we see how very different the conduct of modern republics is from that of the ancients. In consequence of this we daily see remarkable losses, and still more wonderful conquests;

for where men have but little wisdom and valor, Fortune more signally displays her power; and as she is variable, so the states and republics under her influence also fluctuate, and will continue to fluctuate until some ruler shall arise who is so great an admirer of antiquity as to be able to govern such states so that Fortune may not have occasion, with every revolution of the sun, to display her influence and power.

Chapter XXXI

HOW DANGEROUS IT IS TO TRUST TO THE REPRESENTATIONS OF EXILES

IT seems to me not amiss to speak here of the danger of trusting to the representations of men who have been expelled from their country, this being a matter that all those who govern states have to act upon almost daily; and I touch upon it the more willingly, as Titius Livius gives a most memorable instance of it, though in a measure foreign to the subject he treats upon. When Alexander the Great went with his army into Asia, Alexander of Epirus, his brother-in-law and uncle, came with his army into Italy, having been called there by the banished Lucanians, who had held out the hope to him that by their means he would be able to seize that whole country; and when Alexander, upon their assurances and the hopes held out by them, had come into Italy, they killed him, because they had been promised by the citizens of Lucania permission to return to their homes if they would assassinate Alexander. We see, then, how vain the faith and promises of men are who are exiles from their own country. As to their faith, we have to bear in mind that, whenever they can return to their country by other means than your assistance, they will abandon you and look to the other means, regardless of their promises to you. And as to their vain hopes and promises, such is their extreme desire to return to their homes that they naturally believe many things that are not true, and add many others on purpose; so that, with what they really believe and what they say they believe, they will fill you with hopes to that degree that if you attempt to act upon them you will incur a fruitless expense, or engage in an undertaking that will involve you in ruin. The example of Alexander of Epirus, just cited, will suffice to prove the truth of this; but I will add that of Themistocles the Athenian, who, having been declared a rebel, fled to Darius in Asia, and made such representations and promises to him if he would attack Greece, that Darius allowed himself to be persuaded to undertake it. But when Themistocles found that he could not fulfil those promises, he poisoned himself, either from shame or from the fear of punishment. And if so eminent a man as Themistocles could commit so great an error, we may judge to what extent men of less virtue allow themselves to be misled by their desires and their passions. A prince therefore should be slow in undertaking any enterprise upon the representations of exiles, for he will generally gain nothing by it but shame and serious injury. And as cities are rarely taken by surprise or by means of secret intelligence with those within, it seems to me it will not be out of place if I treat of this in the following chapter, and at the same time give some account of the method practised by the Romans in taking cities.

Chapter XXXII

OF THE METHOD PRACTISED BY THE ROMANS IN TAKING CITIES

THE Romans, being much given to war, did everything relating to it in the most advantageous manner, as well in the providing of money as in every other requirement. And therefore they avoided all regular sieges of cities, deeming that the expense and inconveniences of a siege exceeded the advantages of the capture, and consequently they regarded every other mode of taking a city as more advantageous than a regular siege; and thus with all their wars, during so many years, there are but very few instances of regular sieges made by them. Their mode of taking cities was either by assault or by voluntary surrender on the part of the city, the capture by assault being either by open force and violence, or by a mixture of force and fraud. The capture by open force was by assault without breaking the walls; this was termed "attacking the city crown fashion," because they surrounded the city with the entire army and assailed it from all sides at once; and they often succeeded by a single attack of this kind in taking even the strongest cities, as was the case when Scipio took New Carthage in Spain. But when this assault did not succeed, then they breached the walls with battering rams and other engines of war; sometimes they mined subterraneous passages by which they entered the city, and it was in this way that they took Veii; or to bring them on a level with those who defended the walls, they constructed wooden towers, or made earth embankments against the outside of the walls, so as to be at the same height with the defenders. By the first mode of attack the besieged were exposed to the greatest and most sudden dangers; for being attacked on all sides at once they could never have troops enough in any one place for defence, or to relieve those who had been on duty, or if they had, the resistance was not equal at all points, and if the besiegers succeeded in forcing a single point, all the rest was lost. And therefore, as I have said, the open assault was generally the most successful; but when it failed at the first attempt, it was rarely repeated, because it was dangerous for an army to extend itself so considerably that it would not be able to resist a sortie of the besieged; besides, an assault of that kind was very fatiguing to the soldiers, and apt to throw them into disorder, and therefore they usually tried this method of attack but once, and as a surprise to the besieged. The breaching of the walls was resisted by those within, by repairs and by throwing up new ramparts behind the wall that was breached, the same as is done at the present day. The mines were met by countermines, in which the besieged opposed the enemy with arms or other means, one of which was to fill barrels with feathers, which they placed in the mines and set fire to them, so that the stench and smoke might impede the entrance of the enemy. The attack by means of towers the besieged endeavored to thwart by setting them on fire; and as to the embankments against the exterior of the walls, these were counteracted by making openings in the lower part of the wall against which the embankment was being made, through which the earth which the besiegers heaped up against the wall was drawn away from within, thus preventing the raising of the embankment from the outside. This system of attacks cannot be continued long, and if not promptly successful other means must be adopted; or the siege abandoned. This was the course adopted by Scipio on his arrival in Africa; having made an unsuccessful attempt to take Utica, he raised the siege and went to meet the Carthaginian army in the field. And this is the proper course, unless a regular siege is undertaken, as was done by the Romans at Veii, Capua, Carthage, Jerusalem, and other similar places, which they took in that way.

The capture of cities by violence and stealth has been often attempted by the Romans and others, but has proved successful in but few instances. This was the case with Palæpolis, which the Romans carried by means of secret intelligence with the inhabitants. The slightest obstacles often disconcert this plan, and obstacles present themselves at almost every step. For either the secret communications are discovered before the execution of the plan, which happens very easily, either by the treachery of those to whom the secret has been communicated, or by difficulties in the execution, having to deal with enemies with whom it is not permitted to hold any communication. But even if the conspiracy is not discovered in its progress, yet a thousand difficulties will arise in its execution; for if you arrive a little before or a little after the appointed moment, all is spoilt. The least unusual noise, as the cackling of the geese of the Capitol, the slightest change in the order agreed upon, or the least fault or smallest error, will involve the whole enterprise in ruin. To these difficulties add the darkness of night, which naturally increases the apprehensions of those engaged in such hazardous enterprises; and as the greater part of the men employed in such expeditions are wholly unacquainted with the situation of the country or the place where they are led, the slightest unforeseen accident confounds them and fills them with fear and trouble, so that the merest shadow will cause them to turn back. No one has ever been more successful in these stealthy nocturnal expeditions than Aratus of Sicyon, who displayed as much courage in these as he showed cowardice in those that were carried on openly in broad daylight; which may be attributable to some special occult merit which he possessed, rather than to any natural facility in achieving success in such attempts, which are so often projected and but rarely put in practice, and which still more rarely prove successful.

In obtaining possession of cities by surrender, the rendition is either voluntary or forced. The first results from some extrinsic necessity that constrains a city to come to you for protection, as Capua did to the Romans, either from the desire of being well governed, or attracted by the good government which the prince bestows upon those who have voluntarily given themselves to him; it was in this way that the Rhodians, the Massilians, and others submitted voluntarily to the Romans. As to the compulsory surrender of a city, this occurs either in consequence of a long siege, or when a city finds her territory being ruined by incursions, depredations, and every kind of spoliation, which she is unable to prevent except by surrender. Of all the methods described, it was this of which the Romans made use most frequently; and during more than four and a half centuries they thus harassed their neighbors with constant incursions, battles, and depredations, and then by means of treaties obtained all possible advantages over them, as we have already said several times. And they always came back to this system, although they tried all the others, which they found more perilous and less advantageous. For a regular siege involves time and expense; an open assault is doubtful and fraught with danger, and the employment of fraud or conspiracy is most uncertain in its results. The Romans saw that by the defeat of an enemy's army they conquered a kingdom in a day, whilst the siege of a city which is obstinately defended may consume many years.

Chapter XXXIII

THE ROMANS LEFT THE COMMANDERS OF THEIR ARMIES ENTIRELY UNCONTROLLED IN THEIR OPERATIONS

I THINK that, to read the history of Livius with profit, we should carefully reflect upon all the principles that governed the conduct of the Senate and people of Rome. Amongst other things most worthy of consideration is the question as to the power and authority with which they clothed their Consuls, Dictators, and other commanders of the armies whom they sent into the field. This authority was of the most unlimited character, so that the Senate reserved to itself no other power than that of declaring new wars and ratifying treaties of peace, all other matters being remitted to the arbitrament and power of the Consul; so that, when the Senate and the people of Rome had resolved upon a war, (as, for instance, that against the Latins,) all the details of the campaign were left to the discretion and authority of the Consul, who could bring on a battle or not, and lay siege to this or that place, as seemed to him proper. The truth of this is established by very many examples, and more especially by that which occurred on the occasion of an expedition against the Tuscans. The Consul Fabius had defeated them near Sutrium, and intended after that to pass through the Ciminian forest and enter the Tuscan territory. Not only did he not consult the Senate upon this movement, but he did not even notify them of his intentions, although the war had to be carried on in a new, unknown country, full of difficulties and dangers. The course adopted by the Senate on this occasion proves it also; for having heard of the victory gained by Fabius, and fearing lest he might attempt to pass through the forest into Tuscany, they sent two legates to Fabius to advise him not to undertake to enter Tuscany in that way. But when these arrived, Fabius had already passed the forest, and had won a victory over the Tuscans; so that, instead of opposing his operations, they carried back the news of his conquest and of the glory he had achieved.

Now, if we reflect upon this conduct on the part of the Senate, we shall see that it was eminently wise; for if they had required the Consul to conduct the war under orders from them, so to say, from hand to hand, it would have made Fabius less circumspect, and more slow in his operations; for he would not have considered the glory of victory as all his own, but as being shared by the Senate, by whose orders and counsels he had been governed. Besides this, the Senate would have undertaken to advise upon a matter which they could not have understood; for although there were many of the Senators who had great experience in war, yet not being on the spot, and not knowing the endless particulars which it is necessary to know to counsel wisely, they would have been liable to commit the most serious errors in attempting to instruct the Consul. And therefore they were willing that he should act entirely upon his own responsibility, and that he should reap all the glory, the love of which, they judged, would be his best check and rule of conduct.

I have the more willingly remarked upon this subject because I see that the republics of the present day, such as the Venetians and the Florentines, act very differently, so that, if their generals, providers, or commissaries wish merely to place a battery of artillery, they want to know and direct it; a system which is worthy of about the same praise as their conduct in all other respects, and which has brought them to the condition in which they now find themselves.

RELIGION

THIRD BOOK

Chapter I

TO INSURE A LONG EXISTENCE TO RELIGIOUS SECTS OR REPUBLICS, IT IS NECESSARY FREQUENTLY TO BRING THEM BACK TO THEIR ORIGINAL PRINCIPLES

THERE is nothing more true than that all the things of this world have a limit to their existence; but those only run the entire course ordained for them by Heaven that do not allow their body to become disorganized, but keep it unchanged in the manner ordained, or if they change it, so do it that it shall be for their advantage, and not to their injury. And as I speak here of mixed bodies, such as republics or religious sects, I say that those changes are beneficial that bring them back to their original principles. And those are the best-constituted bodies, and have the longest existence, which possess the intrinsic means of frequently renewing themselves, or such as obtain this renovation in consequence of some extrinsic accidents. And it is a truth clearer than light that, without such renovation, these bodies cannot continue to exist; and the means of renewing them is to bring them back to their original principles. For, as all religious republics and monarchies must have within themselves some goodness, by means of which they obtain their first growth and reputation, and as in the process of time this goodness becomes corrupted, it will of necessity destroy the body unless

397

something intervenes to bring it back to its normal condition. Thus, the doctors of medicine say, in speaking of the human body, that "every day some ill humors gather which must be cured."

This return of a republic to its original principles is either the result of extrinsic accident or of intrinsic prudence. As an instance of the first, we have seen how necessary it was that Rome should be taken by the Gauls, as a means of her renovation or new birth; so that, being thus born again, she might take new life and vigor, and might resume the proper observance of justice and religion, which were becoming corrupt. This is clearly seen from the history of Livius, where he shows that, in calling out her army against the Gauls, and in the creation of Tribunes with consular powers, the Romans observed no religious ceremonies whatsoever. In the same way they not only did not deprive the three Fabii of their rank for having, "contrary to the law of nations," fought against the Gauls, but actually raised them to the dignity of Tribunes. And we may readily presume that they made less account of the good institutions and laws established by Romulus and other wise princes, than what was reasonable and necessary to preserve their liberties. It needed, then, this blow from without to revive the observance of all the institutions of the state, and to show to the Roman people, not only the necessity of maintaining religion and justice, but also of honoring their good citizens and making more account of their virtue than of the ease and indulgence of which their energy and valor seemed to deprive them. This admonition succeeded completely; for no sooner was Rome retaken from the Gauls than they renewed all their religious institutions, punished the Fabii for having fought the Gauls contrary to the law of nations; and then they appreciated so highly the valor and excellence of

Camillus that the Senate and the other orders in the state laid aside all envy and jealousy, and confided to him all the burden of the affairs of the republic.

It is necessary then (as has been said) for men who live associated together under some kind of regulations often to be brought back to themselves, so to speak, either by external or internal occurrences. As to the latter, they are either the result of a law, that obliges the citizens of the association often to render an account of their conduct; or some man of superior character arises amongst them, whose noble example and virtuous actions will produce the same effect as such a law. This good then in a republic is due either to the excellence of some one man, or to some law; and as to the latter, the institution that brought the Roman republic back to its original principles was the creation of the Tribunes of the people, and all the other laws that tended to repress the insolence and ambition of men. But to give life and vigor to those laws requires a virtuous citizen, who will courageously aid in their execution against the power of those who transgress them.

The most striking instances of such execution of the laws, anterior to the capture of Rome by the Gauls, were the death of the sons of Brutus, that of the Decemvirs, and that of the corn-dealer, Spurius Mælius; and after the taking of Rome by the Gauls, the death of Manlius Capitolinus, that of the son of Manlius Torquatus, the punishment inflicted by Papirius Cursor upon his master of cavalry, Fabius, and the accusation of the Scipios. As these were extreme and most striking cases they caused on each occasion a return of the citizens to the original principles of the republic; and when they began to be more rare, it also began to afford men more latitude in becoming corrupt, and the execution of the laws involved more danger and disturbances. It would be desirable therefore that not more than ten years should elapse between such executions, for in the long course of time men begin to change their customs, and to transgress the laws; and unless some case occurs that recalls the punishment to their memory and revives the fear in their hearts, the delinquents will soon become so numerous that they cannot be punished without danger.

In relation to this subject it was said by the magistrates who governed Florence from the year 1434 until 1494 that it was necessary every five years to resume the government, and that otherwise it would be difficult to maintain it. By "resuming the government" they meant to strike the people with the same fear and terror as they did when they first assumed the government, and when they had inflicted the extremest punishment upon those who, according to their principles, had conducted themselves badly. But as the recollection of these punishments fades from men's minds, they become emboldened to make new attempts against the government, and to speak ill of it, and therefore it is necessary to provide against this, by bringing the government back to its first principles. Such a return to first principles in a republic is sometimes caused by the simple virtues of one man, without depending upon any law that incites him to the infliction of extreme punishments; and yet his good example has such an influence that the good men strive to imitate him, and the wicked are ashamed to lead a life so contrary to his example. Those particularly, who in Rome effected such beneficial results were Horatius Cocles, Scævola, Fabricius, the two Decii, Regulus Attilius, and some others, who by their rare and virtuous example produced the same effect upon the Romans as laws and institutions would have done. And certainly if at least some such signal punishments as described above, or noble examples, had occurred in Rome every ten years, that city never would have become so corrupt; but as both became more rare, corruption increased more and more. In fact, after Marcus Regulus we find not a single instance of such virtuous example; and although the two Catos arose, yet there was so long an interval between Regulus and them, and between the one Cato and the other, and they were such isolated instances, that their example could effect but little good; and especially the latter Cato found the citizens of Rome already so corrupt that he utterly failed to improve them by his example. Let this suffice so far as regards republics.

Now with regard to religions we shall see that revivals are equally necessary, and the best proof of this is furnished by our own, which would have been entirely lost had it not been brought back to its pristine principles and purity by Saint Francis and Saint Dominic; for by their voluntary poverty and the example of the life of Christ, they revived the sentiment of religion in the hearts of men, where it had become almost extinct. The new orders which they established were so severe and powerful that they became the means of saving religion from being destroyed by the licentiousness of the prelates and heads of the Church. They continued themselves to live in poverty; and by means of confessions and preachings they obtained so much influence with the people, that they were able to make them understand that it was wicked even to speak ill of wicked rulers, and that it was proper to render them obedience and to leave the punishment of their errors to God. And thus these wicked rulers do as much evil as they please, because they do not fear a punishment which they do not see nor believe. This revival of religion then by Saint Francis and Saint Dominic has preserved it and maintains it to this day. Monarchies also have need of renewal, and to bring their institutions back to first principles. The kingdom of France shows us the good effects of such renewals; for this monarchy more than any other is governed by laws and ordinances. The Parliaments, and mainly that of Paris, are the conservators of these laws and institutions, which are renewed by them from time to time, by executions against some of the princes of the realm, and at times even by decisions against the king himself. And thus this kingdom has maintained itself up to the present time by its determined constancy in repressing the ambition of the nobles; for if it were to leave them unpunished, the disorders would quickly multiply, and the end would doubtless be either that the guilty could no longer be punished without danger, or that the kingdom itself would be broken up.

We may conclude, then, that nothing is more necessary for an association of men, either as a religious sect, republic, or monarchy, than to restore to it from time to time the power and reputation which it had in the beginning, and to strive to have either good laws or good men to bring about such a result, without the necessity of the intervention of any extrinsic force. For although such may at times be the best remedy, as in the case of Rome (when captured by the Gauls), yet it is so dangerous that it is in no way desirable. But to show how the actions of some men in particular made Rome great, and produced the most excellent effects in that city, I will make them the subject of the discourses of this Third Book, with which I shall close my reflections upon the first Ten Books of the history of Titus Livius. And although the actions of some of the kings were great and remarkable, yet as history treats of them very fully I shall leave them aside, and not speak of them, excepting so far as regards some things which they did for their personal advantage; and shall begin with Junius Brutus, the father of Roman liberty.

Chapter II

IT MAY AT TIMES BE THE HIGHEST WISDOM TO SIMULATE FOLLY

No one ever displayed so much sagacity, or was esteemed so wise on account of any distinguished act, as Junius Brutus deserves to be esteemed for his simulation of folly. And although Titus Livius gives but one reason that induced him to this simulation, namely, that he might live in greater security and preserve his patrimony, yet if we well consider his conduct we are led to believe that he had another reason, which was that by thus avoiding observation he would have a better chance of destroying the kings, and of liberating his country, whenever an opportunity should offer. And that such was really his thought may be seen, first, from his interpretation of the oracle of Apollo, when he pretended to have fallen and kissed the earth, hoping thereby to propitiate the gods to his projects; and afterwards, when on the occasion of the death of Lucretia, in the midst of the father, husband, and other relatives, he was the first to pluck the dagger from her breast and to make all present swear henceforth to suffer no king to reign in Rome.

All those who are dissatisfied with their ruler should take a lesson from this example of Brutus; they should measure and weigh well their strength, and if sufficiently powerful to be able to declare themselves his enemies, and to make open war against the prince, then they should take that course as the least dangerous and most honorable. But if their condition be such that their forces do not suffice for open war against the prince, then they should seek by every art to win his friendship, and for this purpose employ all possible means, such as adopting his tastes, and taking delight in all things that give him pleasure. Such intimacy will insure you tranquillity without any danger, and enable you to share the enjoyment of the prince's good fortune with him, and at the same time afford you every convenience for satisfying your resentment. True, some people say that one should not keep so close to princes as to be involved in their ruin, nor so far away but what in case of their ruin you might thereby advance your own fortunes. This middle course would undoubtedly be the best to pursue, but as I believe that impossible, one of the above-described modes must be adopted,— either to go away from them entirely, or to attach yourself very closely to them; and whoever attempts any other way, even though he be a personage of distinction, exposes himself to constant danger. Nor will it do for him to say, "I do not care for anything; I desire neither honor nor profit; all I want is to live quietly and without trouble,"—for such excuses would not be admitted. Men of condition cannot choose their way of living, and even if they did choose it sincerely and without ambition, they would not be believed; and were they to attempt to adhere to it, they would not be allowed to do so by others.

It is advisable then at times to feign folly, as Brutus did; and this is sufficiently done by praising, speaking, seeing, and doing things contrary to your way of thinking, and merely to please the prince. And as I have spoken of the sagacity of Brutus in recovering the liberty of Rome, let me now speak of his severity in maintaining it.

Chapter III

TO PRESERVE THE NEWLY RECOVERED LIBERTY IN ROME, IT WAS
NECESSARY THAT THE SONS OF BRUTUS SHOULD HAVE BEEN
EXECUTED

THE severity of Brutus was not only useful, but necessary for
the maintenance of that liberty in Rome which he had restored to her; and certainly it is one of the rarest examples
within the memory of man for a father not only to sit in
judgment and condemn his own sons, but actually to be
present at their execution. Every student of ancient history
well knows that any change of government, be it from a republic to a tyranny, or from a tyranny to a republic, must
necessarily be followed by some terrible punishment of the
enemies of the existing state of things. And whoever makes
himself tyrant of a state and does not kill Brutus, or whoever restores liberty to a state and does not immolate his
sons, will not maintain himself in his position long. Having
already in another place treated this subject at length, I refer
to what I have there said, and confine myself now to citing
a single and most remarkable example, taken from the history of our own country. It is that of Pietro Soderini, who
believed that he would be able by patience and gentleness
to overcome the determination of the new sons of Brutus to
return to another form of government; in which, however,
he greatly deceived himself. And although his natural sagacity recognized the necessity of destroying them, and although the quality and ambition of his adversaries afforded
him the opportunity, yet he had not the courage to do it. For
he thought, and several times acknowledged it to his friends,
that boldly to strike down his adversaries and all opposition

would oblige him to assume extraordinary authority, and even legally to destroy civil equality; and that, even if he should not afterwards use this power tyrannically, this course would so alarm the masses that after his death they would never again consent to the election of another Gonfalonier for life, which he deemed essential for the strengthening and maintaining of the government. This respect for the laws was most praiseworthy and wise on the part of Soderini. Still one should never allow an evil to run on out of respect for the law, especially when the law itself might easily be destroyed by the evil; and he should have borne in mind, that as his acts and motives would have to be judged by the result, in case he had been fortunate enough to succeed and live, everybody would have attested that what he had done was for the good of his country, and not for the advancement of any ambitious purposes of his own. Moreover, he could have regulated matters so that his successors could not have employed for evil the means which he had used for beneficent purposes. But Soderini was the dupe of his opinions, not knowing that malignity is neither effaced by time, nor placated by gifts. So that by failing to imitate Brutus he lost at the same time his country, his state, and his reputation.

In the following chapter I propose to show that it is equally difficult to save a monarchy as to save a republic.

Chapter IV

A PRINCE CANNOT LIVE SECURELY IN A STATE SO LONG AS THOSE LIVE WHOM HE HAS DEPRIVED OF IT

THE assassination of Tarquinius Priscus by the sons of Ancus, and the death of Servius Tullus caused by Tarquinius Superbus, prove how difficult and dangerous it is to deprive any one of a kingdom and leave him his life, even though you try to conciliate him by benefits. We see how Tarquinius Priscus was deceived by the seemingly lawful possession of the sovereignty of Rome, which had been bestowed upon him by the people and confirmed by the Senate. He could not believe that resentment would so master the sons of Ancus that they would not be satisfied to submit to him, to whom all Rome yielded obedience. Servius Tullus in like manner deceived himself in supposing that he could win the sons of Tarquin with benefits. Thus the first may serve as a warning to all princes that they will never be safe so long as those live whom they have deprived of their possessions; and as to the second, it should remind every potentate that old injuries can never be cancelled by new benefits, and the less so when the benefits are small in proportion to the injury inflicted. Certainly Servius Tullus showed little sagacity when he supposed that the sons of Tarquin would remain content to be the sons-in-law of him whose kings they felt themselves entitled to be. And this desire to reign is so powerful that it not only dominates the minds of those born with the expectation of a throne, but also that of those who have no such expectations. This was well illustrated by the wife of Tarquin the younger, daughter of Servius, who, urged on by this mad desire, regardless of all filial piety, stirred up her husband to deprive her father of his life and kingdom; so much more did she value being a queen than being the daughter of a king. If, then, Tarquinius Priscus and Servius Tullus lost the kingdom from not knowing how to assure themselves of those whose thrones they had usurped, Tarquinius Superbus lost it by a disregard of the laws established by his predecessors, as we shall show in the next chapter.

Chapter V

OF THE CAUSES THAT MAKE A KING LOSE THE THRONE WHICH HE HAS INHERITED

SERVIUS TULLUS, having been assassinated by Tarquinius Superbus, left no heirs; so the latter could reign with entire security, not having to fear the dangers to which his predecessors had fallen victims. And although the manner in which he had obtained possession of the kingdom was irregular and odious, still, if he had conformed to the ancient institutions of the former kings, neither the Senate nor the people would ever have risen against him to deprive him of the throne. Tarquin was driven from Rome, not because his son Sextus had violated Lucretia, but because he had disregarded the laws of the kingdom and governed it tyrannically; having deprived the Senate of all authority, which he appropriated to himself, and having diverted the funds intended for the improvement of the public places and buildings, which the Senate had carried on with so much satisfaction, to the construction of his own palace, greatly to the disgust of the Senate; despoiling Rome in a short time of all the liberties which she had enjoyed under previous kings. And not content with having incurred the enmity of the Senate, he also aroused the people against himself, unlike his predecessors, by obliging them to perform all sorts of mechanical labor. So that, having disgusted all Rome by his many acts of cruelty and pride, he disposed the minds of the Romans to revolt against him on the first occasion that might offer. And if the incident of Lucretia had not occurred, some other would have produced the same effect; for had Tarquin conducted himself like the previous kings, when his son Sextus committed that crime Brutus and Collatinus would have appealed to Tarquin for vengeance against Sextus, instead of stirring up the Roman people as they did.

Princes should remember, then, that they begin to lose their state from the moment when they begin to disregard the laws and ancient customs under which the people have lived contented for a length of time. And if, having thus lost their state, they should ever become wise enough to see with what facility princes preserve their thrones who conduct themselves prudently, they would regret their loss the more, and would condemn themselves to greater punishments than that to which others have doomed them. For it is much easier to be beloved by the good than the wicked, and to obey the laws than to enforce them; and if kings desire to know what course they have to pursue to do this, they need take no other trouble than to follow the example of the lives of good rulers, such as Timoleon of Corinth, Aratus of Sicyon, and the like, whose lives they will find to have afforded as much security and satisfaction to him who ruled as to those who were governed; which should make kings desire to imitate them, as is easily done. For when men are well governed, they neither seek nor desire any other liberty; as was experienced by the two above-named princes, whom their people constrained to reign to the end of their lives, though they often wished to retire to private life.

Having discussed in the preceding chapters the evil dispositions that are apt to be stirred up against princes, and the conspiracy set on foot by the sons of Brutus against their country, and those formed against Tarquinius Priscus and Servius Tullus, it seems to me nevertheless not amiss to treat this subject at length in the following chapter, it being a matter well worthy of the attention of princes and subjects.

Chapter VI

OF CONSPIRACIES

IT seems to me proper now to treat of conspiracies, being a matter of so much danger both to princes and subjects; for history teaches us that many more princes have lost their lives and their states by conspiracies than by open war. But few can venture to make open war upon their sovereign, whilst every one may engage in conspiracies against him. On the other hand, subjects cannot undertake more perilous and foolhardy enterprises than conspiracies, which are in every respect most difficult and dangerous; and thence it is that, though so often attempted, yet they so rarely attain the desired object. And therefore, so that princes may learn to guard against such dangers, and that subjects may less rashly engage in them, and learn rather to live contentedly under such a government as Fate may have assigned to them, I shall treat the subject at length, and endeavor not to omit any point that may be useful to the one or the other. And certainly that is a golden sentence of Cornelius Tacitus, where he says "that men should honor the past and obey the present; and whilst they should desire good princes, they should bear with those they have, such as they are";—and surely whoever acts otherwise will generally involve himself and his country in ruin.

In entering upon the subject, then, we must consider first against whom conspiracies are formed; and it will be found generally that they are made either against the country or against the prince. It is of these two kinds that I shall speak at present; for conspiracies that have for their object the surrender of any town to an enemy that besieges it, or that have some similar purpose, have already been sufficiently discussed above. In the first instance we will treat of those that are aimed against the sovereign, and examine the causes that provoke them; these are many, though one is more important than all the rest, namely, his being hated by the mass of the people. For when a prince has drawn upon himself universal hatred, it is reasonable to suppose that there are some particular individuals whom he has injured more than others, and who therefore desire to revenge themselves. This desire is increased by seeing the prince held in general aversion. A prince, then, should avoid incurring such universal hatred; and, as I have spoken elsewhere of the way to do this, I will say no more about it here. If the prince will avoid this general hatred, the particular wrongs to individuals will prove less dangerous to him; partly because men rarely attach sufficient importance to any wrong done them to expose themselves to great danger for the sake of avenging it, and partly because, even if they were so disposed and had the power to attempt it, they would be restrained by the general affection for the prince. The different wrongs which a prince can inflict upon a subject consist either in an attempt upon his possessions, his person, or his honor. In matters of personal injury, threats are worse than the execution; in fact, menaces involve the only danger, there being none in the execution, for the dead cannot avenge themselves, and in most cases the survivors allow the thought of revenge to be interred with the dead. But he who is threatened, and sees himself constrained by necessity either to dare and do or to suffer, becomes a most dangerous man to the prince as we shall show in its proper place. Besides this kind of injury, a man's property and honor are the points upon which he will be most keenly sensitive. A prince, then, should be most careful to avoid touching these; for he can never despoil a man so completely but what he will cherish a determined desire for revenge. As to attacking men's honor, that of their wives is what they feel most, and after that their being themselves treated with indignity. It was an outrage of this nature that armed Pausanias against Philip of Macedon, and such indignities have caused many others to rise against their princes. In our day, Julius Belanti would not have conspired against Pandolfo, tyrant of Sienna, had it not been that the latter, having accorded him one of his daughters in marriage, afterwards took her away from him, as we shall relate in its place. The principal cause of the conspiracy of the Pazzi against the Medici was the inheritance of Giovanni Borromeo, of which they had been deprived by an order of the Medici.

There is another and still more powerful motive that makes men conspire against their princes, and that is the desire to liberate their country from the tyranny to which it has been subjected by the prince. It was this that stirred up Brutus and Cassius against Cæsar; it was this that excited others against the Falari, the Dionysii, and other usurpers. And no tyrant can secure himself against such attacks, except by voluntarily giving up his usurpation. But as none of them ever take this course, there are but few that do not come to a bad end; and thence this verse of Juvenal's:—

"Ad generum Cereris sine cæde et vulnere pauci
Descendunt reges, et sicca morte tyranni." *

The perils incurred by conspirators are great, as I have said above, because they present themselves at every moment. There is danger in plotting and in the execution of the plot, and even after it has been carried into effect. A plot may be

---

* "Few kings descend to the dark abode of Ceres without wounds or slaughter, and tyrants never die a natural death."

formed by a single individual or by many; the one cannot be called a conspiracy, but rather a determined purpose on the part of one man to assassinate the prince. In such case the first of the three dangers to which conspiracies are exposed is avoided; for the individual runs no risk before the execution of his plot, for as no one possesses his secret, there is no danger of his purpose coming to the ears of the prince. Any individual, of whatever condition, may form such a plot, be he great or small, noble or plebeian, familiar or not familiar with the prince; for every one is permitted on occasions to speak to the prince, and has thus the opportunity of satisfying his vengeance. Pausanias, of whom I have spoken elsewhere, killed Philip of Macedon as he was proceeding to the temple, surrounded by a thousand armed men, and having his son and his son-in-law on either side. But Pausanias was a noble, and well known to the prince. A poor and abject Spaniard stabbed King Ferdinand of Spain in the neck; the wound was not mortal, but it showed nevertheless that this man had the audacity as well as the opportunity of striking the prince. A Turkish Dervish drew a scimitar upon Bajazet, the father of the present Grand Turk; he did not wound him, but it shows that this man too had the audacity and the opportunity to have done it, had he so chosen. I believe it is not uncommon to find men who form such projects (the mere purpose involving neither danger nor punishment), but few carry them into effect; and of those who do, very few or none escape being killed in the execution of their designs, and therefore but few are willing to incur such certain death.

But let us leave the plots formed by single individuals, and come to conspiracies formed by a number of persons. These, I say, have generally for their originators the great men of the state, or those on terms of familiar intercourse with the prince. None other, unless they are madmen, can engage in conspiracies; for men of low condition, who are not intimate with the prince, have no chance of success, not having the necessary conveniences for the execution of their plots. In the first place, men of no position have not the means of assuring themselves of the good faith of their accomplices, as no one will engage in their plot without the hope of those advantages that prompt men to expose themselves to great dangers. And thus, so soon as they have drawn two or three others into their scheme, some one of them denounces and ruins them. But supposing even that they have the good fortune not to be betrayed, they are nevertheless exposed to so many difficulties in the execution of the plot, from being debarred free access to the prince, that it seems almost impossible for them to escape ruin in the execution. For if the great men of a state, who are in familiar intercourse with the prince, succumb under the many difficulties of which we have spoken, it is natural that these difficulties should be infinitely increased for the others. And therefore those who know themselves to be weak avoid them, for where men's lives and fortunes are at stake they are not all insane; and when they have cause for hating a prince, they content themselves with cursing and vilifying him, and wait until some one more powerful and of higher position than themselves shall avenge them. Still, if one of this class of persons should be daring enough to attempt such an undertaking, he would merit praise rather for his intention than for his prudence.

We see, then, that conspiracies have generally been set on foot by the great, or the friends of the prince; and of these, as many have been prompted to it by an excess of benefits as by an excess of wrongs. Such was the cause of the conspiracy of Perennius against Commodus, of Plautianus against Severus, and of Sejanus against Tiberius. All these men had been so loaded with riches, honors, and dignities by their Emperors that nothing seemed wanting to complete their power and to satisfy their ambition but the Empire itself; and to obtain that they set conspiracies on foot against their masters, which all resulted, however, as their ingratitude deserved. More recently, however, we have seen the conspiracy of Jacopo Appiano succeed against Piero Gambacorte, prince of Pisa; this Jacopo owed his support, education, and reputation to Piero, and yet he deprived him of his state. The conspiracy of Coppola against Ferdinand of Aragon, in our own day, was of the same character; Coppola had attained such greatness that he seemed to lack nothing but the throne, and to obtain this he risked his life, and lost it. And certainly if any conspiracy of the great against a prince is likely to succeed, it should be one that is headed by one, so to say, almost himself a king, who can afford the conspirators every opportunity to accomplish his design; but, blinded by the ambition of dominion, they are equally blind in the conduct of the conspiracy, for if their villainy were directed by prudence, they could not possibly fail of success. A prince, then, who wishes to guard against conspiracies should fear those on whom he has heaped benefits quite as much, and even more, than those whom he has wronged; for the latter lack the convenient opportunities which the former have in abundance. The intention of both is the same, for the thirst of dominion is as great as that of revenge, and even greater. A prince, therefore, should never bestow so much authority upon his friends but that there should always be a certain distance between them and himself, and that there should always be something left for them to desire; otherwise they will almost invariably become victims of their own imprudence, as happened to those whom we have mentioned above.

But to return to our subject. Having said that conspiracies are generally made by the great, who have free access to the prince, let us see now what their results have been, and what the causes were that influenced their success or their failure. As we have said above, there are in all conspiracies three distinct periods of danger. The first is in the organization of the plot, and as but few have a successful issue, it is impossible that all should pass happily through this first stage, which presents the greatest dangers; and therefore I say that it requires the extremest prudence, or great good fortune, that a conspiracy shall not be discovered in the process of formation. Their discovery is either by denunciation or by surmises. Denunciation is the consequence of treachery or of want of prudence on the part of those to whom you confide your designs; and treachery is so common that you cannot safely impart your project to any but such of your most trusted friends as are willing to risk their lives for your sake, or to such other malcontents as are equally desirous of the prince's ruin. Of such reliable friends you may find one or two; but as you are necessarily obliged to extend your confidence, it becomes impossible to find many such, for their devotion to you must be greater than their sense of danger and fear of punishment. Moreover, men are very apt to deceive themselves as to the degree of attachment and devotion which others have for them, and there are no means of ascertaining this except by actual experience; but experience in such matters is of the utmost danger. And even if you should have tested the fidelity of your friends on other occasions of danger, yet you cannot conclude from that that they will be equally true to you on an occasion that presents infinitely greater dangers than any other. If you attempt to measure a man's good faith by the discontent which he manifests towards the prince, you will be easily deceived, for by the very fact of communicating to him your designs, you give him the means of putting an end to his discontent; and to insure his fidelity, his hatred of the prince or your influence over him must be very great. It is thus that so many conspiracies have been revealed and crushed in their incipient stage; so that it may be regarded almost as a miracle when so important a secret is preserved by a number of conspirators for any length of time. Such however was the case in the conspiracy of Piso against Nero, and in our times that of the Pazzi against Lorenzo and Giuliano de' Medici, of which more than fifty persons were cognizant, and which yet remained undiscovered till the moment of its execution.

Discovery from lack of prudence occurs when any one of the conspirators speaks incautiously, so that a servant or third person overhears it, as happened to the sons of Brutus, who in the arranging of their plot with the messengers of Tarquin were overheard by a slave, who denounced them. Or it may occur from thoughtlessness, when some one communicates the secret to his wife or child, or to some other indiscreet person, as was done by Dinnus, one of the conspirators with Philotas against Alexander, who confided the plot to Nicomachus, a lad of whom he was enamored, who told it to his brother Ciballinus, who at once communicated it to the king. As to discovery by conjecture, we have an instance of it in the Pisonian conspiracy against Nero. The day before he was to have killed Nero, Scevinus, one of the conspirators, made his testament; he ordered his freedman Melichius to sharpen an old, rusty poniard, enfranchised all his slaves and distributed money amongst them, and had bandages made for tying up wounds. Melichius surmised from these various acts what was going on, and denounced it to Nero. Scevinus was arrested, and with him Natales, another conspirator, with whom he had been seen to converse secretly for a length of time. As their depositions respecting that conversation did not agree, they were forced to confess the truth, and thus the conspiracy was discovered to the ruin of all that were implicated. When the number of accomplices in a conspiracy exceeds three or four, it is almost impossible for it not to be discovered, either through treason, imprudence, or carelessness. The moment more than one of the conspirators is arrested, the whole plot is discovered; for it will be impossible for any two to agree perfectly as to all their statements. If only one be arrested, and he be a man of courage and firmness, he may be able to conceal the names of his accomplices; but then the others, to remain safe, must be equally firm, and not lay themselves open to discovery by flight, for if any one of them proves wanting in courage, whether it be the one that is arrested or one of those that are at liberty, the conspiracy is sure to be discovered. Titus Livius cites a very remarkable instance that occurred in connection with the conspiracy against Hieronymus, king of Syracuse. Theodorus, one of the conspirators, having been arrested, concealed with the utmost firmness the names of the other conspirators, and charged the matter upon the friends of the king; and, on the other hand, all the other conspirators had such confidence in the courage of Theodorus, that not one of them left Syracuse, or betrayed the least sign of fear. The conduct of a conspiracy then is exposed to all such dangers before it can be carried into execution; and to avoid these perils the following remedies present themselves. The first and most certain, I should rather say the only one, is not to afford your associates in the plot any time to betray you; and therefore you should confide your project to them at the moment of its execution, and not sooner. Those who act thus are most likely to escape the first of the three dangers, and frequently also the others; and therefore have their enterprises almost always succeeded. And any man of prudence will always be able to govern himself in this wise.

I will cite two examples of this. Nelematus, unable to bear the tyranny of Aristotimus, tyrant of Epirus, assembled in his house a number of friends and relatives, and urged them to liberate their country from the yoke of the tyrant. Some of them asked for time to consider the matter, whereupon Nelematus made his slaves close the door of his house, and then said to those he had called together, "You must either go now and carry this plot into execution, or I shall hand you all over as prisoners to Aristotimus." Moved by these words, they took the oath demanded of them, and immediately went and carried the plot of Nelematus successfully into execution. A Magian having by craft usurped the throne of Persia, and the fraud having been discovered by Ortanus, one of the grandees of the realm, he conferred with six other princes of the state as to the means of ridding themselves of this usurper. When one of them inquired as to the time when they should act, Darius, one of the six assembled by Ortanus, arose and said, "We must either go now at this very moment and carry it into execution, or I shall go and denounce you all," whereupon they all arose, and, without affording any one time to repent, they carried their design into execution without difficulty. The Ætolians acted much in the same way in ridding themselves of Nabis, tyrant of Sparta. They sent Alexamenes, one of their citizens, with thirty horse and two hundred infantry, to Nabis, on pretence of rendering him assistance; but they gave secret instructions to Alexamenes to slay Nabis, and enjoined the others, on pain of exile, strictly and most implicitly to obey the orders of Alexamenes, who accordingly went to Sparta, and kept the secret until the moment when he succeeded in killing Nabis. In this manner

then did Nelematus, Ortanus, and Alexamenes avoid the
dangers that attend the conduct of conspiracies before their
execution, and whoever follows their example will be equally
fortunate in escaping them. And to prove that it is in the
power of every one to act in the same way, I will cite the case
of Piso, to which I have already referred above. Piso was a
man of the highest consideration and distinction in Rome,
and the familiar companion of Nero, who reposed entire
confidence in him, and often went to dine with him at his
villa. Piso then might have attached to himself a few men of
intelligence and courage, well qualified for such an attempt
as he contemplated. This would have been an easy thing to
do for a man of such high position; and then, when Nero
was in his gardens, he might have communicated his project
to them and have stirred them by a few words to do what
they would not have had time to refuse, and which could not
have failed of success.

And thus, if we examine all the other instances, but few
will be found where the conspirators might not have acted
in the same way; but men not accustomed to the affairs of
this world often commit the greatest mistakes, and especially
in matters that are so much out of the ordinary course as conspiracies. One should therefore never open himself on the
subject of a conspiracy except under the most pressing
necessity, and only at the moment of its execution; and then
only to one man, whose fidelity he has thoroughly tested for
a long time, and who is animated by the same desire as himself. One such is much more easily found than many, and
therefore there is much less danger in confiding your secret
to him; and then, even if he were to attempt to betray you,
there is some chance of your being able to defend yourself,
which you cannot when there are many conspirators. I have
heard many wise men say that you may talk freely with one

man about everything, for unless you have committed yourself in writing the "yes" of one man is worth as much as the "no" of another; and therefore one should guard most carefully against writing, as against a dangerous rock, for nothing will convict you quicker than your own handwriting. Plautianus, wishing to have the Emperor Severus and his son Antoninus killed, committed the matter to the Tribune Saturninus; he however, instead of obeying Plautianus, resolved to betray him, and, fearing that in accusing him he would be less believed than Plautianus, he exacted from him an order in his own handwriting to attest his authority. Plautianus, blinded by his ambition, gave him such a written order, which the Tribune used to accuse and convict him. Plautianus denied his guilt with such audacity, that without this written order and other indications he never would have been convicted. You may escape, then, from the accusation of a single individual, unless you are convicted by some writing or other pledge, which you should be careful never to give. In the Pisonian conspiracy there was a woman named Epicaris, who had formerly been a mistress of Nero's. She deemed it advisable to have amongst the conspirators the commander of a trireme, who was one of Nero's bodyguards. She communicated the plot to him, but without naming the conspirators. The commander, however, betrayed her confidence, and denounced Epicaris to Nero; but she denied it with such audacity as to confuse Nero, who did not condemn her.

There are two risks then, in communicating a plot to any one individual: the first, lest he should denounce you voluntarily; the second, lest he should denounce you, being himself arrested on suspicion, or from some indications, and being convicted and forced to it by the torture. But there are means of escaping both these dangers: the first, by denial and

by alleging personal hatred to have prompted the accusation; and the other, by denying the charge, and alleging
that your accuser was constrained by the force of torture
to tell lies. But the most prudent course is not to communicate the plot to any one, and to act in accordance with the
above-cited examples; and if you cannot avoid drawing some
one into your confidence, then to let it be not more than
one, for in that case the danger is much less than if you confide in many.

Another necessity may force you to do unto the prince that
which you see the prince about to do to you; the danger of
which may be so pressing as not to afford you the time to
provide for your own safety. Such a necessity ordinarily in-
sures success, as the following two instances will suffice to
prove. The Emperor Commodus had amongst his nearest
friends and intimates Letus and Electus, two captains of
the Prætorian soldiers; he also had Marcia as his favorite
concubine. As these three had on several occasions reproved
him for the excesses with which he had stained his own
dignity and that of the Empire, he resolved to have them
killed, and wrote a list of the names of Marcia, Letus, and
Electus, and of some other persons, whom he wanted killed
the following night. Having placed this list under his pillow,
he went to the bath; a favorite child of his, who was playing
in the chamber and on the bed, found this list, and on going
out with it in his hand was met by Marcia, who took the list
from the child. Having read it, she immediately sent for
Letus and Electus, and when these three had thus become
aware of the danger that threatened them, they resolved to
forestall the Emperor, and without losing any time they
killed Commodus the following night. The Emperor Antoninus Caracalla was with his armies in Mesopotamia, and
had for his prefect Macrinus, a man more fit for civil than

military matters. As is always the case with bad rulers, they are in constant fear lest others are conspiring to inflict upon them the punishment which they are conscious of deserving; thus Antoninus wrote to his friend Maternianus in Rome to consult the astrologers as to whether any one was aspiring to the Empire, and to advise him of it. Maternianus wrote back that Macrinus was thus aspiring; and this letter fell into the hands of Macrinus before it reached the Emperor. He at once directed his trusted friend, the Centurion Martialis, whose brother had been slain by Caracalla a few days before, to assassinate him, which he succeeded in doing. From this we see that the necessity which admits of no delay produces the same effect as the means employed by Nelematus in Epirus, of which I have spoken above. It also proves the truth of what I said in the beginning of this discourse, that to threaten is more dangerous for princes, and more frequently causes conspiracies, than the actual injury itself; and therefore princes should guard against indulging in menaces. For you must bind men to you by benefits, or you must make sure of them in some other way, but never reduce them to the alternative of having either to destroy you or perish themselves.

As to the dangers that occur in the execution of a conspiracy, these result either from an unexpected change in the order of proceeding, or from the lack of courage in those who are charged with the execution of the plot, or from some error on their part, owing to want of foresight in leaving some of those alive whom it was intended to have killed. There is nothing that disturbs or impedes the actions of men more than when suddenly, and without time to reflect, the order of things agreed upon has to be entirely changed. And if such a change causes embarrassment in ordinary affairs, it does so to an infinitely greater degree in war or in conspiracies; for in such matters nothing is more essential than that men should firmly set their minds on performing the part that has been assigned to them. And if men have their minds fixed for some days upon a certain order and arrangement, and this be suddenly changed, it is impossible that this should not disturb them so as to defeat the whole plot. So that it is much better to carry out any such project according to the original plan, even if it should present some inconveniences, rather than to change the order agreed upon and incur a thousand embarrassments. And this will occur, if there be not time to reorganize the project entirely; for when there is time for that, men can suit themselves to the new order of things.

The conspiracy of the Pazzi against Lorenzo and Giuliano de' Medici is well known. These were to dine on the appointed day with the Cardinal of San Giorgio, and it was agreed amongst the conspirators to kill the Medici at this dinner. They had distributed amongst themselves the several roles, as to who was to kill them, who was to seize the palace, and who was to scour the city to rouse the people to liberty. It happened that whilst the Medici, the Pazzi, and the Cardinal were at some great solemnity in the cathedral church of Florence, it became known that Giuliano would not dine with the Cardinal on that day. Hereupon the conspirators hastily met, and resolved to do in the church what they had intended to do in the house of the Cardinal. This disarranged all their plans, for Giambattisto Montesecco refused to consent to the murder in the church, which obliged them to make an entire change and distribute the roles to different persons, who, not having time fully to prepare themselves, committed such mistakes as to cause themselves to be crushed in the execution.

Want of firmness in the execution arises either from respect, or from the innate cowardice of him who is to commit the act. Such is the majesty and reverence that ordinarily surrounds the person of a prince, that it may easily mitigate the fury of a murderer, or fill him with fear. Marius having been taken prisoner by the Minturnians, they sent a slave to kill him, who was so overcome by the presence of this great man, and by the memory of his glory, that his courage and strength failed him at the thought of killing Marius. Now if a man in chains, in prison, and overwhelmed by misfortune can still exert such an influence, how much more is to be feared from a prince who is free, and clothed in all the pomp and ornaments of royalty, and surrounded by his court? And whilst all this pomp is calculated to inspire fear, an affable and courteous reception may equally disarm you.

Some of the subjects of Sitalces, king of Thrace, conspired against him. The day for the execution of their plot being fixed, they went to the place agreed upon where the king was, but not one of them made a movement to strike him; so that they returned without having made the attempt, and without knowing what had prevented them, and reproached each other. They committed the same fault several times, so that the conspiracy was discovered, and they suffered punishment for the crime which they might have committed, but did not.

Two brothers of Alfonso, Duke of Ferrara, plotted against his life, and employed for the execution of their plot one Giannes, the Duke's almoner and musician, who several times at their request brought the Duke to them; so that they might on each occasion have killed him, but neither of them had the courage to do it. The conspiracy was discovered, and they bore the penalty of their wickedness and their imprudence. Their neglect to profit by the opportunities afforded them for the execution of their design could have arisen only from two causes; either the presence of the prince imposed upon them and filled them with fear, or they were disarmed by some act of kindness on his part. Failure in the execution of such designs results from lack of prudence or courage; men are seized by one or the other of these feelings, which confuse their brains and make them say and do things that they ought not.

And nothing can better prove the fact that men's minds are thus seized and confounded than the fact stated by Titus Livius of Alexamenes the Ætolian, who wanted to kill Nabis of Sparta, of whom I have already spoken. When the time for the execution of his design had come, and he was about to make known to his soldiers what they would have to do, as Titus Livius says, "He collected his own spirits, which were confused by the greatness of the undertaking." For it is impossible that one should not be confused at such a moment, even though possessed of firmness and courage, and accustomed to the use of the sword and to seeing men killed. Therefore only men experienced in such affairs should be chosen as the instruments of execution, and none other should be trusted, though they be reputed to be most courageous; for you cannot be sure of any man's courage in great affairs, unless it has been tested by actual experience. For the confusion of the mind at the important moment may cause the sword to drop from a man's hand, or may make him say things that will be equally ruinous.

Lucilla, the sister of the Emperor Commodus, ordered Quintianus to kill him. He lay in wait for Commodus at the entrance of the amphitheatre; and on stepping up to him with drawn dagger, he cried, "The Senate sends you this!" which caused Quintianus to be arrested before he had time to strike Commodus. Messer Antonio da Volterra, having been appointed to kill Lorenzo de' Medici, as we have related above, called out, on approaching him, "Ah, traitor!" This mere word saved Lorenzo and defeated the attempt.

Conspiracies against single individuals are generally apt to fail, for the reasons I have adduced; but when undertaken against two or more persons, they fail much easier. Such conspiracies present so many difficulties that it is almost impossible they should succeed. In fact, to strike two blows of this kind at the same instant and in different places is impracticable, and to attempt to do so at different moments of time would certainly result in the one's preventing the other. So that, if it is imprudent, rash, and doubtful to conspire against a single prince, it amounts to folly to do so against two at the same time. And were it not for the respect which I have for the historian, I should not be able to believe possible what Herodianus relates of Plautianus, when he charged the centurion Saturninus by himself to kill Severus and Caracalla, who lived separately in different places; for it is so far from being reasonable, that nothing less than the authority of Herodianus could make me believe it. Some young men of Athens conspired against Diocles and Hippias, tyrants of Athens; they succeeded in killing Diocles, but missed Hippias, who avenged him. Chion and Leonidas, of Heraclea, disciples of Plato, conspired against the tyrants Clearchus and Satirus; they slew Clearchus, but Satirus, who remained, avenged him. The Pazzi, whom I have mentioned several times, succeeded only in killing Giuliano. Thus conspiracies against several persons at the same time should be avoided; they do no good to the conspirators, nor to the country, nor to any one, but rather cause the tyrants that survive to become more cruel and insupportable than before. as was the case with those of Florence, Athens, and Heraclea, already mentioned above. It is true that the conspiracy of. Pelopidas to deliver his country, Thebes, from her tyrants, succeeded most happily, despite of all those obstacles; and he conspired not only against two, but against ten tyrants, and, so far from having ready access to them, he had been declared a rebel and had been banished. With all this, he was enabled to come to Thebes to slay the tyrants and free his country. But he succeeded thus mainly through the assistance of a certain Charon, privy counsellor of the tyrants, who facilitated his access to them and the consequent execution of his plot. Let no one, however, be seduced by this example; for it was an almost impossible enterprise, and its success was a marvel, and was so regarded by the historians, who speak of it as a most extraordinary and unprecedented event. The execution of such a plot may be interrupted by the least false alarm, or by some unforeseen accident at the moment of its execution.

The morning of the day when Brutus and his fellow-conspirators intended to kill Cæsar, it happened that the latter had a long conversation with Cn. Popilius Lena, one of the conspirators. This was observed by the other conspirators, who at once imagined that Popilius had denounced the conspiracy to Cæsar, and were tempted to assassinate Cæsar on the spot, and not to wait until he should reach the Senate; and they would have done so, had they not observed that after the conversation Cæsar made no extraordinary movement, which reassured them. These false apprehensions are not to be disregarded and should be carefully considered, the more so as it is very easy to be surprised by them; for a man who has a guilty conscience readily thinks that everybody is speaking of him. You may overhear a word spoken to some one else that will greatly disturb you, because you think it has reference to you, and may cause you either to discover the conspiracy by flight, or embarrass its execution by hastening it before the appointed time. And this will happen the more easily the more accomplices there are in the conspiracy.

As to the unforeseen accidents, of course no idea can be given of them; they can only be illustrated by examples that should serve as a caution. Julio Belanti of Sienna (of whom I have already made mention) hated Pandolfo for having taken his daughter away from him after having first given her to him as his wife. He resolved to kill him, and thus chose his time. Pandolfo went almost daily to visit a sick relative, and in going there he passed before Julio's house, who, having observed it, arranged to have the conspirators there to assassinate Pandolfo when he passed. He concealed them, well armed, behind the house door, whilst one of them was stationed at the window to watch for the coming of Pandolfo, and to give a signal when he should be near the door. Pandolfo came, and the signal was given by the conspirator at the window; but at that moment a friend met and stopped Pandolfo, whilst some who were with him moved on, and, upon hearing the noise of arms within the door of Julio, they discovered the ambush, so that Pandolfo was enabled to save himself, and Julio, with his accomplices, was obliged to fly from Sienna. This accidental meeting with a friend prevented the execution of the plot, and thwarted the designs of Julio. Such accidents, being rare, cannot be foreseen nor prevented; though one should endeavor to foresee all that can happen, so as to guard against it.

It only remains for us now to speak of the dangers that follow the execution of a plot; of which there is really but one, namely, when some one is left who will avenge the prince that is killed. He may have brothers or sons, or other relatives, who inherit the principality, and who have been spared by your negligence or for some of the reasons we have mentioned above, and who will avenge the prince. This happened to Giovan Andrea da Lampognano, who, together with other conspirators, had killed the Duke of Milan, who left a son and two brothers, who in time avenged the murdered Duke. But truly in such cases the conspirators are not to be blamed, because there is no help for it. There is no excuse for them, however, when from want of foresight or negligence they permit any one to escape. Some conspirators of Furli killed the Count Girolamo, their lord, and took his wife and children, who were of tender age, prisoners. Believing, however, that they could not be secure if they did not obtain possession of the castle, which the castellan refused to surrender, the Lady Catharine, as the Countess was called, promised to the conspirators to procure its surrender if they would allow her to enter it, leaving them her children as hostages. Upon this pledge the conspirators consented to let her enter the castle; but no sooner was she within than she reproached them for the murder of the Count, and threatened them with every kind of vengeance. And to prove to them that she cared not for her children, she pointed to her sexual parts, calling out to them that she had wherewith to have more children. Thus the conspirators discovered their error too late, and suffered the penalty of their imprudence in perpetual exile. But of all the perils that follow the execution of a conspiracy, none is more certain and none more to be feared than the attachment of the people to the prince that has been killed. There is no remedy against this, for the conspirators can never secure themselves against a whole people. As an instance of this, I will cite the case of Julius Cæsar, who, being beloved by the people, was avenged by them; for having driven the conspirators from Rome, they were the cause of their being all killed at various times and places.

Conspiracies against the state are less dangerous for those

engaged in them than plots against the life of the sovereign. In their conduct there is not so much danger, in their execution there is the same, and after execution there is none. In the conduct of the plot the danger is very slight, for a citizen may aspire to supreme power without manifesting his intentions to any one; and if nothing interferes with his plans, he may carry them through successfully, or if they are thwarted by some law, he may await a more favorable moment, and attempt it by another way. This is understood to apply to a republic that is already partially corrupted; for in one not yet tainted by corruption such thoughts could never enter the mind of any citizen. Citizens of a republic, then, may by a variety of ways and means aspire to sovereign authority without incurring great risks. If republics are slower than princes, they are also less suspicious, and therefore less cautious; and if they show more respect to their great citizens, these in turn are thereby made more daring and audacious in conspiring against them.

Everybody has read the account written by Sallust of the conspiracy of Catiline, and knows that, after it was discovered, Catiline not only stayed in Rome, but actually went to the Senate, and said insulting things to the Senate and the Consul; so great was the respect in which Rome held the citizens. And even after his departure from Rome, and when he was already with the army, Lentulus and the others would not have been seized if letters in their own handwriting had not been found, which manifestly convicted them. Hanno, one of the most powerful citizens of Carthage, aspired to the tyranny of the state, and arranged to poison the whole Senate on the occasion of his daughter's marriage, and then to make himself sovereign. When this plot was discovered, the Senate did nothing more than to pass a decree limiting the expense of feasts and weddings; such was the respect which the Carthaginians had for so great a citizen as Hanno.

It is true that in the execution of a conspiracy against one's country there are greater difficulties and dangers to surmount. For it is very rare that the forces of a conspirator suffice against so many; and it is not every one that controls an army, like Cæsar, or Agathocles, or Cleomenes, and the like, who by a single blow made themselves masters of their country. For such men the execution is sure and easy, but others who have not the support of such forces must employ deceit and cunning, or foreign aid.

As to the employment of deceit and cunning, I give the following instances. Pisistratus, after the victory which he had gained over the people of Megara, was greatly beloved by the people of Athens. One morning he went forth from his house wounded, and charged the nobility with having attacked him from jealousy, and demanded permission to keep a guard of armed followers for his protection, which was accorded him. This first step enabled him easily to attain such power that he soon after made himself tyrant of Athens. Pandolfo Petrucci returned with other exiles to Sienna, where he was appointed to the command of the guard of the government palace, a subordinate employ which others had refused. Nevertheless, this command gave him in time such influence and authority that in a little while he became prince of the state. Many others have employed similar means, and have in a short time, and without danger, acquired sovereign power. Those who have conspired against their country with their own forces, or by the aid of foreign troops, have had various success, according to their fortune. Catiline, whose conspiracy we have already spoken of, succumbed. Hanno, whom we have also mentioned, having failed in his attempt with poison, armed his partisans to the number of many thousands, and perished with them. Some of the first citizens of Thebes, wishing to obtain absolute control of the state, called to their aid a Spartan army, and seized the government. Thus, if we examine all the conspiracies attempted by men against their country, we find none, or but very few, that have failed in their conduct; but in their execution they have either met with success or failure. Once, however, carried into effect, they involve no other dangers but such as are inherent to absolute power; for he who has become a tyrant is exposed only to the natural and ordinary dangers which tyranny carries with it, and against which there are no other remedies than those indicated above.

Those are the considerations that have presented themselves to me in treating the subject of conspiracies; and if I have noted only those where the sword is the instrument employed, and not poison, it is because the course of both is absolutely the same. It is true that the latter are in proportion more dangerous, as their success is more uncertain, for it is not every one that has the means of employing poison; it must, therefore, be intrusted to such as have, and that very necessity causes the dangers. Furthermore, many reasons may prevent a poison from proving mortal, as in the case of Commodus. Those who had conspired against him, seeing that he would not take the poisoned draught they had offered to him, and yet being resolved upon his death, were obliged to strangle him.

There is, then, no greater misfortune for a prince than that a conspiracy should be formed against him; for it either causes his death, or it dishonors him. If the conspiracy succeeds, he dies; if it be discovered, and he punishes the conspirators with death, it will always be believed that it was an invention of the prince to satisfy his cruelty and avarice with the blood and possessions of those whom he had put to death. I will, therefore, not omit offering an advice to princes or republics against whom conspiracies may have been formed. If they discover that a conspiracy exists against them, they must, before punishing its authors, endeavor carefully to know its nature and extent,—to weigh and measure well the means of the conspirators, and their own strength. And if they find it powerful and alarming, they must not expose it until they have provided themselves with sufficient force to crush it, as otherwise they will only hasten their own destruction. They should therefore try to simulate ignorance of it, for if the conspirators should find themselves discovered, they will be forced by necessity to act without consideration. As an instance of this, we have the case of the Romans, who had left two legions at Capua to protect its inhabitants against the Samnites. The commanders of these legions (as we have related elsewhere) conspired to make themselves masters of the city. When this became known at Rome, the new Consul Rutilius was directed to see to its being prevented; and by way of lulling the conspirators into security, he published that the Senate had resolved to continue the legions in garrison at Capua. The captains and soldiers, believing this, and thinking, therefore, that they had ample time for the execution of their design, made no attempt to hasten it, and thus waited until they perceived that the Consul was separating them from each other. This excited their suspicions, and caused them to expose their intentions, and to proceed to the execution of their plot. There could not be a more forcible example than this for both parties; for it shows how dilatory men are when they think that they have time enough, and, on the other hand, how prompt they are in action when impelled by necessity. A prince or a republic who, for their own advantage, wish to defer the disclosure of a conspiracy, cannot use a more effectual means for that purpose than artfully to hold out to the conspirators the prospect of an early and favorable opportunity for action; so that, whilst waiting for that, or persuaded that they have ample time, the prince or republic will themselves gain time to overwhelm the conspirators. Those who act differently will accelerate their own ruin, as was the case with the Duke of Athens and Guglielmo de' Pazzi. The Duke, having become tyrant of Florence, and being apprised that there was a conspiracy on foot against him, had one of the conspirators seized without further inquiry into the matter. This caused the others at once to take to arms, and to wrest the government from him. Guglielmo de' Pazzi was commissary in the Val de Chiano in the year 1501. Having heard that a conspiracy had been organized in Arezzo in favor of the Vitelli, for the purpose of taking that place from the Florentines, he immediately went there, and without considering the strength of the conspirators or measuring his own, and wholly without any preparation, he had one of the conspirators seized by the advice of his son, the Bishop of Arezzo. Hereupon the others immediately took to arms, declared the independence of Arezzo, and made Guglielmo prisoner.

But when conspiracies are feeble, they can and ought to be crushed as promptly as possible; in such case, however, the two instances we shall quote, and which are almost the direct opposites of each other, should not in any way be imitated. The one is that of the above-named Duke of Athens, who, to prove his confidence in the attachment of the Florentines to him, had the man who denounced the conspiracy to him put to death. The other is that of Dion of Syracuse, who by way of testing the fidelity of some one whom he suspected ordered Callippus, in whom he had entire confidence, to pretend to be conspiring against him. Both, however, ended badly; the first discouraged the accusers, and encouraged those who were disposed to conspire; and the other paved the way for his own destruction, and was, as it were, the chief of the conspiracy against himself, as was proved by experience, for Callippus, being able to conspire with impunity against Dion, plotted so well that he deprived him of his state and his life.

Chapter VII

THE REASONS WHY THE TRANSITIONS FROM LIBERTY TO SERVITUDE AND FROM SERVITUDE TO LIBERTY ARE AT TIMES EFFECTED WITHOUT BLOODSHED, AND AT OTHER TIMES ARE MOST SANGUINARY

THE question may suggest itself to some persons why it is that, in the many changes that carry a state from freedom to tyranny, and from servitude to liberty, some are effected by bloodshed, and others without any. In fact, history shows that in such changes sometimes an infinite number of lives are sacrificed; whilst at other times it has not cost the life of a single person. Such was the revolution in Rome which transferred the government from the kings to the consuls, where only the Tarquins were expelled, and no one else suffered injury. This depends upon whether the state that changes its form of government does so by violence, or not. When effected by violence the change will naturally inflict suffering upon many; these in turn will desire to revenge themselves, and from this desire of revenge results the shedding of blood. But when such a change is effected by the general consent of the citizens, who have made the state great, then there is no reason why the people should wish to harm any one but the chiefs of the state. Such was the case with the government of the kings in Rome, and the expulsion of the Tarquins; and such was that of the Medici in Florence, whose ruin and expulsion in the year 1494 involved none but themselves. Such revolutions are very rarely dangerous. But those that are effected by men from motives of revenge are most dangerous, and have ever been of a nature to make us tremble with fear and horror in reading of them. History is so full of these that I will not dilate upon them here.

Chapter VIII

WHOEVER WISHES TO CHANGE THE GOVERNMENT OF A REPUBLIC SHOULD FIRST CONSIDER WELL ITS EXISTING CONDITION

WE have already shown that an evil-disposed citizen cannot effect any changes for the worse in a republic, unless it be already corrupt. Besides the reasons elsewhere given, this conclusion is confirmed by the examples of Spurius Cassius and Manlius Capitolinus. This Spurius, being an ambitious man and wishing to obtain the supreme power in Rome, endeavored to gain the favor of the people by numerous benefits, such as the selling to them the lands taken from the Hernicians. This opened the eyes of the Senate to his ambitious projects, and he became suspected, even by the people, to that point, that when he offered them the proceeds of the sale of the grain which the government had caused to be brought from Sicily, the people refused it altogether; for it seemed to them as though Spurius offered it as the price of their liberty. But if this people had been corrupt, they would, so far from refusing this offer, have accepted it, and thus have opened the way for Spurius to the tyranny which now they closed against him.

The example of Manlius is even more forcible, and proves how this evil ambition to rule cancels the noblest qualities of mind and body, and the most important services rendered to a state. We see that this ambition had its origin with Manlius in his jealousy of the honors bestowed upon Camillus; and so blinded was he by it, that, regardless of the manners and customs of Rome, and without examining the condition of the state, which was not yet prepared to accept a vicious form of government, he set to work to stir up disturbances in Rome against the Senate and the institutions of his country. Here we recognize the perfection of the constitution of Rome, and the excellent character of its population; for on the occasion of the fall of Manlius, not one of the nobility (so ardent generally in their mutual support and defence) made the slightest effort in his favor; nor did any of his relatives make any attempt to support him. And whilst the families of others accused were in the habit of showing themselves near them, all covered with dust and in deep mourning and sadness, for the purpose of exciting the commiseration of the people for the accused, not one of the family of Manlius appeared near him. The Tribunes of the people, so accustomed always to favor every measure that seemed for the advantage of the people, and the more so in proportion as it was adverse to the interests of the nobility, in this instance united with the nobles for the purpose of suppressing a common enemy. And finally the people of Rome, ever most jealous of its own interests, and eagerly in favor of everything that was adverse to the nobles, had at first shown themselves well disposed towards Manlius; but the moment the Tribunes summoned him and brought his case before them, the same people, having now from defenders become judges, condemned him, without regard to his former services, to suffer the death penalty. I therefore think that there is no fact in history that more effectually shows the excellence of the Roman constitution than this example, where not a single person of the whole city stirred to defend a citizen gifted with the best qualities, and who had rendered the most signal services to the public, as well as to private individuals. For the love of country had more power over them than any other sentiment; and they thought so much more of its present dangers, to which the ambition of Manlius exposed them, than of his past services, that they saw no other way of relieving themselves of those dangers than by his death. And Titus Livius says: "Thus ended the career of this man, who would have been memorable had he not been born in a free community."

This brings us to two important considerations: the first, that the means of attaining glory are different in a republic that is corrupt from what they are in a republic that still preserves its institutions pure; and the second, (which is in a measure comprised in the first,) that men in their conduct, and especially in their most prominent actions, should well consider and conform to the times in which they live. And those who, from an evil choice or from natural inclination, do not conform to the times in which they live, will in most instances live unhappily, and their undertakings will come to a bad end; whilst, on the contrary, success attends those who conform to the times. And doubtless we may conclude from the words of our historian that, if Manlius had been born in the times of Marius and Sylla, when the people were already corrupt, and when he could have moulded them according to his ambition, he would have achieved the same results and successes as Marius and Sylla, and the others who after them aspired to the tyranny. And in the same way, if Sylla and Marius had lived in the times of Manlius, they would have been crushed in their first attempt. For a man may well by his conduct and evil ways begin to corrupt a people, but it is impossible for him to live long enough to enjoy the fruits of it. And even if it were possible that by length of time he should succeed, the natural impatience of the people, which cannot brook delay in the indulgence of their passion, would prove an obstacle to his success, so that by too much haste, or from error, he would be led to engage in his attempt at the wrong time, and thus end in failure.

To usurp supreme and absolute authority, then, in a free state, and subject it to tyranny, the people must have already become corrupt by gradual steps from generation to generation. And all states necessarily come to this, unless (as we have shown above) they are frequently reinvigorated by good examples, and brought back by good laws to their first principles. Manlius thus would have been regarded as a rare and memorable man if he had lived in a corrupt republic. And therefore all such as desire to make a change in the government of a republic, whether in favor of liberty or in favor of tyranny, must well examine the condition of things, and from that judge of the difficulties of their undertaking. For it is as difficult to make a people free that is resolved to live in servitude, as it is to subject a people to servitude that is determined to be free. Having argued above that in any such attempts men should well consider the state of the times and govern themselves accordingly, I will develop this subject more fully in the next chapter.

Chapter IX

WHOEVER DESIRES CONSTANT SUCCESS MUST CHANGE HIS CONDUCT WITH THE TIMES

I HAVE often reflected that the causes of the success or failure of men depend upon their manner of suiting their conduct to the times. We see one man proceed in his actions with passion and impetuosity; and as in both the one and the other case men are apt to exceed the proper limits, not being able always to observe the just middle course, they are apt to err in both. But he errs least and will be most favored by fortune who suits his proceedings to the times, as I have said above, and always follows the impulses of his nature. Every one knows how Fabius Maximus conducted the war against Hannibal with extreme caution and circumspection, and with an utter absence of all impetuosity or Roman audacity. It was his good fortune that this mode of proceeding accorded perfectly with the times and circumstances. For Hannibal had arrived in Rome whilst still young and with his fortunes fresh; he had already twice routed the Romans, so that the republic was as it were deprived of her best troops, and greatly discouraged by her reverses. Rome could not therefore have been more favored by fortune, than to have a commander who by his extreme caution and the slowness of his movements kept the enemy at bay. At the same time, Fabius could not have found circumstances more favorable for his character and genius, to which fact he was indebted for his success and glory. And that this mode of proceeding was the result of his character and nature, and not a matter of choice, was shown on the occasion when Scipio wanted to take the same troops to Africa for the purpose of promptly terminating the war. Fabius most earnestly opposed this, like a man incapable of breaking from his accustomed ways and habits; so that, if he had been master, Hannibal would have remained in Italy, because Fabius failed to perceive that the times were changed. But Rome was a republic that produced citizens of various character and dispositions, such as Fabius, who was excellent at the time when it was desirable to protract the war, and Scipio, when it became necessary to terminate it. It is this which assures to republics greater vitality and more enduring success than monarchies have; for the diversity of the genius of her citizens enables the republic better to accommodate herself to the changes of the times than can be done by a prince. For any man accustomed to a certain mode of proceeding will never change it, as we have said, and consequently when time and circumstances change, so that his ways are no longer in harmony with them, he must of necessity succumb. Pietro Soderini, whom we have mentioned several times already, was in all his actions governed by humanity and patience. He and his country prospered so long as the times favored this mode of proceeding; but when afterwards circumstances arose that demanded a course of conduct the opposite to that of patience and humanity, he was unfit for the occasion, and his own and his country's ruin were the consequence. Pope Julius II. acted throughout the whole period of his pontificate with the impetuosity and passion natural to his character; and as the times and circumstances well accorded with this, he was successful in all his undertakings. But if the times had changed so that different counsels would have been required, he would unquestionably have been ruined, for he could not have changed his character or mode of action.

That we cannot thus change at will is due to two causes;

the one is the impossibility of resisting the natural bent of our characters; and the other is the difficulty of persuading ourselves, after having been accustomed to success by a certain mode of proceeding, that any other can succeed as well. It is this that causes the varying success of a man; for the times change, but he does not change his mode of proceeding. The ruin of states is caused in like manner, as we have fully shown above, because they do not modify their institutions to suit the changes of the times. And such changes are more difficult and tardy in republics; for necessarily circumstances will occur that will unsettle the whole state, and when the change of proceeding of one man will not suffice for the occasion.

Having made mention of Fabius Maximus, and the manner in which he held Hannibal at bay, it seems to me opportune in the next chapter to examine the question whether a general who is resolved anyhow to give battle to the enemy can be prevented by the latter from doing so.

Chapter X

A GENERAL CANNOT AVOID A BATTLE WHEN THE ENEMY IS RESOLVED UPON IT AT ALL HAZARDS

"CNEIUS SULPITIUS, appointed Dictator against the Gauls, protracted the war by refusing to commit himself to the fortunes of battle against an enemy whose position was being daily made worse by time and the disadvantages of the country." When an error is very generally adopted, I believe it to be advantageous often to refute it; and therefore, although I have already several times pointed out how much we differ in our important actions from the ancients, yet it seems to me not superfluous once more to repeat it here. It is especially in matters relating to the art of war that we deviate from the practice of the ancients, for in this respect we do not observe any of the principles that were so much esteemed by them. And this defect arises from this, that the republics and princes of the present day abandon the charge of their armies to others, so as to avoid themselves the cares and dangers attending it. And if we nevertheless occasionally see a king in our times march in person with his army, it must not be supposed that he will introduce a more laudable system; for even if he does expose himself to the fatigue, it is for the sake of pomp only, and not from any praiseworthy motive. And yet these princes in only occasionally showing themselves with their armies, whilst reserving to themselves the title of commander, are less in fault than republics, and most especially those of Italy. These, trusting entirely to others, understand themselves nothing of what pertains to war, and yet wish to decide upon everything, so as to preserve at least the appearance of sovereignty, and in their decisions they commit a thousand errors. And although I have already elsewhere spoken of some, yet I will not refrain here from referring to one of the most important instances.

When these indolent princes or effeminate republics send a general with an army into the field, the wisest order they think they can give him is never to risk a battle, and above all things to avoid a general action. In this they think they imitate the salutary prudence of Fabius Maximus, who by delaying battle saved the Roman republic; but they do not understand that in most cases such a commission is either impracticable or dangerous. For we must hold it as a principle that a general who wishes to keep the field cannot avoid a battle when the enemy is determined upon fighting. And thus such orders are as much as to say to him, "Give battle at your enemy's convenience, but not at your own." To keep the field and yet to avoid a battle there is no other safe way than to keep at least fifty thousand men at a good distance from the enemy, and to keep good watch so that in case of his approach you may have time to retreat farther. Another way is to shut yourself up in a city. But both the one and the other of these courses are replete with danger. In the first case you leave the country open to be pillaged by the enemy; and certainly a brave prince would prefer the fortune of battle rather than to prolong the war with such damage to his people. The second plan will manifestly ruin you; for if you shut yourself up with your army in a city you will be besieged, and in a short time hunger will compel you to surrender. Therefore, to avoid battle by either of these means is equally dangerous. The course taken by Fabius in occupying naturally strong positions is good when you have an army so formidable that the enemy dares not attack you. Nor can it be said that Fabius sought to avoid a battle; all he wanted was to fight when it should be to his advantage. In fact, if Hannibal had attacked him, Fabius would have met and fought him; but Hannibal never dared to offer him battle in the manner that suited Fabius. Thus the one and the other equally avoided a combat; but if either one of them had been resolved to bring it on anyhow, the other would have had but three ways of avoiding it,—the two we have just mentioned, or flight.

A thousand examples attest the truth of what I have advanced, and especially the war which the Romans carried on against Philip of Macedon, father of Perseus. Philip, attacked by the Romans, wished to avoid the combat, and for this purpose, in imitation of Fabius Maximus in Italy, posted himself with his army on the summit of a mountain, where he strongly fortified himself, judging that the Romans would never venture to come and attack him there. But they did attack and drive him from that position, and forced him to fly with the greater part of his troops. And what saved him from being entirely cut to pieces was the irregularity of the country, which prevented the Romans from pursuing him. Philip then resolved not to fight, but, being posted near the Romans, was obliged to fly; and having learnt by this experience that keeping on the heights did not avail him in his wish to avoid a battle, and unwilling to shut himself up in a city, he resolved to adopt the other plan of keeping at many miles' distance from the Roman camp. Thus, when they marched into one province he moved off to another, and whenever the Romans left one country he entered it. But finding in the end that the prolonging of the war by these means only made his condition worse, and that his own subjects were by turns oppressed by the enemy and by himself, he resolved to try the chance of combat, and thus came to a regular battle with the Romans.

It is advantageous, then, not to fight when your army is in the condition of that of Fabius, or that of Cn. Sulpicius; that is to say, when you have so formidable an army that the enemy dares not come to attack you in your intrenchments; or that he is upon your territory without having gained a foothold, so that he suffers from want of provisions. In such cases it is a wise course to follow, for the reason given by Titus Livius; namely, "It is well for a general not to risk the chance of battle with an enemy whose position is daily made worse by time and the disadvantages of the country." But in any other case a battle cannot be avoided without dishonor and danger; for to fly like Philip is the same as being defeated, and is the more humiliating the less proof you have given of your courage. And if Philip succeeded in saving himself by flight, another, unless equally favored by the country, will fail. No one will pretend to say that Hannibal was not a master in the art of war; and if, when he was opposed to Scipio in Africa, he had found it to his advantage to prolong the war, he certainly would have done so. And perhaps, being a good general, and having a good army, he might have done as Fabius did in Italy; but as he did not do so we must suppose that he was influenced by important considerations. But a prince who has an army composed of various materials, and finds that from want of money or friendly support he can no longer keep his army together, must be utterly demented if he does not take his chance of battle before his army shall have fallen to pieces; for by waiting he is sure to lose, but by trying a battle he may possibly be victorious. Another point deserving consideration is, that even in losing a battle a commander should at least endeavor to save his glory; and surely there is more glory in being overcome by force than in losing from any other cause. It was this consideration that must have influenced Hannibal. Scipio, on the other hand, even if Hannibal had wished to protract the war and had lacked the courage to attack him in his strongholds, was not suffering any privations, for he had already defeated Syphax, and had made himself master of so great a part of Africa that he could have held his ground there with as much security and convenience as in Italy. Such was not the position of Hannibal when opposed to Fabius, nor of the Gauls when they were opposed to Sulpicius. Still less can a general avoid coming to battle when he attempts to penetrate with his army into the interior of the enemy's country; if the enemy opposes him he will be obliged to fight, and still more will he be obliged to give battle if he should attempt to besiege a town. This happened in our day to Charles, Duke of Burgundy, who, having pitched his camp before Morat, a town belonging to the Swiss, was attacked and routed by them. The same thing occurred to the French army when encamped before Novara, where they were equally defeated by the Swiss.

Chapter XI

WHOEVER HAS TO CONTEND AGAINST MANY ENEMIES MAY NEVER-
THELESS OVERCOME THEM, THOUGH HE BE INFERIOR IN POWER,
PROVIDED HE IS ABLE TO RESIST THEIR FIRST EFFORTS

The power of the Tribunes of the people in Rome was very great, as has already been said several times, but it was necessary to restrain the ambition of the nobles, who would otherwise have corrupted the republic much more than it was already. Nevertheless, as all human institutions (as has been observed elsewhere) contain some inherent evil that gives rise to unforeseen accidents, it becomes necessary to provide against these by new measures. The Tribunes had become insolent and formidable to the nobility and to all Rome, and would have become dangerous to the liberties of the republic had not Appius Claudius pointed out the way for the Romans to protect themselves against the ambition of the Tribunes. As there was always to be found amongst them some one more easily intimidated or corrupted than the others, or some lover of the public good, Claudius advised that they should oppose such a one to his colleagues whenever these wanted to pass any act contrary to the wishes of the Senate. This expedient tempered the formidable authority of the Tribunes, and for a long while proved most advantageous to Rome; and it has caused me to reflect that the presumption of success should always be in favor of a single power contending against a combination, however superior in numbers and power. For independent of the infinity of circumstances of which an individual can take advantage better than a combination of many, the former will always have the opportunity, with a little address, to create divisions between the latter, and thus to weaken any powerful combination. I will not adduce here any examples of antiquity, of which there are many, but will confine myself to instances of our own times only. In the year 1484 all Italy leagued together against the Venetians; who, after losing everything, and being unable to keep the field any longer, succeeded in corrupting Ludovico Sforza, governor of Milan, and concluded a treaty with him by which they not only recovered all the territory they had lost, but actually seized a portion of the principality of Ferrara. And thus, although they had been losers in war, yet they proved to be gainers in peace. A few years since a general league was formed against France, but before the termination of the war Spain broke from the league, and made terms with France, so that the other confederates were soon afterwards constrained also to come to terms with her. We may therefore with reasonable certainty presume that when a number of princes combine to make war upon a single one, the latter will triumph over the combination, provided he has courage and strength enough to resist the first shock and bide events by temporizing. But if he cannot do this, he is exposed to a thousand dangers, as was the case with the Venetians in 1508. If at that time they could have held their own against the French army until they could gain over some of those who had combined against them, they would have escaped the disasters by which they were overwhelmed. But being without an army that could temporarily hold the French in check, and thus having no time to detach any one power from the league, they were crushed. In fact, we see that the Pope, after having recovered what belonged to him, became their friend; and so did Spain; and both of these powers would gladly have saved to the Venetians their possessions in Lombardy if they could have done it, so as to prevent France from becoming so powerful in Italy. The Venetians might, by sacrificing a part, have saved the rest; this would have been a wise course for them to pursue, provided they had done so before seeming to be forced to it by necessity; but after the war was actually begun, such a course would have been disgraceful, and probably of little advantage. Before the war only a few of the citizens of Venice could discern the danger, still fewer perceived the remedy, and none advised it. But to return to what I said at the beginning of this discourse, I conclude that, as the Roman Senate found the means for saving the country from the ambition of the Tribunes, who were many, so will any one prince find a remedy, when assailed by many enemies, provided he has wisdom and skill, by suitable means, to create such misunderstandings between them as will cause their disunion.

Chapter XII

A SKILFUL GENERAL SHOULD ENDEAVOR BY ALL MEANS IN HIS POWER TO PLACE HIS SOLDIERS IN THE POSITION OF BEING OBLIGED TO FIGHT, AND AS FAR AS POSSIBLE RELIEVE THE ENEMY OF SUCH NECESSITY

WE have already pointed out the advantage of necessity in human actions, and to what glorious achievements it has given rise. Some moral philosophers have even maintained that without it neither the hand nor the tongue of man, the two noblest instruments of his glory, would have served his purpose perfectly, nor carried human works to that height of perfection which they have attained. The ancient commanders of armies, who well knew the powerful influence of necessity, and how it inspired the soldiers with the most desperate courage, neglected nothing to subject their men to such a pressure, whilst, on the other hand, they employed every device that ingenuity could suggest to relieve the enemy's troops from the necessity of fighting. Thus they often opened the way for the enemy to retreat, which they might easily have barred; and closed it to their own soldiers for whom they could with ease have kept it open. Whoever then desires that a city should make an obstinate resistance, or that an army should fight with determination in the field, should above all things endeavor to inspire them with the conviction of the necessity for their utmost efforts. A skilful general, then, who has to besiege a city, can judge of the difficulties of its capture by knowing and considering to what extent the inhabitants are under the necessity of defending themselves. If he finds that to be very urgent, then he may deem his task in proportion difficult; but if the motive for resistance is feeble, then he may count upon an easy victory. Thence it comes that it is more difficult to reduce a country to subjection that has revolted, than it was to conquer it originally. For not having given any special offence before the conquest that would cause them to fear punishment, they yield easily; but having offended by the rebellion and fearing the penalty, they defend themselves with great obstinacy.

Such a determined resistance may also be caused by the natural hatred between neighboring princes and republics, which arises from rivalry and the thirst of dominion. The case of Tuscany proves that this is especially the case with republics. This spirit of rivalry and contention will ever make it difficult for republics to subjugate each other. Whoever, therefore, carefully examines the character of the neighboring powers of the republics of Florence and of Venice will not wonder, as many do, that Florence has expended more money and made fewer conquests than Venice. This is due to the fact that the Venetians have had to do with neighbors less obstinate in defence than those with whom Florence has had to contend, the cities in the vicinity of Venice being accustomed to live under the domination of princes, and not as free states; for those who live in servitude are indifferent to a change of masters, in fact in most cases they rather desire it. So that Venice (although she has had more powerful neighbors than Florence) found these neighboring cities less obstinate in defence than Florence, which is entirely surrounded by free states.

To return to my subject, then, I say that a captain who besieges a city should strive by every means in his power to relieve the besieged of the pressure of necessity, and thus diminish the obstinacy of their defence. He should promise them a full pardon if they fear punishment, and if they are apprehensive for their liberties he should assure them that he is not the enemy of the public good, but only of a few ambitious persons in the city who oppose it. Such a course will often facilitate the siege and capture of cities. Artifices of this kind are quickly appreciated by the wise, but the people are generally deceived by them. Blinded by their eager desire for present peace, they do not see the snares that are concealed under these liberal promises, and thus many cities have fallen into servitude. This was the case with Florence in our immediate times, and in ancient times with Crassus and his army. Crassus well knew that the promises of the

Parthians were not to be trusted, and that they were made merely for the purpose of removing from the minds of the Roman soldiers the impression of the necessity of defending themselves. Yet so blinded were these by the offers of peace that had been made by the enemy, that Crassus could not induce them to make a vigorous resistance.

The Samnites, instigated by the ambition of a few, disregarded their treaties with the Romans; and made incursions upon and pillaged the territory of some of the Roman allies. After that, they sent ambassadors to Rome to ask for peace, offering restitution of what they had plundered, and to deliver up the authors of the disorders and the pillage. Their proposition was rejected by the Romans, and the ambassadors returned to Samnium hopeless of any accommodation. Thereupon Claudius Pontius, at that time commander of the Samnite army, pointed out to them in a remarkable speech that the Romans were resolved upon war under any circumstances, and that, although they themselves desired peace, yet they were thus forced to accept the war, adding these words: "War is just for those who are forced to it by necessity, and Heaven favors those who have no hope but in their arms." It was upon this necessity that he based his hope of victory with his soldiers.

And not to be obliged to return to this subject, I think it well here to cite the most noteworthy examples from Roman history that illustrate my proposition. C. Manilius had led his army against the Veientes, and, a part of the troops of the latter having forced a passage into his intrenchments, Manilius rushed with a detachment to the support of his men, and closed up all the issues of his camp, so that the Veientes could not escape. Finding themselves thus shut in, they began to combat with such desperate fury that they killed Manilius, and would have destroyed the rest of the

Roman army if one of the Tribunes had not the sagacity
to open a way for them to escape. This shows that the Veientes, when constrained by necessity, fought with the most
desperate valor; but when they saw the way open for their
escape, they thought more of saving themselves than of
fighting. The Volscians and Equeans having entered with
their troops upon Roman territory, the Romans sent two
Consuls with armies against them. Becoming engaged in
battle, the Volscian army under command of Vettius Messius suddenly found itself shut in between their own intrenchments, which were occupied by the Romans, and the
other Roman army. And seeing that they would have to
perish or cut their way out with the sword, Messius addressed his soldiers in the following words: "Follow me!
You have no walls nor ditches to encounter, but only men
armed like yourselves. Equals in valor, you have the advantage of necessity, that last and most powerful of weapons!"
It is thus that Titus Livius styles necessity "the last and most
powerful weapon." Camillus, the most experienced of the
Roman generals, had penetrated with his army into the
city of Veii, for the purpose of facilitating its capture; and
to deprive the enemy of the extreme necessity of defending
himself, he ordered his soldiers, in a voice loud enough to
be heard by the Veientes, not to harm those that should be
disarmed. This caused the latter to lay down their arms, and
the city was taken almost without bloodshed. This example
was afterwards imitated by several other generals.

Chapter XIII

WHETHER AN ABLE COMMANDER WITH A FEEBLE ARMY, OR A GOOD ARMY WITH AN INCOMPETENT COMMANDER, IS MOST TO BE RELIED UPON

CORIOLANUS, having been exiled from Rome, went to the Volscians, where he formed an army with which he returned to Rome to revenge himself upon his countrymen. But he soon withdrew again, influenced more by his affection for his mother than by the forces of the Romans. On this occasion Titus Livius says: "It became evident that the Roman republic was more indebted for her aggrandizement to the merit of her generals than to that of their armies, seeing that the Volscians had until then always been defeated, and that they became victorious only when led by Coriolanus." And although Livius advances this opinion, yet we find many instances in history where the soldiers, deprived of their captains, have given wonderful proofs of valor, and displayed more order and intrepidity after the death of their Consuls than before. It was thus with the army which the Romans had in Spain under the Scipios, which, after the loss of both its commanders, not only saved itself by its bravery, but actually defeated the enemy, and saved that province to the republic. So that on the whole we shall find many instances of battles won solely by the valor of the soldiers, and many others where the same result was achieved by the courage of the general alone. So that we may conclude that they are equally dependent one upon the other.

It may be well here to consider which of the two is most to be feared, a good army badly commanded, or a good commander with a bad army. According to the judgment of Cæsar, neither one nor the other is worth much; for when he went into Spain against Afranius and Petreius, who had a good army under their orders, he said that he cared little about that, "as he was marching against an army without a chief," meaning thereby the weakness of the commanders. And, on the other hand, when he went into Thessaly against Pompey, he said "that he was marching against a leader without an army." We may consider here also another matter, namely, whether it be easier for a good captain to form a good army, or for a good army to form a good captain. Upon this point I say that the question would seem to be decided, inasmuch as it is much easier for the many who have merit to find or instruct one to be equally good, than for the one to form the many. Lucullus was wholly inexperienced in war when he was sent against Mithridates; nevertheless, being placed at the head of a good army that had already very superior officers, he soon became a good commander. The Romans, being in want of men, armed a number of slaves and gave them to Sempronius Gracchus to be trained, who in a brief time made a good army of them. After Pelopidas and Epaminondas had delivered their country, Thebes, from the yoke of the Spartans, they made in a very short time the best kind of soldiers out of the Theban peasants; so that they were not only able to sustain the shock of the Spartan troops, but actually to defeat them. Thus the matter is about even; for if either one of the two, the army or the commander, be good, they will be apt to make the other good likewise. But a good army without an able commander often becomes insolent and dangerous, as was the case with the Macedonian army after the death of Alexander, and with the veteran troops in the civil wars of Rome. And therefore I am disposed to believe that you can more safely rely upon a competent general, who has the time to instruct his men and the facilities for arming them, than upon an insolent army with a chief tumultuously chosen by them. Those generals, therefore, deserve double praise and glory who not only had to conquer, but had actually to form and train their troops before meeting the enemy. For in this they have shown that twofold merit the union of which is so rare that many commanders, if they had been obliged to perform the same task, would not have obtained that celebrity which they have achieved.

Chapter XIV

OF THE EFFECT OF NEW STRATAGEMS AND UNEXPECTED CRIES IN THE MIDST OF BATTLE

We have numerous instances of the important effect produced by some unforeseen incident caused by something new that is seen or heard in the midst of a conflict or heat of battle. One of the most striking examples of this occurred in the battle between the Romans and the Volscians, when Quintius saw one wing of his army give way, and cried out to them in a loud voice to stand firm, as the other wing was victorious. These words reanimated the courage of his soldiers, and caused dismay amongst those of the enemy, so that Quintius carried off the victory. And if such a cry can produce such an effect in a well-disciplined army, its influence is infinitely greater upon a tumultuous and undisciplined body, who are all moved by similar impulses. I will adduce a notable example of this, which occurred in our own times. A few years ago the city of Perugia was divided into two factions, the Oddi and the Baglioni. The latter held the government and had exiled the former, who, with the aid of their friends, gathered an army, and established themselves at a convenient place near Perugia. One night they entered the city by the aid of their partisans, and, without being perceived, succeeded in making themselves masters of the public square. As the streets were all barred with chains, they had a man precede them with an iron club to break the fastenings of these chains, so that horses might be able to pass. Only one more that closed the public square remained to be broken, and already the cry of "To arms!" had been raised in the city. Closely pressed by those that followed him, the man who was charged to break the chains, unable to raise his arms for the purpose, called out to those pressing upon him to fall back. This cry of "Fall back!" taken up from rank to rank, caused the hindmost to fly; the others, one by one, followed them with such a rush that it ended in a complete rout. And thus by this slight accident the whole project of the Oddi was thwarted. This shows the necessity of discipline in an army, not only to make them combat with order, but also to prevent any slight accident from creating confusion. And it is just for this reason that an undisciplined multitude is useless in war; for the least unexpected noise or word will throw them into confusion, and make them take to flight. And a good commander should therefore, amongst his other regulations, specially appoint persons to receive his orders and transmit them to the others; and he should accustom his soldiers not to listen to any but their regular officers, and direct the officers to give no orders but such as emanate from the commander. The non-observance of this rule has often caused the greatest misfortunes.

As to new stratagems, when the armies are engaged in conflict, every captain should endeavor to invent such as will encourage his own troops and dishearten those of the enemy.

This is one of the most efficacious means of achieving victory. In proof of which I will cite the example of the Roman Dictator C. Sulpicius, who, being about to come to battle with the Gauls, armed all the teamsters and camp-followers, and mounted them upon the mules and other beasts of burden, and supplied them with standards, so as to seem like regular cavalry. These he placed behind a hill, with orders to show themselves to the enemy at a given signal during the heat of battle. This artifice, being carried out as ordered, so alarmed the Gauls as to cause them to lose the day. A good general, then, has to do two things; the one, to try by novel stratagems to create alarm amongst the enemy; and the other, to be on his guard to discover those that the enemy may attempt to practise upon him, and to render them fruitless. It was thus that the Indian king acted against Semiramis. This queen, seeing that the king had a great many elephants, tried to frighten him by showing him that she had quite as many. She therefore ordered a number of sham elephants made of the hides of buffaloes and cows, which she had placed upon camels and sent to the front. But the stratagem was discovered by the king, and proved, not only useless, but damaging to Semiramis. The Dictator Mamercus was carrying on the war against the Fidenati. These, for the purpose of frightening the Roman army, caused, in the midst of an action, a number of soldiers to issue forth from the city with burning torches at the end of their lances, hoping that the Roman soldiers, struck by the novelty of the thing, might break their ranks, and thus create confusion. Here it is well to observe that such artifices may safely and with advantage be employed when they have more the appearance of reality than of fiction; for then their seeming strength will prevent the prompt discovery of their weakness. But when they are manifestly rather fictitious than real, they should either not be employed, or they should be kept at such a distance that their real character cannot be so quickly discovered, as Sulpicius did with his muleteers. Otherwise, when too near, their real weakness will be quickly discovered, and then they do more harm than good, as was the case with the sham elephants of Semiramis, and the torches of the Fidenati. For although these did at the first moment somewhat disturb the Roman soldiers, yet when the Dictator discovered it he called out to them to be ashamed to fly from the smoke like insects. "Return to the combat," he shouted to them, "and with their own torches burn their city of Fidena, which your benefits could not placate." Thus was the artifice of the Fidenati rendered futile, and the battle won by the Romans.

Chapter XV

AN ARMY SHOULD HAVE BUT ONE CHIEF: A GREATER NUMBER IS DETRIMENTAL

THE Fidenati, having revolted, massacred the colony which the Romans had established at Fidena. To avenge this outrage the Romans appointed four Tribunes with consular powers, one of whom remained to guard Rome, while the other three were sent against the Fidenati and Veientes. These three Tribunes gained nothing but dishonor in this expedition, in consequence of the dissensions that had arisen between them. For this dishonor they were themselves alone responsible; and it was only the valor of their soldiers that saved them from experiencing a serious check. The Romans, having perceived the cause of this disorder, resorted to the creation of a Dictator; so that one man might restore that order which the three Tribunes had destroyed. Thence we may see the uselessness of several commanders in one army, or in a city that is besieged. And Titus Livius could not more forcibly illustrate this than when he says: "Three Tribunes with consular powers proved how useless it is to confide the command of an army to several chiefs; for each one holding opinions of his own, which the others would not adopt, they afforded the enemy the opportunity to take advantage of their dissensions." And although this example proves sufficiently the disadvantages resulting from a plurality of commanders for an army in time of war, yet by way of still further elucidating this truth, I will cite one or two other instances of both ancient and modern times. When Louis XII, king of France, had retaken Milan in the year 1500, he sent his troops to Pisa, with orders to restore that city to the Florentines; whereupon the government of Florence sent there as commissioners Giovanbattista Ridolfi and Luca d' Antonio degli Albizzi. As Giovanbattista enjoyed a great reputation, and was the older of the two, Luca left the entire management of affairs to him; and although he did not exhibit his ambition by opposing him yet he manifested it by his silence and by the indifference and contempt with which he treated everything that was done, so that, neither aiding in the actions in the field nor in council, one would have supposed him to be a man destitute of all ability. But he soon proved the very opposite, when, in consequence of something that had occurred, Giovanbattista was obliged to return to Florence. Then Luca, remaining in sole command, displayed his worth by his great valor, skill, and wisdom; all of which were lost so long as he had a colleague who shared in the command. I will quote once more, in confirmation of what I have advanced, the authority of Titus Livius. This historian, referring to the circumstance that the Romans had sent Quintius and Agrippa against the Equeans, adds, that the latter begged his colleague to take upon himself the sole conduct of the war, saying to him, "In important affairs it is necessary for success that the principal authority should reside in one man only." This is just the contrary of what is done by our princes and republics of the present day; who confide to several commissaries and chiefs the administration of places subject to them, which creates an inconceivable confusion. And if we seek for the causes of the reverses experienced by the Italian and French armies in our times, we shall find that to have been the most powerful of all the causes. So that we may truly conclude that it is better to confide any expedition to a single man of ordinary ability, rather than to two, even though they are men of the highest merit, and both having equal authority.

Chapter XVI

IN TIMES OF DIFFICULTY MEN OF MERIT ARE SOUGHT AFTER, BUT IN EASY TIMES IT IS NOT MEN OF MERIT, BUT SUCH AS HAVE RICHES AND POWERFUL RELATIONS, THAT ARE MOST IN FAVOR

IT ever has been, and ever will be the case, that men of rare and extraordinary merit are neglected by republics in times of peace and tranquillity; for jealous of the reputation which such men have acquired by their virtues, there are always in such times many other citizens, who want to be, not only their equals, but their superiors. The Greek historian Thucydides gives the following striking instance of this. The Athenian republic, having obtained the advantage in the Peloponnesian war, having checked the pride of the Spartans and subjected almost all Greece to their rule, acquired such reputation that she conceived the project of conquering Sicily. This enterprise was much debated in Athens. Alcibiades and some other citizens, thinking more of the honor they could gain by it than of the public good, were much in favor of it, and hoped that the direction of it would be intrusted to them. But Nicias, one of the most influential citizens of Athens, opposed it, and the principal reason which he adduced against it, when addressing the people (who had faith in him), was this: that in advising them against this war he counselled them to what was against his own interest, for he well knew that so long as Athens remained at peace there were many citizens who wanted to take precedence of him; but he also knew that there was not a citizen who would pretend to show himself his superior, or even his equal, in time of war. Thus showing that it is the common fault of republics in tranquil times to make small account of men of merit. And it is a twofold cause of indignation for such men to see themselves deprived of the rank to which they are entitled, and to be associated with, and often even subordinated to unworthy men, who are their inferiors in capacity. This defect in republics has often caused great evils; for those citizens who feel themselves so unjustly depreciated, and knowing it to be the result of the peace and tranquillity which the state enjoys, will stir up troubles and kindle fresh wars to the detriment of the republic.

In reflecting upon the means for remedying this evil, I believe I have found two. The first is to keep the citizens poor, so that their wealth and lack of virtue may neither corrupt themselves nor enable them to corrupt others; and the second, so to organize for war as to be ever prepared for it, and always to have need of men of merit and reputation, as Rome did in her early days. For as this city always kept armies in the field, there was constant opportunity for the employment of men of ability; nor could rank be withheld from a man who deserved it, neither could it be bestowed upon another who did not merit it. And if, notwithstanding this, it was at times done, either by mistake or by way of trial, it caused at once such disorders and dangers that they quickly returned to the regular course. But other republics, which are not constituted like Rome, and who engage in war only when compelled by necessity, cannot avoid this inconvenience, but are rather constantly led into it. And this will always produce evil consequences whenever the meritorious citizen, who has thus been neglected, is disposed to be vindictive, and has influence and partisans in the city. Rome avoided this evil practice for a time; but after she had conquered Carthage and Antiochus, (as we have said elsewhere,) and no longer fearing other wars, she also seems to have confided the conduct of her armies indifferently to whoever aspired to it, looking less to the merits and ability of the man than to such other qualifications as assured him favor with the people. For we see that the consulate was several times refused to Paulus Æmilius, and that he obtained it only when the war with the Macedonians occurred, which being deemed perilous, the command of the army was by general consent committed to him.

When after the year 1490 the city of Florence was involved in many wars, and her citizens had given but indifferent proof of their ability, the city by chance found a man who showed himself capable of commanding her armies. This was Antonio Giacomini; and so long as Florence had difficult wars on hand, all the ambition of her citizens ceased, and Antonio had no competitors for the part of commissary and chief of the army. But when there was a war that presented no dangers, and promised only honors and credit.

then there were so many applicants that, in the appointment of three commissaries for the conduct of the siege of Pisa, Antonio was left out. And although the injury that resulted to the state from not having sent Antonio was not evident to all, yet it could most easily be conjectured. For Pisa, being destitute of munitions and provisions, would quickly have been forced to surrender at discretion to the Florentines, if Antonio had been in command. But the siege, being conducted by wholly incompetent men, was protracted to that degree that the Florentines had to resort to the purchase of the city, which they might otherwise have taken by force. Such an indignity might well have had an effect upon Antonio, and he must have been very good and forbearing not to have desired to revenge himself for it, either by the ruin of the state (which he could have occasioned) or by the destruction of some of his particular rivals. A republic should guard against similar dangers, as we will show more fully in the following chapter.

Chapter XVII

A PERSON WHO HAS BEEN OFFENDED SHOULD NOT BE INTRUSTED WITH AN IMPORTANT ADMINISTRATION AND GOVERNMENT

A REPUBLIC should take great care not to intrust with an important administration one who has been gravely offended. Claudius Nero, who left the army with which he was confronting Hannibal, and, taking a portion of the same, went with it into La Marca to meet the other Consul, in order to engage Asdrubal before he could form a junction with Hannibal, found himself in front of Asdrubal, and surrounded him with his forces in a place where he had to fight at a disadvantage or die of starvation; but he was so craftily entertained by Asdrubal with propositions of an agreement, as to enable him to make his escape and defeat Nero's opportunity of crushing him. This becoming known in Rome, the Senate and people deemed it a grievous blunder, making him the constant topic of conversation about the city, to his great disgrace and shame. But afterwards becoming Consul and being sent against Hannibal he acted in the manner above indicated, which involved such great danger that all Rome was troubled and in doubt until the news came of Asdrubal's rout. Claudius, being subsequently interrogated as to the reasons for taking so dangerous a course, by which without extreme necessity he had jeoparded the liberty of Rome, answered that he did so, knowing that if successful he should regain the glory lost in Spain; and if unsuccessful, and his plan should have an adverse issue, he would be revenged on that city and those citizens who had so ungratefully and indiscreetly offended him. And if such an affront could rouse to such passion a citizen of Rome in those days when Rome was yet incorrupt, we can imagine what might be done by a citizen of a city in a condition unlike that of Rome at that time. Hence, no adequate remedies existing for similar disorders arising in republics, it follows that it is impossible to establish a perpetual republic, because in a thousand unforeseen ways its ruin may be accomplished.

Chapter XVIII

NOTHING IS MORE WORTHY OF THE ATTENTION OF A GOOD GENERAL THAN TO ENDEAVOR TO PENETRATE THE DESIGNS OF THE ENEMY

EPAMINONDAS the Theban said that nothing was more necessary and useful for a general than to know the intentions and projects of the enemy. And the more difficult it is to acquire such knowledge, the more praise he deserves who succeeds in conjecturing it correctly. Nor is it as difficult to understand the designs of the enemy as it is at times to comprehend his actions; and often it is less difficult to appreciate what he is doing at a distance, than what he does at the moment and near by. For it has happened many a time that, when a battle has lasted until nightfall, the victor thinks himself beaten, and the defeated imagines himself to have been victorious. Such errors have caused men to resolve upon acts that proved their ruin; as happened to Brutus and Cassius, the latter of whom perished in consequence of just such an error. For although the wing commanded by Brutus had been victorious, yet Cassius thought that it had been defeated, and that consequently the whole army was beaten; so that, despairing of his safety, he killed himself. We have an instance almost of the same kind in our own times, in the battle of Santa Cecilia (Marignan) in Lombardy, between Francis I, king of France, and the Swiss. Night having come on, that portion of the Swiss troops which had not been broken through believed themselves to be victorious, not knowing that the others had been routed and slain. This error was the cause of their not saving themselves; for they awaited the morning to renew the contest that proved so disastrous to them. And this same error came near causing the loss of the army of the Pope and of the king of Spain, which, upon the false news of victory, had crossed the Po, and, had it advanced any farther, would have become prisoners to the French, who were victorious.

The Roman and Equean armies fell into a similar error. The Consul Sempronius, having attacked the latter, the battle lasted all day until evening, with varying fortunes for both sides. When night came on, both armies, half beaten, did not return to their encampments, but retired to the neighboring heights, where they believed themselves secure. The Roman army divided into two parts; one followed the Consul, and the other a centurion named Tempanius, whose valor had saved the Roman army on that day from being entirely defeated. When morning came, the Roman Consul, without knowing anything more of the enemy, marched towards Rome, and the Equean army retreated likewise. Each of them believed the other to have been victorious, and therefore retreated, regardless of leaving their encampments a prey to the other. It happened that Tempanius, who with the remainder of the Roman army was also retreating, learnt from some wounded Equeans that their captain had withdrawn, and had abandoned their encampments. Upon this news, he returned to the Roman intrenchments, and saved them, and afterwards destroyed those of the Equeans, and then marched to Rome victorious. This victory, as we see, consisted only in his having been the first to learn the discomfiture of the enemy. And this should make us reflect that it may often happen that two armies opposed to each other may both be equally damaged, and suffering from the same necessity; in such case, the victory will be for him who is first informed of the condition of the other.

I will further cite upon this point the following domestic incident of modern times. In the year 1498 the Florentines had a powerful army before Pisa, and pressed that city very closely. The Venetians, having undertaken its protection, and seeing no other means of saving it, resolved to make a diversion by attacking the Florentine territory in the rear. They accordingly entered it by the Val di Lamona with a powerful army, occupied the Borgo di Marradi, and laid siege to the castle of Castiglione, which crowns the hill above. The Florentines, hearing of this, resolved at once to succor Marradi, without, however, reducing their force before Pisa. They organized new infantry and cavalry, and sent them, under command of Jacopo Quarto d' Appiano, Lord of Piombino, and the Count Rinuccio da Marciano. When these forces reached the heights above Marradi, the Venetians withdrew from before Castiglione into the Borgo below. After the two armies had been facing each other for some days, both began to suffer from want of provisions and other necessaries; and neither daring to attack the other, and ignorant of their respective sufferings, both resolved to raise their camp and to withdraw, the Venetians towards Berzighella and Faenza, and the Florentines towards Casaglia and the Mugello. When morning came, and each army had commenced sending off its trains, it chanced that a woman came from the Borgo di Marradi into the camp of the Florentines, (deeming herself protected by her age and poverty,) desiring to see some of her people who served there. From her the Florentine commanders learnt that the Venetian troops were marching off. Encouraged by this news, they changed their intentions, and went in pursuit of the Venetians, as though they had driven them from their intrenchments; and wrote to Florence that they had repulsed the Venetians, and gained a victory. But this victory was due to nothing else than to their having by chance been the first to learn that the enemy was retreating; had this, on the other hand, been first known to the Venetians, it would have given the victory to them.

Chapter XIX

WHETHER GENTLE OR RIGOROUS MEASURES ARE PREFERABLE IN GOVERNING THE MULTITUDE

WHILST the Roman republic was disturbed by the dissensions between the nobles and the people, a war occurred; and they sent their armies into the field under the command of Quintius and Appius Claudius. Appius, naturally cruel and rude in his mode of commanding, was badly obeyed by his troops; so that he had to fly from his province as though he had been beaten. Quintius, on the other hand, being of a gentle and humane disposition, was cheerfully obeyed by his men, and returned to Rome victorious; whence it would seem that a multitude is more easily governed by humanity and gentleness than by haughtiness and cruelty. Nevertheless, Cornelius Tacitus (followed in this respect by many other writers) holds the opposite opinion, and says, "To govern the multitude, severity is worth more than gentleness." In attempting to reconcile these two opposite opinions, we must consider whether the people to be governed are your equals or your subjects. If they are your equals, then you cannot entirely depend upon rigorous measures, nor upon that severity which Tacitus recommends. And as the people of Rome divided the sovereignty with the nobles, any one who had temporarily become chief of the state could not rule them with harshness and cruelty. And we have frequently seen those Roman generals who made themselves beloved by their armies, and managed them with gentleness, obtain more success than those who made themselves feared in an extraordinary manner, unless the latter were gifted with uncommon virtues, as was the case with Manlius Torquatus. But he who has to command subjects, such as Tacitus speaks of, should employ severity rather than gentleness, lest these subjects should become insolent, and trample his authority under foot, because of too great indulgence. This severity, however, should be employed with moderation, so as to avoid making yourself odious, for no prince is ever benefited by making himself hated. And the best way not to excite such hatred is to respect the property of the subjects; as to their lives, no prince ever desires those, unless secretly animated by the spirit of rapine. But when influenced by that spirit, bloodshed will ever occur; and in that case the desire and pretexts for it will not be wanting, as I have elsewhere demonstrated at length. Thus, Quintius was more entitled to praise than Appius; and the judgment of Tacitus can be approved only when confined within just limits, and not applied in the manner of Appius. Having spoken of the effects of severity and gentleness, it seems to me not superfluous to show how an act of humanity had more influence with the Faliscians than the power of arms.

Chapter XX

AN ACT OF HUMANITY PREVAILED MORE WITH THE FALISCIANS THAN ALL THE POWER OF ROME

CAMILLUS was besieging the city of the Faliscians, and had surrounded it, when a teacher charged with the education of the children of some of the noblest families of that city, for the purpose of ingratiating himself with Camillus and the Romans, led these children, on pretence of making them take exercise, into the Roman camp; and presenting them to Camillus, said to him, "By means of these children as hostages, you will be able to compel the city to surrender." Camillus not only declined the offer, but had the teacher stripped and his hands tied behind his back, and then had a rod put into the hands of each of the children wherewith he directed them to whip him all the way back to the city. Upon learning this fact, the citizens of Faliscia were so much touched by the humanity and integrity of Camillus, that they surrendered the place to him without any further defence. This example shows that an act of humanity and benevolence will at all times have more influence over the minds of men than violence and ferocity. It also proves that provinces and cities which no armies and no engines of war, nor any other efforts of human power, could conquer, have yielded to an act of humanity, benevolence, chastity, or generosity. History furnishes many other instances of this besides the one just cited. It tells us how the Roman arms could not drive Pyrrhus out of Italy, but that the magnanimity of Fabricius in making known to him the offer of his confidential servant to poison him caused Pyrrhus to leave it voluntarily. It also shows us that the taking of New Carthage, in Spain, did not give Scipio Africanus so much reputation as the example of chastity which he gave in restoring intact to her husband a young and beautiful wife, whose honor he had respected; which act gained him the hearts of all Spain. History also shows us how much the people desire to find such virtues in great men, and how much they are extolled by historians and biographers of princes, and by those who trace their proper course of conduct. Amongst these, Xenophon takes great pains to show how many victories, how much honor and fame, Cyrus gained by his humanity and affability, and by his not having exhibited a single instance of pride, cruelty, or luxuriousness, nor of any other of the vices that are apt to stain the lives of men. And yet we see that Hannibal, by following the very opposite course, achieved also great fame and great victories; it seems to me well, therefore, to discuss the causes of this in the following chapter.

Chapter XXI

WHY HANNIBAL BY A COURSE OF CONDUCT THE VERY OPPOSITE OF THAT OF SCIPIO YET ACHIEVED THE SAME SUCCESS IN ITALY AS THE LATTER DID IN SPAIN

I THINK it astonishing to see some generals achieve by the very opposite course of conduct the same results that have been attained by those who have conformed to the rules we have recommended above. This would make it seem that victories do not depend upon one or the other course of conduct, and that the virtues which we have extolled in the preceding chapter do not render you more happy nor more powerful, inasmuch as both glory and reputation are often acquired by the very opposite means. Let us return to the case of the two above-named generals for the purpose of better illustrating my idea. Scipio, from the moment he entered Spain, gained the affection and respect of the people of that province by his humanity and benevolence. Hannibal, on the contrary, conducted himself in Italy with violence, cruelty, rapine, and every kind of perfidy. Yet he obtained the same success that Scipio had in Spain. For nearly all the cities of Italy, and entire populations, revolted in his favor. In seeking for the causes of this difference, we find several. The first is the love of novelty, which manifests itself equally in those who are well off and in those who are not. For, as we have said elsewhere, and with truth, men get tired of prosperity, just as they are afflicted by the reverse. This love of change, then, so to speak, opens the way to every one who takes the lead in any innovation in any country. If he is a stranger they run after him, and if he is of the country they surround him, increase his influence, and favor him in every way; so that, whatever his mode of proceeding and conduct may be, he will succeed in making rapid progress. In the second place, men are prompted in their actions by two main motives, namely, love and fear; so that he who makes himself beloved will have as much influence as he who makes himself feared, although generally he who makes himself feared will be more readily followed and obeyed than he who makes himself beloved. It matters little, therefore, to any general by which of these two systems he proceeds, provided he be a man of sufficient courage and ability to have made a great reputation for himself. For when this is as great as was the case with Hannibal and Scipio, it cancels all the errors which a general may commit, either by an excess of gentleness or by too great severity. Either of these extremes may be productive of great evils, that will be apt to prove ruinous to a prince; for he who carries too far the desire to make himself beloved will soon become contemned, if he deviates in the slightest degree from the true path; and the other, who aims at making himself feared, will make himself hated, if he goes in the least degree too far; and our nature does not permit us always to keep the just middle course. Either extreme, therefore, must be compensated for by some extraordinary merits, such as those of Hannibal and Scipio; and yet we see how the conduct of both of these brought them disgrace as well as the highest success.

Of their successes we have already spoken; let us look now at the misfortunes which they experienced. That of Scipio occurred when his soldiers combined with some of his allies and revolted, for which there was no other cause than that they did not fear him. For men are so restless that the slightest opening for their ambition causes them quickly to forget all the affection for him with which the humanity of the prince had inspired them. This was the case with the soldiers and allies of Scipio; so that to arrest the evil he was obliged to adopt measures of the extremest severity, which until then he had so carefully avoided. As to Hannibal, there is no particular instance where his cruelty and perfidy caused him any immediate injury; but we may well presume that Naples and many other cities remained faithful to Rome solely from fear of Hannibal's cruelty. This much is certain, that his ferocity made him more hated by the Roman people than any other enemy which that republic ever had. So that whilst they informed Pyrrhus, even whilst he was still in Italy with his army, of the offer made to them by his physician to poison him, yet they never forgave Hannibal; and, though disarmed and a fugitive, they pursued him so relentlessly that he killed himself to avoid falling into their hands. But if the impiousness, perfidy, and cruelty of Hannibal had such disastrous consequences for him in the end, he had on the other hand a very great advantage from it, and which has excited the admiration of all the historians; namely, that in his army, although composed of men of so many different nations, there never occurred any dissensions amongst themselves, or any sedition against him. This could only be ascribed to the terror which he personally inspired,

and which was so great that, combined with his high reputation for courage and ability, it kept his soldiers quiet and
united.

I conclude, then, that it matters little whether a general
adopts the one or the other course, provided he be possessed
of such high ability as to enable him to achieve success by
either line of conduct; for, as has been said, both have their
defects and their dangers, unless compensated for by extraordinary talent and courage. Having shown that Scipio and
Hannibal, the one by most praiseworthy and the other by
most detestable conduct, attained the same results, I think
I ought not to omit speaking also of two other Roman citizens who acquired equal glory by different methods, though
both most praiseworthy.

Chapter XXII

HOW MANLIUS TORQUATUS BY HARSHNESS, AND VALERIUS COR-
VINUS BY GENTLENESS, ACQUIRED EQUAL GLORY

There were in Rome at the same time two distinguished
generals, Manlius Torquatus and Valerius Corvinus. Equals
in bravery, triumphs, and reputation, they achieved these
advantages, so far as the enemy was concerned, by the same
merits and conduct; but as regards their armies, and the
treatment of their men, their manner differed widely. Manlius commanded with the utmost severity, and subjected
his soldiers without intermission to great labor and fatigue.
Valerius, on the other hand, treated his soldiers with the
highest degree of humanity and affability. Thus the one,
by way of securing the obedience of his troops, had his own
son put to death, whilst the other never injured any one.

Nevertheless, with such difference of manner, both obtained the same success against the enemy and in favor of the republic, as well as in their own interests. For no soldier ever resisted their orders to fight, or ever rebelled against them, or in the slightest way opposed their will; although Manlius commanded with such harshness, that the Romans gave the name of "Manlian decrees" to all such as exceeded the ordinary severity. We have to examine now, first, whence it came that Manlius deemed it necessary to be so rigid, whilst Valerius was so humane; and, next, how it was that both these opposite methods produced the same effect; and, finally, which of the two it is best and most advantageous to imitate.

If we carefully consider the character of Manlius from the time that Titus Livius first begins to mention him, we shall find that he was a man of exceeding courage, devoted to his father and to his country, and most respectful to his superiors. These things we know from his defence of his father against a Tribune; from his single combat with a Gaul, whom he slew; and from the words which he addressed to the Consul before engaging in that combat: "I will never fight against the enemy without your orders, not even if I were perfectly certain of victory." When a man of this character comes to command, he desires to have all men like himself; his vigorous character is reproduced in his orders; and these once given, he will require their strict observance. For it is a certain rule, that he who gives severe orders must see them executed with severity, otherwise he will find himself deceived. And here we may note that he who wishes to be obeyed must know how to command; and those give proof of knowing this who properly estimate their own strength with reference to that of those who have to obey, and who commands only when he finds them to bear a proper proportion to each other, and who abstains from commanding when that proportion is wanting. And therefore it was said by a wise man, that to hold the government of a republic by violence, it was necessary that there should be a proper proportion between him who holds by force and those whom he thus subjects to his control. And whenever that just proportion exists, he may expect his tenure of power to be enduring. But when the oppressed is more powerful than the oppressor, then the latter will daily have occasion to fear his overthrow.

But to return to our subject, I say that to give vigorous orders requires a vigorous mind; and he who has that strength of mind, and commands, cannot enforce the execution of his orders by gentle means. And he who lacks such vigor of mind must be careful not to order anything extraordinary; but in ordinary matters he may act with his natural gentleness, for ordinary punishments are not imputed to the prince, but to the laws and to the necessity of preserving order. We must believe then that Manlius was constrained to the exercise of so much rigor by the excessive severity of his orders, to which he was impelled by his natural character. Such severity is useful in a republic, because it brings her back to her first principles, and to her ancient virtue. A republic would be perpetual that has the good fortune often to find men who by their example restore the laws to their original purity and force, (as we have said elsewhere,) and not only prevent her from falling into decadence, but rather carry her in the opposite direction. Thus Manlius was one of those who by the strictness of his commands kept up the military discipline in Rome; constrained to this, first by his natural character, and next by the desire for the strict observance of those orders which his innate temperament had caused him to issue. Valerius, on the other hand, was able to act according to his naturally gentle and humane character, for he asked nothing more of his troops than a compliance with those duties to which the Roman armies were accustomed. The enforcement of this discipline, being wisely regulated, and not being made onerous to the soldiers, sufficed to make him honored; so that Valerius had no occasion to punish, as there were none that transgressed this discipline; and if perchance there had been any, they would have imputed their punishment (as has been said) to the established regulations, and not to the cruelty of their chief. Valerius was thus enabled to indulge the promptings of his natural humanity, by which he secured the contentment and good will of his soldiers. Thus these two generals, being equally obeyed, achieved the same results by two entirely different methods. Those who attempt to imitate them expose themselves to contempt and hatred, which can only be avoided by the possession of extraordinary merits, as I have said when speaking of Hannibal and Scipio.

It remains for us now to examine which of these two methods is the best, and this I believe to be a debatable question, for both have been equally praised by the writers. Nevertheless, those who have written on the subject of the proper conduct of princes incline more to the method of Valerius than to that of Manlius; and Xenophon, whom I have already quoted, in relating several instances of the humanity of Cyrus, speaks of him very much as Titus Livius does of Valerius. When this distinguished Roman was named Consul and marched against the Samnites, he addressed his soldiers on the eve of battle in the same spirit of humanity that characterized all his acts. After reporting his address, Titus Livius says: "No other general was ever more familiar with his soldiers; he cheerfully shared all the fatigues with the lowest of his men. In the various military games, such as contests of strength or speed, he never objected to measuring himself with the first that offered; and whether victorious or defeated, he ever preserved the same countenance and the same affability. In his actions he was ever courteous and benign, and in speech, ever as mindful of the liberty of others as of his own dignity. In the exercise of the magistratures he was the same as when a solicitant for them, which best characterizes the true friend of popular government." Titus Livius speaks no less honorably of Manlius, and shows that his severity in having his own son put to death rendered the army so obedient to him, that it enabled him to achieve the victory over the Latians; and he goes on to praise him to that degree, that, after having related all the particulars of the battle, and the difficulties and perils which the Roman troops had to encounter in the achievement of that victory, he concludes by attributing it exclusively to the valor of Manlius. And in comparing the forces of the Roman armies, he affirms again that the victory had been assured by that portion which was commanded by Manlius. Thus, in examining all that writers have said upon the subject of our discourse, it is difficult to arrive at a precise judgment. Nevertheless, so as not to leave the matter undecided, I say that the conduct of Manlius is more praiseworthy and less perilous for a citizen who lives under the laws of a republic; inasmuch as it operates entirely for the benefit of the state, and can never favor private ambition. For by such conduct a man can never create any partisans for himself; severe towards everybody, and devoted only to the public good, a commander by such means will never gain any particular friends, such as we have called partisans. Thus this course of conduct can only be of the greatest benefit and value in a republic, as it looks only to the public good, and is in no way open to the suspicion of individual usurpation. But with the system of Valerius, quite the contrary is the case; for although it produces the same effects so far as the public service is concerned, yet it is calculated to inspire doubts and mistrust, on account of the special devotion of the soldiers to their chief to which it will give rise, and which might be productive of bad effects against the public liberty, in case of his being continued in command for any length of time. And if no such evil results were caused by the humane conduct of Valerius Publicola, it must be attributed to the fact, that the minds of the Romans were not yet corrupt, and that he did not remain in continuous command for any great length of time.

But if the question were with regard to a prince, as Xenophon treats it, then we should in all respects take Valerius for a model, and not Manlius; for a prince should aim at having the obedience and affection of his soldiers, as well as of his subjects. His strict observance of the laws will insure him obedience and the reputation of being virtuous; and his affability, humanity, and benevolence, and the other good qualities of Valerius, and of those which Xenophon praise in Cyrus, will make him beloved. For the affections of the people for a prince, and the devotion to him of the army, accord perfectly well with all the other interests of the state. But in a republic, the exclusive devotion of the army to its chief does not accord with the other institutions, which oblige him to observe the laws and obey the civil magistrates. We read in the ancient history of the Venetian republic, that, on one occasion when their galleys returned to the city, a quarrel occurred between the sailors and the people, which increased to a tumult and a resort to arms. Neither the public force, nor the respect for the principal citizens, nor the fear of the magistrates, could quell this disturbance; but the sudden appearance of a gentleman who the year

before had commanded these mariners, and had won their
affection, caused them to desist from the fight and to depart. The prompt submission of the sailors to this gentleman excited the suspicions of the Senate to that degree, that
they deemed it well to assure themselves of him by imprison-
ment and death.

I conclude, then, that the character and conduct of Valerius is advantageous in a prince, but pernicious in a citizen,
not only as regards his country, but also in regard to himself; pernicious for the state, because they prepare the way
for a tyranny; and for himself, because in rendering him
suspect to his fellow-citizens, it constrains them to take precautions against him that will prove detrimental to him.
And, on the other hand, I affirm that the severity of Manlius is dangerous to the interests of a prince, but favorable
to a citizen, and above all to the country. And it seldom
turns to his prejudice, unless the hatred which it excites
should be embittered by the suspicions which his great reputation and other virtues may inspire; as we will show when
speaking of Camillus in the next chapter.

Chapter XXIII

THE REASONS WHY CAMILLUS WAS BANISHED FROM ROME

WE have shown above that a character like that of Valerius
is apt to prove injurious to his country and himself, and that
one like Manlius benefits his country, but at times also injures himself. This is clearly shown by the example of
Camillus, who in his conduct resembled Manlius rather than
Valerius. And therefore Titus Livius in speaking of him
says, "The soldiers hated him, but admired his virtues." His

vigilance, prudence, magnanimity, and the good discipline and order which he observed in all his expeditions and in the command of his army, excited the admiration of his troops; whilst their hatred resulted from his being more severe in his punishments than generous in his rewards. Titus Livius gives the following as the causes of the dislike of Camillus by his soldiers. First, he did not divide with the other spoils the money resulting from the sale of the property of the Veientes, but turned it over to the public treasury. Secondly, on the occasion of his triumphal entry into Rome he had his triumphal car drawn by four white horses, which caused his men to say that his pride was so great that he wished to rival the Sun. And the third was, that he had made a vow to consecrate to Apollo the tenth part of all the booty taken from the Veientes; and to enable him to fulfil this sacred pledge he was obliged to make the soldiers surrender a portion of what they had already appropriated to themselves.

This example shows the causes that most easily render a prince odious to his people, the principal one of which is to deprive them of anything that is advantageous and useful to them; this they never forget, and the least occasion reminds them of it; and as these occur almost daily, their resentment is also daily revived. Another cause is to show yourself proud and presumptuous; this is most hateful to the people, especially to such as live under a free government; and although this pomp and pride may in no way inconvenience them, yet it renders those who indulge in it most odious. Princes, therefore, should carefully avoid this rock; for to incur hatred without any advantage is the greatest temerity and imprudence.

Chapter XXIV

THE PROLONGATION OF MILITARY COMMANDS CAUSED ROME THE LOSS OF HER LIBERTY

IF we study carefully the conduct of the Roman republic, we discover two causes of her decadence; the one was the dissensions consequent upon the agrarian laws, and the other the prolongation of her military commands. If these matters had been better understood in the beginning, and proper remedies applied, the liberties of Rome would have endured longer, and she would probably have enjoyed greater tranquillity. And although the prolongation of these powers does not seem to have engendered any actual disturbances, yet the facts show how injurious the authority which citizens acquired thereby proved to civil liberty. But these inconveniences might have been avoided if those other citizens to whom the prolongation of the magistracies were conceded had been as wise and as virtuous as L. Quintius. His good qualities were indeed a notable example; for when an agreement had been concluded between the people and the Senate, and the military powers of the Tribunes had been extended by the people for one year in the belief that they would be able to restrain the ambition of the nobles, the Senate, from a spirit of rivalry and a desire not to appear less powerful than the people, wanted also to extend the term of the consulate of L. Quintius. But he absolutely opposed this determination, saying that they should strive rather to destroy the evil examples, than to add to their number by others and worse ones; and he demanded the creation of new Consuls. If the citizens of Rome generally had shared the virtue and prudence of L. Quintius, they would never have permitted the practice of the prolongation of the magistracies, which custom led to the prolongation of the military commands, which in time proved the ruin of this republic.

The first to whom such prolongation of a military command was granted was P. Philo, who was engaged in the siege of Palæpolis at the time when his consulate was about to expire. The Senate, believing that he would soon accomplish the capture of that city, instead of sending him a successor named him Proconsul; and thus he was the first who held that office. Although the Senate had been actuated in this matter only by considerations of public utility, yet it was this example which in time caused Rome the loss of her liberty. For the farther the Roman armies went from Rome, the more necessary did such prolongation of the military commands seem to the Senate, and the more frequently did they practise it. Two evils resulted from this: the first, that a less number of men became experienced in the command of armies, and therefore distinguished reputation was confined to a few; and the other, that, by the general remaining a long while in command of an army, the soldiers became so attached to him personally that they made themselves his partisans, and, forgetful of the Senate, recognized no chief or authority but him. It was thus that Sylla and Marius were enabled to find soldiers willing to follow their lead even against the republic itself. And it was by this means that Cæsar was enabled to make himself absolute master of his country. Thus, if Rome had not prolonged the magistracies and the military commands, she might not so soon have attained the zenith of her power; but if she had been slower in her conquests, she would have also preserved her liberties the longer.

Chapter XXV

OF THE POVERTY OF CINCINNATUS, AND THAT OF MANY OTHER ROMAN CITIZENS

WE have argued elsewhere that it is of the greatest advantage in a republic to have laws that keep her citizens poor. Although there does not appear to have been any special law to this effect in Rome, (the agrarian law having met with the greatest opposition,) yet experience shows that even so late as four hundred years after its foundation there was still great poverty in Rome. We cannot ascribe this fact to any other cause than that poverty never was allowed to stand in the way of the achievement of any rank or honor, and that virtue and merit were sought for under whatever roof they dwelt; it was this system that made riches naturally less desirable. We have a manifest proof of this on the occasion when the Consul Minutius and his army were surrounded by the Equeans, and all Rome was full of apprehensions lest the army should be lost, so that they resorted to the creation of a Dictator, their last remedy in times of difficulty. They appointed L. Quintius Cincinnatus, who at the time was on his little farm, which he cultivated with his own hands. This circumstance is celebrated by Titus Livius in the following golden words: "After this let men not listen to those who prefer riches to everything else in this world, and who think that there is neither honor nor virtue where wealth does not flow." Cincinnatus was engaged in ploughing his fields, which did not exceed four acres, when the messengers of the Senate arrived from Rome to announce his election to the dictatorship, and to point out to him the imminent danger of the Roman republic. He immediately put on his toga, gathered an army, and went to the relief of Minutius; and having crushed and despoiled the enemy, and freed the Consul and his army, he would not permit them to share the spoils, saying, "I will not allow you to participate in the spoils of those to whom you came so near falling a prey." He deprived Minutius of the consulate, and reduced him to the rank of lieutenant, saying to him, "You will remain in this grade until you have learned to be Consul."

Cincinnatus had chosen for his master of cavalry L. Tarquinius whose poverty had obliged him to fight on foot. Let us note here how Rome honored poverty, (as has been said,) and how four acres of land sufficed for the support of so good and great a citizen as Cincinnatus. We find also that poverty was still honored in the times of Marcus Regulus, who when commanding an army in Africa asked permission of the Roman Senate to return to look after his farm, which was being spoiled by the laborers in whose charge it had been left by him. These instances suggest two reflections: the one, that these eminent citizens were content to remain in such poverty, and that they were satisfied merely to win honor by their military achievements, and to leave all the profits of them to the public treasury; for if they had thought of enriching themselves by their wars, they would have cared little whether their fields were being spoiled or not; and the other, as to the magnanimity of these citizens, who, when placed at the head of an army, rose above all princes solely by the grandeur of their souls. They regarded neither kings nor republics; nothing astonished and nothing inspired them with fear. Having returned to private life, they were frugal, humble, and devoted to the care of their little properties, obedient to the magistrates, and respectful to their superiors, so that it seems almost impossible that the same mind should be able to bear such great changes. This state of things continued at the time of Paulus Æmilius, and these were the last bright days of the republic, when a citizen who had enriched Rome by his triumphs yet remained himself poor. And so much was this poverty still esteemed at that time, that Paulus, by way of rewarding some one who had distinguished himself in war, presented his son-in-law with a silver cup, which was the first piece of this metal that had ever come into his house.

I might demonstrate here at length that poverty produces better fruits than riches,—that the first has conferred honor upon cities, countries, and religions, whilst the latter have only served to ruin them,—were it not that this subject has been so often illustrated by other writers.

Chapter XXVI

HOW STATES ARE RUINED ON ACCOUNT OF WOMEN

A DIFFERENCE arose in the city of Ardea between the patricians and plebeians, on account of a rich heiress, who had been demanded in marriage by a plebeian and a noble at the same time. The young woman, having lost her father, her guardians wanted to give her to the plebeian, but the mother preferred the noble. This gave rise to such disturbances that they actually came to arms; the entire nobility armed in support of the young noble, and all the people in favor of the plebeian. The latter, having been overcome, left Ardea, and sent to the Volscians for assistance, whilst the nobles applied to Rome. The Volscians, having arrived first, surrounded and besieged Ardea. When the Romans came, they shut in the Volscians between their army and the walls of the town, and pressed them so hard that, constrained by want of provisions, the Volscians were obliged to surrender at discretion. When the Romans entered the city, they put to death all the chiefs of the sedition, and re-established order. This occurrence suggests several points for reflection; first, we see that women have been the cause of great dissensions and much ruin to states, and have caused great damage to those who govern them. We have seen, in the history of Rome, that the outrage committed upon Lucretia deprived the Tarquins of their throne, and the attempt upon Virginia caused the Decemvirs the loss of their authority. Thus, Aristotle mentions as one of the first causes of the ruin of tyrants the outrages committed by them upon the wives and daughters of others, either by violence or seduction; and we have discussed this subject at length when treating of conspiracies. I say, therefore, that absolute princes and rulers of republics should not be indifferent to this subject, but should well reflect upon the disorders that may arise from such causes, and should see that proper remedies be applied in time, ere they involve their state or republic in loss and shame. This happened to the people of Ardea, who, after having permitted the quarrel amongst their citizens (which we have mentioned above) to grow to that degree that it led to civil war, were obliged afterwards, by way of restoring union, to ask the intervention of strangers, which is a great step to a loss of independence. But let us come to another subject for reflection, namely, the means of restoring union and harmony to a city, of which we shall treat in the following chapter.

Chapter XXVII

OF THE MEANS FOR RESTORING UNION IN A CITY, AND OF THE
COMMON ERROR WHICH SUPPOSES THAT A CITY MUST BE KEPT
DIVIDED FOR THE PURPOSE OF PRESERVING AUTHORITY

WE observe, from the example of the Roman Consuls in restoring harmony between the patricians and plebeians of Ardea, the means for obtaining that object, which is none other than to kill the chiefs of the opposing factions. In fact, there are only three ways of accomplishing it; the one is to put the leaders to death, as the Romans did, or to banish them from the city, or to reconcile them to each other under a pledge not to offend again. Of these three ways, the last is the worst, being the least certain and effective; for it is impossible that, after dissensions that have caused so much bloodshed and other outrages, a forced peace should be enduring. The parties meeting each other daily face to face will with difficulty abstain from mutual insults, and in their daily intercourse fresh causes for quarrel will constantly occur.

The city of Pistoja furnishes a most striking example in point. Fifteen years ago that city was divided into two factions, the Panciatichi and the Cancellieri, and this division continues to the present day; but then they were in arms, whilst now they have laid them down. After many disputes, they had come to bloodshed, to the pulling down of houses, plundering each other's property, and every other kind of hostilities; and the Florentines, upon whom it devolved to restore order in that city, always employed for that purpose the third means, namely, conciliation, which, however, invariably led to greater troubles and disorders. So that, tired of this method, they resorted to the second; that is, they removed the chiefs of the factions by imprisoning some and exiling others to various places; and thus they succeeded in restoring order in a manner that could and does, endure to this day. Doubtless, however, the first means (that of putting the chiefs of the factions to death) would have been the most effectual, but would have required a power and courage not to be expected from a feeble republic like Florence, which could with difficulty employ even the second method.

These, as I have said in the beginning, are some of the errors which the princes of our day are apt to commit. When they are called upon on great occasions to take decided measures, they ought to examine the conduct of the ancients on similar occasions. But the weakness of the princes of the present day, caused by an effeminate education and want of instruction, makes them regard the maxims of the ancients as inhuman, or impossible of application. And certainly modern opinions are very far from the truth when they maintain, as some wise men of our city did not long since, that "Pistoja must be controlled by means of factions, and Pisa by means of fortresses." They do not see that both of these means would have been equally useless. I will say nothing here of fortresses, having discussed that subject at length in a former chapter; but I will show how nothing is to be gained by attempting to control cities by means of keeping alive factions. For it is impossible either for prince or republic to preserve an equal influence over both the old factions, it being in the nature of man in all differences of opinion to prefer either the one side or the other. Thus, one of the parties being malcontent, you will lose the city on the occasion of the first war, it being impossible to hold it against enemies from without and within. If the government

of the city is a republic, then there is no surer way of corrupting the citizens, and to divide the city against itself, than
to foment the spirit of faction that may prevail there; for
each party will strive by every means of corruption to secure
friends and supporters, which gives rise to two most serious
evils: first, that a government which changes often, according to the caprice of the one or the other faction, can
never be good, and consequently never can secure to itself
the good will and attachment of its citizens; and, secondly,
that such favoring of factions keeps the republic of necessity
divided. The historian Biondo attests the truth of this when
he says, in speaking of the Florentines and Pistojans: "The
Florentines, whilst endeavoring to restore harmony in Pistoja, became divided amongst themselves." The evils resulting
from such a division are manifest. In the year 1501, Florence
lost Arezzo, the Val di Tevere, and the Val di Chiana, which
were taken from her by the Vitelli and the Duke Valentino.
The king of France sent a Seigneur de Lant to cause a restitution to the Florentines of all the places they had lost. The
Seigneur de Lant, finding in all the castles only men claim-
ing to belong to the party of Marzocco,* censured this division most severely, saying that, if in France any one of the
subjects were to call himself of the king's party, he would
immediately be punished, because such a remark could have
no other meaning than that there were people in the country
who were opposed to the king, who wanted the whole realm
to be his friends, and that it should be united and without
parties. But all these diversities of opinion and modes of
governing spring from the weakness of those who are at

* Marzocco was the name familiarly given by the people of Florence to
the marble lion supporting the arms of Florence, at the door of the Palazzo
Vecchio. Thence the party supporting the government of Florence was
called the party of Marzocco. The marble lion is attributed to the chisel
of Donatello.

the head of governments, and who, lacking the requisite force and energy to preserve their states, resort to such expedients; which in times of tranquillity may occasionally be of service, but when trouble and adversity come, then their fallacy becomes manifest.

Chapter XXVIII

THE ACTIONS OF CITIZENS SHOULD BE WATCHED, FOR OFTEN SUCH AS SEEM VIRTUOUS CONCEAL THE BEGINNING OF TYRANNY

THE city of Rome was afflicted by a famine; and as the public magazines were insufficient to supply the deficiency of food, a citizen named Spurius Melius, who was very rich for those times, resolved to lay in a private stock of grain and feed the people at his own expense. This liberality attracted crowds of people, and so won him the popular favor that the Senate, fearing the evil consequences that might arise from it, and for the purpose of putting an end to the evil before it should grow too great, created, expressly against Spurius, a Dictator, who had him put to death. This shows that very often actions that seem good on the surface, and which cannot reasonably be objected to, may become oppressive and highly dangerous to a republic, unless they are corrected betimes. To explain this matter more fully, I say that a republic that has no distinguished citizens cannot be well governed; but, on the other hand, it is often the great influence of such distinguished citizens that is the cause of states being reduced to servitude. And to prevent this the institutions of the state should be so regulated that the influence of citizens shall be founded only upon such acts as are of benefit to the state, and not upon such as are injurious to the public interests or liberty. And therefore attention must be given to the means employed by citizens for acquiring such influence; and these are twofold, either public or private. The former are when a citizen gains reputation and influence by serving the state well with his counsels or his actions. The way to such honors should be open to every citizen, and suitable rewards should be established, that will be satisfactory and honorable to those who merit them. Reputation and influence gained by such pure and simple means will never prove dangerous to any state. But when they are acquired by private means, then they become most dangerous and pernicious. These private ways consist in benefiting this or the other private individual, by lending them money, marrying their daughters, sustaining them against the authority of the magistrates, and bestowing upon them such other favors as to make partisans of them. This encourages those who are thus favored to corrupt the public and to outrage the laws. A well-regulated republic, therefore, should open the way to public honors to those who seek reputation by means that are conducive to the public good; and close it to those whose aim is the advancement of private ends. It was thus that Rome decreed the reward of triumphs and other honors to such of her citizens as had acted well for the public good; whilst, on the other hand, she ordered accusations to be brought against those who under various pretexts aimed to make themselves powerful for private ends. And when such accusations did not suffice, in consequence of the people's being blinded by a sort of false and illusory advantage, they created a Dictator, who, armed with regal powers, caused them to return to the true path of duty from which they had strayed; as was seen in the punishment of Spurius Melius. And if one such transgression were allowed to go unpunished, it might lead to the ruin of the republic, for it would then be difficult to force back the ambitious to the true path of duty.

Chapter XXIX

THE FAULTS OF THE PEOPLE SPRING FROM THE FAULTS OF THEIR RULERS

LET not princes complain of the faults committed by the people subjected to their authority, for they result entirely from their own negligence or bad example. In examining the people who in our day have been given to brigandage and other vices of that kind, we see that these arise entirely from the faults of their rulers, who were guilty of similar abuses. Before Pope Alexander VI. had crushed the petty tyrants that ruled the Romagna, that country presented an example of all the worst crimes. The slightest causes gave rise to murder and every species of rapine; and this was due exclusively to the wickedness of the princes, and not to the evil nature of the people, as alleged by the former. For these princes, being poor, yet wishing to live in luxury like the rich, were obliged to resort to every variety of robbery. And amongst other dishonest means which they employed was the making of laws prohibiting some one thing or another; and immediately after, they were themselves the first to encourage their non-observance, leaving such transgressions unpunished until a great number of persons had been guilty of it, and then suddenly they turned to prosecute the transgressors; not from any zeal for the law, but solely from cupidity, in the expectation of obtaining money for commuting the punishment. These infamous proceedings caused many evils; the worst of them was that the people became impoverished without being corrected, and that then the stronger amongst them endeavored to make good their losses by plundering the weaker. This gave rise to all the evils of which we have spoken above, and which are chargeable exclusively upon the princes. Titus Livius confirms this assertion when he relates how the Roman ambassadors, who were charged with carrying to Delphos a portion of the spoils taken at Veii and consecrated to Apollo, were captured by the corsairs of Lipari in Sicily, and carried on shore. The Prince Timasitheus, on being informed what gifts these ambassadors were carrying and their destination, conducted himself like a Roman, although a native of Lipari. He pointed out to his people how impious it would be to seize such a gift, and with the general consent allowed the ambassadors to depart with all their things. Upon which the historian remarks in the following terms: "Timasitheus inspired the multitude with a sentiment of religion, and they always imitate their rulers." And Lorenzo de' Medici confirms this idea by saying: "The example of the prince is followed by the masses, who keep their eyes always turned upon their chief."

Chapter XXX

A CITIZEN WHO DESIRES TO EMPLOY HIS AUTHORITY IN A REPUBLIC FOR SOME PUBLIC GOOD MUST FIRST OF ALL SUPPRESS ALL FEELING OF ENVY: AND HOW TO ORGANIZE THE DEFENCE OF A CITY ON THE APPROACH OF AN ENEMY

THE Roman Senate, upon learning that new levies of troops had been made throughout Tuscany for the purpose of attacking Rome, and that the Latins as well as the Hernicians, who until then had been friends of the Romans, had now united with the Volscians, Rome's implacable enemies, judged that this would be a most dangerous war. Camillus, who happened at the time to be Tribune with consular powers, thought that they might dispense with the creation of a Dictator, if his colleagues (the other Tribunes) would yield to him supreme authority. To this they promptly assented, "persuaded," says Titus Livius, "that the adding to the authority of Camillus would not in the least detract from theirs." Camillus at once availed of the powers thus conferred upon him, and ordered the immediate raising of three armies. The first he wanted to command himself against the Tuscans; of the second he made Quintus Servilius general, with orders to remain in the environs of Rome to oppose the Latins and Hernicians in case they should attempt any movement; and the third he placed under command of Lucius Quintus, with instructions to guard the city and defend the gates and the Senate in any event that might arise. In addition to this he ordered Horatius, one of his colleagues, to provide arms and provisions and all other supplies necessary in time of war. He furthermore confided to Cornelius, another colleague of his, the care of presiding over the Senate and public assemblies, so that he might propose the measures which it might be necessary to take from day to day. Thus were the Tribunes in those days equally disposed to command or to obey for the well-being of the state. This example shows us what great services a good and wise man can render to his country, when his virtues and goodness have silenced envy, which so often prevents men from being useful by depriving them of the authority necessary for important occasions.

Envy may be extinguished in two ways: either by some extraordinary and difficult occasion, when every one fears his own destruction, and therefore lays aside all ambition, and eagerly obeys any one whom he supposes capable of averting the danger by his virtues and talents. Such was the case with Camillus, who, having given so many proofs of his eminent merit, was three times made Dictator; and having always administered this high office for the public good and without any selfish views, other men did not fear his greatness and did not deem it discreditable to acknowledge their own inferiority to a man of such distinguished worth and reputation. The observation of Titus Livius upon this circumstance was therefore very just. The other way of destroying envy is, when either violence or a natural death carries off those of your rivals who on seeing you acquire such reputation and greatness cannot patiently bear your being more distinguished than themselves. If men of this kind live in a corrupt city, where education has not been able to infuse any spirit of good into their minds, it is impossible that they should be restrained by any chance, but they would be willing rather to see their country ruined than not to attain their purpose, or not to satisfy their perverse natures. To overcome such envy and evil passions there is no other remedy but the death of those who harbor them. And when fortune is so propitious to a virtuous man as to deliver him from such rivals by their natural death, he becomes glorious without violence, and may then display his virtues to their full extent without hindrance and without offence to anybody. But when he has not such good fortune, he must strive nevertheless by all possible means to overcome this difficulty, and relieve himself of such rivals before attempting any enterprise. And whoever reads the Bible attentively will find that Moses, for the purpose of insuring the observance of his laws and institutions, was obliged to have a great many persons put to death who opposed his designs under the instigation of no other feelings than those of envy and jealousy. Brother Girolamo Savonarola fully understood the necessity of this course, which was recognized also by Pietro Soderini, Gonfalonier of Florence. Savonarola, however, could not put it into practice for want of power and authority; still, he was not remiss in doing all he could, for his sermons abound with accusations and invectives against the wise of this world, for it was thus he styled the jealous opponents of his doctrines. The other, Soderini, believed that he would be able in time to silence envy by his affability and good fortune, and by bestowing benefits upon some of his adversaries. Feeling himself young, and being loaded with public favors on account of his conduct, he hoped to triumph over the jealousy of his rivals without any violence or public disturbance. But he forgot that in such matters nothing is to be expected from time, that goodness does not suffice, and that benefits will not placate envious malignity. So that both these men came to their ruin, which was caused by their lack of knowledge or power to crush envy.

Let us now come to the other part of our subject, namely, the orders given by Camillus, inside and outside of the city, for the safety of Rome. And it is truly with good reason that historians such as Titus Livius give a more exact and detailed account of certain events, so that future generations may learn therefrom how to defend themselves under similar circumstances. And here we must remark that there is not a more ineffectual and hazardous mode of defending a city than to do it in a disorderly and tumultuous manner. This is shown by the precaution which Camillus took to raise a third regular army for the protection of the city, which was then and may still be regarded by some to have been superfluous, inasmuch as the people of the city were warlike and used to arms. And therefore they considered it unnecessary to raise a special army, as it would have been sufficient to arm the citizens when occasion should require it. But Camillus thought differently, and every wise person will share his opinion; for he never would permit a multitude to take to arms without order or discipline. And according to his example, any one charged with the defence of a city should avoid, as a dangerous rock, the arming of a tumultuous multitude; but he should select and enroll those whom he wants to arm, and teach them whom they have to· obey, the places for assembling, and where to march; and then he must order those who are not enrolled to remain at home to protect their houses. Those who adopt this system in a city that is attacked will easily be able to defend it, whilst those who act otherwise and disregard the example of Camillus will surely fail.

Chapter XXXI

GREAT MEN AND POWERFUL REPUBLICS PRESERVE AN EQUAL DIGNITY AND COURAGE IN PROSPERITY AND ADVERSITY

AMONGST the admirable sayings and doings related of Camillus by our historian, Titus Livius, for the purpose of showing how a great man conducts himself, he puts the following words into his mouth: "My courage has neither been inflated by the dictatorship nor abated by exile." These words show that a truly great man is ever the same under all circumstances; and if his fortune varies, exalting him at one moment and oppressing him at another, he himself never varies, but always preserves a firm courage, which is so closely interwoven with his character that every one can readily see that the fickleness of fortune has no power over him. The conduct of weak men is very different. Made vain and intoxicated by good fortune, they attribute their success to merits which they do not possess, and this makes them odious and insupportable to all around them. And when they have afterwards to meet a reverse of fortune, they quickly fall into the other extreme, and become abject and vile. Thence it comes that princes of this character think more of flying in adversity than of defending themselves, like men who, having made a bad use of prosperity, are wholly unprepared for any defence against reverses. These virtues and vices are met with in republics as well as in individuals.

Rome and Venice furnish us an example of this. No ill fortune ever made the former abject, nor did success ever make her insolent. This was clearly shown after the defeat which the Romans experienced at Cannæ, and after their victory over Antiochus. For this defeat, although most alarming, being the third, never discouraged them; but they put new armies into the field, and refused to violate their constitution by ransoming their prisoners. Nor did they sue for peace with either Hannibal or Carthage; and repelling all such base suggestions, they thought only of combating anew, and supplied their want of men by arming their old men and slaves. When the Carthaginian Hanno heard this, he pointed out to the Senate of Carthage of how little importance the defeat of the Romans at Cannæ really was. And thus we see that periods of difficulty neither alarmed nor discouraged the Romans. On the other hand, they were not made insolent by prosperity; for when Antiochus, before engaging in battle with them, in which he was defeated, sent messengers to Scipio to ask for peace, the latter named the conditions on which he was willing to grant it; which were, that Antiochus should retire beyond Syria, and leave the rest of the country to the control of the Romans. Antiochus declined these terms, but accepted battle, and was defeated; whereupon he sent his messengers back to Scipio with orders to accept the conditions previously offered by him. Scipio added no further conditions to those which he had named before his victory, saying: "The Romans do not lose their courage in defeat, nor does victory make them overbearing."

The conduct of the Venetians was exactly the opposite of this; for in good fortune (which they imagined entirely the result of a skill and valor which they did not possess) they carried their insolence to that degree that they called the king of France a son of St. Mark. They had no respect for the Church, nor for any other power in all Italy; and had the presumption to think of creating another empire similar to that of the Romans. Afterwards, when their good fortune abandoned them, and they suffered a partial defeat at Vaila at the hands of the king of France, they not only lost the greater part of their state by a rebellion, but, under the influence of their cowardly and abject spirit, they actually made large concessions of territory to the Pope and the king of Spain, and were so utterly demoralized that they sent ambassadors to the Emperor, and made themselves tributary to him; and by way of moving the Pope to compassion, they addressed him the most humiliating letters of submission. And to this wretchedness were they reduced within the short space of four days, and after a but partial defeat. Their army, after having sustained a fight, retreated; about the half of it was attacked and beaten; but one of their Proveditori saved himself, and reached Verona with over twenty thousand men, horse and foot. If there had been but one spark of true valor in the Venetians, they could easily have recovered from this check, and faced Fortune anew; for they would still have been in time either to have conquered, or to have lost less ignominiously, or to have concluded a more honorable peace. But their miserable baseness of spirit, caused by a wretched military organization, made them lose at a single blow their courage and their state. And thus it will ever happen to those who are governed in the same way that the Venetians were; for insolence in prosperity and abjectness in adversity are the result of habit and education. If this be vain and feeble, then their conduct will likewise be without energy. But if the education be of an opposite nature, then it will produce men of a different character; it will enable them to know the world better, and will teach them to be less elated in good fortune, and less depressed by adversity. And what we say of individuals applies equally to the many who constitute a republic, and who will form themselves according to the manners and institutions that prevail there.

Although I have elsewhere maintained that the foundation of states is a good military organization, yet it seems to me not superfluous to repeat here that, without such a military organization, there can neither be good laws nor anything else good. The necessity of this appears on every page of Roman history. We also see that troops cannot be good unless they are well disciplined and trained, and this cannot be done with any troops other than natives of the country; for a state is not and cannot be always engaged in war, therefore troops must be trained and disciplined in time of peace, and this can only be done with subjects of the state, on account of the expense. Camillus had taken the field with his army against the Tuscans, as has been related above; and when his soldiers beheld the extent of the enemy's army, they were alarmed by their own inferiority in numbers, believing that they would not be able to resist the enemy's onset. When this apprehension of the troops came to the ears of Camillus, he showed himself to his army, and, going through the camp, he spoke personally to the men here and

there; and then, without making any change in the disposition of his forces, he said, "Let every man do what he has
learned, and is accustomed to do." In reflecting upon the
conduct and words of Camillus to reanimate his troops, we
cannot but conclude that he would not have acted and
spoken thus to his troops unless they had been disciplined
and trained in time of peace as well as in war. For a commander cannot depend upon untrained soldiers who have
learned nothing, nor can he expect them to do anything
well. And if a second Hannibal were to command such
troops, he would nevertheless be ruined, for a general cannot be everywhere during a battle. If he have not beforehand
filled his soldiers with the same spirit that animates himself,
and if he have not trained them promptly and precisely to
obey his orders, he will inevitably be beaten. Now, any republic that adopts the military organization and discipline
of the Romans, and strives by constant training to give her
soldiers experience and to develop their courage and mastery
over fortune, will always and under all circumstances find
them to display a courage and dignity similar to that of the
Romans. But a republic unprovided with such military force,
and which relies more upon the chances of fortune than
upon the valor of her citizens, will experience all the vicissi-
tudes of fortune, and will have the same fate as the Venetians.

Chapter XXXII

OF THE MEANS ADOPTED BY SOME TO PREVENT A PEACE

Two of the Roman colonies, Circea and Velitræ had revolted, hoping to be sustained by the Latins; but the defeat
of these deprived them of that hope, and therefore a num-

ber of their citizens advised the sending of deputies to Rome to sue for peace and offer their submission to the Senate. The authors of the rebellion objected to this, fearing that all the punishment would fall upon their heads; and to put an end to all further discussions about peace they stirred up the multitude to take up arms and make incursions into the Roman territory. And certainly, if any one desires a people or a prince to abandon all idea of a peaceful settlement with another, then there is no more certain and effectual way than to make them commit some outrageous act against those with whom you wish to prevent them from making peace. For the fear of punishment which they are conscious of having deserved by that outrage will ever keep them from coming to terms. After the first Punic war the soldiers whom the Carthaginians had employed in Sicily and Sardinia returned to Africa when peace was concluded. Being dissatisfied with their pay, they rose against the Carthaginians, and having chosen two chiefs from amongst themselves, Mathus and Spendius, they seized a number of places belonging to the Carthaginians and sacked several of them. The Carthaginians, anxious to exhaust all other means for reducing these revolted troops to submission before coming to arms, sent their former commander, Asdrubal, to them, supposing him on that account to have some influence with them. Upon his arrival, Mathus and Spendius, for the purpose of destroying all hopes of reconciliation and to make war inevitable, persuaded the soldiers to kill Asdrubal, together with all the other Carthaginian citizens whom they held prisoners. Whereupon they not only massacred them, but first subjected them to every kind of torment, and then crowned this villainy by proclaiming that all the Carthaginians who might thereafter fall into their hands would be subjected to a similar death. This resolve, which they carried into execution, made the contest of these rebels with the Carthaginians most cruel and obstinate.

Chapter XXXIII

TO INSURE VICTORY THE TROOPS MUST HAVE CONFIDENCE IN THEMSELVES AS WELL AS IN THEIR COMMANDER

To make an army victorious in battle it is necessary to inspire them with confidence, so as to make them believe that the victory will be theirs under any circumstances. But to give an army such confidence they must be well armed and disciplined, and the men must know each other; such confidence and discipline, however, can exist only where the troops are natives of the same country, and have lived together for some time. It is necessary also that they should esteem their general, and have confidence in his ability; and this will not fail to be the case when they see him orderly, watchful, and courageous, and that he maintains the dignity of his rank by a proper reputation. All this he will do by punishing faults, by not fatiguing his troops unnecessarily, by strictly fulfilling his promises, by showing them that victory is easy, and by concealing or making light of the dangers which he discerns from afar. These maxims well observed are the best means of inspiring the troops with that confidence which is the surest pledge of victory. The Romans were in the habit of resorting to religion for the purpose of inspiring their armies with confidence; and availed of auspices and auguries in the creation of their consuls, in the levying of troops, and before sending their armies into the field or engaging in battle. Without this no prudent captain would ever have hazarded an action, fearful of defeat if his soldiers had not been assured beforehand that they would have the gods on their side. And any consul or general who would have dared to combat contrary to the auspices would have been punished, as was done in the case of Claudius Pulcher. And although we find evidences of this practice throughout the history of Rome, yet we have still more conclusive proof of it in the words which Titus Livius puts into the mouth of Appius Claudius; who, complaining to the people of the insolence of their Tribunes, points out how by their means the auguries and other religious observances had been neglected and corrupted, saying: "It pleases them now to deride these religious practices, for they care not whether the fowls eat, or whether they come slowly out of their cages, or whether a bird sings; these are trifles for them; but such small matters are not to be contemned, for it was by their strict observance that our ancestors made this republic great." In fact it is little things of this kind that keep the soldiers united and confident, and these are essential elements of victory; though without courage they avail nothing.

The Prænestines, having taken the field against the Romans, took up a position on the river Allia, where the Romans had been defeated by the Gauls; hoping that the memories of that locality would inspire their own soldiers with confidence, and discourage the Romans. Although the probabilities were in favor of this for the reasons above given, yet the event showed that true courage is not affected by such trifling incidents. Our historian expresses this thought extremely well by the words which he puts into the mouth of the Dictator in speaking to his master of cavalry: "You see the enemy, trusting to fortune, has chosen his position on the Allia; do you, trusting to the arms and valor of your men, attack the very centre of their line of battle." For real courage, good discipline, and confidence founded upon so many victories cannot be extinguished by matters of such slight moment; nor can a vain idea inspire men animated by such feelings with fear, or a momentary disorder seriously injure them. This was clearly proven in the war against the Volscians, where there were two Consuls, both named Manlius. Having imprudently sent a part of their army to pillage the country, it happened that those who had been thus sent and those who remained in camp were both surrounded by the enemy at the same time; and from this danger they were delivered by their own valor, and not by the prudence of the Consuls. Whereupon Titus Livius says, "The army, even without a chief, was saved by its own indomitable valor." I will not omit mentioning here an expedient employed by Fabius the first time he led his army into Tuscany. Wishing to inspire them with confidence, which he felt to be the more necessary as they were in a country entirely new to them and opposed to an enemy whom they had not met before, he addressed his troops before going into battle; and after giving them many reasons for anticipating victory, he said "that he could give them other good reasons that would make their victory certain, but that it would be dangerous to reveal them at that moment." This artifice so judiciously employed well deserves to be imitated.

Chapter XXXIV

HOW THE REPUTATION OF A CITIZEN AND THE PUBLIC VOICE AND OPINION SECURE HIM POPULAR FAVOR; AND WHETHER THE PEOPLE OR PRINCES SHOW MOST JUDGMENT IN THE CHOICE OF MAGISTRATES

WE have related elsewhere how Titus Manlius, subsequently called Torquatus, saved his father, Lucius Manlius, from an accusation brought against him by Marcus Pomponius, Tribune of the people. And although the manner of it was somewhat violent and extraordinary, yet so far from censuring him for it, the people were so touched by this display of filial piety that, when they had to nominate military Tribunes, they appointed Titus Manlius as one of the two. This result, I think, should make us reflect upon the manner in which the people form their judgment of the men to be appointed to public offices; so that we may see whether our conclusion is correct, that the people show more wisdom in their selection than princes. I say, then, that the people are guided in their choice either by what is said of a man by the public voice and fame, even if by his open acts he appears different, or by the preconceptions or opinion which they may have formed of him themselves. And these are based either upon the character of the fathers of such men, who were so eminent and influential in the republic that the people suppose the sons will be like them unless by their actions they have given proof of the contrary, or that opinion is founded upon the individual conduct of the parties in question. The best means of judging of this is to ascertain whether they choose for their companions men of known respectability, good habits, and generally well reputed. For there is no better indication of a man's character than the company which he keeps; and therefore very properly a man who keeps respectable company acquires a good name, for it is impossible that there should not be some similitude of character and habits between him and his associates. Or indeed a man acquires this good reputation by some extraordinary act, which, although relating to private matters, will still obtain him celebrity if it be honorably performed. And of these three things that give a man a good reputation, the last is the most influential. For the first, being founded upon the merits of a man's father or relations, is so fallacious, that it makes no lasting impression and is soon effaced altogether, unless sustained by the individual merits of him who has to be judged. The second, which makes a man known by the company he keeps, and by his social conduct, is better than the first, but inferior to that which is founded upon his individual actions; for unless a man has by these given some proof of himself, his reputation will depend merely upon public opinion, which is most unstable. But the third course, being founded entirely upon a man's own actions, will from the start give him such a name that it will require a long course of opposite conduct to destroy it. Men who are born in a republic, therefore, should adopt this last course, and strive to distinguish themselves by some remarkable action.

This is what many of the young men of Rome did, either by proposing some law that was for the general good, or by preferring charges against some powerful citizen as a transgressor of the laws; or by some similar and novel act that would cause them to be talked about. Such conduct is necessary not only for the purpose of achieving a name and fame, but also to preserve and increase it. To do this requires a frequent repetition of similar acts; as was done by Titus Manlius throughout the entire course of his life. For after having gained his first reputation by the gallant and extraordinary manner in which he defended his father, a few years later he slew a Gaul in single combat, and took from him that golden chain which afterwards gave him the name of Torquatus. Nor did this suffice him, for later, when already of mature age, he killed his own son for having engaged in fight without orders, although he had defeated the enemy. These three acts gave to Manlius, and will give him for all time to come, more celebrity than all the victories he won and all the triumphs with which he was honored, and which were not exceeded by any other Roman. And the reason of this is, that in his victories he had many rivals, but in these particular acts he had very few or none. The elder Scipio did not win as much glory by all his triumphs as by the courageous manner in which he, whilst still a youth, defended his father on the Ticino, and by his having, after the defeat at Cannæ, made a number of young Romans swear upon his ensanguined sword that they would not leave Italy, as they had contemplated doing. These two acts were the beginning of his glory, and paved the way for his triumphs in Spain and Africa. He added still greater lustre to his fame by his sending back in Spain a daughter to her father, and a young wife to her husband. Such conduct is necessary not only for those citizens who desire to achieve distinction for the purpose of obtaining honorable employment in their republics, but equally so for princes to enable them to maintain their dignity and reputation in their dominions. For nothing so certainly secures to a prince the public esteem as some such remarkable action or saying dictated by his regard for the public good, showing him to be magnanimous, liberal and just, and which action or saying is of a nature to become familiar as a proverb amongst his subjects. But to return to our first proposition, I say that when the people begin to bestow office upon a citizen, influenced thereto by the three above-given reasons, they act wisely. They do still better, however, when they base their choice upon a number of good actions known to have been performed by him; for in that case they are never deceived. I speak only of such offices and grades as are given to men in the beginning before they have established their reputation by confirmed experience, and before they have time to fall into an opposite course of conduct. Thus the people are always less liable to the influence of erroneous opinions and corruption than princes; although it might happen that the people are deceived by public opinion and the fame and acts of a man, supposing him to be better than he really is, which would not happen to a prince, who would be informed of it by his counsellors. Therefore, so that the people might not lack similar counsel, the wise lawgivers of republics have ordered that, in the appointment of men to the highest positions, where it would be dangerous to place inefficient persons, every citizen should be allowed, and in fact it should be accounted honorable for him, to publish in the assemblies the defects of any one named for public office; so that the people, fully informed, might form a more correct judgment. That such was the established custom at Rome is proved by the speech which Fabius Maximus made to the people at the time of the second Punic war. When the Consuls were to be chosen, popular favor inclined towards T. Otacilius. Fabius deeming him unfit for that important post in such difficult times, spoke against him, and pointed out his insufficiency, so as to prevent the nomination of Otacilius, and caused the popular choice to fall upon one more worthy of that dignity. The people then are influenced in the choice of their magistrates by the best evidences they can obtain of the qualifications of the candidates, and are less liable to error than princes when equally counselled. Every citizen, therefore, who desires to win the favor of the people, should strive to merit it by some notable action, according to the example of Titus Manlius.

Chapter XXXV

OF THE DANGER OF BEING PROMINENT IN COUNSELLING ANY
ENTERPRISE, AND HOW THAT DANGER INCREASES WITH THE
IMPORTANCE OF SUCH ENTERPRISE

IT is too lengthy and important a matter to attempt here to discuss the danger of becoming the chief promoter of any new enterprise that affects the interests of the many, and the difficulties of directing and bringing it to a successful conclusion, and then to maintain it. Leaving such a discussion, therefore, till a more convenient occasion, I shall speak here only of those dangers to which those expose themselves who counsel a republic or a prince to undertake some grave and important enterprise in such a manner as to take upon themselves all the responsibility of the same. For as men only judge of matters by the result, all the blame of failure is charged upon him who first advised it; whilst in case of success he receives commendations, but the reward never equals the punishment. The present Sultan Selim, called the Grand Turk, having prepared (according to the report of some who have come from that country) to make war upon Syria and Egypt, was advised by one of his Pashas, who was stationed on the borders of Persia, rather to march against the Shah. Influenced by this advice, the Sultan started upon that enterprise with a very powerful army. Having arrived in that country, where there are vast deserts and little water, he experienced all the same difficulties that had in ancient times caused the loss of several Roman armies there. These difficulties were so overwhelming, that, although always successful against the enemy, yet he saw a large part of his army destroyed by pestilence and famine. This so infuriated the Sultan against the Pasha who had advised this enterprise that he put him to death. History relates many instances of citizens having been sent into exile for having counselled enterprises that terminated unsuccessfully. Some Roman citizens were foremost in urging the selection of Consuls from amongst the people. It happened that the first one so chosen was defeated with his army in the field, and the originators of that system would certainly have been punished if the party to conciliate which it was adopted had not been so powerful. Certainly those who counsel princes and republics are placed between two dangers. If they do not advise what seems to them for the good of the republic or the prince, regardless of the consequences to themselves, then they fail of their duty; and if they do advise it, then it is at the risk of their position and their lives; for all men are blind in this, that they judge of good or evil counsels only by the result.

In reflecting as to the means for avoiding this dilemma of either disgrace or danger, I see no other course than to take things moderately, and not to undertake to advocate any enterprise with too much zeal; but to give one's advice calmly and modestly. If then either the republic or the prince decides to follow it, they may do so, as it were, of their own will, and not as though they were drawn into it by your importunity. In adopting this course it is not reasonable to

suppose that either prince or republic will manifest any ill
will towards you on account of a resolution not taken contrary to the wishes of the many. For the danger arises when
your advice has caused the many to be contravened. In that
case, when the result is unfortunate, they all concur in your
destruction. And although by following the course which I
advise you may fail to obtain that glory which is acquired
by having been one against many in counselling an enterprise which success has justified, yet this is compensated for
by two advantages. The first is, that you avoid all danger;
and the second consists in the great credit which you will
have if, after having modestly advised a certain course, your
counsel is rejected, and the adoption of a different course
results unfortunately. And although you cannot enjoy the
glory acquired by the misfortunes of your republic or your
prince, yet it must be held to be of some account.

I do not believe that I can give a better advice upon this
point than the above; for to advise men to be silent and to
withhold the expression of any opinion would render them
useless to a republic, as well as to a prince, without avoiding
danger. For after a while they would become suspect, and
might even experience the same fate as that which befell a
certain friend of King Perseus of Macedon. This king having been defeated by Paulus Æmilius, and having fled with
a few adherents, it happened that, in discussing the late
events, one of them began to point out to Perseus the many
errors he had committed, to which he ascribed his ruin.
"Traitor," exclaimed the king, in turning upon him, "you
have waited until now to tell me all this, when there is no
longer any time to remedy it";—and with these words he
slew him with his own hands. Thus was this man punished
for having been silent when he should have spoken, and for
having spoken when he should have been silent: his having

withheld his counsel from the king did not save him from danger. I believe, therefore, that it is best to adopt the course I have advised above.

Chapter XXXVI

THE REASON WHY THE GAULS HAVE BEEN AND ARE STILL LOOKED UPON AT THE BEGINNING OF A COMBAT AS MORE THAN MEN, AND AFTERWARDS AS LESS THAN WOMEN

THE audacity of that Gaul who defied to single combat any Roman of the army on the Arno, and his subsequent combat with T. Manlius, recalls to my mind the saying of Titus Livius, "that the Gauls at the beginning of a fight are more than men, but in the course of the combat they become less than women." In reflecting upon the causes to which this is attributed, I believe the general opinion to be true, that it is owing to their natural temperament. But we must not infer from this that this temperament, which makes them so ferocious in the beginning, may not be so disciplined by training that they will preserve their valor up to the very end of the fight. And to prove this I maintain that there are three different characters of troops. One combines warlike ardor with discipline: this produces true valor, like that of the Romans. All history shows that a proper discipline prevailed in their armies, and had done so for a long time. For in a well-ordered army no one should do anything except in accordance with the regulations; and accordingly we find that the Roman armies (which having vanquished the world may well serve as an example to all others) neither ate nor slept, nor performed any other act, military or civil, unless according to the order of the Consul. And armies that do not observe such a system cannot in reality be called armies; and if nevertheless they sometimes seem to merit the name, it is more by their ardor and a sort of blind impulse than by their steady valor. But where that ardor is properly disciplined, it employs its impetuosity at the right time and with moderation; and no difficulties can abate or disconcert it. For good order sustains the courage and reanimates that ardor with the hope of victory, which will never fail if discipline be preserved. The reverse of this happens to armies that have ardor without discipline: such was the case with the Gauls, who were wholly wanting in discipline during combat. For if they did not overthrow the enemy by their first furious onset, upon which they relied for victory, not being sustained by a well-regulated valor, and having nothing besides their impetuosity to give them confidence, they failed when that first ardor was cooled. But with the Romans it was very different; less mindful of danger because of the good order which they preserved during battle, they felt assured of victory, and continued the fight with firm and obstinate courage, and manifested the same valor at the end as at the beginning of battle, the heat of the contest rather inflaming their courage than otherwise. The third kind of armies are such as have neither natural courage nor discipline. Of this kind are the Italian armies of our time, which are entirely useless. Unless they fall upon an enemy that by some accident has taken to flight, they are never victorious. Without citing any special instances, we have daily proofs of their total lack of valor. The testimony of Titus Livius shows us how good armies are formed, and how bad ones are made. Upon this latter point I will quote the remarks of the Dictator Papirius Cursor, when he wanted to punish Fabius, his master of cavalry. "Let none," said he, "fear either men or the gods; let them disregard the orders of the commanders and the auspices; let the soldiers, unprovided with anything, roam loosely through the country of friend or foe, forgetful of their oaths, from which they absolve themselves at will; let them desert their colors, disregard the orders for assembling; let them fight indiscriminately by day or by night, in favorable or unfavorable positions, and with or without the orders of their commanders; let them be faithless to their flag and disregard all discipline,—and then we shall have a confused and blind assemblage, more like a vile rabble of brigands than a solemn and imposing army."

This discourse will readily show whether our modern troops are a blind and chance rabble, or whether they constitute solemn and imposing armies; and how much they lack from deserving to be called armies, and how far they are from having the impetuous ardor and discipline of the Romans, or even the mere impetuosity of the Gauls.

Chapter XXXVII

WHETHER SKIRMISHES ARE NECESSARY BEFORE COMING TO A GENERAL ACTION, AND HOW TO KNOW A NEW ENEMY IF SKIRMISHES ARE DISPENSED WITH

It seems that in all the actions of men, besides the general difficulties of carrying them to a successful issue, the good is accompanied by some special evil, and so closely allied to it that it would seem impossible to achieve the one without encountering the other. This is evident in all human affairs, and therefore the good is achieved with difficulty, unless we are so aided by Fortune that she overcomes by her power the natural and ordinary difficulties.

I am reminded of the truth of this by the combat between Manlius Torquatus and the Gaul, of which Titus Livius says: "So decisive was the influence of this action upon the whole war, that the army of the Gauls, after having precipitately left their camp, retreated behind the Tiber, and thence into Campania." I consider, then, on the one hand, that a good captain should avoid every unimportant action that may nevertheless produce a bad effect upon his army. For he must be altogether reckless to engage in any action in which he cannot employ his entire force, and where yet he hazards his whole fortune, as I have already demonstrated elsewhere in condemning the guarding of passes. On the other hand, I consider that a prudent general, who has to encounter a new and untried enemy that has a reputation, should, before engaging in a general action, afford his troops the opportunity of testing such an enemy by slight skirmishes; so that, by learning to know him somewhat, and how to meet him, they may be relieved of any fear which the fame and report of the enemy may have caused them. I look upon this as a most essential duty of a general; in fact, he will feel the necessity of it himself when he sees that he would be marching to certain defeat, unless by some such slight experience he first removes the terror which the enemy's reputation may have engendered in the hearts of his troops. When Valerius Corvinus was sent by the Romans against the Samnites, who were new enemies, with whom his troops never before had measured themselves, he made them engage the Samnites first in some slight skirmishes, "lest," as Titus Livius says, "a new war and a new enemy should cause them fear." Nevertheless, there is great danger lest a defeat in such slight combats should increase that fear and apprehension in your soldiers, and thus produce the very opposite effect from what you designed; for in such event, instead of reassuring them, they will be discouraged. So that this is one of those cases where the evil lies so near the good, and is so commingled with it, that it is easy to encounter the one in thinking to take the other.

On this subject, then, I say that a skilful commander should avoid with the utmost care everything that can possibly tend to discourage his army. And as nothing is so likely to do this as a check in the beginning, a general should beware of small combats, and should not permit them unless he can engage in them with decided advantage and the certain hope of victory. He should not attempt to guard any passes where he cannot employ his whole force; nor should he hold any strong places except such as would involve his own destruction in their loss; and then he should manage their defence in such a manner that, in case of their being besieged, he may go to their relief with his entire force. All other places he should leave undefended; for the loss of any place that a general abandons, without his army having experienced any reverse, will neither dim the glory of his arms nor his hope of victory. But the loss becomes a danger and real misfortune when you had intended to defend it, and every one believes that you attempted to do so; it is then that a matter of so little moment may cause the loss of the whole war, as in the case of the Gauls. Philip of Macedon, father of Perseus, a man of warlike character and much renown in his day, having been attacked by the Romans, judged that he would not be able to defend all his possessions, and therefore abandoned a portion of them after having laid them waste, convinced that the loss of his reputation in having failed to defend them would be more pernicious to him than the loss of the country which he abandoned a prey to the enemy as a thing of little value. The Romans, after the defeat of Cannæ, when their affairs were in a very bad condition, refused all aid to a number of their allies, and even to some of their own subjects, advising them to defend themselves as best they were able. This was a much wiser course than to undertake a defence which they could not make good; for in that case they would have sacrificed both their friends and their own strength, whilst as it was they only lost their friends.

But to return to the subject of skirmishes. I say that if a general is unavoidably forced to engage in some against a new enemy, he should do so only with such advantages on his side as to expose him to no danger of defeat. Or rather, he should do as Marius did (which in fact would be the better way) when marching against the Cimbrians. This savage people, who came to plunder Italy, spread general terror before them by their numbers and ferocity, and because they had already defeated one Roman army. Marius, therefore, deemed it necessary, before engaging in battle with them, to do something to disabuse the minds of his army of the erroneous opinion which fear had caused them to form of the enemy. And, as a most sagacious commander, he encamped his army several times in positions where the Cimbrian hordes had to pass in view of them. Thus, he wanted his soldiers, from the security of their intrenchments, to become accustomed to the sight of that enemy; so that, seeing that irregular multitude, encumbered with all sorts of impediments, partly armed with useless weapons and partly without arms, they might be reassured, and become eager to meet them in battle. This was a wise proceeding on the part of Marius, and should be diligently imitated by others, so as to avoid the dangers which I have pointed out above, and not to be obliged to do as the Gauls, "who, alarmed by some slight cause, retreated behind the Tiber into Campania." Having cited Valerius Corvinus in this discourse, I will, as

cording to his own words, point out in the next chapter what
a general should really be.

Chapter XXXVIII

WHAT QUALITIES A COMMANDER SHOULD POSSESS TO SECURE THE CONFIDENCE OF HIS ARMY

VALERIUS CORVINUS, as I have said above, was sent with an
army against the Samnites, who were new enemies to the
Romans. On this occasion, by way of reassuring his soldiers
and to make them know the enemy, he caused them to engage in some slight skirmishes with the Samnites. Not satisfied with this, he harangued his troops before coming to a
general battle; and after recalling their valor and his own,
he pointed out to them, in the most effective manner, how
little importance they should attach to such an enemy. From
the words which Titus Livius makes him say, we may note
what a general should really be in whom an army could
have confidence. These words were as follows: "Consider,
then, under whose lead and auspices you are about to go
into battle, and whether he to whom you are listening is
merely a magniloquent orator, terrible only in words; or
whether he is skilled in military matters and himself able to
deal blows, to lead on the banners, and to combat in the
thickest of the fight. I want you to follow my actions, and
not merely my words; not my orders only, but the example
of him who by his right arm has thrice achieved the consulate and the highest glory." These words, well considered,
will teach any one how to bear himself so as properly to fill
the position of general; and whoever acts differently will,
instead of gaining fame, find himself in time deprived of

that grade which he may have acquired by good fortune or ambition. For it is not titles that honor men, but men honor the titles. We should also bear in mind at the very outset, in treating of this subject, that, if great commanders have employed extraordinary means for reassuring veteran troops, much greater precautions are necessary with fresh troops that have never before met an enemy face to face. For if an unaccustomed enemy can inspire veteran troops with terror, that feeling must be infinitely greater with raw troops, who for the first time encounter an enemy of any kind. And yet we have seen many times able commanders by their prudence. triumph over all these difficulties; as was the case with the Roman Gracchus and the Theban Epaminondas, of whom we have spoken elsewhere, who both with fresh troops vanquished the best disciplined veterans. The course which they adopted to accomplish this was to exercise their raw levies for some months in sham battles, and to accustom them to obedience and order, so that afterwards they led them with the greatest confidence into actual battles. No commander, therefore, need despair of forming good troops so long as he does not lack men; and a prince who has plenty of men, and yet has not good soldiers, has to blame only his own indolence and want of skill, and not the cowardice of the men.

Chapter XXXIX

A GENERAL SHOULD POSSESS A PERFECT KNOWLEDGE OF THE LOCALITIES WHERE HE IS CARRYING ON A WAR

AMONGST other essentials for a general is the knowledge of localities and countries, without which general and particular knowledge he cannot successfully undertake any enterprise. And although the acquirement of every science demands practice, yet to possess this one perfectly requires more than any other. This practice, or rather this special knowledge of localities, is better acquired by the chase than in any other exercise. And therefore the ancient writers say of those heroes who in their day ruled the world, that they were nursed in the forests and brought up to the chase. For, besides this special knowledge of localities, the chase also teaches many other things that are necessary in war. And Xenophon, in his Life of Cyrus, tells us that, when the latter was about to attack the king of Armenia, in assigning to his captains their several parts he recalled to them that this was nothing more than one of those hunting expeditions which they had so often made with him; comparing those whom he placed in ambush in the mountains to the men that are sent into the woods to spread the nets, and those who were sent to scour the plains to the men who rouse the game from its lair to drive it into the nets. I cite this to show that, according to Xenophon, the chase is an imitation of war; and therefore this exercise is honorable and necessary for rulers. Nor is there any better or more convenient means of acquiring a knowledge of countries than the chase; for it makes those who indulge in it perfectly familiar with the character of the country. And it is a fact that a man who has familiarized himself thoroughly with one country afterwards readily comprehends the nature of all other countries; for all countries resemble each other in their general conformation, so that the knowledge of one facilitates the knowledge of others. But a man who has never acquired a practical knowledge of one rarely or perhaps never attains the knowledge of another country, unless after a great length of time. But he who has that practice will at a glance know how such a plain lies, how such a mountain rises, or where such a valley leads; and all similar things which his former practice has taught him.

The truth of this Titus Livius shows by the example of Publius Decius, when he served as military Tribune in the army which the Consul Cornelius commanded against the Samnites. This Consul, having taken position with his army in a valley where they might easily have been shut in by the Samnites, Publius Decius, recognizing the danger, said to him, "Do you see yonder point, that rises above the enemy? That is our only hope of safety if we promptly seize upon it; for the Samnites have blindly neglected it." Before reporting these words of Decius, Livius says: "Publius Decius, the·military Tribune, had observed a hill rising above the enemy's camp, difficult of access for an army with all its impediments, but easy for light troops." Being thereupon sent by the Consul to occupy that point with three thousand soldiers, he saved the Roman army; and intending to take advantage of the night to get away, and save his men also, Titus Livius makes him say these words to his men: " 'Follow me, and whilst yet a little daylight remains, let us examine where the enemy's outposts are placed, and by what passage we may escape.' And lest he should be· remarked by his dress of a general, he clothed himself in the garb of a simple soldier to make this reconnoissance." Whoever reflects upon this passage in Livius will see how useful and necessary it is for a general to know the character of the country; for if Decius had not known and understood it, he would not have been able to judge of the importance for the Roman army to possess themselves of that hill; nor would he have been able to discern from a distance whether that hill was accessible or not. And after having obtained possession of it, he could not have reconnoitred from a distance the issues by which he could rejoin the Consul with the main body of the army, despite of the enemy, who was all around him, nor the places guarded by the enemy. It was therefore of the utmost importance that Decius had such a thorough knowledge of the country, which enabled him, by the taking of that hill, to save the Roman army, and afterwards to save himself and the troops he had with him by knowing how to escape the enemy by whom he was surrounded.

Chapter XL

DECEIT IN THE CONDUCT OF A WAR IS MERITORIOUS

ALTHOUGH deceit is detestable in all other things, yet in the conduct of war it is laudable and honorable; and a commander who vanquishes an enemy by stratagem is equally praised with one who gains victory by force. This is proved by the judgment of those who have written the lives of great men, and who give much credit to Hannibal and others who 'were most remarkable in that respect. History gives so many examples of this that I need not cite any of them here. But I will say this, that I do not confound such deceit with perfidy, which breaks pledged faith and treaties; for although states and kingdoms may at times be won by perfidy, yet will it ever bring dishonor with it. But I speak of those feints and stratagems which you employ against an enemy that distrusts you, and in the employment of which properly consists the art of war. Such was that practised by Hannibal when he feigned flight on the lake of Perugia (Thrasimene), for the purpose of hemming in the Consul and the Roman army; and when he attached blazing fagots to the horns of his cattle to enable him to escape from the hands of Fabius

Maximus. Such was also the stratagem of Pontius, general
of the Samnites, to draw the Romans into the defiles of the
Caudine Forks. Having concealed his army behind a mountain, he sent a number of his soldiers disguised as herdsmen
with droves of cattle into the plains. These, on being captured and interrogated by the Romans as to the whereabouts
of the Samnite army, answered, according to the instructions
of Pontius, that it was engaged in the siege of the town of
Nocera. The Consuls, believing it, entered the defiles of
Caudium, where they were promptly hemmed in by the
Samnites. This victory won by stratagem would have been
most glorious for Pontius had he followed the advice of his
father, who wanted him either to allow the Romans to pass
out entirely free, or to kill them all; but not to take any half-
way measures, which, as we have said elsewhere, are always
pernicious, "and never make a friend nor rid you of an
enemy."

Chapter XLI

ONE'S COUNTRY MUST BE DEFENDED, WHETHER WITH GLORY OR
WITH SHAME; IT MUST BE DEFENDED ANYHOW

As stated above, the Roman Consul and his army were shut
in by the Samnites, who proposed to him the most ignominious conditions, such as to pass under a yoke, and to send the
army back to Rome disarmed; which filled the Consul and
the army with despair. But the Legate Lentulus said, "That
for the purpose of saving the country no propositions ought
to be rejected. The safety of Rome depended upon that army,
and he maintained that it ought to be saved at any price;
that the defence of their country was always good, no mat-

ter whether effected by honorable or ignominious means. That if the army were saved, Rome would in time be able to wipe out that disgrace; but if the army were lost, even if they died most gloriously, Rome and her liberties would also be lost." This advice of Lentulus was followed; and the case deserves to be noted and reflected upon by every citizen who finds himself called upon to counsel his country. For where the very safety of the country depends upon the resolution to be taken, no considerations of justice or injustice, humanity or cruelty, nor of glory or of shame, should be allowed to prevail. But putting all other considerations aside, the only question should be, What course will save the life and liberty of the country? The French follow this maxim by words and deeds in defending the majesty of their king and the greatness of France; for nothing excites their impatience more than to hear any one say that such or such a thing is discreditable to the king. For they say that their king can suffer no shame from any resolutions he may take, whether in good or in ill fortune; for whether he be victor or vanquished is a matter that only concerns the king.

Chapter XLII

PROMISES EXACTED BY FORCE NEED NOT BE OBSERVED

WHEN the Consuls returned to Rome with their troops disarmed and the insult to which they had been subjected at the Caudine Forks, the Consul Sp. Posthumius was the first who said in the Senate, that the peace agreed to at Caudium ought not to be observed. He maintained that this peace did not bind the Roman people, but only himself individually and those others who had assisted in concluding it. And therefore, if the people wished to free themselves from all its obligations, they need only send him and the others back as prisoners to the Samnites. He urged this advice so persistently that the Senate agreed to it, and sent him and the others as prisoners to the Samnites, protesting against the validity of the peace. And fortune so favored Posthumius in this matter that the Samnites declined to keep him, so that when he returned to Rome he was more honored there on account of the reverse he had suffered, than was Pontius by the Samnites for the victory he had gained. This case suggests two points for reflection: the one, that a general may acquire glory in any action; in victory it follows as a matter of course, and in defeat it may be acquired, either by showing that it was not due to any fault of his, or by promptly doing some act that neutralizes the effects of the defeat. The other point is, that there is no disgrace in disregarding promises that have been exacted by force. Promises touching public affairs, and which have been given under the pressure of force, will always be disregarded when that force no longer exists, and this involves no dishonor. History offers us many examples of this, and even in the present times we have daily instances of it. Not only do princes pay no attention to pledges which they have been forced to give, when that force has ceased to exist, but they frequently disregard equally all other promises, when the motives that induced them no longer prevail. Whether such conduct be praiseworthy or not on the part of princes, has been so fully discussed in our treatise of "The Prince," that we will not touch upon that question any further here.

Chapter XLIII

NATIVES OF THE SAME COUNTRY PRESERVE FOR ALL TIME THE SAME CHARACTERISTICS

WISE men say, and not without reason, that whoever wishes to foresee the future must consult the past; for human events ever resemble those of preceding times. This arises from the fact that they are produced by men who have been, and ever will be, animated by the same passions, and thus they must necessarily have the same results. It is true that men are more or less virtuous in one country or another, according to the nature of the education by which their manners and habits of life have been formed. It also facilitates a judgment of the future by the past, to observe nations preserve for a long time the same character; ever exhibiting the same disposition to avarice, or bad faith, or to some other special vice or virtue. Whoever reads attentively the history of our city of Florence, and observes the events of our more immediate times, will find that the Germans and the French are full of avarice, pride, cruelty, and bad faith, from which evil qualities our city has suffered greatly at various times. As to the want of good faith, everybody knows how often the Florentines have paid money to King Charles VIII., upon his promising to restore to them the citadel of Pisa; which promises, however, he never fulfilled, thereby exhibiting his want of good faith and his greed of money. Let us come, however, to more recent events. Everybody may have heard of what happened in the war which the Florentines carried on against the Visconti, Dukes of Milan; and how Florence. having no other resources left, thought of calling the Emperor into Italy, in the expèctation that he would devote his reputation and forces to assailing Lombardy. The Emperor promised to come with a sufficient force to carry on the war against the Visconti, and to defend Florence against their power, on condition that the Florentines should pay him one hundred thousand ducats before starting, and a like sum after he should have entered Italy. The Florentines agreed to these terms and made both the first and the second payment; but when the Emperor had reached Verona, he turned back without doing anything, alleging as a reason that the Florentines had not fulfilled their part of the agreement.

Thus, if Florence had not been constrained by necessity, or carried away by passion, and had studied and known the ancient habits of the barbarians, she would not have allowed herself to have been deceived by them on this occasion, as well as on several others. For the Gauls have constantly preserved the same characteristics, and have on every occasion, and towards everybody, displayed the same conduct as according to history they did in ancient times towards the Tuscans. These being hard pressed by the Romans, having been several times routed and put to flight by them, and finding their own forces insufficient to resist the assaults of the Romans, called to their aid the Gauls from beyond the Alps, agreeing to give them a sum of money on condition that they should unite their forces to those of the Tuscans, and march together against the Romans. Thereupon the Gauls, after having received the money from the Tuscans, refused to take up arms in their behalf; pretending that they had received this money, not for the purpose of making war against the Romans, but to induce them to abstain from plundering the country of the Tuscans. And thus were the Tuscan people deprived, by the avarice and bad faith of the Gauls, both of their money and of the assistance upon which they had counted from them. So that we see from this example of the ancient Tuscans, and by that of the Florentines of the present day, that the Gauls of old and the modern French have ever conducted themselves in the same manner; and thus we may readily judge to what extent princes may place confidence in them.

Chapter XLIV

IMPETUOSITY AND AUDACITY OFTEN ACHIEVE WHAT ORDINARY MEANS FAIL TO ATTAIN

THE Samnites being hard pressed by the Romans, and unable to keep their army in the field against them, resolved, after having garrisoned their towns, to pass with their entire army into Tuscany. They hoped thus by the presence of their army to induce the Tuscans, notwithstanding the truce between them and the Romans, to take up arms against them, which they had refused to the ambassadors sent by the Samnites. In the interview which these had with the Tuscans, and especially in their efforts to explain the reasons that had induced them to take up arms again, they made use of a remarkable expression, saying "that they had revolted against the Romans, because peace was more burdensome for men that are enslaved than war is for men that are free." And thus partly by persuasion, and partly by the presence of their army, they induced the Tuscans also to take up arms. From this we should conclude that, when one prince wishes to obtain something from another, he must not, when the occasion permits, give him time for deliberation. But he must act so as to make the other see the necessity of prompt decision, and that a refusal or delay may cause an immediate and dangerous indignation.

We have seen this course successfully practised in our time by Pope Julius II. towards the French; and by Gaston de Foix, general of the king of France, towards the Marquis of Mantua. For Julius II., wishing to drive the Bentivogli from Bologna, deemed it would be necessary for him in this matter to secure the assistance of the French army and the neutrality of the Venetians. Having for some time solicited the one and the other, and having received only evasive answers, he resolved, by not giving them any further time, to force both the French and the Venetians to a compliance with his wishes. He therefore left Rome with as many troops as he could gather, and marched upon Bologna, and sent word to the Venetians to remain neutral, and to the king of France to send his forces to aid him. Pressed by the short time given them for deliberation, and seeing that, if they refused or temporized, they would excite the indignation of the Pope, they yielded to his wishes; the king of France sent him troops, and the Venetians remained neutral. The Count de Foix was with his army at Bologna, when he heard of the revolt of Brescia; and wishing to go to recover that city, there were two routes open to him. The one lay through the dominions of the king, but it was long and difficult; the other and shorter route was through the territory of the Marquis of Mantua. He was obliged not only to traverse the dominions of this Marquis, but to enter them he had to pass over certain dikes raised between the lakes and swamps of which that region is full, and which are closed and guarded by fortresses. Gaston de Foix resolved to take this shorter route, and by way of removing all obstacles, and not to give the Marquis time for deliberation, he at once put his army on the march, and signified to the Marquis to send him the keys to the fortresses that commanded this passage. The Marquis, surprised by this prompt and unexpected determination on the part of the Count de Foix, sent him the keys; which he would never have done if the French general had displayed less impetuositv. For the Marquis would have had a good excuse for refusing his demand, being in alliance with the Pope and the Venetians, and one of his sons being in the hands of the Pontiff. But being taken aback by the prompt action of Gaston de Foix, he yielded, for the reasons which we have given above. The Tuscans acted in the same way towards the Samnites, being forced by the presence of the Samnite army to take up arms against Rome, which till then they had refused.

Chapter XLV

WHETHER IT IS BETTER IN BATTLE TO AWAIT THE SHOCK OF THE ENEMY, AND THEN TO ATTACK HIM, OR TO ASSAIL HIM FIRST WITH IMPETUOSITY

THE Roman Consuls Decius and Fabius were with their respective armies opposed to the Samnites and the Tuscans; and as they both delivered battle on the same day, it is well to examine which of the two different methods adopted by these Consuls was the best. Decius attacked the enemy with his entire force, and with the utmost impetuosity; whilst Fabius contented himself with merely sustaining the shock of the enemy, judging a slow and deliberate attack to be the most advantageous, and reserved the ardor of his troops for the last, when the enemy's eagerness for combat and his fire had somewhat cooled down. The result proved the plan of Fabius much more successful than that of Decius. Exhausted by their first impetuous efforts, Decius saw his troops more disposed to flight than to combat; and to achieve by death that glory which he had failed to win by victory, he sacrificed himself for the Roman legions in imitation of his father's example. When Fabius heard this, he determined to achieve no less glory living than what his colleague had acquired by dying; and throwing all his forces, which he had reserved for that purpose, upon the enemy, he gained a most signal victory. From this we see that the method of Fabius is the most certain and most worthy of imitation.

Chapter XLVI

THE REASONS WHY THE SAME FAMILY IN A CITY ALWAYS PRE-SERVES THE SAME CHARACTERISTICS

It seems that not only do cities differ from each other by their manners and institutions, producing either men of harsh or gentle character, but such differences are observable also between families of the same city. The proof of this may be found in every city; and we read of many instances of it in Rome. For we find that the men of the family of Manlius were severe and inflexible; the Publicoli were affable and lovers of the people, whilst the Appii were ambitious and hostile to the people; and so on, each family having its own distinctive characteristics. This cannot be attributed only to the blood, for that is necessarily modified by marriage; but must be the result of the difference of education in the several families. For it is of great importance whether a youth in his tender years hears any act praised or censured; this necessarily makes a lasting impression upon his mind, and becomes afterwards the rule of his life for all time. For if

this were not so, it would not have been possible that the
Appii should all have had the same inclinations, and have
been agitated by the same passions. Titus Livius has observed this in several of them, and especially in that Appius
who was made Censor. When his colleague, after the ex-
piration of eighteen months, laid down that magistracy, in
accordance with the provisions of the law, he declined to do
the same, alleging that, according to the first law made by
the Censors, he was entitled to hold that office for five years.
And although several public meetings were held on the subject, and numerous disturbances occurred in consequence,
yet they found no means to make him resign, and he held
the office in opposition to the will of the people and the
majority of the Senate. In reading his speech against P.
Sempronius, the Tribune of the people, we cannot fail to
note throughout the real Appian insolence, and at the same
time we cannot but remark the goodness and gentleness displayed by an infinite number of citizens in respecting the
auspices and obeying the laws of their country.

Chapter XLVII

LOVE OF COUNTRY SHOULD MAKE A GOOD CITIZEN FORGET PRIVATE WRONGS

THE Consul Manlius was wounded in a fight during the war
against the Samnites, and as his army, in consequence of his
being disabled, were exposed to great danger, the Roman
Senate judged it necessary to send Papirius Cursor as Dictator to supply the place of the Consul. But as the law required
that the Dictator should be named by Fabius, who was at
that time at the head of the armies in Tuscany, and being

known to be hostile to Papirius, the Senate feared that he might refuse to nominate him. They therefore sent two deputies to entreat him to put aside his personal hatreds, and to nominate Papirius Consul for the general good. Moved by his love of country, Fabius made that nomination, although he manifested, by his silence and other indications, his aversion to him. This should serve as an example to all who desire to be regarded as good citizens.

Chapter XLVIII

ANY MANIFEST ERROR ON THE PART OF AN ENEMY SHOULD MAKE US SUSPECT SOME STRATAGEM

FULVIUS, having been left as lieutenant of the Roman army in Tuscany, whilst the Consul had gone to assist at some religious ceremonies, the Tuscans attempted to draw him into an ambush which they had placed near the Roman camp. For this purpose they sent some soldiers, disguised as herdsmen, with a drove of cattle, who approached the intrenchments within sight of the Romans. The lieutenant, wondering at their presumption, which did not seem reasonable to him, suspected and discovered the deceit, and thus defeated the design of the Tuscans. This instance will serve to show that the commander of an army should always mistrust any manifest error which he sees the enemy commit, as it invariably conceals some stratagem. For it is not reasonable to suppose that men will be so incautious. But the desire of victory often blinds men to that degree that they see nothing but what seems favorable to their object. After their victory over the Romans on the Allia, the Gauls marched upon Rome, and, finding the gates open and unguarded they remained a whole day and night without entering, fearing some stratagem, and unable to believe that the Romans were so cowardly and so ill-advised as to abandon their city. When the Florentines, in 1508, went to besiege Pisa, Alfonso del Mutolo, a citizen of that town, who had fallen into their hands, promised, if they would grant him his liberty, to deliver to them one of the gates of Pisa. His offer was accepted, and he was set free. Afterwards he came several times to confer on the subject with the deputies of the commissaries, but never concealed his visits, coming openly and accompanied by several Pisans, whom he left apart whilst conferring with the Florentines. From this circumstance his duplicity might readily have been conjectured; for it was not reasonable that he should have treated a matter of this kind so openly if he had been acting in good faith. But the eager desire to possess Pisa so blinded the Florentines that, under his guidance, they advanced to the gate of Lucca, where, by the double treason of the said Alfonso, they lost in a discreditable manner a number of their officers and men.

Chapter XLIX

A REPUBLIC THAT DESIRES TO MAINTAIN HER LIBERTIES NEEDS
DAILY FRESH PRECAUTIONS: IT WAS BY SUCH MERITS THAT
FABIUS OBTAINED THE SURNAME OF MAXIMUS

WE have already said elsewhere, that in a great republic there are constantly evils occurring requiring remedies which must be efficacious in proportion to the importance of the occasion. And if ever any city experienced strange and unforeseen ills, it was Rome. Such, for instance, as the plot which the Roman ladies seem to have formed to kill their husbands, so that many had actually poisoned them, whilst others had prepared the poison for the purpose. Such was also the conspiracy of the Bacchanals, discovered at the time of the Macedonian war, in which many thousands of men and women were implicated. This conspiracy would have proved very dangerous to Rome had it not been discovered in time; and if the Romans had not been accustomed to punish the guilty, even if they were in great numbers. Even if we had not an infinity of other evidences of the greatness of this republic, it would be made manifest by the extent of her executions, and the character of the punishment she inflicted upon the guilty. Rome did not hesitate to have a whole legion put to death according to a judicial decision, or to destroy an entire city, or to send eight or ten thousand men into exile with such extraordinary conditions as could hardly be complied with by one man, much less by so many. It was thus she banished to Sicily the soldiers that had unfortunately allowed themselves to be defeated at Cannæ, imposing upon them the conditions not to live in any cities, and to take their meals standing. But the most terrible of her executions was the system of decimation in her armies, when, by lot, one soldier out of every ten was put to death. It was impossible to devise a more terrible punishment, where a great number were involved, than this. For when any crime is committed by a multitude, where the individual authors cannot be ascertained, it is impossible to punish them all, there being so many. To chastise a part, leaving the others unpunished, would be unjust to the first, whilst the others would feel encouraged to commit fresh crimes. But where all have merited death, and only every tenth man is punished by lot, these will have occasion to complain only of fate; whilst those who escape will be careful not to commit other crimes, for fear that the next time the lot might fall *on* them. The poisoners and the Bacchanals were punished as the greatness of their crimes merited.

Although the consequences of such evils in a republic are bad, yet they are not mortal, for there is always time to correct them. But it is not the same with such evils as affect the state itself; for unless they are checked and corrected by some wise hand, they will cause the ruin of the state. The liberality with which the Romans used to grant the privileges of citizenship to strangers had attracted a great many new families to Rome. These began to exercise so great an influence in the elections that it sensibly changed the government, and caused it to deviate from the institutions and principles of the men who had been accustomed to direct it. When Quintus Fabius, who was Censor at that time, observed this, he had all the new families that had caused this disorder enrolled into four tribes; so that, being confined to such narrow limits, they should not corrupt all Rome. Fabius had well comprehended the evil, and promptly and without difficulty applied a suitable remedy; which was so well received by the republic, that it earned him the surname of Maximus.

MODERN LIBRARY COLLEGE EDITIONS

HEGEL, GEORG WILHELM FREIDRICH: *The Philosophy of Hegel* (30976)

HERODOTUS: *The Persian Wars* (30954)

IBSEN, HENRIK: *Eight Plays* (32865)

JAMES, HENRY: *The Bostonians* (30959)

JAMES, HENRY: *The Portrait of a Lady* (30947)

JOHNSON, JAMES WELDON, (Ed.): *Utopian Literature* (30996)

LOOMIS, ROGER SHERMAN AND LOOMIS, LAURA HIBBARD, (Ed.): *Medieval Romances* (30970)

MACHIAVELLI, NICCOLO: *The Prince and the Discourses* (30925)

MALRAUX, ANDRE: *Man's Fate* (30975)

MANN, THOMAS: *Death in Venice* (30999)

MANN, THOMAS: *The Magic Mountain* (30993)

MELVILLE, HERMAN: *Moby Dick* (30926)

MILTON, JOHN: *Paradise Lost* (30994)

MOLIERE: *Eight Plays* (30929)

OATES, WHITNEY J. AND O'NEILL, EUGENE, JR., (Ed.): *Seven Famous Greek Plays* (30930)

O'NEILL, EUGENE: *The Later Plays* (30991)

PLATO: *The Work of Plato* (30971)

POE, EDGAR ALLAN: *The Selected Poetry and Prose* (30958)

PROUST, MARCEL: *Swann's Way* (30967)

QUINTANA, RICARDO, (Ed.): *Eighteenth-Century Plays* (30980)

SHELLEY, PERCY BYSSHE: *Selected Poetry and Prose* (30950)

SOLOMON, ROBERT C., (Ed.): *Existentialism* (31704)

SWIFT, JONATHAN: *Gulliver's Travels and Other Writings* (30932)

TACITUS: *The Complete Works* (30953)

TENNYSON, ALFRED LORD: *Selected Poetry* (30960)

THACKERAY, WILLIAM MAKEPEACE: *Vanity Fair* (30933)

THOREAU, HENRY DAVID: *Walden and Other Writings* (32666)

THUCYDIDES: *The Peloponnesian War* (32978)

TOCQUEVILLE, ALEXIS DE: *Democracy in America* (32675)

TOLSTOY, LEO: *Anna Karenina* (30936)

TROLLOPE, ANTHONY: *Berchester Towers and The Warden* (30937)

TURGENEV, IVAN S.: *Fathers and Sons* (30938)

VOLTAIRE: *Candide and Other Writings* (30964)

WHITMAN, WALT: *Leaves of Grass and Selected Prose* (32661)

WINE, M. L., (Ed.): *Drama of The English Renaissance* (30866)

WORDSWORTH, WILLIAM: *Selected Poetry* (30941)